Approaching *Silence*

D1337857

Approaching *Silence*

New Perspectives on Shusaku Endo's Classic Novel

Edited by
Mark W. Dennis and Darren J. N. Middleton

Bloomsbury Academic
An imprint of Bloomsbury Publishing Inc

B L O O M S B U R Y
NEW YORK • LONDON • NEW DELHI • SYDNEY

Bloomsbury Academic

An imprint of Bloomsbury Publishing Inc

1385 Broadway	50 Bedford Square
New York	London
NY 10018	WC1B 3DP
USA	UK

www.bloomsbury.com

BLOOMSBURY and the Diana logo are trademarks of Bloomsbury Publishing Plc

First published 2015

Library of Congress Cataloging-in-Publication Data
Approaching Silence : new perspectives on Shusaku Endo's classic novel / edited by Darren J. N. Middleton, Mark Dennis.
pages cm
Includes bibliographical references and index.
ISBN 978-1-62356-280-9 (hardback)– ISBN 978-1-62356-983-9 (pb) 1. Endo, Shusaku, 1923-1996. Chinmoku. English 2. Endo, Shusaku, 1923-1996–Criticism and interpretation. 3. Japanese fiction–20th century–History and criticism. I. Middleton, Darren J. N., 1966- editor. II. Dennis, Mark W., editor.
PL849.N4C5337 2015
895.6'35–dc23
2014037300

ISBN: HB: 978-1-6235-6280-9
PB: 978-1-6235-6983-9

Typeset by Fakenham Prepress Solutions, Fakenham, Norfolk NR21 8NN
Printed and bound in the United States of America

Introduction: *Silence* in the World

Mark W. Dennis and Darren J. N. Middleton

Scholarly anthologies like the present one come into existence for numerous reasons. Perhaps an archaeological discovery is made revealing an earlier version of a canonical text, or a group of scholars decide to observe the anniversary of the birth or death of a famous author or the publication of one of their novels. Such moments frequently facilitate a book's or a writer's re-entry into the world, as it were. In 2005, Middleton edited a volume of essays dedicated to the fiftieth anniversary of the publication, in Greek, of Nikos Kazantzakis's allegedly blasphemous Jesus-novel, *The Last Temptation of Christ* (1955), and this collection included an afterword from Martin Scorsese, in which he re-examined his controversial cinematic version of Kazantzakis's story (1988).[1] Although *Approaching Silence* adopts a similar strategy, in that it celebrates Shusaku Endo's modern literary classic, it also anticipates rather than remembers. Put differently, our book forestalls Scorsese's 2015 filmic adaptation of *Silence* (1969; Japanese title *Chinmoku*, 1966), and its essays expect this film will help to re-situate the novel's being in the world.[2] In another context, Edward Said explains this intricate process,

> The point is that texts have ways of existing that even in their most rarefied form are always enmeshed in circumstance, time, place, and society—in short, they are in the world, and hence worldly. Whether a text is preserved or put aside for a period, whether it is on a library shelf or not, whether it is considered dangerous or not: these matters have to do with a text's being in the world, which is a more complicated matter than the private process of reading. The same implications are undoubtedly true of critics in their capacities as readers and writers in the world.[3]

As editors, we have long been fascinated by *Silence*'s being in the world, and our contributors concur. This shared interest has stimulated many questions: Why do critics consider *Silence* a "classic novel"? As a text, does *Chinmoku/Silence* exist in the world solely in its words? What is the relationship between Endo's "original" Japanese text and the English translation? If there are, as some essayists note, significant differences in the Japanese and English versions are they the same text? And how should we understand the paratextual material—the Translator's Preface, cover, publicity blurbs, and such—that surrounds the text, enabling it to appear to us in the form of a book?

Questions about the figure of the author intrigue us: How, for example, are we to understand the historical Endo, Kazantzakis, or Graham Greene, whose names and works live on in the present but all of whom have died? What is their relationship to the works they published? To what degree can they influence the reception and interpretation of their work? Several contributors to our volume take up these questions, noting, for example, that Endo offered varied public comments on *Silence,* ranging from his description of the change in the protagonist's image of Christ being the novel's most important element, to his desire, as Van C. Gessel notes, to persuade Scorsese to adapt his novel for the silver screen. Furthermore, what is Endo's literary significance as a writer influenced by Roman Catholicism but writing from a country whose dominant religious traditions are non-Christian?

We are also interested in the diversity of reading practices, whether one reads a religious text, like the Bible or the *Dhammapada,* or a novel, like *Silence, The Last Temptation of Christ,* or *The Power and the Glory* (1940). Some readers will engage a text alone and in silence, while others will read as part of a community, as members of a book club or as participants in a study session. Moreover, we read different types of texts in distinct ways: a cell phone text message is read differently from a comic book, a legal document, or a sacred myth. For many reasons, some texts seem to demand our undivided attention, calling us back, again and again, to their words and their many, drifting meanings. Exceptional texts frequently invite us to read slowly and purposefully. We believe *Silence* is an exceptional text, and thus *Approaching Silence* represents our deliberate attempt(s) to listen *for* as well as *to* Endo's multifaceted story.

Measured, careful reading repays our best efforts, scholars say. Zhu Xi, who codified the neo-Confucian canon in *The Four Books,* told his students that reading a single text even one hundred times was not excessive, and that if their readings "were slow and deliberative, penetrating ever deeper layers of significance ... students [could] 'savor' the true flavor of the text and come to appreciate its true taste."[4] Furthermore, Paul Griffiths describes "religious reading" as a practice wherein one seeks not simply to extract pieces of information from the text, which he calls "consumerist reading," but to open oneself to being existentially transformed in the process.[5] We hold that nuanced and moving literature, like Endo's *Silence,* inclines readers to scrutinize it carefully, and thus we have sought to emerge from our work on the novel with new perspectives on what it means to read it.

Whatever else our anthology accomplishes, we hope it galvanizes readers of all kinds, whether religious or not, and serves to bring them back to the novel, to *Silence* in the world, even to other examples of Endo's acclaimed literary art.

A Brief Sketch of Endo's Life and Literary Art

Born in Tokyo in 1923, Endo spent much of his childhood in Dalian, part of Japanese-occupied Manchuria.[6] After his parents' divorce, he returned with his mother to Japan in 1933 and lived in Kobe where he and his mother, through the influence of his aunt, converted to Catholicism. Endo was baptized in 1934 at the tender age of 11, and his experience as a Japanese Catholic, which he described as clothes that were ill-fitting, deeply colored his later literary art, as our collection shows. Endo eventually studied at Keio University, an elite private university founded by Fukuzawa Yukichi in 1858, just ten years before Japan's Meiji Restoration, which focused on *rangaku,* or Western learning. Endo received a Bachelor's degree in French Literature in 1949, an interest that led him to travel to France where he studied Catholic fiction at the University of Lyon. His experience as a Japanese living in the West and his attempt to assimilate French culture, informed his work, as did his regular bouts of illness, some of them quite serious. He contracted tuberculosis while in France for a second stay, for instance, and was hospitalized for more than two years.

Endo burst onto the Japanese literary scene in 1955 when *White Man* (*Shiroi Hito*) won the Akutagawa Prize, one of Japan's most prestigious literary awards given to young and emerging authors. Over the next 40 years, Endo published a substantial body of fiction that includes short stories and novels; indeed, some of the former serve as the basis for extended consideration in the latter. A number of Endo's works have been translated into English by Van C. Gessel and Mark Williams, two of our contributors, William Johnston, and others. Gessel, for example, has translated a number of Endo's novels, including *Deep River* (*Fukai Kawa*), *Scandal* (*Sukyandaru*), and *Kiku's Prayer* (*Onna no Isshō*), as well as the short-story collection entitled *The Final Martyrs* (*Saigo no Junkyōsha*). Other works, such as *A Life of Jesus,* translated by Richard A. Schuchert, are also available in English and have been well received by English-speaking literary critics and theologians.

Complications brought on by an outbreak of hepatitis led to Endo's death in 1996, aged 73; today, he lies buried in Huchu Catholic Cemetery, located in Fuchu City, which is part of Tokyo's metropolis. Endo was nominated for, but did not win, the Nobel Prize in Literature, yet was the recipient of other literary prizes during his lifetime. Those awards include the Tanizaki Prize for Japanese Literature, which he won in 1966 for *Silence*, the novel that is the subject of our collection and that is considered by many Japanese and Western critics to be his masterpiece.

Silence describes the activities of Fr. Sebastian Rodrigues, a Portuguese Jesuit priest who travels to Japan in the mid-seventeenth century. He goes to the archipelago not only to minister to the *kakure kirishitan*, or "hidden Christians," who are forced to conceal their faith in an era of brutal persecution of that faith, but also to search for Fr. Christovao Ferreira, his mentor. Ferreira was a key figure in the early Jesuit mission in Japan, and the reader learns through his letters of the initial success of these efforts. But those letters abruptly stop. Word eventually reaches Lisbon that the Japanese military government had suddenly cracked down on the missionaries and that Ferreira may have apostatized while being tortured by the authorities. After the crackdown began, Christians were forced to renounce their faith by stepping or spitting upon an image of Christ that had been placed on the ground before them. This act and its object are both known as the *fumie* (the word is sometimes rendered *efumi*), "to step on an image." Those who refused were tortured or executed: some were hung upside down in an excrement-filled pit, eventually bleeding to death through tiny slits made on their temples and foreheads. Others were boiled alive in the water of the Mt. Unzen *jigoku*, or "the hell of Mt Unzen," while some were crucified at sea.

Rodrigues and another priest eventually arrive on the archipelago with the help of a drunken, weak-willed Japanese man, Kichijiro, whom they meet in Macao. In Japan, Rodrigues witnesses the persecution of the hidden Christians and is angered by the silence of God in the face of their immense suffering. To buoy his spirits, Rodrigues often imagines a beautiful, blue-eyed face of Christ as he endures hardships in a land described as dark and foreboding, unforgiving and hostile. Japan's inhospitability comes not only from its harsh natural terrain but also from the people: the samurai, and their devilish leader Inoue (our essayists also refer to him as magistrate, persecutor, and Lord Chikugo) but also from a group of unnamed Buddhist monks, who appear to Rodrigues as undifferentiated and lifeless, indistinct and flat characters who continually harass the missionaries.

After being betrayed by Kichijiro for 300 silver pieces, Rodrigues is taken to prison where he meets his teacher in a dramatic scene in which Ferreira explains that the rumors were true—he had apostatized. His act was motivated not by weakness or cowardice, however. It was, he tells his student, an act of compassion for the Japanese Christians who were being tortured. By waving his hand to signal his apostasy, they had been spared.

opus, we must situate *Silence* and his other novels "within this great transformative moment in the history of the Catholic Church."

Elizabeth Cameron Galbraith examines how Endo's life experience—for instance, his struggles with illness and racism in France—and his sense that Western forms of Christianity were ill-suited with Japanese religious sensibilities inform the novelist's literary work. Focusing on *Silence* and *Deep River*, Galbraith analyzes how Endo seeks to retailor "the Western suit his mother had put on him into a Japanese garment that would fit his Japanese body." Galbraith draws from Christian and Buddhist models to examine Endo's efforts to effect this transformation through the Japanese preference for the softness of a maternal Christ and a "mother religion."

Dennis Hirota examines Endo's use of marshland, or swamp, imagery, which pervades *Silence* and the author's other writings. Hirota's chapter "seeks to probe the nature of the 'marshland of Japan' by considering Endo's perception of a Christianity transformed under its influence, a Christianity that finds resonance in the space between two modalities of religious sensibility." In addition, Hirota argues that when we view these two modalities—Japanese Buddhism and Western Christianity—as distinct modes of religious perception, we can appreciate the "complexity and ambiguity that *Silence* embodies." In that context, Hirota interprets the characters of Rodrigues and Kichijiro in the second part of his chapter through the lens of the Pure Land teachings of Shinran, a Japanese Buddhist monk, especially the Primal Vow of the Buddha Amida.

Mark W. Dennis interprets *Silence* through the lens of Buddhist thought, focusing first on the story and then on the text, the story's "vehicle." Both parts draw from Middleton's use of Steiner's characterization of the role of the literary critic as being that of the "pilot fish." After introducing key Buddhist concepts, Dennis uses a Buddhist lens to interpret the transformation of Rodrigues as he confronts the many faces of suffering while pursuing a glorious Christian martyrdom.

The second part of his chapter draws from *The Questions of King Milinda,* a Buddhist text that considers "real" things—a key issue in Steiner's statement about the literary critic—through the lens of Buddhist teachings on emptiness and interdependence. Dennis writes, "This Buddhistic approach to the study of things, which resonates with poststructuralist thought, focuses on change and interdependence over stasis and singularity, and highlights the ambiguity of language, whether we use it to represent a wooden chariot to convey a king or a wooden cross to crucify a messiah, whether it appears in a story about a seventeenth-century Jesuit priest who imagines the face of that messiah to be beautiful and blue eyed."

The chapters in Part Three, "Endo's Theology," offer sustained interpretations of the Christian doctrinal issues that arise in an oblique way in the first two parts, taking up a reading of Endo's apparently paradoxical use of laughter by characters in the novel at seemingly odd places, but also the intellectual and spiritual implications of the changing face of Christ as the novel progresses.

Jeff Keuss considers the novel as a form of missionary literature through the lenses of phenomenology and theology. Here, Keuss reads the changing face of Christ in the novel as a literary strategy used by Endo to "sublimate Japanese notions of the Sacred through the propagation of essentialist Christian doctrines." To illustrate this process, Keuss draws from the Japanese notion of *dōhansha*, or "companion," arguing that "Endō releases the sacred into the poetics of *Silence* through what I will explore as 'textual *dōhansha*'—that is, as a constant companion of the text that *suffers* with the reader, therein offering a poetics of Christ fully realized beyond received doctrinal formulations."

Dennis Washburn takes up the climactic scene in which Rodrigues tramples upon the face of Christ in the *fumie*. Noting that this act of "apostasy invites and sustains multiple interpretations," Washburn describes the many sorts of interpretive frames readers may bring to bear when reading *Silence* as a historical novel: as a "meditation on moral choice," and as a "novel on the question of the translatability of values," among other possibilities. To account for these multiple readings, which are part of the novel's history and are necessary to "a more complete and sensitive engagement with *Silence*," Washburn focuses on how the novel's meaning emerges from two of Endo's key choices: the use of a narrative structure that is multi-perspective and multi-vocal (for example, switching from a first to a third-person discourse in the novel), and a narrowly focused character study.

Frances McCormack's chapter explores Endo's ambiguous use of water as a motif in *Silence*. Whereas Christian traditions, especially when drawing from the New Testament, have viewed water as a symbol of faith and grace, Endo employs it to shape his narrative by drawing from an array of theological imagery. In *Silence*, water not only provides relief from the intense heat but also serves as a place to torture the hidden Christians; the multivalence of water "echoes the moral and spiritual ambiguities of the novel." McCormack shows how Endo's use of water thereby "problematizes interpretation and adds a richness of theological nuance to the text." She concludes by reconsidering Rodrigues's character "through the motif of tears and the monastic doctrine of compunction."

Jacqueline Bussie investigates the significance of laughter, or "risibility," in Endo's novel. Although *Silence* is filled with pain and darkness, the "oppressed characters … repeatedly exhibit the same incongruous behavior: they laugh in the face of their own suffering." Even so, scholarly literature has ignored this "fascinating yet dislocated and unanticipated risibility." To make up for that lacuna, Bussie's chapter considers why these characters laugh at unexpected moments, the significance of laughter by the faithful at the "horrible" and at their own suffering, and how *Silence* helps "Christian thought elucidate the theological and ethical significance of the laughter of the oppressed as well as a nuanced understanding of a theology of the cross." Bussie concludes that laughter serves as a theological and ethical mode of resistance, a "hidden transcript," used by the oppressed when facing suffering, when they have entered a state in which language and traditional beliefs have been ruptured. She writes, "In particular, Endo's novel reveals that the laughter of the oppressed not only protests evil and unmasks the limits of theodicy, but also deconstructs the dominant consciousness."

Since Endo's novel routinely appears on university syllabi addressing everything from World Literature to East Asian Religions, and from Global Christianity to Japanese Studies, Part Four addresses the teaching of *Silence* in the college classroom, emerging with several pedagogical suggestions for seminar discussions. John Kaltner begins by describing his experience while a student reading Endo's novel for the first time: "*Silence* was clearly one of the most influential and memorable books I read during that time of my life." Since moving to the professor's chair, Kaltner has regularly taught the novel to undergraduate students, and seeks in the chapter "to describe some of my experiences using the novel as a pedagogical tool to identify and explore questions of meaning and value for students." To this end, he takes up four pivotal scenes from the novel that have been useful for generating discussion and debate. In examining these scenes, Kaltner "comments on the plot, characterization, and other literary features of the novel that make it such an accessible and fertile resource for both teachers and students. The chapter also describes an assortment of questions, conversation starters, and assignments I have developed over the years that are meant to encourage students to explore the richness and relevance of Endo's masterpiece."

The anthology's final part, which addresses the novel's adaptation for the stage and screen, is meant to suggest how *Silence* has been transformed through its adaptation and representation in other forms and media, such as translation, artwork, comic books, Facebook pages, but especially stage and screen. As noted above, we have included comments from Martin Scorsese on his adaptation of the novel, which is being filmed in Taiwan over summer/autumn 2014, is slated for release in 2015, and is set to star Andrew Garfield, Liam Neeson, and Ken Watanabe. Here, we also include the unabridged script of Steven Dietz's play, which was showcased at the Milwaukee Repertory Theater in 1995. Dietz, a playwright at the University of Texas at Austin who has produced more than 30 plays, won the Yomiuri Shimbun Award (the Japanese "Tony") for this adaptation. *Variety* described it as follows:

> The Milwaukee Rep's season-opening collaboration with the Subaru Acting Company is an erudite and intellectually stimulating new adaptation by Steven Dietz of a Japanese novel by Shusaku Endo. Performed by a cast of American and Japanese actors, the resulting bilingual production is a beguiling, beautifully designed mix of Eastern and Western dramatic styles that's appropriate for a play that explores the cultural constraints of European Christianity.[9]

Issues in Translation, Linguistics, and Sources

A number of our chapters address linguistic issues that arise in relation to William Johnston's translation of the novel from Japanese into English—languages with distinct grammar, syntax, and modes of representation. Unlike the Latin script used to represent the English language, the Japanese language is written using a combination of *kanji*, or "Chinese characters," and two syllabaries: *katakana* and *hiragana*. A single *kanji* can generally be read with one or more *on*, or Chinese, and *kun*, or Japanese, readings. For example, the Japanese title of Endo's novel is *Chinmoku* (*Silence*), the combination of the characters 沈 (*chin*: "to sink," "to subside") and 黙 (*moku*: "silence"). The latter character, which appears on the cover of Johnston's translation to represent the Christian cross, has *on* readings of *moku* and *boku*, and *kun* readings of the verbs *damaru* and *modasu*, meaning "to be silent" and "to stop speaking," but it can also appear in other forms: for example, *damare* is the imperative form, and thus, "Silence!"

Moreover, Japanese names are generally written, surname first, in *kanji*: for example, the author's name is written in *kanji* as 遠藤 (Endō) 周作 (Shūsaku); long vowel sounds, which appear in both his names, are indicated in transliterations with a macron over the vowel, although these diacritical markings can be omitted in some renderings, giving us Shusaku Endo. We respect both renderings in our anthology, as we make clear elsewhere, leaving individual essayists to adopt their own style.

One final, important translation issue concerns the dramatic scene in which Rodrigues confronts the face of Christ in the *fumie*; in that scene, Christ tells the priest in Endo's Japanese, 踏むがいい, transliterated as

Before *Silence*: Stumbling Along with Rodrigues and Kichijiro

Kevin M. Doak

In this chapter, I explore the prototypes of the characters for Rodrigues and Kichijiro in *Silence* as they were developed in a variety of earlier works, particularly in short stories that have garnered much less attention than Endō's major novels. Re-tracing the precursors to these key characters from *Silence* brings us to a new view of Endō's unusual style of literary development in which themes and even characters themselves recur in surprising contexts across different works over a span of years. But the main goal of this chapter is not merely an exercise in the study of literary development or narratology. Rather, I suggest that only by understanding the evolution of these prototypes across time and texts can we come to a full appreciation of what *Silence* is really about. Moreover, I argue that it is certainly legitimate to explore the meaning of Endō's literature from a Roman Catholic perspective. The reason is not because Endō was always a perfect Catholic in his personal life or because he was trying to proselytize through his fiction: clearly, neither was the case. Rather, it is because, regardless of the vicissitudes in Endō's own spiritual life, he never abandoned his Catholic perspective on life and, most importantly, this Catholic perspective is deeply embedded in his literature. Ultimately, the question of what Endō's literature means rests on an interpretation of his texts, but it is certainly not irrelevant to take into consideration the life experiences and values that Endō himself drew from. In short, the goal of this chapter will be to present key elements in Endō's fiction that develop over ten years or more leading up to the 1966 publication of *Silence* as a way of gaining a better understanding of Endō as a Catholic Japanese writer.

The first step in appreciating Endō as a Catholic writer is to explore the question of whether he endorsed a form of cultural relativism that would undermine the claims of the Catholic Church to be, as its name implies, "universal." Some critics have turned to Endō's early novellas, "Yellow Man" and "White Man," both published in 1955, as proof that he believed in a determinant racial sense of difference from "White Europeans," some even going so far as to suggest that Endō's difficult experiences as a student in France led him to move slowly but surely into a nostalgia for Japan's traditional pantheism, which he coded in his theme of a "maternal" spirituality versus a paternalistic ("Western") Catholicism.[1] When Tsuge Teruhiko suggested, in an important roundtable discussion on postwar Catholic Japanese writers, that the apostate priest Fr. Durand in "Yellow Man" expressed Endō's own views in opining that Japan was poor ground for Christianity to set down roots, Ōsugi Shigeo offered the following: "I feel the narrative structure of 'Yellow Man' seems a bit more complicated in that the Japanese optic and the foreigner optic are both interwoven here."[2] Whether or not one believes Endō agreed with his character Fr. Durand about the incompatibility of Christianity and Japanese climate (an issue that comes up again in *Silence* and other works), Ōsugi makes an important point: Endō is a skilled and cosmopolitan writer, not easily given to national stereotypes. And to their credit, Mark Williams, Francis Mathy, and John T. Netland reject the cultural particularism of the swamp metaphor in favor of an interpretation, like Ōsugi's, that transcends cultural boundaries and reads the swamp as indicative of a more general human condition.[3]

Nonetheless, arguments that Endō proposes a dichotomy between a monotheistic Christian West and a pantheistic Japanese culture persist, and his 1958 novel *The Sea and Poison* is held up as the best evidence.[4] And why not? The narrative itself—based on an actual incident in which Japanese doctors during the war performed vivisections on American POWs—seems an instructive example of the moral difference that results from acts based on Christian ethics and acts that are not. But is that really what Endō was trying to say? In a rare exception to his usual stance of leaving the meaning of his fiction to his readers' interpretation, Endō spoke out against Yamamoto Kenkichi's claim that *The Sea and Poison* showed that because the Japanese people do not have faith in God they are easily drawn into evil acts. Endō said:

> I do not think that the Japanese people's current condition of a loss of humanity is due to Japan's premodernity or our nationality but rather I think it is a manifestation of the decadent phenomena of today's late modernity. … Faith is a constant conversion. At a minimum, I've never thought that seeking God and possessing God are separate things. Man, no matter who he is, is always seeking God. … The distinction I want to make is the difference between "seeking God and the kind of god one seeks."[5]

Among the kinds of "gods" people often seek, Endō lists the pantheists' worship of nature, the aesthetes' worship of beauty as a surrogate for God, and the rationalists' worship of "god" as merely a symbol for human-ity's intellect. His point is reminiscent of Heidegger's distinction between *Sein* and *Dasein*, between Being (God) and "being thrown into Being." Understandings of God, literature, human life—indeed, symbolic represen-tations *per se*—are all at the level of "*Dasein*," and thus subject to tremendous freedom of interpretation, which is also to say, a responsibility to get it right (or, if one does not, as the character Suguro in *The Sea and Poison* illustrates, to bear the costs of getting it wrong). Endō himself was "thrown into God" with his famous "forced baptism" as a youth. But he did not really raise the question of "what kind of God" he had been thrown into until he started to write. The question came to the fore most in *The Sea and Poison* where he highlighted this concern with a God that may (or may not) intervene in the face of evil (that is, the topic of theodicy).[6] This theodicy unfolds in a particular pattern through much of Endō's writing up to *Silence*. However, with the publication of *The Samurai* in 1980, the problematic shifts in a dramatically new way, making the discussion of Endō's works after *Silence* a matter that will have to be taken up on a separate occasion.

The Rodrigues Prototype

Silence has been portrayed as Endō's "first fruits" in burying the sense of distance Japanese have from Christianity, as Yamane Michihiro put it, or as an experiment in inculturating Christianity into Japanese culture, as others would have it. But Yamane also points out that *Silence* can be located in an important way in Endō's literary motif of foreign priests who abandon their faith.[7] Indeed, Yamane quotes Endō as saying that he had intended to title the work not "*Silence*" but "*Hinata no nioi*" (the scent of sunshine) to evoke, among other things, the "smell of loneliness" of Fr. Ferreira whose entire life had turned out poorly.[8] This theme of the foreign apostate priest and the fate that befalls him can be traced through works like "Yellow Man," *Volcano* (1960), "Eihōshi" (1968), and *The Golden Country* (1969). The theme of the foreign apostate priest continues in works after *Silence*, most notably with Fr. Velasco in *The Samurai*. Yamane argues that in post-*Silence* works there is a different significance to the apostate priest than in pre-*Silence* works. This is a complex issue, one that requires an extensive and nuanced consideration of both Velasco and Ōtsu in *Deep River* (1993). Due to space and other limita-tions, I will only treat those pre-*Silence* apostate priest characters here.

The Rodrigues prototype has a basis in Endō's biography. There were two foreign priests who, Endō felt, had betrayed him. The first was a French missionary at the Shukugawa Catholic Church to whom Endō's mother gave music lessons and who came to Endō's house to tutor him when he was young. He has never been identified by name. However, from the available information, we can conclude that this incident happened some time between 1934, when Endō was baptized at the Shukugawa church, and 1941 when he matriculated at Sophia University in Tokyo. In 1955 Endō wrote this priest into his first work that took up the character of an apostate priest, "Yellow Man." Yamane argues that this work, also the first by Endō that is set in Japan, is built on Endō's own memories of his boyhood hometown of Kobe, particularly the Shukugawa church. The Fr. Durand character, Yamane suggests, was composed on the basis of the French apostate priest at the Shukugawa church. And Yamane points out that Fr. Durand's violation of his vow of life-long celibacy with an immoral relationship with a woman named Kimiko torments him with thoughts of hell. Fr. Durand begins to resemble Judas in his torment until he is killed by a B29 bomb, a pitiful death that indeed recalls the end of Judas who "fell off a cliff and burst open his stomach with his intestines falling out."[9] While Fr. Durand tries to justify his betrayal of Christ by the idea that Judas's betrayal was necessary for Christ's plan to redeem humanity through his death on the cross, Fr. Durand's final tragic end tells the reader that in fact his own act of betrayal was not one oriented towards life but death.

The next work that treats this theme of the apostate priest is *Volcano*, which Endō published five years later. In between these two works was the actual incident of the second foreign priest who betrayed Endō, Fr. Petrus Herzog, S. J. (1905–96). He was a close friend of the Endō family who served as the spiritual director to both Endō and his mother, Iku. Fr. Herzog came to Japan in 1935 and met her at Mass at the Sacred Heart Convent in Takarazuka. He then went to Fordham University to study law and returned to Japan in 1940 as a professor at Sophia University, one year before Endō matriculated there. Endō's mother translated Fr. Herzog's "The Glory of God" as *Kami no Eikō* (1944). It was Fr. Herzog who took Endō in his car to the Shinagawa embarkation point when Endō sailed for France in 1950. Meanwhile, Iku became deeply involved in Fr. Herzog's publications. In December 1953, immediately after Endō's return from France, his mother died of a brain hemorrhage after an argument with Fr. Herzog. Still, Fr. Herzog officiated at Endō's marriage to Okada Junko in September 1955. In 1957, when Herzog became the subject of rumors regarding a woman working in his office, he suddenly resigned his position at Sophia, left the Jesuits, married the woman, and was naturalized as a Japanese the following year, taking on the name Hoshii Iwao. The woman involved happened to be divorced from Endō's cousin. Endō Junko has related how shocking Fr.

embracing a theological justification for falling away from the Church (the so-called Christ not taught in the churches); and, a strong attraction to community rather than an isolated, individualistic life. Most importantly, Tōgorō's voice calls him to community whereas Rodrigues's voice calls him to break from community. And his community of fellow Catholics comes to accept Tōgorō the weakling even after he apostatized yet again: "Kashichi was relieved to know that his suspicions about Tōgorō being a spy has [*sic*] been mistaken. 'It's all right. It's all right,' he thought."[37] And like Kichijiro, Tōgorō's end is uncertain. The surviving Catholic prisoners were released in 1871 by the Meiji government but "no one knows what happened to Tōgorō."[38] In contrast, we know all too well, unfortunately, what happened to Rodrigues.

Building on this historical character of Tōgorō, Endō took a decisive step in the formation of the Kichijiro prototype two years later in the short story "Unzen" (1965), which Endō himself has called a "prelude" to *Silence*.[39] For the first time, the character carries the name Kichijiro. Like "The Day Before," "Unzen" is a pseudo-*watakushi-shōsetsu* story that starts off again with Suguro (the recurring character who closely resembles Endō) traveling to Unzen in Nagasaki prefecture to research the persecution of Catholics in the early seventeenth century. Unzen is an infamous site where Catholics were tortured with the scalding waters of the hot springs. Also, as in "The Day Before," a book (this time, Collado's *Christian Confessions*) opens a window onto a subplot that takes the reader to another narrative about events several centuries earlier.[40] Here, Endō skillfully interweaves the two narratives, the two time periods, even two characters to make a point: "Suguro diligently searched the Christian histories for someone like himself ... [who] was more than adequately aware of his own spiritual slovenliness and pusillanimity ... [until] finally he had stumbled across the *Christian Confessions* ... and had been moved by the account of a man whose name Collado had concealed. The man had the same feeble will and tattered integrity as Suguro."[41] This unnamed man had hidden his Catholic faith, chanted Buddhist prayers, and ultimately publicly renounced his faith to save his wife and children from death—all information that, significantly, came from his later confession to Fr. Collado. In short, he was repentant for his sins in this matter. Like Tōgorō he was drawn back to his Catholic community and sought reconciliation, in his case, through the Sacrament of Reconciliation.

Yet, if Suguro's identification with this unnamed seventeenth-century Catholic Japanese frustrates the conventions of the *watakushi-shōsetsu* genre, Endō pushes the challenge even further. While Suguro looks on at the site of torture at Unzen, the ominously named Valley of Hell, and thinks of the man who had confessed his sins to Fr. Collado, we find:

the image of another individual had overlapped with that of the first man and now stumbled along with his head bowed. There was a little more detailed information about this second man. His name was Kichijirō and he first appeared in the historical records on the fifth day of December, 1631, when seven priests and Christians were tortured at the Valley of Hell. ... Standing on tiptoe, he had witnessed the cruel punishments which the officers inflicted on his spiritual mentors.[42]

From this point on, there is a superimposition of a trinity of persons, as it were: Suguro, "the unnamed seventeenth century Japanese man," and Kichijirō. This superimposition of persons is made explicit when we are told that "the only tangible piece of information he [Suguro] had about Kichijirō was that he had forsworn his religion to the officers, 'so that his wife and children might live'" and "Suguro could almost see the look on Kichijirō's face as he stood at the back of the crowd, furtively watching his former companions with the tremulous gaze of a dog, then lowering his eyes in humiliation. That look was very like Suguro's own."[43] The narrative continues to shift back and forth, particularly between Kichijirō and Suguro, as Suguro explicitly wonders whether the whole reason for his visit to this place was to understand Kichijirō's emotions as he watched his fellow Catholics suffer martyrdom. Our last sight of Kichijirō is when he follows after the Catholic prisoners and tries to offer them some food, wondering whether he will be able to enter Paradise with them. In the final lines, we encounter an anonymous man (Kichijirō?) who rushed toward the Catholics who were being burned at the stake. After fearfully denying he was one of them to the guards, we hear him praying "Forgive me! Forgive me!" Then Suguro walks away from the site, "his spine bent like Kichijirō's."[44] Again, in "Unzen," Endō reinforces the prototype sketched earlier with Tōgorō as one of human frailty, a propensity to sin (apostasy), but a simultaneous desire for reconciliation with the Catholic *ecclesia*.

Conclusion: Kichijiro and Rodrigues, Together in the End?

How can we better understand Kichijiro and Rodrigues in *Silence* from the patterns that emerge from these earlier prototypes? Suekuni Yoshimi argues that Kichijiro represents Endō's perspective of the weak.[45] But "weakness" alone does not quite cover the significance of the Kichijiro character. There are various kinds of weaknesses, and Kichijiro's typical kind of weakness is a weakness of the flesh and a fear of physical pain, whereas Rodrigues's weakness is the mortal kind: the capital sin of pride. Kichijiro's weakness does not prevent him from desiring reunion with the Catholic Church, and he expresses this desire with a cry for forgiveness and his constant returning to the Catholics. The pivotal scene is at the end of Chapter 10 when Kichijiro tearfully begs the apostate priest Rodrigues for the Sacrament of Reconciliation. Receiving absolution, he leaves. But contrast his attitude and actions with those of Rodrigues, who is actually laughing at being called "the Apostate Paul" just when Kichijiro approaches in tears of repentance, seeking the Sacrament of Reconciliation.[46] And as Kichijiro leaves confession, absolved and weeping softly, Rodrigues adopts a defiant attitude, desperately justifying his act even while admitting he had betrayed his fellow Catholic priests (*alter Christus*, as they would be known to him). Here Rodrigues declares he was able to betray the Catholic Church but not betray his Lord. Yet his declaration that "he loved him now in a different way from before"[47] exposes an interesting nuance: the Japanese text reads "*ano hito*" ("that man") for "him," leaving open to question whether he means "Jesus as only a man, not God" or if in fact "his Lord" is someone else, a "man" who is not God at all (Satan). It is well-known that Endō referred to Jesus as "that man" in other writings. But here the question is internal to the text, and the text leaves open a range of possible interpretations of Rodrigues's final position after his apostasy.

Yamane takes seriously Endō's well-known complaint that readers of *Silence* too often overlook the final sections of the novel after Rodrigues's stepping on the *fumie*. He turns to the "Appendix" where he finds a "decisive conversion" by *Kichijirō* who is now a servant of Rodrigues (who is given the Japanese name Okada San'emon): "in a word, *Kichijirō*'s soul has now been freed from the darkness of solitude and has had a conversion of faith that has deeply attached him to the love of Christ."[48] Yamane agrees with Akifu Kasai's view that *Kichijirō* has come around to accepting Rodrigues's new understanding of a "Christ of a maternal religion" instead of his earlier "Christ of a paternal religion," a new theological view that emphasizes the salvation of the weak.[49] This is not going so far as to say Endō is endorsing a Christ without the Catholic Church, however, as others have claimed.[50] Rather, Yamane emphasizes the connection to St. Peter in the amulet case discovered among *Kichijirō*'s belongings (Johnston's translation says it had the image of both St. Peter and St. Paul), suggesting that, like St. Peter, *Kichijirō* had finally made a full conversion of faith through repentance and was a "rock" for the Church in Japan, and like the first Pope of the Catholic Church, this former weakling was now a "leader of the faith community" and ready to give his life for his faith—as St. Peter did.[51] Yamane's interpretation of *Kichijirō* as one who comes home to the Church is supported by the pattern of return in the Kichijiro prototype in Endō's earlier works. It is also supported by the ambiguous final information about *Kichijirō* in *Silence*: we leave *Kichijirō* in prison for being a Catholic in violation of the prohibition of the religion. Will he apostatize again? Or will he persevere to martyrdom this time? Endō leaves the question open. I tend to think the evidence suggests that he will not give up the faith this time.

But in a sense, whether *Kichijirō* falls again is not really the question. As the history of the Rodrigues and Kichijiro prototypes attests, Endō's concern is not with condemning sinners—and it certainly is not with justifying sin! Rather, Endō tries to make a more important, overarching point through these characters who fail to live up to their ideals, a point that I believe has often been missed by his readers who seek in *Silence*, not what Endō offers, but rather justification for their own sins, heresies, and other personal comforts. Endō shows over the course of his writings about apostasy that what ultimately matters is not whether one falls or not, but rather what one does after one (inevitably) falls. Some will suggest that failure is an invitation to redefine the goals more "realistically" (for example, the so-called Christ without the dogmas of the Catholic Church). Others will suggest that failure means inevitable condemnation of the one who falls. But Endō looks more to *Kichijirō* than to Rodrigues and finds in this child-like sinner a model for how to live, whether as a Christian or simply as a man. When one falls, one should just get up again and seek forgiveness. This is not a radical new theology, but a time-honored teaching of the Catholic Church. It is as ancient as the Sacrament of Confession. St. Josemaría Escrivá said it best: "the saint is not the person who never falls, but rather the one who never fails to get up again, humbly and with a holy stubbornness."[52] Or, as Endō himself said, "faith is a constant conversion."[53]

Notes

1   See Shin Sunhi, "Haha naru mono," *Kokubungaku: kaishaku to kanshō* 71.2 (2006): 128, 132.

2   Ōsugi Shigeo, "Zadankai: daisan no shinjin 21 seiki kara no shōsha," *Kokubungaku: kaishaku to kanshō* 71.2 (2006): 15.

3   Mark B. Williams, *Endō Shūsaku: A Literature of Reconciliation* (London and New York: Routledge, 1999); Francis Mathy, "Shusaku Endo: The Second Period," *Japan Christian Quarterly* 40 (Fall 1974): 214–20; John T. Netland, "From Cultural Alterity to the Habitations of Grace: The Evolving Moral Topography of Endo's Mudswamp Trope," *Christianity and Literature* 59.1 (Autumn 2009): 27–48.

4 Takao Hagiwara, "Return to Japan: the Case of Endō Shūsaku," *Comparative Literature Studies* 37.2 (2000): 135–6.

5 Endō, "Nihonjin no shinkō ni tsuite," *Yomiuri shimbun*, June 10, 1958; reprinted in Endō, *Kirishitan jidai: junkyō to kikyō no rekishi* (Tokyo: Shōgakkan, 1992), 220–1. Endō's affirmation of the traditional Catholic dictum that "faith is a constant conversion" needs to be borne in mind when considering Dennis Washburn's argument that Rodrigues's act of stepping on the *fumie* in *Silence* is "both an apostasy and a conversion." See Washburn, "The Poetics of Conversion and the Problem of Translation in Endō Shūsaku's *Silence*," in Washburn and A. Kevin Reinhart, eds., *Converting Cultures: Religion, Ideology, and Transformations of Modernity* (Leiden: Brill, 2007).

6 On the general topic of theodicy in Endō's work, see Adelino Ascenso, *Transcultural Theodicy in the Fiction of Shūsaku Endō* (Rome: Editrice Pontificia Università Gregoriana, 2009).

7 Yamane Michihiro, *Endō Shūsaku: sono jinsei to Chinmoku no shinjitsu* (Tokyo: Chōbunsha, 2005), 220. Dating Endō's publications is notoriously problematic because Endō sometimes first published the work in a serial form in journals, often a year before the completed work was published in monograph form in Japanese. For my project, the date of a volume being published is less an accurate measure of what Endō was thinking about than when he was writing (and first publishing) on a topic in the original Japanese. My source for dates of publication is the Yamane chronology, 431–93.

8 Ibid., 220–1. Quotations are from Yamane quoting Endō.

9 Ibid., 226–7.

10 Endō Junko, "Otto Endō Shūsaku to sugoshita hibi," quoted in Yamane, *Endō Shūsaku*, 224–5.

11 Yamane, *Endō Shūsaku*, 227–8.

12 I have revised Richard Schuchert's translation (cf. *Volcano*, London: Peter Owen, 1978), 67 in line with Yamane's points. See Yamane, *Endō Shūsaku*, 228.

13 Yamane offers the insightful reading that Fr. Brou may have been modeled after Fr. Alfred Mercier, M.E.P. of the Shukugawa Catholic Church who was conscripted during the war, and then afterwards arrested by Japanese police on suspicion of espionage. Yamane, *Endō Shūsaku*, 235–6.

14 Ibid., 231, 235.

15 Williams, *Endō Shūsaku*, 231.

16 Here, I disagree with Yamane's reading of Fr. Sato as only expressing an attitude of "duty," and not true Christian charity, toward Durand. See Yamane, *Endō Shūsaku*, 236. Whether his reluctant visit to Durand in the hospital (39–46), the scene where Fr. Sato asks a rude Durand to stop harassing his parishioners after giving Durand a small Christmas gift (95–100), or when Fr. Sato "unobtrusively" gives him money (125), I

think Endō is showing how charity can coexist with temptations toward resentment and rejection of others. But the actions of Fr. Sato speak louder than his private temptations to completely cut ties to Durand, thus demonstrating the Catholic teaching that love is a rational decision taken for the betterment of others, not a mere "feeling." Endō expresses this Catholic understanding of love in "My Belongings," written just four years after *Volcano*, when he wrote "people were drawn to beautiful things, attractive things. But that feeling was not really love" ("My Belongings," in *Stained Glass Elegies*, trans. Van C. Gessel (New York: New Directions Books, 1984), 54. Indeed, the whole point of this short story, which ostensibly is about whether Suguro still "loves" his middle-aged wife, is that true love means taking ownership over the decisions you have made.

17 Endo, *Wonderful Fool*, trans. Francis Mathy (London: Peter Owen, 1974), 234.

18 Ibid., 237.

19 Fuda-no-tsuji, near Keio University, remains a pilgrimage site today, complete with a stone marker and inscription that commemorates the incident. It is known for being a prominent site in Edo where Jesuit and Franciscan missionaries were martyred alongside Japanese Catholics like John Haramondo.

20 Endo, "Fuda-no-tsuji," *Stained Glass Elegies*, 68.

21 Shusaku Endo, *Silence*, trans. William Johnston (New York: Taplinger Publishing Company, 1980). The key line for those who see Rodrigues's "apostasy" as liberation is when he muses, "I know that my Lord is different from the God that is preached in the churches." Yet, one must not only be attentive to the ambiguity in this line (it might mean that his real "Lord," even though Rodrigues may not be aware of the fact, is not Jesus Christ at all, but somebody else, for example, Satan), but also to the context of this musing, which begins with Rodrigues wondering "if there is any difference between Kichijiro and myself" (175). As I argue below, there is.

22 On the language of the body and the moral imperative that it speak consistently with the language of the mind, see John Paul II, *The Theology of the Body: Human Love in the Divine Plan* (Boston: Pauline Books, 1997).

23 Endo, *Silence*, 171.

24 Mt. 26.75.

25 Endo, *Silence*, 176.

26 Dennis Washburn, "The Poetics of Conversion and the Problem of Translation in Endō Shūsaku's *Silence*," 352.

27 Ibid., 350.

28 Christopher Shannon has elucidated the "Catholic insistence on the priority of community to the individual" in ways that underscore the Catholic nature of Endō's fiction. I must also note that Shannon does so while touching on Martin Scorsese's films and major works on Japanese culture. Although he is not a specialist on Japan, his remarks on Japanese

culture are also among the best I have read. See Christopher Shannon, "Catholicism as the Other," *First Things* (January 2004): 52.

29 The debate over whether there exists a "Catholic novel" is a long and contentious one. See for example, Toby Garfitt, "What Happened to the Catholic Novel?," *French Studies: A Quarterly Review* 66.2 (April 2012): 222–30; Gerald R. Russello, "A Different Discipline: The American Catholic Novel," *Renascence* 51.3 (Spring 1999): 205–15; Bernard Bergonzi, *The Myth of Modernism and Twentieth Century Literature* (New York: St. Martin's Press, 1986), 172–87.

30 Reflecting on Lodge's *How Far Can You Go?*, Marian Crowe has noted that "the novel has no single protagonist, for it follows the lives of eight young Catholics, their spouses, and a priest over a period of twenty-three years." Marian Crowe, "Catholicism and Metaphor: the Catholic Fiction of David Lodge," *Logos* 15.3 (Summer 2012): 133.

31 One important exception to this Orientalist reading of *Silence* is that of Van Gessel, who subtly draws our attention from Rodrigues to Kichijiro: "the surface drama of the novel, the portion that captures the most attention, may focus on the questions of whether Christianity or transformative pantheism will win the battle for souls in Japan, but *events in the shadows, the actions among the weak and groveling, are of greater significance to Endō*" (emphasis added). Van C. Gessel, "Shusaku Endo," ed., Gessel, *Japanese Fiction Writers Since World War II, Dictionary of Literary Biography* 182 (Detroit: Gale Research, 1997), 48.

32 If, as Stefan Tanaka has argued, Japan has its own form of Orientalism (*tōyōshugi*), even Japanese readers may not be immune from this Orientalist reading of *Silence*, particular since Rodrigues is a European priest in a novel set in the time when Christianity was fairly "exotic" in Japan. See Tanaka, *Japan's Orient: Rendering Pasts into History* (Berkeley: University of California Press, 1993).

33 Edward W. Said, *Orientalism* (New York: Vintage Books, 1979), 190.

34 Kenneth B. Pyle, "Japan and the United States: An Unnatural Intimacy," *The Journal of Japanese Studies* 37.2 (Summer 2011): 377–95.

35 One intriguing aspect of this blended time in "The Day Before," which I do not have sufficient space to adequately treat here, is the superimposition of the sacred image of the absent *fumie* with its substitute, the vulgar pornographic images pushed by the sketchy peddler who visits the hospital room and who evokes the Kichijiro prototype.

36 Endō, "The Day Before," *Stained Glass Elegies*, 77.

37 Ibid., 78.

38 Ibid.

39 Endō, *Kirishitan jidai*, 38.

40 The author appears to be Fr. Diego Collado, O.P. (a missionary in Japan from 1619–22 who died in a shipwreck on his way from Spain to Manila in 1638) and the work referred to was his *Modus confitendi et examinandi*

paenitentem japonensem formula suamet lingua japonica (Rome 1631, 1632), which was translated into Japanese by Ōtsuka Mitsunobu as *Koriyādo zangeroku* (Tokyo: Kazama Shobō, 1957). I have not been able to consult this work to see whether a person named Kichijiro actually appears in this source or whether Endō invented the name, as his story suggests.

41 Endō, "Unzen," *Stained Glass Elegies*, 98.

42 Ibid., 100–1. Kichijirō in Gessel's translation of "Unzen" has the macron; Kichijiro in Johnston's translation of *Silence* omits it (except for the last section of the book—see below, note 48); to keep the two characters distinct in my discussion, I will follow the practice of each translator for the Kichijiro in his work.

43 Ibid., 102.

44 Ibid., 107. The similarities in reasons for apostasy in the time period suggest that Kichijirō and the unnamed man might be one and the same.

45 Suekuni Yoshimi, "Endō Shūsaku no rekishi ninshiki o megutte: Sengoku sanbu saku o tegakari ni," *Kokubungaku: kaishaku to kanshō* 71.2 (2006): 139.

46 Endo, *Silence*, 190.

47 Ibid., 191.

48 Yamane, *Endō Shūsaku*, 422. Yamane's argument about a converted *Kichijirō* is underscored, perhaps unintentionally, by Johnston's translation. *Kichijirō* in the "Appendix" appears in italics and with the macron, whereas Kichijiro prior to that point in *Silence* does not. In any event, I have followed Johnston's practice below in representing the Appendix *Kichijirō* in italics with the macron.

49 Yamane, *Endō Shūsaku*, 422. Yamane cites with approval Akifu Kasai, *Endō Shūsaku ron* (Tokyo: Sōbunsha, 1987).

50 Richard Durfee argues that Endō begins to show as early as *Volcano* and *Wonderful Fool* "a growing conviction that the locus of genuine Christianity is not necessarily in either European culture *or the Catholic Church*" (emphasis added; 49). Durfee's argument that in *Volcano*, the "love of God is something now subtly portrayed as … beyond … the Catholic Church" (50) is a possible reading of the apostate priest Durand, but it misses the character of the Japanese Catholic priest Fr. Sato and the fact that in *Volcano* Catholicism is limited to neither Western men nor Western culture. Moreover, his interpretation of *Wonderful Fool* is also a possible one (although it must minimize Gaston's own Catholic seminary training and his European cultural identity), but Durfee's position cannot explain why Endō himself remained in the Catholic Church. These points must be addressed by anyone wishing to claim in *Silence* a similar "Christ without the Church" position as anything other than Rodrigues's self-delusion based on pride. Richard E. Durfee, Jr., "Portrait of an Unknowingly Ordinary Man: Endo Shusaku, Christianity and Japanese Historical

Consciousness," *Japanese Journal of Religious Studies* 16.1 (March 1989): 41–62.

51 Yamane, *Endō Shūsaku*, 423.

52 St. Josemaría Escrivá, *Friends of God* (New York: Scepter Publishers, 2002), 138.

53 Endō, "Nihonjin no shinkō ni tsuite," 220.

2

Silence on Opposite Shores: Critical Reactions to the Novel in Japan and the West

Van C. Gessel

Today, nearly 50 years since the publication of Endō Shūsaku's novel *Silence* (*Chinmoku*, 1966; trans. 1969), there is widespread agreement among readers both in Japan and those who have read it in translation that it is a modern masterpiece—deftly told, movingly dramatic, and filled with challenging spiritual insights. That was by no means the case when the book was first published, either in its native land or overseas. I will examine here some of those early reactions and then offer a few of my own perspectives on the novel as a student of Endō's work for some four decades now.

The initial Japanese and Western responses to the book stood almost diametrically opposed to one another: Some within the Roman Catholic Church in Japan sought to "silence" the novel's message through tacit censorship, while outside Japan the English translation of the novel was, for several years, greeted with what can only be termed critical "silence."

"Silenced" on Japanese Shores

In Japan, the native Catholic clergy denounced the work, horrified at what they regarded as the aesthetic glorification of apostasy, and some voices recommended that the novel be listed on a local equivalent of the *Index Librorum Prohibitorum* (List of Prohibited Books).[1] A Catholic father, Kasuya Kōichi, argued that the novel appears to "not only acknowledge apostasy, but even praise it. ... The greatest merit of this work is that it clearly identifies the existence of one of the most fundamental problems that Christianity faces in Japan. But its greatest danger is that it bears within itself the potential to destroy the will to solve that very problem."[2] Kasuya suggested that if the novel is read as an affirmation of, even an exhortation to, apostasy then it takes on a uniquely Japanese, Protestant-like definition of "salvation" that negates the fundamental responsibility of Christians to be the salt of the earth.[3] Other Christian readers of the novel in Japan were equally incensed: Yanaihara Isaku, a professor of philosophy at Protestant-founded Dōshisha University, insisted that the faithful martyrs of Japan's "Christian century" had, indeed, heard the voice of God, but that the apostate priests Ferreira and Rodrigues were denied that blessing because they did not have faith in Him from the beginning.[4]

Given the negative reaction to the novel by the tiny Christian community in Japan (comprising, when both Catholic and Protestant tallies are included, less than 1 per cent of the Japanese population in the 1960s), it may seem remarkable that it became a healthy best seller soon after its publication: The initial hardback edition sold approximately 750,000 copies, and the paperback edition to date has sold 1,770,000 copies.[5] The reality is, indeed, remarkable. *Silence* was appropriated and hailed by college-aged left-wing readers upon its publication in Japan. They saw in the novel an allegory for their intellectual predecessors in 1930s Japan: devout believers in the newly imported ideology of Marxism who were hounded by the Japanese thought-control police, interrogated, beaten, sometimes even brutally murdered if they would not publicly renounce their "seditious" political views.[6] The suffering Catholic priests in Endō's novel were thus seen as metaphors for all the martyrs of the nascent Marxist movement in prewar Japan, and young leftist readers of the 1960s were profoundly stirred as they superimposed the faces of their own radical heroes atop those of Ferreira and Rodrigues.

There was no shortage of Japanese critical responses to the novel that praised the intricate narrative structure of the work or expressed admiration for the dialectical oppositions between Western and Asian spiritual cultures that are so deftly depicted in the debates between Rodrigues and his perse-cutors—primarily the Nagasaki magistrate, Inoue, and his own apostate mentor, Ferreira. The power of the dramatic conflict Endō offers up in the novel was easily recognized and widely appreciated by both critics and readers. Perhaps the most insightful reading at the time came from the critic Etō Jun who wrote that the "mournful gaze" from the image in the *fumie* was the gaze of a "maternal" figure, and that by trampling on that image, Rodrigues was able to obliterate the image of the "Father" who heads the Westernized Church and thereby embrace a forgiving "Mother" who is more compatible with Japanese religious sensibilities.[7]

And yet, however much the construction and the execution of the novel impressed critics and readers, and however many copies of the novel were purchased, a major problem of interpretation still remained. In 1992, Endō felt compelled to write a lengthy essay, titled "Chinmoku no koe" (The voice in the silence), in which he lamented the fact that he yielded to the demands of his publisher and called the novel *Silence*. His original title, *Hinata no nioi* (The scent of a sunny place)[8] was intended to emphasize the loneliness of a defeated man such as Ferreira, who stands beneath the harsh rays of the sun, arms folded, and reflects back on all he has lost.[9] By changing the title to *Silence*, however, Endō felt that he had thrown open the door for readers to interpret the author's intent as the portrayal of the silence of *God*—not merely the silence that haunts Rodrigues as he passes through his trials, but an ultimate, unbroken silence that justifies the priest's decision to trample on the image of a deity who has demonstrated His lack of interest in the human predicament by callously refusing to speak. In other words, the title *Silence* has the potential to facilitate an atheistic reading of the novel that might sit well with the non-Christian audience in Japan but could also drain the crucial meaning from the pivotal *fumie* scene itself—the scene in which Rodrigues, as he is poised to grind his foot into the sacred image, hears Christ break His silence and gently sanction the act of love the priest is about to perform.[10]

Because neither the young liberals who scooped the novel from bookstore shelves nor the Japanese critics who focused on the literary qualities of the book were concerned with the subtle spiritual nuances of Endō's work, it was a simple matter for them to accept without argument the conclusion that the book's title said it all: God is silent when men suffer because He does not exist. Stripping the novel of any religious trappings and imposing a political reading onto it, as leftist readers did, or denying the possibility that the deity actually *did* speak from the bronze image, as critics and general readers in Japan have often done since its publication, is to impose an edict of "silence" on the spiritual essence of the work, the element that was of greatest importance to its author and to a significant majority of its readers outside Japan.[11]

"Silent" on Western Shores

If attempts were made in Japan to muffle the vocal religiosity of *Silence* after its debut, the publication of the novel in translation in the English-speaking West was initially greeted by little more than … silence. Only three years after the book appeared in Japan, William Johnston's translation was published by a veritable trinitarian cooperative effort between Sophia University (a Catholic institution in Tokyo); *Monumenta Nipponica*, an academic journal devoted to Japanese studies and published at Sophia; and the Charles E. Tuttle publishing company, a small firm established in Tokyo in 1948 by a member of the U.S. Occupational forces with the aim of publishing "books to span the East and West." Because of copyright and distribution limitations, many of Tuttle's original imprints could only be sold within Japan. Such was the fate of *Silence* when the English translation appeared in Japan. Although it could be purchased at a few of the larger bookstores in Tokyo and Osaka that carried a small number of volumes about Japan in English, the novel was not accessible outside Japan until 1976, when the independent London publishing firm of Peter Owen Ltd. obtained overseas rights and brought the book out in the U.K. It would be unfair to argue that the publication of the novel in England attracted no attention: several leading newspapers carried reviews of *Silence*, and notable among the critical responses were Graham Greene's decision to include it in his list of the three best novels he had read that year and Francis King's declaration that the work ranked as a masterpiece because of the universality and grandeur of its themes and its literary attainments.[12] Yet even these distinguished voices of praise did little to raise interest in a novel translated from Japanese.

A U.S. edition did not appear until 1979, and the fact that the American firm which acquired the rights, Taplinger Publishing, can best be described as "obscure"[13] surely indicates that the book had not yet attracted the attention of the reading public or critics. By this time, Western readers had begun to show an interest in Japanese literature thanks to translations of major modern novels by Tanizaki Jun'ichirō, Kawabata Yasunari, and Mishima Yukio. But Endō's name was essentially unknown outside Japan at the end of the decade, and he might have remained an obscure figure had the celebrated American novelist, John Updike, not chosen to write a major article on *Silence* in the January 14, 1980 issue of *The New Yorker*.

It is not surprising that Updike, himself sometimes labeled a "Christian writer," should be sensitive to the spiritual underpinnings of the novel, which he said "harrowingly dramatizes immense theological issues."[14] *Silence*, he wrote,

is a remarkable work, a somber, delicate, and startlingly empathetic study of a young Portuguese missionary during the relentless perse-cution of the Japanese Christians in the early seventeenth century. ... Endo has conceived a narrative more orthodox, in texture and thought, than most novels by twentieth-century Christians. ... [T]he Japanese author brings to his Pascalian themes, and even to his descriptions of torture and execution, a tact as inexorable and hypnotic as his steady gray murderous sea, a tact that glazes his dark story lustrously.[15]

There is, no doubt, a degree of danger in trying to interpret the intent of an imaginative writer such as Updike when he spoke of an "orthodox" narrative written with "inexorable and hypnotic" tact—though I choose to regard these assessments as positive statements about the literary quality and impact of the novel. What I think is largely beyond debate, however, is that in introducing Endō's novel to *The New Yorker*'s very large, highly educated readership in the United States, Updike's high praise for *Silence* attracted many readers interested in works that treat "immense theological issues." And although I do not have sales figures for the Taplinger edition in the United States, it would not be surprising to find that Updike's acclaim for the work significantly and persistently boosted sales of *Silence* here.[16] Certainly the enthusiastic responses from reviewers such as Updike played a part in the November 1999 selection of *Silence* by HarperCollins's San Francisco publishers as one of the "100 Best Spiritual Books of the 20th Century."[17]

In the same review, Updike appeared to take a (preemptory?) swing at readers of the English translation, or perhaps at the ways in which he believed the Euro-American brand of Christianity had moved away from the religion's origins. He wrote: "In a culture where Christianity has established itself as an institution of the comfortable, it can be forgotten that its prime appeal was to the wretched. 'Christ did not die for the good and beautiful,' Rodrigues realizes. 'It is easy enough to die for the good and beautiful; the hard thing is to die for the miserable and corrupt.'"[18] What I find compelling about Updike's approach is that he did a remarkable job of preparing readers for the most dramatic moment in the novel— that juncture at which Rodrigues must decide whether to cling to the Church's definitions of his duties as a priest or to set aside his own institutional commission and perform a "painful act of love"[19] on behalf of the "miserable … wretched" Japanese Christians who are suffering excruciating torture.

Another important Christian writer from the United States, Philip Yancey, observed: "Not the least of the paradoxes surrounding Endo is that no important novelist today works so unashamedly and exclusively with overt Christian themes. … Outside Japan, he has shed new light on the faith—at once a harshly revealing light that exposes long-hidden corners, and a softening light that erases dark shadows."[20] It is worth noting that both Updike and Yancey appeared to consider the translations of Endō's novels into English as correctives to the ways in which Christianity is apprehended and practiced in the West. For Updike, *Silence* was a call to Western Christians to awaken and return to the origins of a faith that placed its primary emphasis on compassion and care for the downtrodden; in Yancey's view, the novel was distinguished by the "unashamed" manner in which Endō wrote about his adopted religion.

The Voice in the Wilderness

Interestingly, neither of these Christian critics acknowledged the fact that Endō was essentially forced by the spiritual climate of Japan to write "unashamedly" and "overtly" about the themes that were of greatest concern to him. Japan is both animistic (thanks to its Shinto roots) and largely unaccommodating of monotheistic faiths that demand unwavering adherence to a single religious organization. Because Japan is devoid of a layer of knowledge about Christian dogma, history, and symbolism, the only route open to a writer such as Endō was to bring his themes and images to the forefront. In *Silence*, the core image he employs is, of course, the face of Christ, and on this subject Yancey commented,

> Endo locates the theme of the novel in the transformation of the face of Jesus, not the transformation of the characters. "To me the most meaningful thing in the novel is the change in the hero's image of Christ," [Endo] says. The image of Jesus that had appeared to [Rodrigues] more than 100 times was pure, serene, heavenly. Gradually, though, as Rodrigues's mission fails—and indeed, causes the death of many Japanese—the face of Jesus begins to change into one marked by human despair.[21]

And when Rodrigues, fleeing from the pursuit of Japanese officials, catches a glimpse of his own haggard face in a pool of water, Yancey noted that "From that point on, the novel uses words like *suffering, emaciated, worn down,* and *ugly* to describe the face of Jesus."[22] And, Yancey emphasized, it is *that* face, the pained face of Christ who observes Rodrigues's moral battle with great compassion, that speaks to the priest from the *fumie.*

While careful readers in Japan certainly could have noticed the abrupt shift from Rodrigues's repeated musings about the "beautiful" face of Jesus to that of the "ugly, emaciated" figure that is most often depicted on the cross,[23] there is little likelihood that they would have been familiar with the iconographic history of Christian art and literature or have been expected to identify "Christ figures" or references to New Testament events embedded in a work of fiction. Endō wrote about his isolation as a Christian writer in a non-Christian country:

> I like to use double-layered, even triple-layered images. ... When Rodrigues is forced to trample on the *fumie*, dawn breaks. After passing through a torturous night, the dawn comes as he steps on the *fumie*, and a cock crows. Nearly every Japanese reader took that to mean nothing more than: "A rooster crowed." But when you write that a cock

crows just as a painful night comes to an end, in foreign lands virtually everyone would recognize in that scene a reference to the episode in the Bible where Peter betrays Christ. ... It's humiliating for me as a writer to complain that I'm not understood, but the fact is that it's been a real uphill battle for me.[24]

It was a unique burden for Endō to bear. Much of the power of *Silence*, particularly for Western readers who have been raised within (or at least adjacent to) a Christian culture, lies in the overlays of religious meaning that he places on his core narrative. Whether it be the obvious identification between Kichijirō and Judas, or the ways in which Rodrigues's journey to the *fumie* is modeled on Christ's Passion, or the manner in which Rodrigues's agony in stepping on the *fumie* is deftly presented as an act of love that echoes Jesus's sacrifice, Endō's conscious inclusion of New Testament parallels enriches the book for readers in the Western world. But few readers in Endō's homeland have the background in Christology to recognize the references. This is, perhaps, yet another example in which an author is not without honor, save in his own country.

On the "Greene-ing" of Endō

Many Western readers and critics, upon reading *Silence*, noted some key similarities between Endō and Graham Greene. In *The New Yorker's* review of Endō's novel *Scandal* (*Sukyandaru*, 1986; trans. 1988), the American writer Brad Leithauser tried to identify some of these congruities. He wrote:

> Both men are not merely Catholics but Catholic writers, whose books are an open, ongoing meditation on the meaning of their faith. Both are obsessed with physical pain and the ways in which the body—that mere envelope of the everlasting soul—can distort or canker our spiritual convictions. In selecting a hero, both show a penchant for loners who undertake long journeys that quickly become spiritual pilgrimages. And in bidding their heroes farewell both can be unsentimental to the point of coolness.[25]

Leithauser moved beyond these points of comparison to identify some of what he saw as Endō's strengths as a writer: "He is a craftsman of organization. Pick up any of his books and you are likely to discover that the narrative proportions feel right, that subplots tuck neatly into the larger plot, that the story advances with the surefootedness of someone who understands pacing. He can also be admirably relentless; he does not blink or flinch when handling cruelty, selfishness, or betrayal. ...."[26] Of *Silence* he wrote, "In moral terms, 'Silence' is as complex and instructive as almost any novel I know."[27] Interestingly, while displaying such admiration for Endō as a novelist, Leithauser concluded that Rodrigues's decision to apostatize "leaves the reader feeling let down. Where is the struggle that we have been promised? A hunger inside us for combat and adventure has been stirred but not sated."[28]

A common thread linking Western reactions to the novel—and, particularly, the climactic *fumie* scene—is this sense that there is something truly disturbing, even depressing, about Rodrigues's decision to trample. Is there, perhaps, a lingering preference in Judeo-Christian cultures for the hero to stand firm on his principles? Granted, there are numerous examples in American and European literature—especially since World War II—in which the protagonist fails to hold to his convictions. But in some ways, *Silence* tends to be read as the antithesis to Arthur Miller's *The Crucible* in which John Proctor chooses death over betraying the values he holds sacred.[29] But as Gary Wills pointed out, Rodrigues is unlike either Proctor or the literary character to whom Endō's protagonist is most frequently compared: the whiskey priest in Greene's *The Power and the Glory*. Wills observed:

> some of the criticism directed at Endo by Japanese Catholics resembles early Catholic attacks on Greene, who was accused of glorifying sinners and mocking the pious. But Greene's fascination with sin and guilt looks very tame when put beside Endo's. The whiskey priest of *The Power and the Glory* does not defect or lose his faith; he maintains a priestly ministry despite his own unworthiness, which partially qualifies him for serving other weak people. Endo explores a more interesting paradox; his priest does defect, not from weakness but from love, to spare Christian converts the persecution mounted against them.[30]

It is startling, I think, to hear Graham Greene's obsession with sin and guilt described in any context as "very tame," yet the observation is both apt and telling. Here Wills, like many other Western commentators, argued that Rodrigues "defects" or "loses his faith," in contrast to Greene's whiskey priest. Perhaps as a Catholic thinker, Wills uses "defection" in reference to Rodrigues's inevitable expulsion from the priesthood and the scorn that will be heaped on him by the Church, but the comparison with Greene's protagonist strongly implies that Rodrigues abandons his faith in Christ, choosing instead the weaker path of apostasy in the name of love for those who suffer around him.[31]

"Apostasy" or Epiphany?

Yet that is, I believe, Endō's vital point: that Rodrigues, in debasing himself and making of himself a sacrifice because of his intense love for others, is performing the most Christ-like of the options (imprisonment, ongoing torture, even martyrdom) placed before him. In interpreting Rodrigues's act of trampling on the *fumie*, it is important to view Endō in the context of his generational experience. Japan had been fighting a fierce war in China since around the time of Endō's baptism, and he was almost 19 years old when Pearl Harbor was bombed. One of the most common characteristics ascribed to Endō's generation (individuals born sometime between about 1920–5, who as teenagers were disinclined to believe the wartime military propaganda, making them perhaps the most ambivalent of any of their countrymen toward the war effort)[32] is a profound distrust of all terrestrial institutions—and for Endō, this came to include the institutional Church, in contrast to the spiritual Church. This antipathy is most evident in his 1980 novel, *The Samurai*, but I contend that it manifests itself in *Silence* as well. Also important is the fact that the sectarian battles between Catholics and Protestants waged on Japanese soil after the ban on Christianity was lifted in 1873 were anathema to most Japanese, and this internecine strife likely contributed to the creation and long-term popularity of a *mukyōkai* (non-church, non-sectarian) brand of the religion that made allowance for any individual approach to belief so long as it was centered in Jesus Christ.[33] It has been common in both Japan and the West to refer to Endō's interpretation of Christianity in *Silence* as more "Protestant" than "Catholic."[34] I submit that it is more revealing to look at Rodrigues's act of love as a manifestation of anti-institutional, *mukyōkai* attitudes, what we could, perhaps, label as "Endōism," since the ultimate faith that Rodrigues embraces seems freed from institutional constraints and focused on his true conversion in the wake of the personal encounter he has with Christ when he hears the voice speaking from the *fumie*.

In that respect, though Endō is rightfully praised as one of the few Japanese authors who has been able to create believable, fully rounded Western characters in his novels, we cannot overlook the fact that the character in *Silence* with whom Endō most closely identified is Kichijirō.[35] And the novel can certainly be read as a journey in which the aggressive, fervently faithful Western priest Rodrigues is transformed by his painful experiences in Japan into a much weaker, more passive, yet significantly more compassionate human being, virtually indistinguishable from Kichijirō by the end of the book.[36] Endō emphasizes the identification between these two frail-but-believing figures from different parts of the world in the oft-misread final section of the novel, the "Diary of an Officer at the Christian Residence"[37] (a "residence" that is actually a prison). In oblique terms, Endō hints that Rodrigues has become even more like Kichijirō during his incarceration. Although he has publicly renounced Christianity, Rodrigues continues ministering to the Japanese Christians in the cell, but each time the authorities discover his activities, he is again tortured in the pit and coerced into signing an oath of apostasy.[38] This cycle of falling and rising, only to fall and rise again, can be read as another subtle comparison of Rodrigues and the Apostle Peter. Jesus's admonition to Peter, "When thou art converted, strengthen thy brethren" (Lk. 22.32 in King James Version), is given in the Japanese translation of the Bible (taken from Martin Luther's rendition into German) as "When you are once again standing on your feet, strengthen your brethren." This is all the more poignant in the context of the novel where the colloquial term Endō most frequently employs for what is translated into English as "apostasy" is the word *korobu*, which etymologically has no religious connotations but simply means "to trip and fall; to tumble; to take a spill," with the tacit sense that the fallen one will rise up again. There could scarcely be a better verb to describe Kichijirō's actions throughout the novel and Rodrigues's stubborn cleaving to his belief in Christ with a willing spirit but weak flesh.[39]

Indeed, as others have pointed out, the "conversion" that results from Christ breaking His silence just as Rodrigues tramples on His face is not merely the singular transformation of one priest's heart from dogmatism to compassion, but also an embodiment of Endō's long-held conviction that it is the stern, "paternal" nature of Western Christianity that does not appeal to the Japanese, who prefer forgiving, "maternal" deities.[40] Japanologist Leith Morton wrote:

> Endō … has repeatedly linked his vision of Christ with images that strike a deep resonance from Japanese tradition. … In Endō's fictions we apprehend a grand dream, a dream of a Japanese Christ, more feminine than masculine, a Christ reminding us more of a Mother than a Father. Such a dream may frighten us or fascinate us, but its source surely derives from the same desire that rests within us, within all people, a desire profoundly spiritual that looks to the divine, to the good.[41]

Narrating *Silence*

Silence powerfully speaks to readers throughout the world irrespective of their religious affiliations or national cultures because of the compassionate humaneness of the Christ image that the author depicts and also because of the subtle manner in which the narrative structure of the book delineates, one step at a time, the journey that Rodrigues must make from confident, loquacious preacher to chastened, empathetic crypto-disciple.

After the novel's brief "Prologue," which sets the stage for the ensuing dramatic events, Rodrigues speaks in the first person—in the form of letters addressed to his superiors in Rome—for four consecutive chapters, representing nearly a third of the novel's length. We have immediate access to—in fact, we have no means to escape from!—the proud, confident, faithful voice of Rodrigues. We see what he sees, we hear what he hears, we think what he thinks: His is the only voice that is audible throughout the first section of the novel. We may be impressed by him, we may be annoyed by his egotism and zeal, but we cannot help but accept him as our guide through the opening events of this drama.

After Rodrigues is betrayed to the Japanese authorities by Kichijirō and obviously can no longer send dispatches to Rome, the narrative voice steps away from him, and our only access to his thoughts thereafter is indirect. In cinematic terms, we started this journey with the camera tightly focused on Rodrigues, but beginning in Chapter 5, the camera pulls back to give us a broader viewpoint—one less dominated by Rodrigues's gaze and voice. The "I" has been arrested and incarcerated, with the result that we only see and hear about "he." The "priest," as he is now called, has lost his commanding, capitalized personal pronoun and no longer exerts control over the progress of the narrative.

This detached perspective persists through the climactic *fumie* scene and into Chapter 9, where we still have some third-person limited access to Rodrigues's thoughts, though the only name that is applied to him comes via the taunts of neighborhood children who call him "Apostate Paul!"[42] The dolly bearing the narrative camera seems to continue its slow tracking away from the priest; the first two paragraphs of the chapter are scarcely even populated with human figures. By the time we reach the extracts from the diary of the Dutch clerk at Dejima in Chapter 10, the protagonist has become "Padre Rodrigues, the apostate Portuguese," an appellation well in keeping with the contemptuous attitude that many Dutch traders held toward the Catholic missionaries who had almost ruined their chances for commercial activities in Japan. Rodrigues scarcely shows up at all in the diary entries; it is not until the latter part of the chapter that he has his final interview with Lord Inoue, who informs him that hereafter he will be known as Okada San'emon, the name of a recently deceased Japanese man whose wife will be handed over to him. This is the last opportunity Rodrigues has to speak for, and as, himself in the novel, and it is in his final internal dialogue with

Christ that Endō reaffirms what has been most important to him throughout the work. Rodrigues speaks to Christ: "Lord, I resented your silence"; the response is: "I was not silent. I suffered beside you."[43]

In moving from the unavoidably audible voice of Rodrigues at the beginning of the novel, the gaze of the narrator progressively pulls away from him, and accompanying this movement, his voice grows more and more indistinct. By the final chapter, the Portuguese priest "Sebastian Rodrigues" no longer exists. The camera dolly has withdrawn so far from him that he is now only a pin-point in the mute records of history. The officer at the Christian Residence makes a handful of references to "Okada San'emon" over a period of ten years, until he finally notes in the Ninth Year of Enpō that "*Okada San'emon* died of illness at 2–3 past the hour of the Monkey."[44] Rodrigues's very existence has been removed from the pages of the story. Not once in the final years of his life does the narrative give him the opportunity to speak a word.

To what, then, does the novel's title refer? And what is the function of this cinematic mode of narration that renders the protagonist less and less central to the story? Since I am certain that Endō was *not* ultimately writing about "the silence of God," I can only conclude that it is the voice of Rodrigues— the voice of his overly confident ego, of his aggressive determination to encourage the violently persecuted flock of Japanese Christians to maintain their faith, of his escalating demands that God break His silence—that must be stilled before the voice of Christ can finally speak to him in his extremity. Once that Voice has spoken, Rodrigues is freed from all his preconceptions about the Church as a stern, paternal taskmaster and can now embrace his newfound faith rooted in compassion, sacrifice, and forgiveness. Herein, I believe, lies the power of *Silence* as a novel to move readers among every kindred, tongue, and people.

Notes

1   This is noted in the chronology of Endō's life edited from several sources by Yamane Michihiro and included in the *Endō Shūsaku bungaku zenshū* [Collected literary works of Endō Shūsaku], published in 2000 by Shinchōsha; the chronology is in volume 15, the reference on page 353. The *Index Librorum Prohibitorum*, originally issued in 1559 to identify books banned by the Catholic Church, was virtually ignored in modern times until it was officially abolished by Pope Paul VI, ironically in the same year that *Silence* appeared in Japan.

2   Cited in Masamichi Inoue, "Reclaiming the Universal: Intercultural

Subjectivity in the Life and Work of Endo Shusaku," *Southeast Review of Asian Studies* 34 (2012): 158.

3   Father Kasuya's reflections on *Silence* were published in the July 1966 issue of the journal *Seiki*; cited in Takeda Tomoju, *Endō Shūsaku no sekai* [The world of Endō Shūsaku] (Tokyo: Kōdansha, 1971), 283. The term Father Kasuya used to suggest the Japanese "Protestant-like" sensibilities he is describing is "Jōdo Shinshū-teki," referring to the True Pure Land Sect of Buddhism that emphasizes the universality of salvation through a single utterance of the name of Amida, the saving Buddha.

4   "Translator's Preface," in Endō Shūsaku, *Silence*, trans. William Johnston (Tokyo: Sophia University and Charles E. Tuttle, 1969), 16–17. In his "Afterword" to the original hardback edition of *Silence*, Endō wrote, "Some may consider Rodrigues's ultimate faith to be close to that of Protestantism, but that is my own current position. I'm well aware that I'll be criticized from a theological perspective for this, but I can't help it." *Chinmoku* (Tokyo: Shinchōsha, 1998), 256.

5   I obtained these figures from Miyabe Hisashi, a senior editor at Shinchōsha Publishing Company.

6   Endō mentioned this in "Sekai ni okeru Nihon bungaku, Nihon ni okeru Kirisuto-kyō bungaku" [Japanese literature in the world, Christian literature in Japan], an interview with me that appeared in *Endō Shūsaku to SHUSAKU ENDO* (Tokyo: Shunjūsha, 1994). The Japanese term for this forced renunciation of political beliefs is *tenkō* (転向), which means to make an "about-face."

7   Etō Jun, *Seijuku to sōshitsu: "Haha" no hōkai* [Maturity and loss: The collapse of the "Mother"] (Tokyo: Kawade Bungei Sensho, 1975), 180–1. Etō approaches the novel heavily influenced by his reading of Erik H. Erikson's *Childhood and Society* (1950), an interesting blend of psychology and cultural anthropology. Although I take issue with a number of Etō's observations about *Silence*—particularly his characteristically Japanese critical approach of trying to probe the psyche of the author through his fictional characters—he does a remarkable job of identifying a feature common to many of the writers of Endō's postwar generation: a quest for a mother figure who can take the place of the father who has been either killed or emotionally emasculated as a result of the war and Japan's defeat.

8   An infuriatingly impossible title to translate in a way that would encourage the sales of even a single copy of a novel!

9   Endō Shūsaku, "Chinmoku no koe," in *Chinmoku no koe* [The voice in the silence] (Tokyo: Purejidentosha, 1992), 66–7. In a video titled *Haha naru mono* [Mothers] that was packaged with this essay collection, Endō stated: "Because I titled the novel *Silence*, both readers and critics in Japan have gotten the mistaken impression that I was writing about God's silence. And though I've written that, no, God does speak, there are still many people who misread the novel as treating the silence of God. As a result,

they overlook the portion of the novel where God does speak, the part that is most significant to me .... What I ultimately wanted to write was that within the silence there comes a voice ... that a voice emerges through the silence."

10 Much has already been written about the misinterpretation of Christ's words from the *fumie* because of William Johnston's incorrect rendition in his English translation; *Fumu ga ii* does *not* mean "Trample!" It is a tender expression of Christ's empathy for the priest's pain, a loving admonition that "It is all right to trample."

11 I am not ignorant of the pitfalls of discussing something like "authorial intent." Rather, I am emphasizing the ways in which the relationship between author and readers varies between Japan and the Europeanized West. I am also cognizant of the explicit ways in which Endō in his late years wrote about what he was hoping to achieve in the novel—an achievement which I, among many other critics, accept as valid. Endō commented after the novel was published, "What I was trying to say was that, by allowing those who have been silenced by history or by the church to relate their own life's experiences, God is speaking of His own existence." From the Summer 1966 issue of the journal *Hihyō*; cited in Takeda, 293.

12 Cited in Takadō Kaname, "Kaigai ni okeru Endō bungaku hyōka" [Overseas reviews of Endō's literature], *Kokubungaku: Kaishaku to Kyōzai no Kenkyū* (September 1993): 84. Francis Henry King was the senior book reviewer for the London *Sunday Telegraph* for 25 years.

13 Taplinger Books, currently represented in the United States by Parkwest Publishers, has a backlist catalog consisting of 12 books on calligraphic styles, five on vocal exercises, and works about Buckminster Fuller, Italian architect Ettore Sottsass, and industrial designers Harley Earl and Raymond Loewy. *Silence* is the only work of literature on its list.

14 John Updike, "From Fumie to Sony," *The New Yorker* (January 14, 1980): 97.

15 Ibid., 94, 98.

16 In a 1982 review of Endō's novel, *The Samurai*, Irving Howe wrote as a second witness to Updike's assessment: "*Silence* I regard as a masterpiece, a lucid and elegant drama." "Mission from Japan," *The New York Review of Books* (November 4, 1982): 31. It is worth noting that, despite these words of approbation for *Silence*, Howe concluded his review of *The Samurai* by expressing his inability to understand where Endō is coming from as a novelist: "He is a very strange figure, profoundly alienated, and moving in ways I can't entirely explain. ... [His is] a mind lost to itself. I have before me the image of a remarkable figure, standing neck-deep in his native mudswamp, but head still aflame with stories of the crucified god. It is hard to believe that more than a few can live by so lacerating a vision" (32–3).

17 The selection was announced in November 1999. Phillip Zaleski, the editor of the Best Spiritual Writing series, obtained nominations from a variety

of writers of spiritually oriented works. The list included works by such figures as Gandhi, C. S. Lewis, Viktor Frankl, G. K. Chesterton, J. R. R. Tolkien, Elie Wiesel, Graham Greene, Mother Teresa, T. S. Eliot, Pope John XXIII, Tagore, Martin Buber, Thomas Merton, and D. T. Suzuki.

18 Updike, "From Fumie to Sony," 97.

19 Ferreira uses this expression. See Endo, *Silence*, 170.

20 Philip Yancey, "Japan's Faithful Judas," *Books & Culture* (January/February 1996): 6.

21 Ibid., 7.

22 Ibid. Emphasis in the original.

23 It is worth noting here that in Endō's next major historical novel, *The Samurai* (1980), the image of Christ that repeatedly hounds the Japanese protagonist during his voyages through the nations of the West is that of the scrawny, wasted figure of Jesus hanging in defeat on the cross. On a number of occasions, the samurai sees a carving of "an emaciated man with both hands nailed to a cross [hanging] with drooping head," and he wonders, "A man like this. ... Why do they worship him?" And the narrator records that the samurai "could detect nothing sublime or holy in a man as wretched and powerless as this." Shusaku Endo, *The Samurai*, trans. Van C. Gessel (New York: Vintage Books, 1989), 159–60.

24 Endō, "Chinmoku no koe," 69, 78–9.

25 Brad Leithauser, "An Ear for the Unspoken," *The New Yorker* (March 6, 1989): 107.

26 Ibid., 108.

27 Ibid., 109.

28 Ibid., 110.

29 This observation emerged from a conversation in which I participated among Joseph Hanreddy, Steven Dietz, and Kent Dorsey—who were, respectively, the American director, playwright, and scenic designer for the stage adaptation of *Silence* that was produced through a collaboration between the Subaru Company in Tokyo and the Milwaukee Repertory Theater in 1998. The conversation took place in Japan in July 1997.

30 Gary Wills, "Embers of Guilt," *The New York Review of Books* (February 19, 1981): 21.

31 Darren J. N. Middleton and Mark Bosco explore the Endō-Greene alliance in more detail elsewhere in this volume.

32 For further discussion on the characteristics of this generation of Japanese, see the first chapter in my *The Sting of Life: Four Contemporary Japanese Novelists* (New York: Columbia University Press, 1989).

33 Generally, the founding of the *mukyōkai* movement in Japan is credited to Uchimura Kanzō (1861–1930), a Christian evangelist, writer, and pacifist who was baptized in 1878 while attending Sapporo Agricultural College.

34 Kevin Doak addresses the theme of Protestant readings of Endō's novel elsewhere in this volume.

35   It is illuminating that on several occasions—one of which I witnessed at
a symposium on his works in which Endō participated at John Carroll
University in Cleveland, Ohio in May of 1991—he responded to protests
that the novel glorified the apostate Kichijirō with the simple declaration:
"Kichijirō is me."

36   I would similarly argue that, though the priest Velasco in *The Samurai*,
too, endures many trials and ultimately retains more of his Western-style
confidence than does Rodrigues, he also learns greater humility and
compassion as a result of his afflictions. What is most different about this
novel compared to *Silence* is that Endō gives equal regard to the glaringly
dramatic martyrdom of Velasco when he is burned at the stake as he does
to the quiet, essentially off-stage suicide that his Japanese counterpart,
Hasekura, is ordered to commit because of his conversion to Christianity.

37   Although the English translation designates this section as an "Appendix,"
the original Japanese text does not segregate it off this way. Assigning it
the title of "Appendix" makes it appear to be a less-important part of the
novel, and I have seen many instances in which readers of the translation
overlook or ignore it altogether. That said, it represents a challenge for
Japanese readers of the original as well: It is written in seventeeth-century
documentary-style language, which is largely inaccessible to contemporary
readers.

38   Unfortunately, in the early editions of Johnston's translation of *Silence*, the
recantation oath that Rodrigues was forced to sign was rendered as "He
wrote a book."

39   This is, of course, the point at which Endō's two major themes—religious
faith and the travails of physical illness—merge, reflecting the Christian
baptism that he was persuaded by his mother to accept at a young age,
the unspoken disapproval he sensed during the war years because of his
allegiance to a foreign God, and the many hospitalizations and surgeries he
had to endure through his entire adult life.

40   Endō actually borrows this dialectical view from an earlier Japanese
novelist, Masamune Hakuchō (1879–1962), who was baptized during his
college years but later abjured his adopted faith, rebelling against what he
saw as a stoic overemphasis on the vengeful God of the Old Testament.
Endō discussed Hakuchō's views of "paternal" Christianity in his essay,
"Chichi no shūkyō, haha no shūkyō: Maria Kannon ni tsuite" [Paternal
religion, maternal religion: On the images of Maria as Kannon], published
in the journal *Bungei* 6.1 (1967): 234–9.

41   Leith Morton, "The Image of Christ in the Fiction of Endō Shūsaku,"
Working Papers in Japanese Studies 8 (Melbourne: Japanese Studies Centre,
1994): 13.

42   I cannot resist noting that Endō's baptismal name was Paul.

43   I cannot overemphasize the significance of this brief exchange. When I
translated *The Samurai*, the only passage in my translation which Endō

inquired about (and the only time I can remember him ever asking me how I had rendered any passage in his works) was the scene after which Hasekura has been ordered to commit *seppuku*; as he walks down a darkened corridor toward his fate, his loyal servant Yozō, who has also secretly converted to Christianity, speaks to him: "'From now on … He will be beside you.' Suddenly he heard Yozō's strained voice behind him. 'From now on … He will attend you'" (Endō, *The Samurai*, 262). To my mind, "He will attend you" is a clear echo of Christ's words to Rodrigues: "I suffered beside you."

44 Endō, *Silence*, 305.

3

The "Formality" of the *fumie*?:
A Re-Consideration of the Role
of the *fumie* Scene in *Silence*

Mark Williams

The priest raised his foot [over the *fumie*]. In it he felt a dull, heavy pain. This was no mere formality. He was about to trample on what he had considered the most beautiful thing in his life, on what he had believed most pure, on what was filled with the ideals and dreams of man. How his foot ached! And then at that moment, the man in bronze spoke to him. "You may trample. I, more than anyone else, know the pain in your foot. You may trample. It was to be trampled on by you all that I was born into this world. It was to share your pain that I carried my cross."

As the priest placed his foot on the *fumie*, dawn broke. In the distance, a cock crowed.[1]

There can be few passages in the entirety of postwar Japanese literature to have excited as much critical attention—and indeed controversy—as this short narrative section that appears toward the end of Endō Shūsaku's classic work, *Silence*. In the build-up to this scene, the protagonist, the Portuguese missionary Rodrigues, having knowingly defied the Tokugawa shogunate ban on all Christian proselytization, has endured the whole gamut of human emotions. Arriving in Japan fired with the archetypal missionary zeal of a young seminarian and determined to save as many Japanese peasants as possible in rural western Japan before his inevitable capture and presumed martyrdom, it is not long before Rodrigues finds himself betrayed to the authorities by his solitary guide and interpreter, Kichijirō. He is then confronted, broadly speaking, with the choice for which he had spent his entire adult life preparing: agree to the authorities' demands that he apostatize by placing his foot on the crucifix (a technique that had become the standard shogunal treatment of those suspected of clinging to the proscribed faith) and thereby abandon all that his life to date had sought to espouse, or cling to his faith in the knowledge of the inevitable consequences.

The scenario may not be unique. But in Endō's fictional world, the situation is further complicated by a series of measures that have been introduced by the wily local magistrate, Inoue, himself a former believer but now determined to eradicate the imported faith once and for all. Two, in particular, exercise a peculiar influence on the crucial *fumie* scene introduced above. First, Inoue has determined that the most effective way to the missionaries' hearts was not to bring physical pressure to bear on the priests themselves: they were, after all, well schooled in the importance of "turning the other cheek" and, in most cases, ready to martyr themselves for their faith. Instead, rather than subjecting Rodrigues to the unspeakable *ana-tsurushi* torture (whereby the victim is suspended upside down in a foul-smelling pit), this cruelty is inflicted, rather, on several of the Japanese converts, the so-called "Kirishitan," all of whom have long since renounced any ties to the faith, but whose destiny is linked, overtly and deliberately, to Rodrigues's response. At no time, therefore, is Rodrigues subjected to any of the physical torture for which he has sought so hard to prepare; rather, he is confronted by the psychological torture of knowing that the groaning outside his cell, which he mistakes for the snoring of callous guards, can only be stopped by his agreeing to perform the hitherto unconscionable act of placing his foot on the *fumie*. The second measure introduced by Inoue to add to the dramatic tension of the moment is his insistence that the entire scenario is a "mere formality" (*honno katachi dake no koto*).[2] Inoue is insistent that there is no imperative for Rodrigues to genuinely renounce his convictions: he simply has to "go through the motions of trampling [on the *fumie*]."[3]

As noted, the passage above has stimulated a variety of responses—and opinion remains divided. All too frequent in this discussion, however, has been an overwhelming tendency to discuss this scene as marking the "climax" of the novel. The implications of such a reading are profound, since it suggests that, in ultimately succumbing to the pressure to place his foot on the *fumie*, Rodrigues is destined to follow the route already traveled by his erstwhile mentor, Ferreira, who, confronted by the *fumie*, had succumbed under similar duress and had gone on to settle down with a Japanese home and a wife provided to him by the authorities and to cooperate with them in the shogunate's attempts to eradicate any further intrusion of the "Western" religion into Japan. Indeed, a cursory glance at much of the initial criticism of the novel—or a viewing of the movie version by Shinoda Masahiro (1971), which does indeed accentuate the psychological drama of the *fumie* scene and concludes with Rodrigues seemingly resigned to a similar future—is likely to leave the reader with the distinct impression of such "closure."

Significantly, however, the novel does not end at this point and, in later years, Endō himself was at pains to highlight the significance he attributed to the concluding section(s) of the novel, those that follow the *fumie* scene.[4] Of particular concern to the author was the movie version, hence his concerted attempts, even as his health failed him in the early 1990s, to persuade Martin Scorsese to make a new movie version of the novel.[5] To that end, the discussion that follows will attempt to place the *fumie* scene in its context within Endō's narrative, and to offer a close reading of the conclusion of the novel in an attempt to underscore its significance. In so doing, a sharp distinction will be drawn between the ultimate destinies of Rodrigues and Ferreira. At the same time, moreover, the thorny question of whether the *fumie* scene is best described as a portrayal of Rodrigues's "apostasy" or rather as his "conversion" to a more personal faith will remain as a constant refrain.

A Variety of Responses

Turning first to the varied, and often conflicting, interpretations of the *fumie* scene, these span the gamut of possible readings—from those who would describe Rodrigues's decision to trample as a simple act of apostasy, to those who consider it, rather, as a vital step on a journey of "conversion." At one end of this spectrum is the "orthodox Catholic" reading of this section, whereby the two core arguments that had been employed by Ferreira to elicit Rodrigues's cooperation ultimately prevail. In the preceding pages, Ferreira had been at pains to persuade his former pupil both that Japan was a "swamp" in which the roots of Christianity are destined to "grow yellow and wither,"[6] and that God had maintained His silence, even in the face of the torture and martyrdom of so many believers. With this reading, the *fumie* scene merely marks Rodrigues's final acknowledgment of the inevitable.

The logic here is clear: to such critics, Rodrigues, like his mentor Ferreira, was guilty of self-delusion in believing that he had something to offer Japan whereas, in reality, his faith had never been firm enough to resist such severe provocation: faced with the horrible reality of the *fumie*, he finally shows his true colors. The argument is close to that advanced by the Bishop of Nagasaki who, in a sermon in 1971, urged the faithful not to read Endō's latest novel.[7] A similar argument was articulated by the critic, Francis Mathy, who argued:

> In *Chinmoku*, too, the Christians are presented as something less than true Christians—even the martyrs—while the defecting priest is

from the first weak in his faith and easily moved to apostasy. Japanese critics reviewing the novel have pointed out that Roderigo [*sic*] is more Oriental than Western.[8]

For those in this camp, Rodrigues's action would have led to his immediate excommunication from the Roman Catholic Church—and this certainly appears to represent a concern that preys on the mind of the protagonist portrayed in the immediate aftermath of the *fumie* incident. Here, however, it is important to note that the rumors of excommunication that reach his ears are sown only by the Dutch traders (who historically had exclusive access to the port of Dejima in Nagasaki at the time), who serve, very specifically, as symbols of the rival Protestant tradition. With Rodrigues uncertain as to how much of his action has been reported to the Catholic authorities back in Europe and in what guise those reports had been couched, these doubts augment the protagonist's sense of having sinned in the eyes of the establishment. He accepts that he is no longer in a state of grace, hence the portrayal of the protagonist, struggling to the end of his days with doubt, confusion, and uncertainty.[9]

A second reading of this scene places greater emphasis on the words offered by the emaciated figure on the *fumie*.[10] Here, the psychological tension that had been building within Rodrigues ever since his betrayal to the authorities by his guide Kichijirō reaches a crescendo, and the words sanctioning him to "trample" do indeed register with Rodrigues, inspiring him to proceed as all the onlookers would have it. In short, it is at this moment that God breaks the silence that had so troubled Rodrigues, enabling the latter to convince himself that he is indeed acting in accordance with God's will. Typical of such a reading is that of the Catholic critic, Kasuya Kōichi, who argues:

> Rodrigues heard God's words encouraging him to trample and obeyed. … The decisive moment in the novel is when God breaks His silence and it is significant that He calls on Rodrigues to trample on the *fumie*. … When God speaks about the most precious of things, He maintains His silence. To me, the most disappointing aspect of the novel is that God breaks His silence.[11]

A similar reading is offered by the Protestant critic, Sako Jun'ichirō, who suggests:

> If I may be allowed to express my personal wish based on my spiritual realism, I would rather that Jesus had not urged [Rodrigues] to trample—but that Endō had had Rodrigues trample on the *fumie* in spite of his inner anguish. … In short, I wish God had not broken His

silence in the portrayal of Rodrigues trampling on His face. I would rather have had those words of God thrown at Rodrigues as he endured "the pain in his foot."[12]

It is probably fair to say that this interpretation is the most prevalent. A third, alternative perspective is offered, however, by critics such as Ōzato Kyōsaburō, who makes the following suggestion:

> Of course, the voice of the bronze Jesus represents an auditory illusion on the part of Rodrigues. But there is no doubt that it is on the basis of this that he abandons his faith and Endō supports his [subsequent] action.[13]

A reading of this scene as Rodrigues's responding to some kind of auditory hallucination is certainly compelling given the circumstances in which the protagonist finds himself. Alone in a cell and disturbed only by the groaning of the peasants suffering on his behalf, Rodrigues has long been crying out for guidance: he has been desperate for some words of encouragement in his time of greatest need. At the same time, confronted by the all too human desire to capitulate and thereby end both the psychological anguish that he is enduring and the physical agony being experienced by those whose destiny lies entirely in his hands, all he requires now is some form of justification for proceeding in the direction in which he feels himself being inexorably led. He is, in short, desperate for some kind of suggestion of divine sanction for his pending action—and, according to this reading, this is introduced into the narrative at the most logical moment.

There remains, however, a fourth reading of this passage, one advanced by the critic Kasai Akifu. According to this interpretation, Rodrigues responds less to the words of encouragement offered by the figure on the *fumie*, and more to that which he reads into the facial expression with which he finds himself confronted. Schooled during his Western seminary education to worship the paternalistic face of Old Testament authority, Rodrigues has found himself troubled, ever since his arrival in Japan, by the "ugly face of Christ, crowned with thorns and the thin, outstretched arms."[14] Thereafter, as he finds himself "star[ing] intently at the man in the center of the *fumie*, worn down and hollow with the constant trampling,"[15] Rodrigues is overwhelmed by the image, one that was to become a mainstay of Endō's subsequent *oeuvre*, of Christ as the *dōhansha*, the constant companion figure who shares the pain and suffering of His creations—and who "speaks" by coming alongside them in their hour of need. It is this that leads Kasai to conclude that "Rodrigues *felt as though it were the face* of the 'bronze man' who uttered the words, 'You may trample.'"[16]

Such an interpretation of this passage would seem to be supported by subsequent comments made by the author. In a 1973 discussion with the critic Miyoshi Yukio, for example, Endō acknowledged:

> What [Rodrigues] confronted on the *fumie* was the exhausted and emaciated face of Jesus. And *the face said to him*, "Since this is how I am, there is no problem in your trampling on me."[17]

Of greater significance than any authorial pronouncements, however, is the text itself—and, in this regard, it is interesting to note that, in the concluding sections of the narrative (that is, those following the "climactic" *fumie* scene), there are two subsequent passages in which the narrative returns to focus on Rodrigues overtly reflecting on the "sad face" he recalls from the *fumie*. The first of these occurs about a year after the *fumie* incident—with Rodrigues released from his cell but living under house arrest in the Sotoura-machi district of Nagasaki. With little to occupy his time but "to lean against the window and watch the people going to and fro,"[18] Rodrigues's mind is inevitably drawn back to the incident that had shaped his destiny so dramatically. However, what Rodrigues recalls is "the concave face on the *fumie* that had looked up at the priest in sorrow. In sorrow, it had gazed up at him as the eyes spoke appealingly. 'You may trample. You may trample. It is to be trampled upon by you that I am here.'"[19] Significantly, the passage here focuses on the face—and in particular on the eyes—of the figure on the *fumie* pleading with Rodrigues: there is no recollection by the protagonist of his having been prompted by any audible stimulus.

The second narrative section in which Rodrigues recalls the *fumie* scene occurs some five years after the event, as he finds himself revisited by Kichijirō, his fickle translator and guide. Despite numerous occasions on which he had found himself succumbing to the authorities' demands, elicited by his suspicious behavior, that he defile the *fumie*, he finds himself returning to the protagonist's living quarters in search of absolution. At this stage, Rodrigues has just been informed by Inoue that he should assume the name of a recently deceased Japanese man, Okada San'emon, marry this man's widow, and establish himself in a residence in Kobinatachō in the shogunal capital of Edo. To the protagonist, this all represents a direct and inevitable consequence of his decision to trample on the *fumie* half a decade earlier. And as, once more, he finds himself confronted by Kichijirō, beseeching the protagonist to hear his confession, Rodrigues finds himself again recalling that "face":

> Even now the face is looking at me with eyes of pity from the wooden plaque rubbed flat by many feet. "You may trample. Your foot suffers in

pain; it must suffer like all the feet that have stepped on this plaque. ... I will take upon myself some of your pain and your suffering. It is for that reason that I am here."[20]

By this stage, as Rodrigues relives the *fumie* scene yet again, the objective portrayal of the "dull, heavy pain"[21] he had experienced at the time has been replaced by a "tremendous onrush of joy."[22] The dramatic tension may have disappeared, and his "resentment"[23] at the perceived silence of God in the face of the suffering of His creations has been assuaged. In their stead has emerged a more self-critical approach, one that leads him to question whether his self-justification of his decision to trample on the *fumie* as an act of "love" was merely an "excuse to justify [his] own weakness."[24] At the same time, Rodrigues comes to acknowledge that he cannot—and must not—conceal his weakness and cowardice. As a priest, he had been obliged to hide his weaknesses from the world; here, for the first time, he confronts himself as a weakling, possessed of cowardice, fear, and other negative attributes. On the one hand, therefore, his feelings for Ferreira have changed very little: despite the fact that they now meet on a regular basis in the service of the Nagasaki authorities, his feelings of contempt for his erstwhile mentor remain unattenuated. His understanding of these raw emotions has, however, evolved considerably—as he comes to acknowledge that these feelings were derived, not from resentment that this man "had led him to his fall ... but because in Ferreira he could find his own deep wound just as it was."[25] The two have indeed emerged, certainly in the eyes of the world, as "two inseparable twins."[26]

There exists, however, a rhetorical level to the text in this section, one that highlights the transformation, to which so many critics have alluded, of the stern, "paternal" face that had represented the focus of Rodrigues's earlier faith to the more compassionate, "maternal" form that Endō subsequently embodied in his trope of the constant companion, *dōhansha*.[27] At the same time as seeking to analyze his continued feelings of contempt and hatred for Ferreira, for example, Rodrigues now finds himself openly questioning "if there is any difference between Kichijirō and [him]self."[28] Similarly, as he finds himself once more confronted by his nemesis, Inoue, he is able to bring himself to admit that he had been fighting, not the "mudswamp" of Japan, as Inoue would have it, but his own faith: as he confesses, "my struggle was with Christianity in my own heart."[29]

The evolution is, of necessity, portrayed as a gradual process of self-awakening, one that is marked at the textual level by a subtle shift in the focus of the protagonist's persistent calls: he no longer cries out to "God," but to the being he comes to address as "my Lord." Such textual markings are important. Without them, Rodrigues's claim, as he mulls over Inoue's proposal for his future—that "my faith in you is different from what it was; but I love you still"[30]—would remain unconvincing. Moreover, the narrative assertion, following his decision, taken in spite of his own "fallen" status in the eyes of the church, to administer the sacrament of confession to Kichijirō—that "everything that had taken place until now had been necessary to bring him to this love"[31]—would appear unsubstantiated. As it is, however, in the short narrative section that follows the *fumie* scene—a section that admittedly encompasses more than five years of personal development—Rodrigues has been transformed and now finds himself possessed, as Dennis Washburn asserts, of "a more self-reflective, critical consciousness that permits a new understanding of the nature of his faith."[32]

According to this logic, the *fumie* scene can be seen as representing a theological triumph for Rodrigues, as he emerges from his experience armed with a more personal relationship with the human figure he had encountered on the cross, one that is foundational—and separable—from the institution of the Catholic church. At seminary, Rodrigues would have been schooled in the belief that the church constituted Christ's mystical body; at the same time, he would have been reminded that there can only be one interpretation of any form that claims to be Christ (which would include the figure on the *fumie*) while at the same time contradicting Him, and thus the church: such a form can only be Satan, taking on the appearance of Christ for the purpose of leading the individual away from Christ and His body, the church.

The question that emerges from this is whether this "Satan" succeeds in achieving this separation of Rodrigues from Christ when he suggests that Christ can be separated from the church. And it is here that a more nuanced reading of the remainder of Endō's text is so crucial. Most immediate in this regard is the conclusion to the *fumie* scene itself—which, following depiction of Rodrigues placing his foot on the *fumie*, ends with the following narrative depiction: "dawn broke. In the distance, a cock crowed."[33] The allusion to the gospel accounts of Peter's being confronted with the reality of his having denied Christ three times is overt.[34] And this, in turn, militates against any reading of this scene as simply portraying Rodrigues at his moment of theological triumph. The decision to trample on the *fumie* may indeed represent a moment of insight, as the protagonist establishes a more mature and personal relationship with Christ, freed from the constraints of the institutional church. But then comes the reality check—in which Rodrigues is brought face-to-face with the implications of his act. With this seemingly innocuous aside, therefore, the narrative signals that the protagonist's decision to defile the *fumie* will somehow not be the end of the matter. At the same time, as Washburn notes, it is this depiction that shifts the narrative focus on to the image of Rodrigues as a fusion of "betrayer and betrayed, apostate and convert."[35] Seen thus, it serves a crucial role in presaging the ensuing text in which the simplistic portrayal of Rodrigues consigned to the shadows as an apostate priest is steadily undermined.

"The Diary"

Regardless of how one reads the *fumie* scene, the image with which we are left at the conclusion of the narrative section of the novel is of Rodrigues, having administered the sacrament of confession to Kichijirō, clinging desperately to his conviction that he "remains the last priest in the land." Fully aware that his "fellow priests would condemn his act as sacrilege," he is nevertheless possessed of a conviction that his "life until this day would have spoken of [our Lord]."[36] However, as the author himself was at pains to stress—particularly following the appearance of the movie version of that dramatic scene, which leaves Rodrigues at the end aggressively seeking to consummate his relationship with his recently acquired wife—the novel does not end at this point. There follows a concluding section—"The Diary of an Officer at the Christian Residence"—which, for all its literary awkwardness,[37] nevertheless serves an essential hermeneutical function.

In his "Atogaki" (Postscript) to the novel, Endō acknowledged the non-fictional provenance of the "Diary." It is, he indicates, "extracted and adapted" from the *Sayō Yoroku* (Miscellanies on the Search for Evil Religions) section included in the *Zoku-zoku gunsho ruiji* (Additional Collection of [*Kirishitan*] Documents).[38] And, by way of further explanation, he notes, in a reflective piece following publication of the novel, that this original diary, the *Yoroku*, was penned by one of the clerks at the Christian residence in Edo as a report on the movements of the foreign priests and others with strong earlier connections to the proscribed religion who were confined there under close surveillance. And of greatest relevance to the current discussion are the sections dealing with the historical figure of Giuseppe Chiara (1610–85), Endō's acknowledged model for Rodrigues. According to the author, his sole contribution was to "transpose the original *kanbuntai* (Chinese style text) into classical Japanese."[39]

Comparison between the original *Yoroku* version and Endō's fictional "Diary" section makes for interesting reading.[40] Indeed, consideration of those sections that Endō has chosen to transcribe verbatim from the *Yoroku* and those areas where he has opted to amend the original material provide invaluable insights, not merely into the narrative provenance of the "Diary," but also, more significantly for the purposes of this discussion, into the nature of the protagonist's faith in the aftermath of his decision to trample on the *fumie*.

Both works begin their biographical account of the protagonist's movements in the year Kanbun 12 (1672), more than a quarter of a century after Rodrigues—now renamed Okamoto San'emon in *Yoroku*, Okada San'emon in the "Diary"—had been brought up to Edo in 1646. And both accounts paint a similar picture of San'emon living in the Christian residence with his wife and maidservant. From the outset, the portrait is of the protagonist's living, despite the restrictions on his movements, in relatively relaxed circumstances: he has been "granted the ration of ten persons" and is reunited with Bokui, Juan, Nanho, and Jikan, described in the *Yoroku* as four of Chiara's original traveling companions from Europe who had been arrested almost immediately on arrival in Japan and apostatized in the face of Inoue's cruel torture, but here introduced into Endō's narrative for the first time.[41]

For all Endō's faithfulness to the original historical record, however, there are at least three areas in which the *Yoroku* and the "Diary" versions differ significantly, with all these amendments serving to augment the sense of the protagonist, San'emon, having arrived at a "new understanding of the nature of his faith." The first of these concerns the nature of the writings with which Chiara/San'emon is frequently described as being engaged. In both cases, the protagonist is portrayed as penning a *shūmon no shomotsu* ("book/document on religion"), a depiction that has inspired considerable discussion in Japan as to the nature of the document concerned.[42] To some, including Kasai, the issue appears clear: given that San'emon is portrayed as writing this document "at the command of Tōtōminokami,"[43] the shogunal official with overall responsibility for the Christian residence, such critics see this as a formal document, a pledge of apostasy disavowing all connection with the protagonist's former faith—but with the clear implication that, even now, more than 25 years after his initial encounter with the *fumie*, San'emon continues to waver.

To others, however, such an interpretation remains anathema. Why, they argue, would an act that should, in theory, comprise affixing a simple signature to a formal document take so long to complete and, more significantly, how are we to account for the repeated references to San'emon writing such a document over an extended period?[44] To critics such as Miyao Toshihiko, there is no way that "it could take 81 days (*sic*) to write a pledge of apostasy"; the work on which San'emon was engaged was, rather, he suggests, a "report on Christianity," including an unequivocal denunciation of the core tenets of his erstwhile faith, along the lines of the *Kengiroku*, the anti-Christian tract written by Sawano Chūan, the post-apostasy name granted to Ferreira.[45]

The distinction is subtle, but crucial. Endō would certainly have been aware that the *shūmon no shomotsu*, as portrayed in the *Yoroku*, represented a generic reference to a report that could be demanded of anyone about whom the authorities retained concerns of a religious nature, in which the signatory was expected to create a full and incontrovertible denunciation of his or her faith. At the same time, moreover, as an author renowned for the meticulous research that underpinned his historical novels, he would surely have been aware of the entry given for "Chiara" in the standard historical reference work, *Nihon kirisutokyō rekishi daijiten* (Historical Dictionary of Christianity in Japan), which includes the following detail:

> The *Kirishito-ki* and *Sayō Yoroku*, two documents written by the Inspectorate of Religious Conversion, contain many sayings by Okamoto. These documents are now missing, but, in the second year of Enpō (1674), Okamoto wrote three books about his religion at the command of the authorities. In his *Tenshukyō Taii*, Arai Hakuseki said that these three books contain references to Christianity, but that each makes clear that he is engaged in no anti-Bakufu subversion. In short, it seems that Okamoto had not renounced his faith.[46]

In the years following publication of the novel, Endō himself appeared to advocate both interpretations: on the one hand, in his short story, "Meshitsukai-tachi" (Servants, 1972), he specifically describes a *shūmon no shomotsu* as a "report on Christianity written at the command of the Bakufu."[47] In his subsequent discussion with the critic Miyoshi Yukio, however, he was at pains to stress the significance of this document: the *shomotsu* was, he argued, no mere guide to Christianity, but a *seiyakusho* (covenant, pledge [of apostasy]).[48] More germane to the current discussion, however, is the following explanation, offered by the author in his study, *Kirishitan jidai no chishikijin: haikyō to junkyō* (Intellectuals of the *Kirishitan* Era: Apostasy and Martyrdom, 1967), penned shortly after completion of *Silence*:

> In the *Shūmon-aratameyaku kiroku* (Record of Religious Conversion) by Inoue-chikugo, reference is made to a document similar to a pledge of apostasy, to which Okamoto San'emon affixed his seal ... roughly speaking, this document denounces Christianity as a heretical religion, acknowledges that the Christian missionaries had been spreading unfounded information and that the signatory had come to Japan fully believing in the faith.[49]

The depiction of San'emon signing a formal pledge of apostasy is here explicit. As with Endō's novel, however, the story does not end here. Instead, the record ends with the following notification:

> In consideration of such matters, we carried out an investigation of the *bateren* (padres) and *iruman* (brothers), and had them discuss religion on the tenth and fifteenth days of the month. I then ordered them to be tortured.[50]

Consideration of the timeline of events offered in the "Diary" makes for an interesting comparison. But ultimately a reading of the "Diary" that appears to be in keeping with the supporting documentation is of San'emon, having made clear his determination to revert to his erstwhile beliefs, being confronted with another document of apostasy (the *shūmon no shomotsu* of the "Diary" text), of his subsequent wavering and of the authorities' consequent decision to engage him in religious debate and to subject him to torture. And, in sharp contrast to the *Yoroku*, which makes specific mention of the fact that this *shomotsu* was finished and signed by the following year, the "Diary" not only emphasizes that this process is repeated on at least two further occasions, it also offers no apparent closure: the narrative deliberately leaves open the possibility that, even at the end, San'emon was continuing to refuse to sign such a pledge. The image is that of a torn man, continuing to waver to the end of his life—and this adds poignancy to the final portrayal of San'emon, laid to rest in a Buddhist ceremony at Muryōin temple at Koishikawa and conferred the posthumous Buddhist name of Nyūsen Jōshin-shinshi.

The second change effected by Endō on the *Yoroku* original concerns the figure of Juan, a seemingly minor player in the novel, whose only brief appearances in Endō's text occur in the "Diary" section, but who, when compared with the wavering figure who appears in the *Yoroku*, is portrayed in the "Diary" as possessed of an unshakable faith and thus serves as a useful counter to the vacillating San'emon. Apart from his initial introduction as one of Rodrigues's original traveling companions, the only other references to this figure concern his being sent to gaol, firstly on September 5 in Enpō 2 (1674) and subsequently again on December 10 in Enpō 4 (1676). On both occasions, he is described as being jailed for his "perverse" (*wagamama*) behavior—with the second edict adding that he was "a most insolent person."[51]

The portrait is of a man of unwavering faith, one determined to cling to the orthodox tradition from start to finish. This, however, is in sharp contradiction to the Juan figure who populates the pages of the *Yoroku*—and there would appear to be two specific changes made, designed to augment the sense of constancy personified by Juan in the "Diary." The first of these relates to the decision to omit entirely any reference to events of the third year of Enpō in the "Diary," despite the fact that this section in the *Yoroku* is relatively lengthy. Significantly, the depiction here is of Juan being released from gaol and of his being paid a relatively generous monthly allowance, both of which would militate against the image of a man refusing to relent. The second change made to the *Yoroku* version in this regard relates to the timing of Juan's return to gaol. In the *Yoroku*, this occurs following the death of San'emon: the "Diary," however, has San'emon die with Juan seemingly still in prison, a subtle shift which nevertheless serves to emphasize the contrast between the two men.

The other important variant between the two texts concerns the reintroduction into the drama of Kichijirō. In the *Yoroku* account, the protagonist is served in jail by his loyal attendant, Kaku. In choosing to change this in order to place renewed focus on the role of Kichijirō, Endō would appear to be shining the spotlight on the question of why San'emon is still continuing to redeclare his faith. As already noted, in the immediate aftermath of Rodrigues's initial decision to trample on the *fumie*, it had been Kichijirō who had remained at his side, albeit, for the most part, he is carefully depicted as too scared to venture out from the shadows. As Rodrigues awaits his transfer to Edo, however, it is Kichijirō who re-emerges as a thorn in the authorities' side and who, continuing to defy their proscription of all communication between the two men, turns up unexpectedly at Rodrigues's temporary residence asking for the sacrament of confession. The incident represents a crucial stage on Rodrigues's journey toward his new "critical consciousness": determining that he is "the last priest in the land,"[52] he finds himself inexorably drawn to the mental anguish being betrayed by Kichijirō. Confronted by the latter's haplessness, Rodrigues is reminded that his own fall from grace does not necessarily prevent him from offering the sacrament. The two men are here depicted as possessed of a faith emerging from what the theologian William Hamilton has described as the "crucible of doubt."[53]

In keeping with the narrative portrayal of San'emon struggling with the issue of the nature of his faith for the rest of his life, therefore, it is entirely appropriate that it should be Kichijirō who is reintroduced into the "Christian residence" section. Not only is he thereby depicted as pathologically incapable of putting his past involvement with Christianity totally behind him; in this portrayal, moreover, Kichijirō succeeds in drawing San'emon's attention to the need for a reassessment of so many of the black and white distinctions that the latter had brought with him on his initial journey to Japan. Gone, for example, is the unshakable belief in a division between "the strong," embodied in the person of Garrpe, Rodrigues's fellow priest, and the various Japanese converts who resolved to martyr themselves for their faith, and "the weak," including Rodrigues and Ferreira, who had ultimately succumbed to the pressure to defile the *fumie*: as Rodrigues argues: "Can anyone say that the weak do not suffer more than the strong?"[54] Gone too is the uncompromising image of the "paternalistic" God who might have been expected to stand in judgment over Rodrigues's act of "betrayal." Instead, the "Diary's" focus is as much on Kichijirō who, in choosing—or rather finding himself drawn—to remain with San'emon, not only takes over from Ferreira the mantle of the protagonist's "inseparable twin," but also comes to stand, in many ways, as the physical embodiment of the protagonist's newfound image of a "maternal" God, seeking nothing else than to exist as a constant companion, *dōhansha*. In this way, he offers San'emon the rays of hope and optimism that enable the latter to keep debating with himself and with the authorities.

Conclusion

We have, of necessity, covered the concluding sections of Endō's narrative in considerable detail. This is, I believe, essential, not merely to problematize a literal reading of the *fumie* scene as a simplistic portrayal of an act of apostasy, but also to transform the rather one-dimensional view of Rodrigues that a reading of the protagonist simply following in the footsteps of his former mentor, Ferreira, would engender. Until this moment in the novel, the narrative focus has remained largely on the psychological vacillating betrayed by Rodrigues: as he awaits his moment of destiny, he oscillates between times when he finds "solace and support in the thought of that other man who had also tasted fear and trembling" with a concomitant sense of "joy in the thought that he was not alone"[55] and occasions when his despair threatens to overcome him. It is, however, only with the *fumie* scene that Rodrigues's psychological torment truly comes alive—as the narrative focus shifts from objective, external depiction of the scene before the protagonist to a closer emphasis on his interior dialogue. And it is only in the sections that follow this scene that the full significance of this shift in narrative perspective is fully appreciated. As Washburn suggests, "the elements of Rodrigues' character that made him plausibly susceptible to apostasy also establish the ground upon which his conversion becomes possible."[56] Without the focus on Rodrigues/San'emon's ongoing journey of spiritual transformation that follows the *fumie* scene, however, this plausibility would be brought into question.

In many ways, therefore, we are left at the end of the novel with the portrayal of San'emon dying, seemingly of old age,[57] still struggling with the same doubts that had plagued him since his arrival in Japan. On the one hand, as Kevin Doak has noted, Rodrigues's journey following his public act of renunciation differs markedly from that pursued by Peter in the gospel accounts: unlike Peter, San'emon never comes to an acceptance of his own identity as a sinner in need of forgiveness and he seemingly betrays very little by way of contrition.[58] At the same time, however, he is now a far cry from the determined, unquestioning young man who had first set foot in Japan: he is now shown as possessed of a depth of humanity which, however flawed, nevertheless speaks to those around him. Here for the first time in Endō's *oeuvre* is a concerted attempt to consider the "logic of the weakling."[59] The stage was set for a broader examination, a task that would be honed in subsequent Endō narratives, notably *Samurai* (*The Samurai*, 1980) and *Fukai kawa* (*Deep River*, 1993).

Notes

1   Endō Shūsaku, *Chinmoku* [*Silence*] (Tokyo: Shinchōsha, 1966), 219; *Silence*, trans. William Johnston, (Tokyo: Sophia University and Charles E. Tuttle, 1969), 271. In citing the novel, in cases where I differ from the published English translation, I shall give page numbers from both the Japanese and English versions of the text. In all other cases, I cite directly from the English translation.
2   Endō, *Silence*, 271.
3   Endō, *Chinmoku*, 219; Endō, *Silence*, 271.
4   Personal discussion with the author in the early 1990s.
5   Endō mentioned this possibility several times in the 1990s. Scorsese started work on this venture in early 2014. For testimony to the personal commitment Scorsese has invested in this task, see his "Foreword" in the latest English edition of the novel (London: Peter Owen Modern Classics, 2007).
6   Endō, *Silence*, 237.
7   Confirmed in discussion with Katō Muneya on September 21, 2013.
8   Francis Mathy, "Endō Shūsaku: *White Man, Yellow Man*," *Comparative Literature* 19.1 (1967): 73.
9   I should like to thank Kevin Doak for help with these and the various insights concerning Catholic theology that follow.
10 For more on these alternative readings, see Kasai Akifu, "*Chinmoku* o dō yomu ka? Rodorigo no efumi-bamen to 'Kirishitan yashiki yakunin nikki'" (A Reinterpretation of *Silence*, pertaining to the *fumie* Scene and the

"Diary of an Officer at the Christian Residence"), in *Endō Shūsaku kenkyū* 5 (2012).

11 Kasuya Kōichi, "*Chinmoku* ni tsuite" (Concerning the Novel, *Silence*), *Seiki* 18.7 (1966): 7.

12 Sako Jun'ichirō, "*Chinmoku* ni tsuite" (Concerning the Novel, *Silence*), *Seiki* 18.9 (1966): 78.

13 Cited in Kasai, "*Chinmoku* o dō yomu ka?," 89.

14 Endō, *Silence*, 270.

15 Ibid., 271.

16 Kasai, "*Chinmoku* o dō yomu ka?," 89; emphasis in original.

17 Cited in ibid., 91; emphasis in original.

18 Endō, *Silence*, 273–4.

19 Endō, *Chinmoku*, 224; Endō, *Silence*, 276.

20 Endō, *Chinmoku*, 240; Endō, *Silence*, 297.

21 Endō, *Silence*, 271.

22 Ibid., 297.

23 Ibid.

24 Ibid., 275.

25 Ibid., 278.

26 Ibid., 279.

27 For a full discussion of this transition, see Etō Jun, "Seijuku to sōshitsu: 'haha' no hōkai" [Maturity and Loss: The Collapse of "the Mother"], *Gendai no bungaku* [*Modern Literature*] 27 (Tokyo: Kōdansha, 1972).

28 Endō, *Silence*, 275–6.

29 Ibid., 292.

30 Ibid., 295.

31 Ibid., 298.

32 Dennis Washburn, "The Poetics of Conversion and the Problem of Translation in Endō Shūsaku's *Silence*," in Dennis Washburn and Kevin Reinhart, eds. *Converting Cultures: Religion, Ideology and Transformations of Modernity* (Leiden: Brill, 2007), 346.

33 Endō, *Chinmoku*, 219; Endō, *Silence*, 271.

34 As Endō noted, however, this reference was lost on the vast majority of his Japanese readership, cf. Endō *Chinmoku no koe* [The Voice of *Silence*] (Tokyo: Purejidentosha, 1992).

35 Washburn, "The Poetics of Conversion," 350.

36 Endō, *Silence*, 298.

37 Endō himself acknowledged some of these problems in his *Chinmoku no koe*, 88. *Inter alia*, Endō suggested that he "should have translated the 'Diary' into modern Japanese," that the narrative "lacks passion" (*minetsu*) and that the various characters "fail to come alive" (*ikite inai*). Also, significantly, as noted by Van Gessel, it is important to note that there is no indication in the Japanese original that the author intended this "Diary" as an "Appendix" to the novel: in the original, it is presented simply as a final chapter.

38 This appears in the hardback edition (1998) of the novel, 256.

39 Cited in Kasai, "*Chinmoku o dō yomu ka?*," 98. At this point, I should
like to refer the reader to Gessel's essay in the present volume.
It is clearly imperative to avoid the pitfalls of searching for "authorial intent." But, as
with Gessel, I too believe that the author's voice should also be included as
an integral part of the hermeneutical process.

40 Here too I wish to acknowledge the interpretive work conducted by Kasai
in this regard; cf. Kasai, "*Chinmoku o dō yomu ka?*"

41 Endō, *Silence*, 299.

42 Cf., for example, Arase Yasunari, "Endō Shūsaku *Chinmoku* ni okeru
Rodorigo no saigo no shinkō: 'Kirishitan yashiki yakunin nikki' ni
egakareta sakusha no bungakuteki ito" (The Faith of Rodrigues at the End
of Endō Shūsaku's Novel, *Silence*: The Author's Literary Intent as Portrayed
in the "Diary of the Official at the Christian Residence"), *Hanshin kindai
bungaku kenkyū* 3 (July, 2000); Ikeda Jun'itsu, "Endō Shūsaku *Chinmoku* no
kenkyū: 'Kirishitan yashiki yakunin nikki'—'Kyo' to 'jitsu' to no aida" (A
Study of Endō Shūsaku's *Silence*: Between "Fiction" and "Reality" in "The
Diary of the Christian Residence"), *Jōchi-daigaku kokubungaku ronshū*
26 (January, 1993); Kasai, "*Chinmoku o dō yomu ka?*"; Miyao Toshihiko,
"*Chinmoku* oboegaki: 'Kirishitan yashiki yakunin nikki' to *Sayō Yoroku*"
(Thoughts on the Novel, *Silence*: "The Diary of the Christian Residence"
and *Miscellanies on the Search for Evil Religions*), *Nagano-ken tanki-daigaku
kiyō* 36 (December, 1981).

43 Endō, *Silence*, 300.

44 In the "Diary," all three references to San'emon working on such a
document occur in the second year of Enpō (1674): the first occasion takes
place between January 20 and February 8, the second during February, and
the third between June 14 and July 24. The issue is further complicated
by the fact that the English translation describes the second of these
references as simply referring to San'emon's "writing a book," while the
other two portray him writing a "disavowal of his religion" (300).

45 Cited in Arase, "Endō Shūsaku *Chinmoku* ni okeru Rodorigo no saigo no
shinkō," 64.

46 *Nihon kirisutokyō rekishi daijiten* [Historical Dictionary of Christianity in
Japan] (Tokyo: Kyōbunkan, 1988), 354.

47 Endō Shūsaku, "Meshitsukai-tachi" (Servants); reprinted in *Endō Shūsaku
bungaku zenshū* (The Complete Works of Endō Shūsaku) 8 (Tokyo:
Shinchōsha, 2000), 140.

48 Endō Shūsaku and Miyoshi Yukio, "Bungaku: Jakusha no ronri"
(Literature: The Logic of the Weakling), *Kokubungaku: Kaishaku to kyōzai
no kenkyū* 18.2 (1973): 22.

49 Endō Shūsaku, *Kirishitan jidai no chishikijin: haikyō to junkyō* [Intellectuals
of the Kirishitan Era: Apostasy and Martyrdom] (Tokyo: Nihon keizai
shinbunsha, 1967), 169. Here it is important to remember, as Arase notes,

that this represents a reference to a fictional document: it was the scholar of religion, Anesaki Masaharu, who reprinted a section of the *Kirishito-ki* in his study, *Kirishitan shūmon no hakugai to senpuku* [Persecution and Secrecy in the Kirishitan Faith] (Tokyo: Dōbunsha, 1926) and "chose to call it the *Shūmon-aratameyaku kiroku* out of expediency"; cited in Arase, "Endō Shūsaku *Chinmoku* ni okeru Rodorigo no saigo no shinkō," 65.

50   Cited in Arase, "Endō Shūsaku *Chinmoku* ni okeru Rodorigo no saigo no shinkō," 66.

51   Endō, *Silence*, 304.

52   Ibid., 298.

53   Cited in Rowan Williams, *Dostoevsky: Language, Faith and Fiction* (London: Continuum, 2008), 2.

54   Endō, *Silence*, 297–8.

55   Ibid., 252–3.

56   Washburn, "The Poetics of Conversion," 349.

57   Here it is interesting to note that some Japanese critics (for example, Arase, "Endō Shūsaku *Chinmoku* ni okeru Rodorigo no saigo no shinkō, 72ff.) have picked up on the fact that San'emon is described at the end as *"fujiki itasu"*; this can refer to his simply "losing his appetite" due to ill health (as the English translation has it, 306), but can equally be seen as referring to a religious act of fasting/refusing food. Clearly, this latter interpretation opens up the possibility of San'emon ultimately choosing to martyr himself.

58   Remark made in an email to myself, July 16, 2013. Doak states this point more explicitly in the present volume.

59   "Logic of the Weakling" appears in the title of Endō's discussion with Yukio Miyoshi ["Bungaku: Jakusha no ronri"].

4

Endo and Greene's Literary Theology[1]

Darren J. N. Middleton

Shusaku Endo and Graham Greene met once, almost by accident, standing in the lift at London's Ritz Hotel, circa 1985. Describing the event in a letter to George Bull, onetime director of the Anglo-Japanese Economic Institute, Endo recalls the "tall gentleman with blue eyes" but reveals that the authors exchanged few words; pressed for time, their elevator encounter was little more than casual and cordial.[2] Fortunately, Endo and Greene's literary alliance transcends this passing moment. Pen friends since the 1960s, they spent several years approaching each other's work with fierce regard—an admiration that shows up in several places: in publicity blurbs, formal interviews, inscriptions in books given to friends, and in correspondence housed in the special collections libraries associated with Boston College, Georgetown University, and the University of Texas at Austin. After noting selected, brief examples of Endo and Greene's mutual appreciation, this chapter delves into particular fiction and non-fiction to establish three points of theological agreement between the two writers. Endo and Greene may best be seen as united by a desire to (i) stress sin's mystery; (ii) affirm God's wide mercy; and (iii) emphasize faith as troubled commitment.

Mutual Appreciation

In the Graham Greene Collection at Boston College's Burns Library, two folders in Box Eight contain letters between Endo and Greene. The first (folder 19) comprises 35 letters, penned between July 1969 and April 1971; the second (folder 20) houses 34 letters of the same nature as the letters in folder 19, this time spanning June 1971 to April 1986. Even if most are short letters of thanks, all under one page, they nonetheless reflect a sustained, affectionate correspondence between the two writers. Elsewhere in the same collection, other letters enable us to see stronger or deeper evidence of the

Endo-Greene alliance; consider Greene's February 12, 1973 letter to Peter Owen, Endo's British publisher.

Besides noting Greene's willingness to endorse the English translation of *Wonderful Fool*, Endo's novel about an inexperienced, gentle Frenchman visiting postwar Tokyo, this communication also reveals Greene's assessment of *Silence*, which Greene declares "a marvellous book—so much better than my own *Power and the Glory*."[3] Such words echo Greene's blurb for William Johnston's English translation of *Silence*—"in my opinion one of the finest novels of our time," Greene announces on the book's dust jacket. Many who have read *Silence*, and appreciate its calibration of faith and doubt, concur with Richard Greene (no relation) when he claims that "Endo could hardly have written it without serving an apprenticeship to Graham Greene."[4] At the close of his 2003 interview with the editor-in-chief of one of Japan's most celebrated literary journals, the Caribbean-born British writer Caryl Phillips discovered how Endo learned his trade:

> Mr Muneya Kato stands and gives me a small bow, which I—somewhat self-consciously—return in kind. Mr Kato clears his throat. 'Before Endo writes any book he always picks up Mr Graham Greene's *The End of the Affair* and reads it through. I think maybe you should know this.' I thank Mr Kato for his time, and smile. There is more bowing, and then I watch him thread his way through the crowded foyer of the hotel and disappear through the glass doors and out into the busy streets of the Shibuya shopping area.[5]

If *The End of the Affair* (1951) lies behind *Silence*, illustrating Endo's apprenticeship to Greene, then *Silence*, together with *The Samurai* (Endo's novel about a seventeenth-century Japanese diplomat's mission to Mexico and Europe), lies behind the camaraderie between Greene and Leopoldo Durán, his closest friend and confidant. "Greene was an admirer of the Japanese novelist Shusaku Endo," Durán claims, and, "in my copy of *Silence*, he [Greene] wrote: '... My pen-friend Endo would love to know that he was read by my travel companion in Spain ...' and *The Samurai* was: 'this book by one of my favourite friends and novelists ...'"[6]

William Johnston confirms the Endo-Greene connection. Johnston underlines at least one important difference between them, however, and this contrast stems from what he takes to be their vocational self-understanding. In the end, though, he praises Endo's and Greene's bracingly candid Catholicism. Here, Johnston describes dining with Endo and an English journalist:

After asking many innocuous questions, the journalist suddenly asked, 'Mr. Endo, you are an admirer of Graham Greene?' Endo nodded in agreement. 'But Greene,' said the journalist, 'had many problems with the Catholic Church. What about you, Mr. Endo?'

Endo answered with a smile, 'I have had problems. They appear in my books. But my mother died a Catholic. My brother died a Catholic. And I would like to die a Catholic too.'

Of course, he did admire Graham Greene and was influenced by *The Power and the Glory*. Once when Endo was in London he ran into Graham Greene by accident in a hotel and this was one of the big days in his life. Yet there were differences, pointed out to me by a bishop in Finland who was a fan of Endo. The bishop said that Greene was a novelist who happened to be a Catholic, while Endo was a Catholic who happened to be a novelist. This may be true. Still, both of these authors worked out their religious problems in powerful novels and will go hand in hand through the centuries as honest but committed Catholics.[7]

Some interpreters disfavor this apparent "Greene-ing of Endo."[8] Writing in his introduction to the 2006 re-issue of *Scandal*, Endo's novel about a Tokyo-based Catholic novelist embroiled in sexual intrigue, critic Damian Flanagan notes that back in the 1980s and 1990s, Western readers described Endo as "the Japanese Graham Greene," and he concedes that Endo often enjoyed the comparison, but, in the end, Flanagan contests the label's usefulness. He feels that "Endo deserved better," and, moreover, that "Greene might be lucky to be remembered as 'the British Endo.'"[9] I do not see the point of this observation, to be honest, but I concur with Flanagan when he says: "Now that both writers are dead it is easy to see that both Greene and Endo have established an unassailable position in twentieth-century literature."[10] For my part, I think Endo and Greene secure their "unassailable position" through their Catholic literary modernism's fierce intelligence and terrifying lucidity. But Flanagan seems unconvinced. Endo's and Greene's "obsessive grappling" with Catholicism has become, "in a world increasingly stripped of Christian belief," the "most yawn-inducing aspect of their work."[11] I disagree.[12] Neither Endo nor Greene provides customary Catholic comforts in their fiction; rather, as John Updike observes, their stories chronicle "the bewilderment and panic, the sense of hollowness and futility, which afflicts those whose search for God is not successful. And are we not all, within the churches and temples or not, the more searcher than finder in this regard?"[13] It is to their searching work that I now turn, beginning with the first of three basic points of theological agreement: sin's mystery.

Sin's Mystery

While Greene said that "a ruling passion gives to a shelf of novels the unity of a system," critics have found it difficult to define and discuss this "ruling passion."[14] Perhaps this is because Greene's own character seems so ironic. In many of his recorded interviews, for example, he comes across as a taciturn man both haunted and fortified by an inner core of faith and doubt, of self-interest and self-effacement, and of loyalty and disloyalty. He looks for evidence of humanity in what most of us would think of as inhuman characters. Moreover, he seems to believe that evil contains within itself the seeds of good and that authentic faith pulsates at the heart of the unconventionally pious. This paradoxical spirit explains Greene's well-known narrative sleight-of-hand, as well as his fondness for creating characters marked by manifold incongruities: the unorthodox clergyman who experiences the gratuity of the divine Self-gift and the secret agent who embodies sincerity in the midst of his duplicity. As one of Greene's reviewers writes: "He is moved most by characters who have to be strong because they are weak, who have to be good because they think themselves sinners."[15]

"I have always been preoccupied with the mystery of sin," Greene remarked in 1949, "it is always the foundation of my books."[16] Greene's interest in sin's mystery stems from his awareness of life's ambiguities. Not black and white, Greene insists, human nature is black and gray, which entails that both good and evil can always find a place in human existence. Women and men are marked by an intricate duality that stains and pains them and from which they desperately seek some way of escape.[17] Greene's literary art is replete with examples of this struggle. Consider Major Scobie, Greene's symbol of fragmented consciousness in *The Heart of the Matter* (1948), who feels torn between the competing values of pity and pride, or else Alden Pyle, Greene's symbol of innocence and experience in *The Quiet American* (1955), who feels caught on the borderland between naïve intrusiveness and informed engagement, never sure exactly which way to turn. Pyle and Scobie eventually escape their predicament. But we, as readers, come to their stories' end to find that Greene has challenged us to ponder the ambiguous nature of their salvation or escape.

Like Greene, Endo appears preoccupied with sin's mystery. This fascination displays itself in the double-dealing, nefarious characters that appear in *Stained Glass Elegies*, Endo's first collection of short stories, published in 1984 but representing his best work from the period of the late 1950s to the mid-1970s. And yet, Endo's novel *Scandal*, which features Suguro, an aging, married Japanese Catholic writer, telegraphs this theme most thoughtfully. Accused of frequenting Tokyo's red-light district, Suguro spends the novel's greater part salvaging his reputation as well as saving his sanity from what appears to be an uncanny *doppelgänger*—a creepy, lascivious spitting image of himself. This battle seems oddly fitting because, at the novel's onset, we are informed that Suguro's writerly vocation involved thrusting "his hands into aspects of life that his Church undoubtedly abhors—the evil, loathsome, filthy acts of men."[18] And in a remark that might summarize Endo's and Greene's ruling passion, one of Suguro's associates describes how Suguro's "pen somehow persisted in depicting the black, ugly realms within his characters. As a novelist he could not bring himself to skirt over or ignore any of the components of a human being."[19] Thinking in this manner inclines Suguro, like Endo and Greene, to believe in "the notion that a true religion should be able to respond to the dark melodies, the faulty and hideous sounds that echo from the hearts of men."[20] And even though he struggles to sustain Catholic Christianity in his Japanese context, Suguro treats his religion as true, as an authentic overlay or way of looking at the world, because it recognizes sin as a dangerously unpredictable ugliness lurking within humankind, akin to magma inside people's hearts, liable to erupt at any moment.[21]

Suguro builds on this theological anthropology when he asserts that vice stimulates virtue. Midway through *Scandal*, he appears on television and, despite his Greenean dislike for interviews, Suguro declares that a longing for rebirth lies concealed within every aberrant act:

> 'Rebirth?' The interviewer's eyes again flashed with undisguised interest.
>
> Suguro nodded. 'It's true that my characters squirm in suffocating circumstances and then commit their sins, but if you think about those sins … in the lives of the characters, they turn out to be …' As Suguro groped for the right words, he also seemed to be plumbing the interviewer's response. 'Their sins, in the final analysis, end up being … an expression of their craving for a new way of life.'
>
> 'Can that be called salvation?' the confused interviewer asked.
>
> 'Maybe it can't be styled salvation, but the potential for salvation is contained within the sin.'[22]

Greene upholds analogous thoughts. Although he disliked the word "sin," he uses it recurrently, and often as a precursor to talk about salvation, which inclines commentator Kenneth Tynan to think "Greene believes that sin holds within it the seeds of virtue, and the paradox of evil breeding sanctity, of dunghills sprouting daisies, has become one of the trademarks of his work."[23] Returning to Suguro, and thus to Endo, now compare Tynan's remark with the following summary of Suguro's fiction, which someone offers during an evening when Suguro receives a literary award:

'After a period of groping his way through the darkness, during which time he gleefully depicted the sins of mankind, Suguro began to assert that a yearning for rebirth lies concealed within each act of sin. Within every sin, he suggests, lurks the desire of men to find a way of escaping from the suffocating lives we lead today. I think that's what is original in Suguro's literature. And in his latest novel these unique conceptions are portrayed with considerable maturity.'[24]

Silence is riddled with Endo's sense of sin. And the novel's multifaceted depiction of weakness, betrayal and guilt makes most sense when we view it through the lens of Endo's troubled connection to the Jesuit priest who baptized him, William Johnston avers. Erstwhile rector of Tokyo's Sophia University, Fr. Peter Herzog scandalized his superiors by leaving the priesthood to marry his administrative assistant. "This was in the 1950s, and to Endo it was a terrible shock. He could not fathom it."[25] Over time, however, Endo came to see Herzog's forbidden love differently:

By chance he saw Herzog in a restaurant, no longer the handsome, well-dressed cleric but a slightly disheveled old man who, at the end of his meal, blessed himself. Was he not much better, much more humble than the proud prelate of the past?

Deeply impressed, Endo tells us that he made Herzog the hero of some of his novels. In the novel *Silence*, the noble misfit tramples on the image of the Christ he loves—not to save his life but to save the lives of his Christians. The hero does not lose his faith. He steps on the cross for love. This is Endo's Herzog.[26]

Endo found Herzog's weakness mesmerizing, and his sin oddly elucidatory, because in or through such frailty and iniquity he, Endo, heard the first soundings of an edifying hymn to discipleship's difficulties. Johnston continues:

Chinmoku [*Silence's* Japanese title] ends with the emptiness or *kenosis* of Jesus who cries out that he came into the world to be trampled on. It ends with the *kenosis* of the priest who, out of compassion and love, empties himself completely. And now I believe that *Chinmoku* is a story of the *kenosis* of Endo himself.

In short, I see in Endo the *kenosis* of the Epistle to the Philippians, where Jesus empties himself, taking the form of a slave, becoming obedient unto death, even death on the cross [Phil. 2.5-8]. I see in Endo the *todo y nada* of St. John of the Cross, the 'all or nothing' of *The Cloud of Unknowing*. I now realize that most of Endo's works center on the weak Jesus who emptied himself, and Endo, always conscious of his own sinfulness and admitting that he would have stepped on the *fumie*, looks on himself as the weak follower of Jesus.[27]

God's Wide Mercy

God's wide mercy is the antidote to sin's poison, according to Endo and Greene. Indeed, their fictional characters often find themselves embroiled in situations, everyday circumstances really, where anxiety provokes sin and from which only faith appears able to save them, though often the specific form salvation takes appears ambiguous. In *Brighton Rock* (1938), Pinkie Brown embodies senseless wickedness; sin always seems right there with him, and nor does Pinkie ever strive to cultivate those impulses that promote human flourishing: friendship, truth, and peace of mind. Yet we arrive at the novel's end to find ourselves confronted by the startling possibility that there is no limit to God's mercy—no limit to the pure, unbounded Love that will not let such characters go and that invades the space "between the stirrup and the ground" to redeem them, even them, however appallingly strange such charity seems to us.[28] "The strange mercy of God was an obsession with Greene," critic William Cash states; "the more unlikely the recipient the better."[29] Endo's recipients of divine favor also appear unlikely. Consider the title story in *The Final Martyrs* short fiction collection, which introduces us to spineless Kisuke, an early study for the cowardly Kichijiro in *Silence*, and an arresting symbol of Christian faith buckling under torture's pressure. Set free after recanting his Catholicism, Kisuke soon finds that divine forgiveness dogs his every irresolute step, and that God's generous as well as peculiar providence pushes him to return to prison and seek salvation from the other believers he let down:

> He heard a voice calling to him from behind. He turned round, but no one was there. It was neither the voice of a man nor a woman. But he had heard the voice echoing clearly amidst the sound of the black ocean waves.
>
> 'All you have to do is go and be with the others. If you're tortured again and you become afraid, it's all right to run away. It's all right to betray me. But go follow the others …'
>
> When Kisuke had finished his story, the Christians in the cell were silent, emitting not even a cough. As they sat in confinement they knew from the sharp stab at their skin that the snow was gradually piling up outside. Kanzaburo felt that the torture he had endured these two years, and the fact that his brother had died without abandoning the faith, had not been in vain.

The next morning the officers unlocked the door to the 1-metre cell to interrogate Kisuke. If Kisuke would not agree to apostatize, he would be thrown into the icy lake in the garden of the temple. As he listened to the rasp of the lock and to Kisuke's faltering footsteps, Kanzaburo whispered: 'Kisuke. If it hurts you, it's all right to apostatize. It's all right. The Lord Jesus is pleased just because you came here. He is pleased.'[30]

It is the same Jesus whose gentle judgment pursues Otsu, a failed seminarian in *Deep River*, Endo's pilgrimage to India novel, and it is Jesus, oddly enough, who appears to alert Otsu to the startling possibility of discovering sacred truth in non-Christian religions. Relaxing in an ashram close to the River Ganges, Otsu recalls the scorn of his superiors at the seminary and the novitiate, those who first heard but soon repudiated his apparently aberrant belief that religions are culturally different responses to God's wide mercy:

> As he snored, he had a dream. Even in his dreams he saw the pallid face of Jacques Monge, the brilliant upper classman who had berated him incessantly in the religious community at Lyon.
>
> 'God was fostered in this world of ours. In this Europe you detest so.'
>
> 'I don't believe that. After he was crucified in Jerusalem, he began to wander through many lands. Even today he roams through various countries. Through India and Vietnam, through China, Korea, Taiwan.'
>
> 'Enough! If our teachers knew you were such a heretic …!'
>
> 'Am I… am I really a heretic? Was any religion truly heretical to him? He accepted and loved the Samaritan.'
>
> Only in his dreams could he defy Jacques Mongue and his superiors, plead his case and refute their arguments; in reality his face turned tearful and he lapsed into silence. He was, in sum, no more than a loser, a coward.[31]

Major Scobie, the angst-ridden protagonist of Greene's *The Heart of the Matter*, resembles Otsu, in that both battle constantly with their short-comings and possess a passion to do right. Only faith separates them. While Otsu claims that he cannot leave the Church because "Jesus has me in his grasp,"[32] Scobie feels abandoned, unable to hope:

> Some words she [Louise] was reading momentarily caught his attention:
>
> *We are all falling. This hand's falling too—*
> *all have this falling sickness none withstands.*
>
> *And yet there's always One whose gentle hands*
> *this universal falling can't fall through.*

They sounded like truth, but he rejected them—comfort can come too easily. He thought, those hands will never hold my fall: I slip between the fingers, I'm greased with falsehood, treachery. Trust was a dead language of which he had forgotten the grammar.[33]

Scobie eventually commits suicide, a mortal sin, but is there a wideness in God's mercy? Do those gentle hands hold Scobie's fall? "For goodness sake, Mrs Scobie, don't imagine you—or I—know a thing about God's mercy," Father Rank protests; and, "It may seem an odd thing to say—when a man's as wrong as he was—but I think, from what I saw of him, that he really loved God."[34] The depths of misery and the call to grandeur, both of which appear integral to the human experience, and vital to the Second Vatican Council's theological reflections on human nature and dignity, find their fictional elaboration in Endo and Greene—"Catholic writers in non-Catholic cultures," to cite critic Bates Hoffer.[35]

In the autumn of their careers, Endo and Greene connected the issue of God's wide mercy to the task of living in a modern, religiously plural society, where rival claims exist side by side, all claiming to be true. Are such claims felt to need argument or resolution, so that one religion may be seen as absolutely true to the exclusion of all others? Or are such truths simply different overlays held by different people, who then must learn to coexist? To answer such questions, Endo and Greene consulted Christian theology. Endo read John Hick and Ninian Smart, for example, and Greene studied Fr. Teilhard de Chardin as well as Hans Küng.[36] Briefly, Hick and Teilhard favor a pneumatological or theocentric way of viewing life. On this model, all the world's religions represent different manifestations of one common experience: the human response to Transcendent Spirit or Mystery. God as Spirit sacralizes creation by dispersing grace everywhere, which implies there is a wideness to God's mercy in the sense that there is more to God's Christic agency than Jesus of Nazareth. Put differently, God works within and through different cultures to gather different peoples and their different faiths back to Godself. Scholars like Mark Williams and Emi Mase-Hasegawa describe how and why Endo's theocentrism materializes in his late fiction, especially *Deep River*, even though they stress that Endo always affirmed Jesus's finality in our universe of faiths. In short, they think Endo may best be understood as a *Christian* pluralist.[37] Greene's Teilhardian theocentrism, which sees the Spirit everywhere, active in the here and now, surfaces in his letters and interviews, where he appeals to sacred mystery, doubt, and an ecumenical approach to spirituality.[38] With Endo and Greene, then, the pluralism principle seems strong; in life, numerous different truths exist side by side, and there is a wideness to God's mercy.[39]

Faith as Troubled Commitment

Greene's construal of faith as troubled commitment has a personal history, one that begins with his conversion in 1926, when he took the spiritual name of the doubting disciple Thomas. Greene the Doubter went on to model a faith marked by skepticism.[40] He cared very little for the so-called proofs of God's existence, for example, and this dis-ease was a trait shared by many of his characters, especially the protagonist in his 1963 short story "A Visit to Morin."[41] According to Greene, all attempts to conceptualize God, especially God's providence, yield little or no positive result, because life is replete with those seemingly inexplicable moments that reason appears powerless to explain. Consider the V1 blast, which shatters Sarah Miles's and Maurice Bendrix's infidelity in *The End of the Affair*. Here Sarah's voice reveals that during the first few moments following the explosion, she experienced sheer terror, the sort of nervous tension that inclines even the most skeptical soul to close his or her eyes and pray to God:

> I knelt and put my head on the bed and wished I could believe. Dear God, I said—why dear, why dear?—make me believe. I can't believe. Make me. I said, I'm a bitch and a fake and I hate myself. I can't do anything of myself. *Make* me believe. I shut my eyes tight, and I pressed my nails into the palms of my hands until I could feel nothing but the pain, and I said I will believe. Let him be alive, and I *will* believe. Give him a chance. Let him have his happiness. Do this and I'll believe. But that wasn't enough. It doesn't hurt to believe. So I said, I love him and I'll do anything if you'll make him alive. I'll give him up for ever, only let him be alive with a chance, and I pressed and pressed and I could feel the skin break ...[42]

With her love in the ruins, literally and figuratively, Sarah lays some kind of Pascalian wager, gambling her happiness against Bendrix's survival, her actual doubt against her potential faith. In time her bet with God appears to pay off. Not only does Bendrix live, Sarah experiences the first stirrings of faith—a troubled commitment, one torn by the existential fissure between that which her mind can verify and the sheer trust that God now seems to demand. In contrast to Sarah, Bendrix hates God, especially the seemingly sneaky manner in which God inclines Sarah to proceed out from adultery and toward a kind of sainthood. Not surprisingly, the hues of Bendrix's bitterness fleck the novel's final pages. Standing before numerous characters, especially Fr. Crompton, Bendrix decries God's peculiar providence. And yet Bendrix eventually arrives at his tale's end to find himself at the brink of faith, delivered there by a series of extraordinary events, against which his studiously ironic detachment seems immobilized. In *The End of the Affair*, then, divine providence is deeply inscrutable. And faith is troubled commitment—an unsettled, tenuous, and quizzical approach to matters of the spirit. It was ever thus for Greene, the self-styled Catholic agnostic. "One is attracted to the *Faith*," he revealed in 1989, "Believing is the problem."[43]

In Endo's *Silence*, faith as troubled commitment appears in Fr. Rodrigues, who struggles to model Christian presence in a hostile, non-Christian environment. Prepared as he is himself to endure pain for God at the hands of his incongruously cruel Buddhist captors, to heed the angst-ridden howls of Japanese Christians being tortured close by is excruciating. Rodrigues believes in God. But he finds it hard to pray to God, harder to wait on God to unfold God's plan and practically impossible to cling by faith to traditional theology's belief that instant suffering has an eventual purpose. Rodrigues struggles because God appears to be silent and absent, at least for the greater part of the novel, leaving the beleaguered priest alone with his spiritual quandary: should he safeguard his faith's integrity, and thus hasten his congregation's suffering, or should he betray Christ publicly, trample on the bronze replica of Christ's face, the *fumie*, and thus save his people from persecution? Eventually, Endo's Christ breaks His silence, and He encounters the priest in his betrayal and his parish in their weakness, entering into such suffering with them.[44] For this formal act of betrayal, of course, the Church condemns Rodrigues. He is a fallen priest, weak in faith, yet Christians who have read *Silence* often find themselves energized by Endo's image of Christ as the fellow-sufferer who understands, the eternal companion who loves wastefully and identifies with them when their spiritual journey seems beset with difficulties. "Endo explores the crevices of failure and betrayal that every person on earth lives with and often seeks to hide," Philip Yancey declares, and "in doing so, Endo sheds new light on the Christian faith—at once harshly revealing light that exposes long-hidden corners, and also a softening light that erases shadows."[45] In Rodrigues's agonized faith, that is, many Christian readers of *Silence* sense an edifying parallel to their own troubled commitment; and in Endo, they find an artist who illustrates discipleship's always arduous and often costly road.

Conclusion

The literary critic's function, George Steiner declares, is to behave like "pilot fish, those strange tiny creatures, which go out in front of the real thing, the great shark or the great whale, warning, saying to the people, 'It's coming.'"[46] I find this image intriguing. What is the "real thing" in Endo's or Greene's work? What signifies the "it" that is "coming"? I am not sure. Whatever else it does, Endo's and Greene's fiction opens out to many interpretations—to those who construe it humanistically, as locating the enormous within the everyday, and to those, like me, who read it theologically, as gesturing toward Transcendence. I am not sure of the "real thing" in Endo's and Greene's art. But I suspect that reading defies stasis, and reading the chapters in this volume has helped me along, has prepared me for whatever is on its way, is coming, and therein lies no small virtue.

Notes

1   This chapter is a revised and expanded version of "Graham Greene and Shusaku Endo: Friends, Novelists, Theologians," in Vincent Giroud, ed. *Graham Greene: un écrivain dans le siècle* (Besançon, France: Presses de l'université de Franche-Comté); forthcoming.

2   George Bull, "A literary love affair: Graham Greene's brief encounter with Shusaku Endo," *The Chesterton Review* 27.1/2 (February/May 2001): 176. I intend my chapter, structured as it is around three major points of theological consanguinity, to supplement the work of other scholars who have explored the Endo-Greene alliance. See Bates Hoffer, "Shusaku Endo and Graham Greene: Cross-Cultural Influences in Literary Structure," *Language and Literature* 28 (2003): 127–33. Also see Christopher Link, "Bad Priests and the Valor of Pity: Shusaku Endo and Graham Greene on the Paradoxes of Christian Virtue," *Logos: A Journal of Catholic Thought and Culture* 15.4 (2012): 75–96.

3   Richard Greene, ed., *Graham Greene: A Life in Letters* (London: Little, Brown Book Group, 2007), 322–3.

4   Richard Greene, "Over the Border: The Letters of Graham Greene," in Greene, ed., *Graham Greene: A Life in Letters*, xiii.

5   Caryl Phillips, *Color Me English: Migration and Belonging Before and After 9/11* (New York and London: The New Press, 2011), 214.

6   Leopoldo Durán, *Graham Greene: An Intimate Portrait by His Closest Friend and Confidant*, trans. Euan Cameron (San Francisco: HarperSanFrancisco, 1994), 305. Similar references appear in Fr. Leopoldo Durán, "The Human Aspects of Graham Greene Revealed Through Our Friendship," in Wm. Thomas Hill, ed., *Lonely Without God: Graham Greene's Quixotic Journey of Faith* (Bethesda, MD: Academica Press, 2008), 25–33.

7   William Johnston, *Mystical Journey: An Autobiography* (Maryknoll, NY: Orbis Books, 2006), 110–11.

8   Van Gessel and others note this disfavor elsewhere in our volume.
9   Damian Flanagan, "Introduction" to Shusaku Endo, *Scandal*, trans. Van C.
    Gessel (London: Peter Owen, 2006), i.
10 Ibid.
11 Ibid.
12 Reasons for why I think Endo and Greene speak to us appear in Darren
    J. N. Middleton, "Dead Serious: A Theology of Literary Pilgrimage," *Cross
    Currents* 59.3 (September 2009): 300–18.
13 John Updike, *More Matter: Essays and Criticism* (New York: Random
    House, 1999), 852. Updike's comments come from an address that he gave
    upon receiving the Campion Medal from the editors of *America* in 1987.
    Endo was a Campion medalist in 1990.
14 See Henry J. Donaghy, ed., *Conversations with Graham Greene* (Jackson,
    MS: University of Mississippi Press, 1992), 41. For an instructive,
    well-written summary of Greene's life and work, see Andrew W. Hass,
    "God and the Novelists 5. Graham Greene," *Expository Times* 110.3
    (December 1998): 68–72.
15 Donaghy, ed., *Conversations with Graham Greene*, 152.
16 Ibid., 17.
17 Ibid., 17, 35. Also see K. C. Joseph Kurismmootil, S. J., *Heaven and Hell on
    Earth: An Appreciation of Five Novels of Graham Greene* (Chicago: Loyola
    University Press, 1982), 199–214. Kurismmootil provides an excellent
    outline of Greene's theological convictions, especially the twin notions
    of sin and salvation, gathered together in a chapter he calls "A Novelist's
    Creed."
18 Shusaku Endo, *Scandal*, trans. Van C. Gessel (Boston: Tuttle Publishing,
    1986), 12.
19 Ibid. Also see 151.
20 Ibid., 13.
21 Ibid., 144.
22 Ibid., 96.
23 A. F. Cassis, ed., *Graham Greene: Man of Paradox* (Chicago: Loyola
    University Press, 1994), 107. Also see 168, 330, 333, 349, 460.
24 Endo, *Scandal*, 13.
25 Johnston, *Mystical Journey*, 109.
26 Ibid., 81.
27 Ibid., 109. Johnston ties such remarks to Herzog: "According to Endo,
    the proud, almost arrogant, priest who had baptized him had undergone
    kenosis and was now a better, humbler man." And Endo's appraisal causes
    Johnston to wonder: "Is *Chinmoku* a defense of Herzog? Is Herzog the
    man who abandons everything for love?" (109). For details on kenotic
    Christology, and the exemplarist soteriology that this doctrine seems to
    inspire in Christians, see the essays in C. Stephan Evans, ed., *Exploring
    Kenotic Christology: The Self-Emptying of God* (Oxford: Oxford University

Press, 2006). Of course, there are some critics who disfavor what we might call the "kenotic reading" of *Silence*. See Bradley Baurain, "Shusaku Endo and the Great Temptation," *Christianity and the Arts* 6.3 (Summer 1999): 18–20. "But to act as Rodrigues did is to say that we know better than God how to remedy suffering and overcome evil. This is the great temptation: to claim to act for God in a way that denies God," Baurain writes (20). On Endo's kenotic Christ, see Emi Mase-Hasegawa, *Christ in Japanese Culture: Theological Themes in Shusaku Endo's Literary Works* (Leiden and Boston: Brill, 2008), 147–51.

28 Graham Greene, *Brighton Rock* (London: William Heinemann & The Bodley Head, 1970), 110, 308.

29 William Cash, *The Third Woman: The Secret Passion That Inspired Graham Greene's The End of the Affair* (New York: Carroll & Graf Publishers, Inc., 2000), 138.

30 Shusaku Endo, *The Final Martyrs*, trans. Van C. Gessel (New York: New Directions, 2009), 27.

31 Shusaku Endo, *Deep River*, trans. Van C. Gessel (New York: New Directions, 1994), 191.

32 Ibid.

33 Graham Greene, *The Heart of the Matter* (London: William Heinemann & The Bodley Head, 1971), 311.

34 Ibid., 320.

35 For details, see Pastoral Constitution on the Church in the Modern World *Gaudium et Spes*, promulgated by His Holiness, Pope Paul VI on December 7, 1965. See: http://www.vatican.va/archive/hist_councils/ii_vatican_ council/documents/vat-ii_cons_19651207_gaudium-et-spes_en.html (accessed March 2014). Also see Mark Bosco, S. J., *Graham Greene's Catholic Imagination* (Oxford and New York: Oxford University Press, 2005), 71–96.

36 Mark Williams reveals that Endo read Hick's *The Problem of Religious Pluralism* (1985), which appeared in Japanese in the late 1980s. See Williams, "Crossing the Deep River: Endō Shūsaku and the Problem of Religious Pluralism" in Kevin M. Doak, ed., *Xavier's Legacies: Catholicism in Modern Japanese Culture* (Vancouver, BC: UBC Press, 2011), 115–33; see 117 especially. Also see Emi Mase-Hasegawa, *Christ in Japanese Culture*, 168–80. On Greene and Teilhard de Chardin, see Dermot Gilvary and Darren J. N. Middleton, eds., *Dangerous Edges of Graham Greene: Journeys with Saints and Sinners* (London and New York: Continuum, 2011), 182–92. Mark Bosco describes Küng's influence on Greene in Bosco, *Graham Greene's Catholic Imagination*, 25, 84–9, 93–5, 111, 143. It seems Greene admired Küng's *On Being a Christian* (1974), although at least one letter from Greene to Küng indicates that Greene housed no fewer than five Küng texts in his personal library. See Richard Greene, *Graham Greene: A Life in Letters*, 409.

37   See Williams, "Crossing the Deep River," 130–1. Also see Mase-Hasegawa, *Christ in Japanese Culture*, 181–7. Dissenting views may be seen in Adelino Ascenso, *Transcultural Theodicy in the Fiction of Endō Shūsaku* (Rome: Editrice Pontifica Università Gregoriana, 2009), 11. For a critique of Hick's Christian pluralism in light of Endo's fiction, see Anri Morimoto, "The (More or Less) Same Light but from Different Lamps: The Post-Pluralist Understanding of Religion from a Japanese Perspective," *International Journal for Philosophy of Religion* 53.3 (June 2003): 163–80.

38   Besides the many interviews and correspondence in Richard Greene and A. F. Cassis, cited above, see Ian Thomson, ed. *Articles of Faith: The Collected Tablet Journalism of Graham Greene* (Oxford and New York: Oxford University Press, 2006), 121–45, 151–63.

39   Elizabeth Cameron Galbraith explores pluralism in Endo's literary art elsewhere in this collection.

40   Michael G. Brennan, *Graham Greene: Fictions, Faith and Authorship* (London and New York: Continuum, 2010), 8.

41   Graham Greene, *Collected Stories* (London: William Heinemann & The Bodley Head, 1972), 238–56.

42   Graham Greene, *The End of the Affair* (Harmondsworth, England: Penguin, 1962), 95. For a religious reading of this novel, see Darren J. N. Middleton, *Theology after Reading: Christian Imagination and the Power of Fiction* (Waco, TX: Baylor University Press, 2008), 15–47.

43   Cassis, ed., *Graham Greene: Man of Paradox*, 465. On Greene's Catholic agnosticism, see 435–7, 458. Also see Darren J. N. Middleton, "Graham Greene, Believing Skeptic," in Marc DiPaolo, ed., *Unruly Catholics from Dante to Madonna: Faith, Heresy, and Politics in Cultural Studies* (Lanham, MD: The Scarecrow Press, Inc., 2013), 17–31.

44   Shusaku Endo, *Silence*, trans. William Johnston (New York: Taplinger Publishing Company, 1980), 171.

45   Philip Yancey, *Soul Survivor: How Thirteen Unlikely Mentors Helped My Faith Survive the Church* (New York: Doubleday; Colorado Springs, CO: Water Brook Press, 2003), 282.

46   George Steiner, cited in George Plimpton, editor, *The Writer's Chapbook: A Compendium of Fact, Opinion, Wit, and Advice from the Twentieth Century's Preeminent Writers*, edited from *The Paris Review* interviews and with an introduction by George Plimpton (New York: The Modern Library, 1999), 265. Elsewhere in this volume, Mark Dennis explores Steiner's pilot fish trope.

5

Charting Endo's Catholic
Literary Aesthetic

Mark Bosco, S.J.

Late in Shusaku Endo's writing career, in making his remarks after receiving an honorary degree from an American university, he recalled that "one or two months after *Silence* was published in English, I unexpectedly received a letter from Graham Greene in which he wrote of his impressions of my book and kindly suggested an English publisher for my future work. We corresponded occasionally. But I met him just once."[1] Some years later at a memorial for her husband, Endo's widow, Junko, noted that when her husband met Greene in London, Endo told Greene "how greatly he had been influenced by his works and that he might not even have been a novelist had he not read his novels."[2] Greene, for his part, was quite taken with Endo's novel and true to his word, wrote his publisher at Bodley Head that Endo's *Silence* "is so much better than my own *Power and the Glory*."[3] The comparison of *Silence* to Greene's novel (1940) has been noted countless times and suggests how Endo's early literary imagination was affected by what might be called a Catholic literary aesthetic. Both Greene and Endo set their novels in a time of extreme persecution of Catholics, the Mexico of the 1930s and Japan in the seventeenth century, respectively; each follows a fugitive priest carrying out his priestly duties of Mass and Confession while trying to avoid being captured. The chase and pursuit motif, the skillful dialogue between priest and captors, and the suspenseful climaxes are all elements of both novels.[4] If Greene's novel situates the drama of *The Power and the Glory* in a deeply Catholic culture at odds with the new and aggressive secular regime of Mexico, Endo sets his work in a non-Christian culture, interrogating the very ability of European Catholicism to ever find a home in what Endo called the "mudswamp" of Japan.

Often framed in essentialist terms as the dialectical resistance of Japanese culture to the colonizing power of Westernized Christianity, *Silence* (1969) is frequently read and critiqued as Endo's attempt to make a statement concerning the unsuitability of Christian faith with Japan's traditional sensibility. The novel explores the gulf between East and West—particularly concerns about religious, cultural, and political difference. Endo's earliest written comments on his faith support this assessment, as he likened his baptism into the Catholic Church at the age of 11 to the forced imposition of a "ready-made suit, a Western suit, ill-matched to his Japanese body."[5] Unable to throw off his new faith, Endo produced an entire *oeuvre* characterized by what he calls "a confrontation of my Catholic self with the self that lies underneath."[6] Though there is much to be gained from this reading, it often overshadows Endo's fascination and engagement with the theological tropes, symbols, and narrative strategies of the Catholic literary revival in which he took part. Indeed, Catholicism is as much a hermeneutical lens of interpreting the world as it is a religious faith, a dynamic cultural construction that has shaped a transnational community of writers throughout the world, from the French novels of François Mauriac and Georges Bernanos, the British novels of Greene and Evelyn Waugh, the American writers Flannery O'Connor and Walker Percy, and, for our purposes, the novels and short stories of Shusaku Endo. Endo draws from a tradition that encompasses traits that are deep within the logic and technique of what might be called the Catholic imagination. I would like to trace the genealogy of this twentieth-century Catholic literary aesthetic from its European roots to Endo, noting key elements important to the theological discourse that supports Greene's claim that *Silence*, understood from the vantage point of this unique Catholic literary moment, is indeed "so much better" and so much more pervasive in Endo's novel than in Greene's own work. I will first offer ways to reckon with the impact of Catholic aesthetic literary strategies in the twentieth century, and then suggest a reading of *Silence* in light of these theological foci.

The Twentieth Catholic Literary Revival: France to Japan

As a university student in Tokyo during the waning years of the Second World War, Endo had been a resident at a Catholic hostel under the direction of the leading prewar Catholic intellectual, the theologian-philosopher Yoshihiko Yoshimitsu (1904–45). An important early mentor for Endo, Yoshimitsu's intellectual journey toward the French Catholic revival would later be repeated by Endo when he himself went to study in Lyon 20 years later. Yoshimitsu, while finishing his university studies, befriended the charismatic Catholic priest Iwashita Sōichi, and was baptized into the Catholic Church in 1927. At Fr. Sōichi's suggestion, Yoshimitsu moved to

Paris after graduation in order to study under the Catholic philosopher, Jacques Maritain, whose brand of Neo-Thomistic thought deeply influenced Yoshimitsu's own affirmation of religious faith lived within the exigencies of modern life. He returned to Japan to teach theology in 1931 at the Jesuit-sponsored Sophia University, and then at Tokyo Imperial University from 1940 until his death from tuberculosis in 1945.[7]

Committed to universal values at a time when Japan was governed by right-wing ethnocentrism and militarism, Yoshimitsu argued that traditional Japanese culture was actually closer to early (Catholic) European culture than a post-reformation, post-enlightenment Europe that had produced ideologies of liberalism, individualism, and capitalism, elements foreign to Japanese culture. His anti-modernist stance aligned him philosophically with the ultra-nationalist voices of Japanese life that promoted a purified Japan free of the effects of European contamination. In 1942 Yoshimitsu participated in a famous symposium called *Overcoming Modernity* (*Kindai no chōkoku*) that was soon used as an intellectual justification for military aggression against the West. As the leading Catholic intellectual of Japan, though, Yoshimitsu saw Catholicism as a positive force for Japan's future and he forcefully argued that the Catholic tradition showed a way to retrieve a deeper, more comprehensive Japanese humanism. Nevertheless, he stayed clear of any statements about the war in his teaching and writing. The scholar Adrian Pinnington notes that while the young Endo was being tutored under Yoshimitsu, Endo remembers his mentor "refusing either to criticize or countenance the war, simply advising students not to answer foolish questions posed to them by the police."[8]

Yoshimitsu's understanding of Catholicism as both a faith tradition and a philosophical apparatus that could critique modernity emerged during his formative years in France, under both the tutelage of Maritain and through his great love of French literature. Yoshimitsu's experience was just one part of a larger movement in Catholicism's reappearance on the cultural and intellectual stage in the early twentieth century. The triumph of science and secularization in European society during this time brought to many artists and intellectuals a feeling of disenchantment with a highly industrialized and impersonal world. Many found sustenance and encouragement in the artistic heritage of Catholic faith. A flurry of noted writers converted or reconverted to Catholicism in both France and England.[9] They found in this literary and philosophical turn to Catholicism a way to narrate the odd disruptions and mystical effusions of life in an age beholden to Enlightenment rationalism and crass materialism. By returning to Catholic belief and themes as the material for their work, these artists and intellectuals created a specific vision of Catholic modernity. Many of them gained the attention of a wider European audience because Catholicism was never served up with triumphant, epistemological certainty or as morally uplifting drama; rather, Catholicism was inscribed in the midst of fallen, poor humanity, a place of constant struggle where the mysterious irruptions of grace might shine forth or manifest in profound ways in the characters they portrayed.

This is most evident in the French literature of Joris-Karl Huysmans, Leon Blóy, and Charles Péguy in the late nineteenth century, and continuing on in Paul Claudel, Georges Bernanos, and François Mauriac into the mid-twentieth. These artists made Catholic literature into an accomplished literary form that offered both criticism of the modern condition, and also a powerful philosophical and artistic alternative to it. As the contemporary scholar Ellis Hanson suggests in his review of the Catholic literary revival in both France and England at the turn of the century, the aesthetic and historical heritage of Catholicism—its theology, its cathedrals, its communion of saints, its rituals and sacraments, its music and art—spoke more powerfully of the full range of human experience. Hanson provocatively remarks, "Catholicism is itself an elaborate paradox ... The Church is at once modern and yet medieval, ascetic and yet sumptuous, spiritual and yet sensual, chaste and yet erotic, homophobic and yet homoerotic, suspicious of aestheticism and yet an elaborate work of art."[10] Hanson proposes that it is these lived paradoxes that made Catholicism such a powerful alternative to the rationalized, bourgeois state: to have a Catholic vision of life was to make of one's life an artistic adventure. Catholic faith becomes a material culture that could hold together the paradoxes of the "modern" individual. Ironically, Catholicism becomes for these artists and converts not so much a reaction *against* the modern but a new way to understand the modern, to consciously negotiate the discourses of modernity.

This French-inspired Catholic literary aesthetic was deeply felt in England a generation later, interpreted and reinterpreted in light of Catholicism's minority status in a Christian, but Protestant tradition. One can trace Greene's own literary pedigree to the influence of the French Catholic intellectuals and novelists during the interwar years of Europe. In Greene's *Collected Essays* (1969), he chose to include one on Mauriac and another on Bernanos. Indeed, Greene had forged an intellectual friendship with François Mauriac, in particular. As editor of a British publishing house after the war, Greene was responsible for having Mauriac's works translated into English. Upon winning the Nobel Prize for Literature in 1950, Mauriac confessed that he owed much of it to Greene, who widened his readership beyond the shores of France.[11]

These influences also reached the shores of Japan, for Yoshimitsu's earlier turn to Catholicism exerted a great influence on Endo's decision to accept a scholarship in 1950 to study French literature at the University of Lyon, especially the novels of Mauriac and Bernanos. Endo's many remarks about his stay in France and his return to Japan suggest that the distance traveled between the French Catholic world of his studies and the vast expanse of ocean that differentiated Japanese culture was quite difficult for him. Endo had always felt homeless as a Catholic in Buddhist/Shinto-dominated Japan, so there was much hope that his immersion into the religious culture of France would be a sort of spiritual homecoming for him.[12] But from the very beginning of his studies, Endo was painfully mindful of his otherness. If he suffered on account of his faith while in Japan, he suffered in France due to racial prejudice and the overwhelming humiliation of being Japanese in postwar Europe. While tuberculosis ravaged his body—he would return to Japan after only two years of studies because of this—a spiritual crisis distressed him even more: his faith made him an outsider in Japan while his racial features upset his French Catholic hosts. Yet these pivotal years in France became the inspiration for *Silence*.

Catholicism as a Modern(-ist) Literary Strategy

Endo's inner turmoil between his Catholicism and his Japanese sensibility is amplified by a distinctive aesthetic vision that gave rise to the twentieth-century Catholic novelist. Endo's research and reading of French literature enabled him to absorb key ideas and images of the Catholic revival that would become part of his own artistic development. In terms of theme and plot, what made the Catholic novel "Catholic" in its mostly French and British varieties? In an important essay on Mauriac's novel *The Viper's Tangle* (1933), the writer David Lodge succinctly describes four key attributes of the modern Catholic novel: the idea of the sinner at the heart of Christianity, the doctrine of "mystical substitution," the implied criticism of materialism, and the tireless pursuit of the erring soul by God, the "Hound of Heaven" motif in Francis Thompson's well-known metaphor.[13] Lodge takes the French Catholic poet Charles Péguy's famous phrase, the "sinner at the heart of Christianity," as the premier attribute of the modern Catholic literary aesthetic. Far from the moralism and sentimental pieties of what might produce heroic tales, novelists like Mauriac dramatized the story of great sinners—thieves, prostitutes, drunks, derelicts, and apostates. Mauriac's novel *Thérèse* (1927), for instance, valorizes the title character, a woman married to a boorish husband. She is discovered to be slowly poisoning her husband with arsenic, and is quickly locked up by the two families in order to save face. After much suffering, she gives up her daughter and is banished to Paris. Though she stands as a criminal and outcast, Mauriac's sympathy—and the reader's—is with Thérèse, making the novel's condemnation rest firmly on her family. She is one of Mauriac's tragic studies of a woman who risks all to get out of her encaged life, becoming, in the end, a sort of saint. Mauriac subverts orthodox notions of saintliness in order to offer a kind of Catholic vision that fulfills Peguy's axiom that the sinner—and not the righteous believer—is the heart of the Christian story, the reason why Christ came to save. This is where the real drama is manifested. Endo, in an interview, reflected upon the impact of this profound idea: "I learned from these two writers [Mauriac and Greene] that there exists a possibility of salvation even in sin."[14]

A second property of a modern Catholic aesthetic that Endo absorbed in his creative imagination is the notion of "mystical substitution," perfected by the novelist Georges Bernanos. Works such as *Under Satan's Sun* (1926) and *Diary of a Country Priest* (1937) illustrate what Bernanos thought modern Christian life was like when lived "under Satan's sun." The protagonists of his novels are often saint-heroes whose virtues lie not in super-heroic, conventional saintliness but in their human frailty. This is dramatized in the way Bernanos's characters willingly participate in Christ's agony on the cross by giving their life up for another person. In *The Diary of a Country Priest*, the priest cries out impulsively, "I'll answer for your soul with mine."[15] In theological language, this articulates the doctrine of *kenosis*, an act of self-sacrifice made out of love for another as rehearsed in Paul's hymnic proclamation that Jesus "emptied himself and became a slave" (Phil. 2.7). The Christian doctrine refers to Christ's renunciation of his divine nature in order to live among humanity. Yet, the abasement of the second person of the Trinity in the Incarnation paradoxically and dramatically reveals the assumption of weakness by divine omnipotence. This understanding of *kenosis* is a fundamental idea for Endo's literary imagination, for it places the power of the divine presence among the poor and marginalized: "A person begins to be a follower of Jesus only by accepting the risk of becoming himself one of the powerless people in this visible world."[16] The intense climax of *Silence* is an act of *kenosis* on two levels: the apostasy of Fr. Sebastian Rodrigues as an act of love that mystically substitutes his own righteousness for those being tortured for his sake; and Rodrigues's realization of the larger drama of Christ's willing acceptance of his humiliation and debasement when he looks upon the *fumie* and hears Christ invite him to trample upon his image. This mystical compassion is the fundamental motif of Endo's ongoing literary imagination.

Another property of a Catholic aesthetic vision key to Endo's work is an understanding of a God that "hounds" us "with unhurrying chase and unperturbed pace," in the words of Thompson's celebrated poem.[17] The "Hound of Heaven" vividly illustrates the soul fleeing from a God it both fears and rejects, desperately hiding itself, only to feel at the end a final despairing turn toward this divine presence. What seems like crisis and anxiety in a character's ability to master oneself dramatically becomes another form of *kenosis*, an un-mastering of the self's importance, not so much a defeat as much as a new awareness and acceptance of a deeper reality at work. The Hound of Heaven motif raises the puzzling sense that even in one's freedom to disavow God or a divine agency, this God continues to pursue the soul. Very much in the vein of Fyodor Dostoevsky's thematic enterprise, this anxious hounding is a theological strategy that brings to the fore the personal struggle and torment in characters about the meaning of life. An unwanted or unheeded divine pursuit becomes a principal tactic of the Catholic literary revival. Endo's experience of Catholicism resonates with this existential hounding, for he notes, "That [faith] which brings peace and calm to others has brought me rather contradiction, conflict and anguish … Claudel says: 'God will never permit you to be lazy. He will always provide something to shake you up and worry over.'"[18] If the French Catholic writers helped to give this dramatic form a place of honor in the modern novel, it will be the divine pursuit and chase motif of Greene's *The Power and the Glory* and, later, Endo's *Silence* which will see it perfected. Endo's literary vision, then, is an evangelical one as much as it is personal and mystical, formed within the categories that predominate the twentieth-century Catholic literary revival: the sinner at the heart of Christianity, a climactic gesture of *kenosis* or mystical substitution, and the hounding of the divine until the soul rests, however uneasily, in God. Endo consciously placed himself in this genealogy of writers when he claimed one year after *Silence* was published:

> If there is a God, God can be found not only in the back streets of London where Greene writes, or in the scenery of France where Mauriac writes, but also in the streets of Shibuya or Shinjuku which seem to have nothing to do with God. It is my work to find it [God] in such an ordinary Japanese place, and if I could accomplish it, my "suit" would become my cloth.[19]

Modern Catholic Aesthetics in *Silence*

Like Greene's *The Power and the Glory* set in the religious persecutions of Mexico in the early twentieth century, Endo's novel is based on fact and

brings to light the historical context of early Christian evangelization in
Japan. The Jesuit missionary, Francis Xavier, arrived there in 1549 and
within 50 years native Christians numbered nearly 300,000. The Japanese
shogunate, fearing that the spread of Western cultural ideas would disrupt
its hegemony over Japanese society, became suspicious of the missionaries
who, until that time, had enjoyed the good will of the islands' magistrates
and rulers. All foreign missionaries were ordered to leave Japan, and the
magistrates began an offensive to rid Japan of all Christians. Those who did
not apostatize were brutally tortured in "the pit."[20] Between 1597 and 1650,
over 4,000 Japanese Christians died for their faith, the first by mass cruci-
fixions and then later through the torture of the pit. When the Jesuit leader of
the mission in Japan, Christóvão Ferreira, apostatized under torture in 1632,
the repercussions were felt both in the Jesuit centers of Europe as well as the
areas of hidden Christians who had gone underground in Japan. Into this
history Endo inserts the fictional Fr. Sebastian Rodrigues, an inexperienced
Portuguese priest, whose missionary fervor is tempered by his desire to see
if reports are correct that his mentor, Fr. Ferreira, had truly apostatized. The
novel thus begins with the weary encounters of a zealous missionary with
a variety of ideological factions in this strange Japanese "swampland," and
with the priest's own need to discover and test the truth of his convictions
about his faith.

Endo structures the novel in four parts: a short historical prologue; a
longer first-person epistolary journal of Rodrigues's nine months (October
to June) hiding while secretly ministering to Japanese Christians; a much
longer third-person narrative of Rodrigues's capture and eventual apostasy;
and a short appendix written by a Japanese officer as a diary documenting
Rodrigues's final days of house arrest until his death. Taken together, the
different perspectives problematize any simple treatment of the novel that
would frame it in terms of Western religious imperialism upon the indigenous
peoples of Japan. The critic John Netland notes that if the novel depicts the
tension between religion, culture, and the discourses of power, it also "resists
the reductionism of attributing this complicity solely to western hegemony.
Instead, [the novel] portrays a radically Christian alternative to the worst
impulses of both eastern and western political ambition."[21] Rodrigues's first-
person accounts prepare the reader for the triumphalist posturing of Western
evangelization in the East, and yet the Japanese authority whose shadow
underlies the novel, Inoue, the Lord of Chikugo, immediately undercuts
this sentiment. Through the debates between Rodrigues and Inoue, Endo
raises the issue of enculturation of Christianity in Japan, but it serves only
as a pretext for Inoue to use his authority to eradicate Christianity from
penetrating what he sees as a homogenous Japanese culture.

Endo exposes the reader to the spiritual transformation of Rodrigues through his encounters with the cowardly Kichijiro who betrays him, through Inoue who exercises control over him, and through his former teacher, the apostate Fr. Ferreira, who tries to convince him to apostatize by stepping on the image of Christ. Following the pattern of Greene's whiskey priest in *The Power and the Glory*, Fr. Rodrigues's religious journey operates as a form of deconstructive therapy: his faith must be stripped both of its Western cultural trappings and the personal vanity of his missionary zeal in order to recover a deeper, more orthodox understanding of Christian discipleship. As the Japanese state attempts to eliminate any trace of Christian presence, the priest is finally pushed to find that trace in the very presence of those persecuted and tortured. The delay in capturing the priest in the structure of the novel gradually allows for this unfolding.

Rodrigues is first portrayed as a man ready to prove himself worthy of his faith but his ulterior motive is to redress the dishonor of Ferreira, to offer himself as atonement for the appalling offense of his mentor's apostasy. Rodrigues's spiritual pride, hidden behind his self-abnegating journey toward martyrdom, sets up the climactic scene in the novel. His early letters ponder with both dread and fascination the perils that await him. Rodrigues feels himself pulled toward Japan by an intense vision of the face of Christ filled with majesty and glory. It is the resurrected Christ in triumphant vigor and strength that inspires his vocation. Though the reader initially admires the Jesuit's willingness to face up to any torture, that courage is overplayed until it touches on the priest's ambition and pride, for he wants his martyrdom to be a glorious achievement. And yet in the Christian tradition, one cannot seek out martyrdom: it must be thrust upon one as an act of solidarity with Christ. However noble is Rodrigues's vision of martyrdom, it is ultimately disordered. As T.S. Eliot might say, this "last temptation is the greatest treason: to do the right deed for the wrong reason."[22]

Already suspicious of Kichijiro, the man who had helped him elude capture, Rodrigues discovers that this Japanese man is, in fact, an apostate. His entire family had been burned at the stake for their faith; only Kichijiro submitted to treading on the *fumie*, the image of Christ, as a sign of his apostasy. Rodrigues regards him with a mixture of contempt and pity, a coward without the strength to fight for his faith. Nevertheless, Kichijiro's predicament articulates Rodrigues's theological difficulty, which gives the novel its name. Rodrigues ruminates:

> Everything our Lord does is for our good. And yet, even as I write these words I feel the oppressive weight in my heart of the last stammering

words of Kichijiro on the morning of his departure: "Why has Deus Sama imposed this suffering on us?" ... I suppose I should simply cast from my mind these meaningless words of the coward, yet why does his plaintive voice pierce my breast with all the pain of a sharp needle? Why has our Lord imposed this torture and this persecution on poor Japanese peasants? No, Kichijiro was trying to express something different, something even more sickening. The silence of God."[23]

Kichijiro continues to return to Rodrigues, even after the Jesuit has apostatized, asking for the sacrament of confession for his lack of strength: "Father, I betrayed you. I trampled on the picture of Christ," he says to the priest. Perplexed, he asks the priest, "In this world are the strong and the weak. The strong never yield to torture, and they go to Paradise; but what about those, like myself, who are born weak?"[24] Kichijiro is poor of faith and weak in spirit but readers also sense that he, without any of the spiritual heroics that ground Rodrigues's desire for martyrdom, is genuine in his repeated return to the faith. In suffering over his apostasy, he signifies the presence of grace in his human frailty. It is an insight fully realized through the priest's own journey toward trampling the *fumie*. Agreeing to hear his confession, even though it is forbidden, he responds to Kichijiro, "There are neither the strong nor the weak. Can anyone say that the weak do not suffer more than the strong?"[25] The narrative ends with the affirmation of faith in these two unlikely characters: an apostate priest hearing the confession of his betrayer, Kichijiro. Like the novels of Mauriac, Bernanos, and Greene, Endo offers the reader the trace of God in the poor of faith, characters completely humbled by their inability to master themselves or their situation.

If Rodrigues's encounter with Kichijiro places the sinner at the heart of the Christian message, then his confrontation with Inoue, his captor, stresses the conflict between Japan and European Christianity. Styled as a dialogue between the Shinto/Buddhist and the Christian, Inoue refers to Japan as a hopeless "swamp" that will inevitably subvert Christianity from within. Once the missionaries leave or die, Inoue argues, the Christians will twist the Christian faith. Inoue boasts that even though large numbers of Christian farmers remain on the remote islands of Goto and Ikitsuki, he will not apprehend them, for "If the root is cut the sapling withers and the leaves die. The proof of this is that the God whom the peasants of Goto and Ikitsuki secretly serve has gradually changed so as to be no longer like the Christian God at all."[26] Inoue shrewdly exploits Rodrigues's own misgivings about the compatibility of Eastern and Western cultures, for early on in his letters, Rodrigues had worried about the excessive veneration the Japanese have for icons and that "the peasants sometimes seem to honor Mary rather than Christ."[27] Troubled by the tension between the particularity of the Christian message and the way it is performed by the Christian peasants, he admits that their simple faith irritates him while at the same time he feels a dim awareness that their suffering is increased because of his presence. The entire confrontation between the two men is an attempt to undermine what Netland calls the "Christian claim to universality. [Inoue] challenges the trans-cultural normativity of Christianity, suggesting instead that Japanese culture inevitably syncretizes and hence distorts Christianity."[28]

It is in meeting Ferreira that Rodrigues becomes most disturbed, for this Portuguese provincial has not only apostatized but is collaborating with his former persecutors. He presents himself as "an old missionary defeated by missionary work."[29] Ferreira's defeatism gives credibility to Inoue's argument, echoing the irreconcilability between Christianity and the Japanese mind. To get Rodrigues to defect, he argues that even the successes of past conversions were more illusory than real, since the Japanese quickly recast the new religion in the mold of the old. Ferreira's pessimistic assessment is summed up in the linguistic confusion between the European word for God—*Deus*— and the Japanese word *Dainichi*, meaning "the Great Sun," that was used by the earliest converts: "From the beginning those same Japanese who confused 'Deus' and 'Dainichi' twisted and changed our God and began to create something different."[30]

Endo here gives the novel's drama a decidedly modernist feel, as Ferreira and Inoue try to convince Rodrigues that holding on to his religious faith is really an escape from reality, an escape from the political contingencies at work around him. Religious conviction, they insinuate, is ultimately a subjective experience without any relationship to objective reality. Ferreira presses this line of thought by explaining that his apostasy will only be a matter of form, that, in fact, he does not really have to give up his faith, only empty it of any external relevance. Indeed, Rodrigues's public devotion to his faith puts the Japanese Christians in grave danger and he is urged to perform this apostasy as a great act of compassion, just as Ferreira himself has done. Netland again summarizes the strategy's appeal to the wavering Rodrigues: "The command to apostatize comes not primarily as an invitation to escape suffering, but paradoxically as an appeal to his deepest Christian values. What is more Christ-like than to lay down one's life for others?"[31] Ferreira makes his case by way of the Christian doctrine of *kenosis* but warps the notion of self-abasement in such a way that it ends up serving a Japanese xenophobic strategy to eradicate the Christian faith from the land. In asking Rodrigues to make this gesture, giving up his public faith for the good of those suffering, Ferreira tells him "you are now going to perform the most painful act of love that has ever been performed."[32] This distortion of *kenosis*—to make a compassionate choice of apostasy that terminates religious hope and identity—is a coercive tactic that suggests Rodrigues's complicity and agreement with Ferreira's absent, silent God, and with the inevitability of Inoue's notion of a Japanese swampland.

And yet this strategy will be ultimately undermined, for it is not the arguments of his captors that make Rodrigues trample on the *fumie*. Ferreira's reasoned plea to alleviate the suffering of the tortured Christians around him does seem to resonate with the key concern of mystical substitution—giving up one's own integrity for the sake of others—which is so much a part of twentieth-century Catholic literature, but Endo deepens the theological point of *kenosis* as a participation in the image and form of the suffering Christ. The pain Rodrigues feels when he steps on the worn-out face of Christ breaks the haunting silence of God, for he hears the voice of Christ penetrate his consciousness saying, "Trample! Trample! I more than anyone know of the pain in your foot. Trample! It was to be trampled on by men that I was born into this world. It was to share men's pain that I carried my cross."[33] Rodrigues grasps that Christ's invitation to trample upon his image affects his own sacrifice of pride and position of authority. It is not his personal achievement that is important but the abandonment of his own notions of self-sufficiency. He understands his martyrdom not in ordinary or heroic acts of goodness but as one who is despised and trampled upon, like his Lord Jesus.

Thus Rodrigues's transformation comes not through escape from suffering but in the realization that God shares in his suffering. The logic of this theological insight can be stated in the following terms: Jesus's mission is to proclaim the love of God, but experience of life gives the appearance that there is no God of love but only a universe filled with suffering; how then does God reconcile love with the experience of suffering? He sacrifices himself as a manifestation of presence, of compassion, and companionship. Through this *kenosis*, this surrendering of his life, Christ enables the human person to see again a horizon of love. Salvation is reconfigured into a sharing in this likeness of God, a matter of becoming Christ's image, a broken body as much as a glorified one. Paradoxically, though, Rodrigues the priest becomes an *alter Christus* through the humiliation of his apostasy, another manifestation of the suffering Christ in and for the Japanese people. And this itself becomes not only the modern trace of God in the Catholic imagination of twentieth century writers, but also the particular trace of God in Japanese culture. Netland concludes, "The apparent defeat of Christianity by the mudswamp of Japan ironically validates the very Kingdom it seeks to destroy. It is the moral authority of the suffering Christ that confirms Rodrigues' act, as if to say that the topsy-turvy Kingdom of God, in which the first are last and the last first, can take even Inoue's cynical manipulation of Christian ideals and use it to keep the spark of faith flickering."[34] Endo filters European triumphalism out of the Christian missionary enterprise with something far more supra-cultural and universal, the self-effacing ethic of the cross, in whose mysterious economy of power the weak are exalted and the mighty judged. As Hans Urs von Balthasar, one of the great interpreters of the French Catholic literary tradition, notes, the drama of the Cross "is not the crowning of a human drama with divine victory: rather the drama of human dissolution as a whole becomes the expression of eternal love."[35] The tragedy of the human condition becomes the mode of revealing a God of love over a God of power.

Silence thus extends the literary genealogy of the Catholic genre but with an interesting twist. Whereas the most influential Catholic writers who made an impact on Endo's literary imagination—Mauriac, Bernanos, and Greene— situated their stories in the wasteland of a bourgeois religious modernity, Endo looks back through the historical confrontation of Christianity with Japanese culture.[36] Greene once clarified that his own twentieth century wasteland "is inhabited by the pious 'suburbans' ... the piety of the educated, the established, who seem to own their Roman Catholic image of God, who have ceased to look for Him because they consider they have found Him."[37] Endo's literary wasteland is most certainly the metaphorical swampland of Japan articulated by the novel's cosmopolitan Inoue and the defeated Ferreira, but it is also framed in the wasteland of the same pious Catholicism that Greene rejects. When asked if he had ever suffered conflicts with Church authorities Endo responded, "Well, the Catholic Church in Japan used to be 'old,' but not now. When I wrote *Chinmoku* [*Silence*], I was much rebuked, and some priests even preached at Mass to the congregation telling them not to read my novels."[38] He added that the Christianity that he learned early in his life "was under the shadow of the end of the nineteenth century and of the beginning of the twentieth," a time that "seemed to indicate that God was outside man [*sic*]. We felt as if we did not look within to find God, but looked out of ourselves up to God." He concluded, "The image of God which the old Christianity seemed to present was that of a God of punishment and anger."[39] Endo's image of Christ, the trampled-upon of the *fumie*, the eternal companion accompanying Rodrigues, is as ancient as the Suffering Servant motif of the Book of Isaiah in Hebrew scripture (Isa. 53). Endo's genius, following upon the French writers he studied and admired that went before him, is to invite the reader into a transformed perception of that sorrowful image. It is surprisingly modern in its orientation, even as it harkens back to a more ancient and orthodox image of God. By revealing a God who does not take away suffering but is found in one's suffering, Endo creates an aesthetic strategy that deconstructs the preconceptions of this "old Christianity," inviting the reader to reconsider religious faith and how we evaluate religious experience. *Silence* forces one to relinquish any rationalized and distorted faith in order to encounter the image of God in unlikely places, and among unlikely people.

Notes

1   Shusaku Endo, "These the Least of My Brethren: The Concern of Endo Shusaku: Response," *The Journal of the Association of Teachers of Japanese* 27.1 (April 1993): 86. The honorary doctorate was from John Carroll University in Cleveland, Ohio.
2   Quoted in Bates Hoffer, "Shusaku Endo and Graham Greene: Cross-Cultural Influences in Literary Structure," *Language and Literature* 28 (2003): 132.
3   Letter dated February 12, 1973. *Graham Greene Archives*, Boston College. Box D7.
4   For an early and thorough comparison of Greene and Endo see Francis Mathy, "Shusaku Endo: Japanese Catholic Novelist," *Thought* 42.4 (Winter 1967): 585–614.
5   Endo, quoted in Jean Higgins, "East-West Encounter in Endo Shusaku," *Dialogue and Alliance* 1.3 (Fall 1987): 13. Endo explores this in *Scandal* (1986) where the *doppelgänger* becomes the primary metaphor.
6   Endo, quoted in Mathy, 592.
7   For a fuller account of Yoshimitsu and his influence on Japanese Catholicism and Endo, see Adrian Pinnington, "Yoshimitsu, Benedict, Endo: Guilt, Shame and the Post-war Idea of Japan," *Japan Forum* 13.1 (2001): 91–105.
8   Ibid., 94–5.
9   For a good introduction to this Catholic resurgence in Europe see Steven Schloesser, *Jazz Age Catholicism: Mystic Modernism in Postwar Paris, 1919–1933* (Toronto: University of Toronto Press, 2005), and see Patrick Allit, *Catholic Converts: British and American Intellectuals Turn to Rome* (Ithaca, NY: Cornell University Press, 1997).
10 Ellis Hanson, *Decadence and Catholicism* (Cambridge: Harvard University Press, 1997), 7.
11 For the link between Mauriac and Greene, see Mark Bosco S.J., *Graham Greene's Catholic Imagination* (Oxford and New York: Oxford University Press, 2005), 46–9.
12 For a concise discussion of this tension in Endo's life while in France and his first years back in Japan, see Emi Mase-Hasegawa, *Christ in Japanese Culture: Theological Themes in Shusaku Endo's Literary Works* (Boston: Brill Press, 2008), 61–73.

13 David Lodge, "Introduction," *The Viper's Tangle* by François Mauriac (New York: Carroll & Graf, 1987), 7.

14 Endo, "These the Least of My Brethren," 87.

15 Georges Bernanos, *The Diary of a Country Priest*, trans. Pamela Morris (Cambridge, MA: Da Capo Press, 2002), 255.

16 Jean Higgins, "The Inner Agon of Endo Shusaku," *Cross Currents* 34 (1984–5): 145.

17 Francis Thompson, "The Hound of Heaven," verse 10–11. The poem was first published in 1893 and included in the *Oxford Book of English Mystical Verse* in 1917.

18 Endo, "These the Least of My Brethren," 86.

19 Endo, "My Literature" in *Complete Series of Endo Shusaku's Literature* (Tokyo: Shincho Publishing, 2000), 967.

20 Called *ana-tsurushi*, the "pit" was a form of public torture in which the victim hangs upside down in a trench filled with excrement, while a small incision behind each ear and on the forehead allows the blood to drain slowly and painfully from the person's body until death.

21 John Netland, "Encountering Christ in Shusaku Endo's Mudswamp of Japan," in John C. Hawley, ed., *Christian Encounters with the Other* (New York: New York University Press, 1998), 168.

22 T. S. Eliot, *Murder in the Cathedral* (New York: Harcourt Brace, 1935), 44.

23 Shusaku Endo, *Silence*, trans. William Johnston (New York: Taplinger Publishing Company, 1980), 50.

24 Ibid., 190.

25 Ibid., 191.

26 Ibid., 188.

27 Ibid., 56.

28 Netland, "Encountering Christ," 171.

29 Endo, *Silence*, 146.

30 Ibid., 148.

31 Netland, "Encountering Christ," 172.

32 Endo, *Silence*, 170.

33 Ibid., 130. Numerous scholars and translators, including some in the present volume, note that the original Japanese for "Trample! Trample!" is in the permissive rather than the imperative mood, so that a better translation would be "You may trample. I allow you to trample." Free will is preserved in this rendering. Junko Endo, Shusaku Endo's widow, confirms that her husband wanted a voice that is juxtaposed to a triumphal, patriarchal voice of Jesus. See Junko Endo, "Reflections on Shusaku Endo and *Silence*," *Christianity and Literature* 48.2 (Winter 1999): 145–8.

34 Netland, "Encountering Christ," 172.

35 Hans Urs von Balthasar, *The Glory of the Lord: Seeing the Form* 1 (San Francisco: Ignatius Press, 1982), 504.

36 Of course, Endo's later works take on a contemporary cast, especially his final novel, *Deep River* (1993).
37 Graham Greene, *Ways of Escape* (New York: Simon and Schuster, 1980), 265.
38 Quoted in Kazumi Yamagata, "Mr. Shusaku Endo Talks About His Life and Works as a Catholic Writer," *The Chesterton Review* 12.4 (November 1986): 503–4.
39 Ibid., 496.

6

Forbidden Ships to Chartered Tours: Endo, Apostasy, and Globalization

Christopher B. Wachal

The twentieth century renaissance in Roman Catholic literary arts, of which Shusaku Endo's novels are a part, unfolded over the course of several decades across a large stretch of global literary culture. With such extensive geographic reach—from Endo's Japan to Graham Greene's Britain to Flannery O'Connor's American South—the Catholic literary revival cannot be understood within critical structures that rely on local traditions for their explanatory framework. The global character of this movement requires that scholars think in new ways about the role of place and the experience of encountering cultural otherness in religious literature. At the peak of an extensive literary career covering both forbidden colonial ships sitting idly in Japanese harbors as well as chartered flights of Japanese tourists seeking spiritual adventures abroad, Endo's *Silence* provides readers of Catholic literature a unique narrative of responsibilities in a globally connected era.

Histories of this global era are as numerous as the theories of globalization's impact on literary development in postcolonial nation-states. The most widely cited theorists tend to emphasize three imbricated dimensions of globalization. First, they emphasize that understanding globalization requires a robust effort to historicize cross-cultural and transnational contact. Globalization emerges from colonialism, through modern nationalism, and into the contemporary era of post-industrial market capitalism. Global connectedness caps a long history. Second, theorists largely agree that the processes that define globalization displace the nation as the primary arbiter of identity. In its place may be other transnational forms of identification (for example, religion, class consciousness) or a multiplicity of non-national identities. Third, the cultural experience of globalization involves annexing and adapting concepts that flow with international symbolic and material exchanges. Writers and other artists appropriate and *re-present* forms with origins in other places. The world these theorists describe is one crisscrossed by transnational connections and defined less by localized traditions than by processes of adapting ideas from foreign lands to the needs of specific locations.

It is a world the contours of which Endo would certainly recognize. If Endo's literary career manifests an intellectual heritage, it is a decidedly transnational one with roots in Britain and France as well as Japan. Within *Silence* Endo dramatizes a struggle particular to the global era—how to reconcile a foreign faith with an antagonistic local culture, or how to plant a sapling in a swamp without eroding its roots, to invoke the novel's most famous metaphor. The anxieties Fr. Rodrigues wrestles with arise from both the ancient Catholic theological tradition and the modern experience of cross-cultural contact that defines globalization. His ultimate apostasy is the most challenging scene in Endo's theological narratives. It forces readers to consider a fundamental conflict between Western Christianity and Japanese national culture. The argument here, however, is that we must read Rodrigues's apostasy in light of Endo's global concerns—a context in which cross-cultural contact is a fact the religious imagination must accommodate, not a challenge to the conquest narrative of a universalizing Church. The moral imperative Endo finds appropriate to this global era and first represents in *Silence* is one of conscientious transgression of cultural/ national borders, of accessing transcendence by embodying other forms of religious life. Moving beyond cultural pride and into the life of a powerless other, as Rodrigues does in his apostasy, demonstrates Endo's adaptation of a Christian ethic to the exigencies of the globalized era.

Fitting Two Suits

Giving shape and depth to a Japanese Christian experience is the project of Endo's literary career. It is an enterprise that requires a model of the interaction between Japan and Western Christianity. In a well-known metaphor introduced in a 1967 article, Endo refers to Christianity as an "ill-fitting suit" imported from the West and in need of tailoring to fit his Japanese contours. "I tried several times to remove the suit," he writes, "but in the end I was unable to do so. ... Later I decided not to try to remove the suit. Instead I would try to refashion it into Japanese style clothing that would fit me."[1] The most notable aspect of this metaphor is Endo's insistence that the suit must change to fit him, that Christianity must adapt to Japan. Molding Catholicism to suit the Japanese imagination requires the kind of cultural adaptation characteristic of the global era, as well as narratives that can represent the resistance of many to changes wrought by cross-cultural contact.

Appropriately enough, Endo uses a similar metaphor to describe his understanding of the craft of fiction. "To stand naked and find a set of clothes for yourself, to make that choice on your own—that is literature," he writes. "But I came to feel that literature also exists in the lifelong effort to take a suit of baggy clothes that someone has given you and tailor it to fit your own body."[2] Here again, Endo concerns himself with making that which does not "fit" correspond to the shapes and habits of mind that define him. As with his orientation toward his Christian faith, Endo's thoughts on writing begin with the recognition of difference and the need to reconcile foreign concepts with local patterns of thought. Perhaps it should not be surprising that here, too, Endo's concerns arise from an encounter with Western ideas—in this case literary ones. Much of Endo's engagement with Western literature—and the Catholic literary revival in particular—begins with his studies in France in the 1950s. Studying François Mauriac and Georges Bernanos at Keio University initiated Endo's interest in work by French Catholic writers. Presented with one of the first opportunities to study in France offered to Japanese students after World War II, Endo chose to study French Catholic literature at the University of Lyon. In his two years there (1950–2), Endo studied Mauriac earnestly with additional interest in writers such as Julien Greene, Paul Bourget, and Henri Bourdeaux.[3] What these writers share, Endo's writing from the time reveals, is the experience of the conflict between "the desire, as author, to scrutinize human beings" and "the Christian yearning for purity."[4] His studies at Lyon led Endo to reconsider the tension between his Christian faith and his Japanese identity—a conflict he had previously thought of as unique to those from his background—as part of this much more widespread conflict between the demands of ephemeral culture and the orientation of the person of faith. He comes to realize, as John Netland puts it, "that all Christians are citizens of two worlds."[5] The challenge for the Catholic writer lies in representing this duality without resorting to proselytization or despair.[6]

To make the baggy clothes of the Catholic literary tradition fit his Japanese mind, Endo turned primarily to Mauriac. As he did for Greene, Mauriac serves Endo as a model for the Catholic writer whose focus is the "creation of living human beings" and whose interest is "to understand not only the characters' psyche and personality, but also their true flavor, their pains and struggles, everything about them."[7] In Mauriac, he finds twin emphases on restraint and realism. "Catholic literature involves not a literary portrayal of God and angels, but must limit itself to scrutiny of human beings," Endo writes in "The Problems Confronting the Catholic Author."[8] By restraining himself to the world of the human present, Endo, like Mauriac and Greene before him, participates in the Catholic literary tradition of seeing "godless man as human beings."[9] This commitment to realism fixes Endo squarely within the aesthetic orthodoxy of the Catholic literary revival.

Endo's aesthetic strategies do not derive exclusively from the French, however. Greene's influence on Endo is so profound that references to "the Japanese Graham Greene" have become pervasive in Endo criticism.[10] Endo's widow Junko recalls the one time her husband met Greene in London, saying he "leapt for joy" and that "he told Greene how greatly he had been influenced by his works and that he might even not have been a novelist had he not read his novels."[11] In Greene, Endo finds an aesthetic strategy that marries the realism of Mauriac and his French Catholic colleagues to a dialectical sensibility that highlights the consequentiality of sin and faith. In "The Problems Confronting the Catholic Author," Endo distills his view of the Catholic writer's dual commitments to realism and mystery:

> The Catholic author views this world as a shadow of the supernatural world, and, even whilst observing human psychology, he will detect, behind the second dimension psychology of Freud, Bergson, and Proust, the 'third dimension' of which Jacques Riviere happened to make mention. As a result, the Catholic writer can conceive as reality the introduction of the supernatural world into the world of human interaction, even if the non-Catholic reader is apt to misrepresent this as a distortion of reality.[12]

Both writers choose aesthetic strategies that emphasize dialectical environments occasionally transcended by analogical moments. On this point, Endo critic and translator Van Gessel highlights *The Power and the Glory* as having an especially profound effect on Endo. He notes, as have many critics, the parallels between *The Power and the Glory* and *Silence*. More importantly, he points to a larger aesthetic strategy common to the work of both writers. "The plots are secular, the discourse celestial" is Gessel's formulation.[13] Both Endo and Greene "trap their characters in a neutral zone between concerns of the flesh and those of the spirit" and there "impel them to battle."[14] Bates Hoffer goes even further, claiming that both authors structure their analogical moments around moments of sin and vice.[15] What is most important to take away from both Gessel and Hoffer is the influence Greene's dialectical sense of place wields over Endo's novels.

A Globalizing Sensibility

The picture of Endo painted here is a decidedly transnational one. He conceives of his work in transcultural terms—of adapting Western

Christianity for the Japanese mind. His aesthetic influences originate in both French and English literatures. He studies the Catholic literary tradition while one of the first Japanese students in Europe after World War II. Perhaps more so than Catholic authors from the Anglo-American context, Endo's life and work reflect the increasingly globally transient character of the second half of the twentieth century. His work inhabits the intersection of traditional Japanese culture and the aesthetic and thematic concerns of the international Catholic literary revival. Examining how Endo "refashions" the suit of the Catholic literary tradition to fit his Japanese context reveals a writing imagination wrestling with obligations to multiple traditions. In *Silence*, Endo both dramatizes and maps the tensions such obligations incur in a narrative appropriate to a global era.

The global character of Endo's Catholic vision is apparent from the trajectory of his plots from *Wonderful Fool* through *Silence* to *Deep River*. In the earlier novels, Endo focuses on Japan and the encounters generated by foreign ideas encroaching on Japanese terrain. *Wonderful Fool* describes how the arrival of Gaston—a poor French failure of a man who claims to be descended from Napoleon—disrupts the lives of many native Japanese, calling into question postwar Japanese morality. *Silence*, as we shall see, examines a particular moment in Japanese history when a burgeoning national culture seemingly emerges victorious from a conflict with colonial European Christianity. What these plots share, of course, is a common narrative of Japanese encounter with foreign ideas in Japan. By the end of his career, however, Endo's examinations of cross-cultural experiences move beyond Japanese borders. Most notably, *Deep River* takes a company of Japanese tourists to Buddhist and Hindu holy sites in India, putting them in contact with religious traditions indigenous to India, as well as a particular version of Catholicism professed by a Japanese priest named Otsu. It is a decidedly multi-national, multicultural mix—one set in neither Japan nor Europe but a third liminal space. The point of tracing this trajectory is to highlight the evolution of Endo's global sensibility—from *Silence's* colonial ships forbidden to enter Japanese harbors to *Deep River's* confident Japanese tourists reaching out to the rest of the world for spiritual insight. John Netland traces this same history and finds Endo's views evolving from an emphasis on conflict to one of larger cultural rapprochement in *Deep River*. Here, I want to emphasize instead the increasingly multifaceted nature of Endo's theology. The narrative shifts over time mark the development of a complex model of narrating and representing cross-cultural exchanges, such as the particular cultural intersection Endo himself occupies, which moves beyond both peaceful coexistence and colonial dialectic.

The global model Endo develops reaches its fullest expression in the theological discourse of *Deep River*. The exemplary figure of Otsu voices a theological vision that simultaneously elevates intercultural contact as sanctifying and rejects cross-cultural dialogue as hopelessly ineffective. Crucially, Otsu occupies multiple cultural positions—Japanese, European, Indian, Christian, pantheist, heretic, priest, outcast, *sadhu*, and so on. His cultural identity is decidedly complex and, more importantly to this chapter, transnational. When at the novel's conclusion, Otsu lives in a Hindu ashram and transports those too poor or sick to make it to the holy River Ganges on their own, he does so not by turning on his Christian faith or rejecting his Japanese identity. Instead, on his private bookshelf he keeps "a prayer-book; the Upanishad; a book by Mother Theresa ... a book of sayings by Mahatma Gandhi" next to his Bible.[16] He imagines the bearing of the dying to the river as a Christic act, imitative of carrying the cross.[17] He tells the tourist Mitsuko that the life of the *sadhu* is the life Jesus would assume had he lived in Varanasi.[18] He imitates Christ by performing the rites of Hinduism. He is a Christian to the extent that he lives as a *sadhu*.

What Endo presents in *Deep River* is a model of cross-cultural engagement premised on practice rather than dialogue or new forms of community. This is an approach that recognizes and reveres cultural and religious difference while asserting that both can be meaningful to those from other contexts. For Endo, experiencing this meaning is a prerequisite for productive cross-cultural dialogue, engagement, or community. Otsu voices this in religious terms familiar to readers of *Silence*. In one episode early in his training for the priesthood, Otsu responds to his European superiors' challenge on the need for dialogue among world religions. He posits that European Christianity assumes an access to truth unavailable to other cultures or religious traditions—"One can hardly call this a dialogue among equals," he says. "Real dialogue," Otsu argues, "takes place when you believe that *God has many faces*, and that he exists in all religions."[19] The invocation of "many faces" is very telling. Here, Otsu does not refer to God having one face seen many different ways, as Mark Williams posits.[20] Nor does he claim God's face is an amalgam of many disparate faces, as Netland intimates.[21] Instead, Endo, in the voice of Otsu, presents a vision of religious and ethnic pluralism that respects difference while insisting on a more fundamental analogical similarity. In this formulation, cross-cultural, interfaith, and transnational dialogue requires a commitment by all parties to the truths of the others. It is a precursor to meaningful engagement, not the result of it.

Forbidden Ships

Within the world of *Silence*, however, resistance to any engagement with foreign thought defines Japanese power. When Rodrigues attempts to dialogue with Inoue, the feared persecutor of Japanese Christians, the nationalist pride implicit in Inoue's responses is not his alone. Indeed, historically, Japanese resistance to Christian influence reflected a more fundamental concern with defining and stabilizing Japanese cultural identity. The first decades of the Tokugawa shogunate were marked by efforts geared toward politically unifying what had been a network of warring states spread across Japan. Part of fostering a new nationalist spirit among the Japanese involved expelling foreign influences, including Western Christianity. The first Christian missionaries in Japan, mostly Spanish and Portuguese Jesuits, arrived in the middle of the sixteenth century when the Dutch and Spanish began trading with Japanese textile makers. At the time, feudal rulers (*daimyō*) viewed opening their lands to Catholic proselytizing as a way of appeasing the European crowns who sponsored them. By granting permission to the Jesuits, each hoped to bring traders to his territory rather than the neighbors with whom he was likely at war. Following the unification of much of Japan under the Tokugawa shogunate in 1603, Christianity was formally banned as unwelcome European meddling in Japanese affairs.[22] The tension between Japanese cultural identity and the Christian churches of Europe arises not from irreconcilable philosophical disputes but from the efforts to centralize administrative power under a single ruling family. It is telling, then, that Jesuits were expelled from the country following the establishment of the shogunate, but traders from Holland and other European powers were allowed to remain in Japanese ports. There is no doubt Endo is aware of this history. As he notes in the first chapter of *Silence*, despite dozens of Dutch vessels anchored in Japanese ports, "Portuguese ships were forbidden to enter the harbors of Japan."[23] The question, of course, is what was so threatening about European Christianity? What did Catholic missionaries carry with them in their forbidden ships that made them a threat to Japanese sovereignty while Dutch traders were welcomed openly?

The Japanese response to the threat of Christian ships was the persecution dramatized in *Silence*. Ritualized public apostasy (*efumi*) was an annual experience for many of Japan's Christians during the early part of the Edo period. It is the demand that he apostatize by stepping on an image of the face of Jesus (*fumie*) that plagues Rodrigues. Why is this particular form of religious transgression so threatening? An answer takes shape when examining the descriptions of the *fumie* and its emotional impact on Rodrigues. Throughout the novel, Rodrigues is haunted by the face of Jesus staring at him silently. His first night imprisoned by the shogunate, Rodrigues contemplates the image:

> From childhood the face of Christ had been for him the fulfillment of his every dream and ideal. The face of Christ as he preached to the crowd the Sermon on the Mount. The face of Christ as he passed over the Lake of Galilee at dusk. Even in its moments of terrible torture this face had never lost its beauty. Those soft, clear eyes which pierced to the very core of a man's being were now fixed upon him. When the vision of this face came before him, fear and trembling seemed to vanish like the tiny ripples that are quietly sucked up by the sand of the sea-shore.[24]

Over the course of his imprisonment and mental anguish, however, Rodrigues's vision of Jesus's face transforms into something decidedly less comforting and helpful. Witnessing Japanese Christians trample the *fumie*, he imagines "the face of Christ, wet with tears. When the gentle eyes looked straight into his, the priest was filled with shame."[25] Believing other Christians will be executed the following day because he will not apostatize, he sees "the face now before his eyes. Hundreds and hundreds of times it had appeared in his dreams; but why was it that only now did the suffering, perspiring face seem so far away?"[26] When Fr. Ferreira tells him that he has apostatized, "that face seemed close beside him. At first it was silent, but pierced him with a glance that was filled with sorrow."[27] In these episodes, Endo charts a profound change in how Rodrigues interprets the Christian drama. As a child he had focused on the face that performed miracles, pronounced great sermons, and comforted the pained. Faced with actual danger and suffering, Rodrigues shifts his attention to the Jesus who suffers and experiences sorrow. Perhaps it should be expected, then, that the face he tramples on in his moment of apostasy is not the beautiful, comforting face of his previously naïve European faith. With the *fumie* at his feet, "Before him is the ugly face of Christ, crowned with thorns and the thin outstretched arms. Eyes dimmed and confused the priest silently looks down at the face which he now meets for the first time since coming to this country."[28] As he steps on the *fumie*, the face commands, "Trample! Trample! It was to be trampled on by men that I was born into this world!"[29] The transformation of the face of Christ from source of comfort and beauty to abused image demanding further mistreatment caps a dramatic shift in Rodrigues's theological imagination.

Silence's representation of "that man's face" also manifests Endo's desire to adapt his Christian religious commitments to a form sympathetic to the Japanese cultural imagination.[30] Crystallized most concisely in *A Life of Jesus*, Endo's interpretation of the Catholic theological tradition begins with the doctrine of the Incarnation. Endo's Christ suffers, fulfilling the Incarnation's demands for a suffering and grotesque hanging from the cross; however, Endo's incarnate Christ also exercises free will. This is especially significant given Endo's stated purpose in writing *A Life of Jesus*. From the "Preface to the American Edition":

> I wrote this book for the benefit of Japanese readers who have no Christian tradition of their own and who know almost nothing about Jesus. What is more, I was determined to highlight the particular aspect of love in his personality precisely in order to make Jesus understandable in terms of the religious psychology of my non-Christian countrymen and thus to demonstrate that Jesus is not alien to their religious sensibilities.[31]

In adapting the Christian narrative to a Japanese audience, Endo begins with the picture of a human Jesus who chooses, decides, experiences ambivalence, and otherwise exercises free will. Japanese religious sentiments have "little tolerance for any kind of transcendent being who judges humans harshly, then punishes them."[32] Consequently, Endo's Christ is one whose most significant choices align him with the poor, the downcast, the oppressed, and the lonely. His Jesus is one whose teachings place him at odds with political power and whose miracles are largely "ineffectual."[33] Fumitaka Matsuoka argues, "Endo's Christology appeals to the contemporary Japanese because of the depiction of Jesus as participating fully in the human condition of vulnerability. So Christianity is the story of one who failed, was rejected and alienated."[34] So how does the ineffectual failure called Jesus become the "Christ of Glory?"[35] Endo's answer seems to lie in a paradox. Only by participating in the lives of the oppressed—by "laying his head" among them—does the embodiment of human weakness transcend human limitations. For example, Endo's *A Life of Jesus* connects the Christian mystery with Jesus living among lepers rather than with healing them.[36] What we find in Endo's interpretation of Catholic theology is a fundamental connection between transgressing social boundaries and transcending human frailty. The "fact of the resurrection," Endo argues, is only significant because it involves a "carpenter who grew up in the back country of a weak nation."[37] The Christ who chooses weakness does so by participating in the lives of those with whom he would be least expected to identify.

Becoming Silenced

It is this analogy of transgression, I argue, that Endo holds out as necessary in the global era. It is what makes Rodrigues's apostasy the only possible response to his situation. Within the world of *Silence*, apostasy in the form of trampling on the *fumie* symbolizes the despair of those who could no longer tolerate the tortures of the shogunate. For the local Japanese Christians, it is the only path out of the pains inflicted by the fearsome Inoue, Lord of Chikugo, and his underlings.[38] Throughout the novel, Rodrigues imagines his journey will end with him either dying at the hands of the state or trampling on the *fumie*. His choices lead to martyrdom or apostasy. For many early commentators as well as contemporary critics, these options seem strange ones for a Catholic author like Endo. Why tell the story of one who despaired? Why valorize apostasy? The view implicit in these questions is one Endo sought to correct in many of his contemporary critics. One critic asserts that Endo has not written a story of faith but a narrative of men whose faith is an illusion. "The martyrs heard the voice of Christ," he asserts, "but for Ferreira and Rodrigues God was silent. Does this not mean that from the beginning those priests had no faith?"[39] As Endo acknowledges, a reading such as this makes sense if one believes that Rodrigues's act of apostasy is the culmination of the novel. Of course, he steps on the *fumie* at the end of Chapter 8. In a later postscript, Endo emphasizes the fact that there are still two chapters following Rodrigues's apostasy.[40] Apostasy, then, is not the end Rodrigues believed it to be or the finale many critics assumed it must be. Instead, it is a conduit to something else. As many critics concerned with Catholic literature have pointed out, what Endo presents is a new form of faith stripped of Rodrigues's many delusions.[41] The priest who had been obsessed with martyrdom and angered by God's silence in the face of so much suffering among "His people" embraces a new faith drained of Western pride and unconcerned with making suffering and death something glorious or religiously edifying. By performing "the most painful act of love that has ever been performed," [42] Rodrigues comes to believe, "I know that my Lord is different from the God that is preached in the Churches."[43] As numerous critics have pointed out, the version of faith Endo presents in these final chapters is decidedly at odds with European Christianity and corresponds in meaningful ways with the Christian narrative in *A Life of Jesus*.[44] In the paradox of finding faith in one's weakest moments, Endo begins to shape the Catholic tradition to the demands of Japan.

My contention here is that we must understand apostasy as a transgression of traditional Western Christian teaching *and* as a means of entry into a new form of Christian life annexed and adapted to this context. Jean Higgins conceives of this change as the difference between the former "Rodrigues of the West" and the new "Rodrigues of the East." The Western Rodrigues is characterized as "the young missionary who comes to Japan with dedicated aggressiveness, bearing in heart and mind the image of a transcendent God of power and might. The image of Christ constantly before his mind's eye is that of the risen Christ, serene in conquest; a Christ of glory, whose example calls for heroism in his followers, for fidelity unto death, even in martyrdom."[45] His faith is triumphalist, conquering, and universal. What "Rodrigues of the East" finds in the face of the *fumie*, conversely, is "a kenotic God … a weak and powerless Christ who shows himself understanding of the weak, who has compassion with the betrayer, who knows well the pain in the foot of the apostate who tramples upon his face."[46] While I would certainly quibble with Higgins's use of "East" and "West" as totalizing categories, and although I agree with Netland that this formulation too easily elides the emphasis on *kenosis* in many Western Christian traditions,[47] I find it useful to conceive of Rodrigues's evolving religious imagination in terms of his locality. The longer he spends in Japan, the more his vision of Christ changes. Put another way, the more Rodrigues experiences the life of a Japanese Christian—complete with torture, oppression, and demands of apostasy—the more Japanese his interpretation of Christianity becomes. When Endo says in *A Life of Jesus* that the Japanese mind is amenable to a God "who suffers with us" and "allows for our weakness," the image on the *fumie* is what he has in mind.[48] Rodrigues comes to this view in the end when, reflecting on his apostasy, he has a final vision of Christ's face saying, "I was not silent. I suffered beside you."[49]

To understand finally how Christ's face appears to Japanese Christians, Rodrigues must experience the pains of apostasy they have been forced to suffer. Only by sharing in this experience can he adapt his faith to this context. Thus the most powerful sign of the necessity of cross-cultural experience in the life of globalized Catholicism is the experience of Okada San'emon, the Japanese name assigned to Rodrigues during the years in Japan following his apostasy. His experience connects to the title of the novel. Initial criticism of the novel took "silence" to refer to God remaining silent in the face of human suffering. For this reason, many early responses to the novel considered it an indictment of indifference in European Christianity.[50] Endo, of course, was quick to question this interpretation, insisting that, just as the novel documents the paradox of finding strength in weakness, it also insists on the need to "hear God's voice in the silence" of one who suffers with the oppressed and the pained.[51] Apostasy, then, is the way into silence—a way to quiet oneself as other Japanese Christians have been forced to do. Other than Kichijiro, Japanese Christians almost never speak within the pages of the novel. They are talked to, ministered to, and talked about, but they never themselves speak of their faith. Those whose faith is secret dare not speak of it for fear of torture. Those who have publicly apostatized but remain secretly faithful do so in order to maintain the appearance of the proper apostate. They silently maintain their faith through the practices and rituals brought to them from abroad. In their silence, these communities present another model of cross-cultural practice. Theirs is one that eschews public proclamations of faith or identity in favor of the quiet lived experiences of the cultures they inhabit. This is the silent faith lived by the apostate Rodrigues. The missionary abandons zeal and the strength of the martyr's convictions for the weakness and quiet of the oppressed Church in Japan. "Our Lord was not silent," Rodrigues tells Kichijiro in one of the novel's final scenes. Instead, Rodrigues himself must be silent to experience the life of faith demanded by the culture he has come to inhabit. He does not speak nor is his consciousness narrated in the novel's final pages. Even his thoughts are silenced.

Throughout *Silence*, Japanese authorities, attempting to centralize and localize cultural power, assert that the Christian faith is incompatible with the Japanese imagination. They cannot see or hear what Rodrigues experiences—namely, the silent transformation of the Christian suit to the Japanese form. By submitting to the demands of power but maintaining the silent faith of the Japanese Christian, Rodrigues models a cultural encounter absent the power dynamics of both colonialism and proselytization. Silence is powerlessness. In embracing this weakness—an orientation Endo figures as Christic—he lives a Christian narrative drained of the universalizing triumphalism of European Christianity. Here, then, is the hope Endo offers to a globalized era. To live the life of the other—to live across cultural/national borders—is to live without regard for the structures of power on which those borders are built. If globalization requires annexing and adapting foreign forms of culture in order to navigate a reconfigured cultural terrain, Endo holds out hope that we can do so without the pride of power. Before the travelers of our global era can affirm that "God has many faces," we must first learn to see "that man's face" from new perspectives.

Notes

1   Shusaku Endo, "Ill-Fitting Clothes," *Endo Shusaku bungaku zenshū* 10 (1975): 374.

2   Quoted in Van C. Gessel, "Hearing God in Silence: The Fiction of Endo Shusaku," *Christianity and Literature* 48.2 (Winter 1999): 149–64.

3   Mark Williams, *Endō Shūsaku: A Literature of Reconciliation* (London: Routledge, 1999), 36.

4   Shusaku Endo, "François Mauriac," *Endo Shusaku bungaku zenshū* 10 (1975): 94.

5   John T. Netland, "From Resistance to *Kenosis*: Reconciling Cultural

Difference in the Fiction of Endo Shusaku," *Christianity and Literature* 48.2 (Winter 1999): 179.

6   Williams, *Endō Shūsaku: A Literature of Reconciliation,* 37.

7   Shusaku Endo, "Religion and Literature," *Endo Shusaku bungaku zenshū* 10 (1975): 119.

8   Shusaku Endo, "The Problems Confronting the Catholic Author," *Endo Shusaku bungaku zenshū* 10 (1975): 20-1.

9   Ibid., 23.

10 See, for example, Gessel, Williams, Hoffer, and Netland. Interestingly, each of these critics goes to great lengths to trouble this designation, pointing to the influences of other writers, both Catholic and Japanese. There seems to be a sense among many critics that referring to Endo in this way is reductive or ignores his Japanese heritage, despite "Japanese" appearing in the phrase.

11 George Bull, "A literary love affair: Graham Greene's brief encounter with Shusaku Endo," *The Chesterton Review* 27.1/2 (February/May 2001): 176.

12 Endo, "The Problems Confronting the Catholic Author," 27.

13 Van C. Gessel, *The Sting of Life: Four Contemporary Japanese Novelists* (New York: Columbia University Press, 1989), 239.

14 Ibid.

15 Bates Hoffer, "Shusaku Endo and Graham Greene: Cross-Cultural Influences in Literary Structure," *Language and Literature* 28 (2003): 132. Hoffer's argument is more complex than this, of course. His reading of the influence of *The Power and the Glory* on the structure of *Silence* asserts that Endo takes Greene's exploration of sin and reverses it, so that Rodrigues, unlike the whiskey priest, ends with the ultimate sin of despair, abandoning the community he has come to serve at the same time.

16 Shusaku Endo, *Deep River*, trans. Van C. Gessel (New York: New Directions, 1994).

17 Ibid., 193.

18 Ibid., 184.

19 Ibid., 122. Emphasis added.

20 Mark Williams, "Endō Shūsaku: Death and Rebirth in *Deep River*," *Christianity and Literature* 51.2 (Winter 2002): 230.

21 Netland, "From Resistance to *Kenosis*," 189.

22 Much of this comes from Brett L. Walker's study of Japan's relations with the rest of the world in the Sengoku and early Edo periods, entitled "Foreign Affairs and Frontiers in Early Modern Japan," *Early Modern Japan: An Interdisciplinary Journal* 10.2 (Fall 2002): 44-62.

23 Shusaku Endo, *Silence*, trans. William Johnston (New York: Taplinger, 1980), 11.

24 Ibid., 103.

25 Ibid., 116.

26 Ibid., 137.

27 Ibid., 161.

28 Ibid., 170.

29 Ibid. With the novel's emphasis on faces, it cannot be coincidental that Endo begins *A Life of Jesus* with, "We have never seen his face. We have never heard his voice. We do not really know what he looked like." See Shusaku Endo, *A Life of Jesus*, trans. Richard A. Schuchert (New York: Paulist, 1978), 7.

30 Endo, *Silence*, 175.

31 Shusaku Endo, "A Preface to the American Edition," in Endo, *A Life of Jesus*, 1.

32 Ibid.

33 Endo, *A Life of Jesus*, 79.

34 Fumitaka Matsuoka, "The Christology of Shusaku Endo," *Theology Today* 39.3 (October 1982): 298.

35 Ibid., 296.

36 Endo, *A Life of Jesus*, 73.

37 Ibid., 177.

38 The most feared of these tortures, referred to by locals only as "the pit," involves hanging by one's ankles and being slowly bled over several days (145). Williams notes that there are many analogs for this form of torture in the historical record of Edo Japan.

39 Quoted in William Johnston, "Preface to *Silence*," in Endo, *Silence*, xvii.

40 Williams, *Endō Shūsaku: A Literature of Reconciliation*, 109.

41 Here I have in mind readings produced by Netland, Higgins, and Gaughan. Many others examine Rodrigues in the aftermath of his apostasy, but few assert as these do the unusual position that Endo presents apostasy as a path to a more authentic faith.

42 Endo, *Silence*, 170.

43 Ibid., 175.

44 See Netland, Gessel, Higgins, Williams, and Matsuoka, among others.

45 Jean Higgins, "The Inner Agon of Endo Shusaku," *Cross Currents* 34 (1984–5): 421.

46 Ibid.

47 Netland, "From Resistance to *Kenosis*," 185.

48 Endo, *A Life of Jesus*, 1.

49 Endo, *Silence*, 190.

50 Gessel summarizes many of these early responses in his chapter on Endo in *The Sting of Life*.

51 Van C. Gessel, "Hearing God in Silence," 149. Gessel goes one step beyond Endo, asserting that what Rodrigues requires in order to experience a renewal of faith in line with his new cultural context is the "silencing" of his ego. Otherwise, he cannot hear the unique voice with which the Divine speaks in Japan (152). I do not intend to disagree with any of these interpretations of *Silence*, as they are all in one form or another validated by the text. To them I would simply like to add the silent suffering of the secret Christian communities of Japan.

Part Two

Christianity and Buddhism

7

The Catholic Shift East: The Case of Japan

Christal Whelan

Introduction

The mid-twentieth century marked the beginning of a definite shift in orientation in the Roman Catholic Church. Among other possible interpretations, it could be described as an age of exploration in which a newly emerging mystical Christianity entered into dialogue with various streams of Asian spirituality, most notably with Buddhism and Hinduism. Exemplary of the trend was the Benedictine monk Bede Griffiths (1906–93), who, in his later years, came to preside over Shantivanam Ashram in southern India where Hindu *pūjā* played a part in the Christian liturgy as did daily teachings from the Vedas. The barefoot British monk, dressed in the saffron robes of a *sannyasin*, sought to create an Indian Christian theology by divesting the faith of its alien European signifiers that he felt ultimately had served only to exoticize the Christian message.[1] Instead, he constantly aspired to find the Christ within India's own customs and scriptures by employing Vedanta and yoga to awaken the inner life and shed new light on traditional forms of Western Christianity.

In Japan, the German Jesuit Hugo Enomiya-Lassalle (1898–1990) established the Christian Zen temple of Shinmeikutsu on the outskirts of Tokyo where Japanese Catholics could experience the spiritual treasures of their own Buddhist cultural heritage within the perimeters of their Christian faith, while Western Catholics living in or just visiting Japan could push the boundaries of their own. Missionary priests based in Asia were not the only clerics thus engaged. On the U.S. front, from within a Cistercian monastery in Kentucky, a monk named Thomas Merton (1915–68) wrote eloquently about contemplative Christian prayer and Zen meditation, while the Trappist abbot, Thomas Keating (b. 1923), organized the first monastery-to-monastery exchanges between Tibetan Buddhist and Catholic monks with the loyal assistance of another Trappist priest, Theophane Boyd (1929–2003). Other notable pioneers of this ecumenical movement were the Catholic priests: Anthony de Mello (1931–87), Raimon Panikkar (1919–2010), John Main (1926–82), and William Johnston (1925–2010).

The Church itself officially sanctioned the trend toward greater inter-religious rapprochement in the Second Vatican Council's 1965 declaration on "Non-Christian Religions," that acknowledged the truths in other religions in these words: "She [the Catholic Church] regards with sincere reverence those ways of conduct and of life, those precepts and teachings which, though differing in many aspects from the ones she holds and sets forth, nonetheless often reflect a ray of that Truth which enlightens all men."[2] The declaration also affirmed the unity of the spiritual quest on the grounds that all people share common existential questions that concern the purpose of life, the nature of being human, and what happens after death. Therefore, "through dialogue and collaboration with the followers of other religions, carried out with prudence and love … they preserve and promote the good things, spiritual and moral … found among these men."[3] Perhaps the most apt image for this new dialogue-centered orientation was Raimon Panikkar's "rainbow of religions," a metaphor that nicely summed up in a vivid image the affirmation of a newfound unity of purpose within the diversity of the world's religions.[4]

Finally, Pope John Paul II's 1986 invitation to religious leaders of diverse faiths to convene in Assisi to pray for peace further demonstrated that common ground had been found, but on the deeper level of prayer rather than the more divisive ones of dogma or belief. The fact that the floodgates of communication had been willingly opened by the Church, however, did not mean that it would not occasionally reprimand some of its advocates for having crossed an invisible yet poorly defined critical line. Dialogue was deemed good but the possibility of being absorbed by the partner-in-dialogue, diluting one's own tradition in the process, or losing one's own moral compass remained ever-present dangers. Neither De Mello nor Enomiya-Lassalle escaped ecclesiastical censure during their careers. Nevertheless, the importance of the dialogue for all of these men of the cloth seemed to be the conviction that certain aspects of the Gospel could only be brought to light through sustained contact with the interiority characteristic of Eastern ways of thinking and being in the world.

Endo: His Life, Literary Work, and the Zeitgeist

Shusaku Endo's literary opus needs to be situated within this great trans-formative moment in the history of the Catholic Church in order to be properly understood. For within his own medium of literary fiction, Endo also played a major role in the burgeoning religious dialogue between Eastern and Western religious traditions. After all, the English translator of Endo's masterful novel *Silence* was the Irish Jesuit William Johnston, a passionate proponent of interreligious dialogue from his base at one of Japan's most elite institutions of higher learning, Sophia University in Tokyo, and no doubt a significant conduit to a much broader discussion for the novelist.

In a conversation between the two men recorded by Johnston, Endo notes that prior to the Second Vatican Council there was little interest in Zen and the retreat center built by Enomiya-Lassalle. However, the emerging interest in Buddhism among Christians had roused Endo's curiosity. Aside from the immensely appealing techniques of meditation that are not typically part of the education of most Christians, Johnston discussed with Endo the need for a new indigenous Japanese Christian theology in the following terms, "Theology ... is reflection on religion at a given time and in a given culture. It changes from culture to culture and from age to age, as we have seen so dramatically in the twentieth century. Our task at present is to create an Asian theology."[5] Endo's response was characteristically more measured: "Theology has been based on Western thought patterns for too long. We Japanese were taught that it was dangerous to depart from them. That was good medicine, but like all good medicine it had unpleasant side effects."[6]

Endo's comment sums up a lifetime of spiritual tensions and dilemmas that play out dramatically and longitudinally in his novels and short stories. This tension could be described as living with an "uncomfortable Christianity" in which one size, expected to fit all, never quite fits anyone. Becoming Christian in Japan had always meant first undergoing some degree of Westernization (or, given a more positive spin, "internationalization") in order to grasp the cultural context of the faith. Apart from its deep historical roots in Kyushu among rural people, in urban areas Christianity has more often been associated with the affluent and well educated. Though the novelist evidently did not live comfortably with his own Catholicism, he nevertheless remained loath to deny it. At times, Endo interprets the problem as a deep-seated cultural incompatibility—the Japan as a "mud swamp" idea expressed by Fr. Ferreira in *Silence* in which the sapling of Christianity can never grow in the wet soil (of "monsoon cultures"?) because the plant rots from the very roots.[7] At other times, Endo seems to suspect his uncomfortableness to be the result of an unfortunate series of personal calamities—his parents' divorce and his subsequent repatriation with his mother to Kobe from Manchuria where his father remained. Driven by a deep sense of loss and abandonment, his mother finds solace through conversion to a religion with only one true God. Either for the sake of plausibility or from sincere and zealous devotion, she then insists that her young son also be baptized into the faith. The ambivalence for Endo toward his religion then is rooted in images of his mother and her devotion at once morbid and disconcerting as described in the autobiographical story "Mothers": "I truly could not understand why my mother believed in such a religion. The words of the priest, the stories in the Bible, the crucifix—they all seemed like intangible happenings from a past that had nothing to do with us. I doubted the sincerity of the people who gathered there each Sunday to clasp their hands in prayer."[8]

From *Silence* to *Deep River*

Endo spent the greater part of his life in an attempt to understand the meaning of his own conversion to Christianity no matter the nature of its having been imposed on him initially by his mother. While the search for a specifically Japanese Christianity can describe Endo's early works, by the time he wrote *Deep River* the novelist had moved beyond even a search for a pan-Asian Christianity of the sort Johnston was recommending to one with a God large enough to contain all religions and even those souls who operate without any explicit religious framework but nevertheless grope in the dark for some truth that might liberate them from the prison of their ego-confined lives. This section charts the spiritual distance traveled from the perspective Endo expresses in early works, such as *Silence*, to that of his last work *Deep River*, an arc that represents a considerable shift in his thinking, and a kind of literary, if not wholly personal, *metanoia*.

First, Endo's exploration into the nature of a Japanese Christianity finds its initial focus and abiding interest in the *kakure kirishitan*, or "hidden Christians," of Japan. This group of people is undoubtedly one of the perennial vehicles of his exploration of what a genuine Japanese Christian identity might actually look like. Sometimes disdainful of this orphaned group, at other times his identification with them is nearly seamless: "Sometimes I catch a glimpse of myself in these *kakure*, people who have had to lead lives of duplicity, lying to the world and never revealing their true feelings to anyone."[9] These secret Christians are unique among Christians because their contact with European missionaries was cut short by the onslaught of brutal persecutions, the expulsion of the foreign priests, the demolition of the churches, and, by 1640, an enforced policy of national isolation that did not end until the mid-nineteenth century. Nevertheless, while remaining hidden for over two hundred years with the threat of execution hanging over their heads if discovered, the descendants of these early Christians perpetuated the faith through camouflaged traditions. They chanted Christian prayers using the *kata*, or "form," and rhythm of *sutra* chanting. They did this before a Buddhist altar with memorial tablets bearing *kaimyō*, or posthumous Buddhist names, painted in gold on the front and baptismal names of the deceased inked on plain slabs on the back.

For Endo, the hidden Christians represented a test-case since the Christianity they preserved (at the price of apostasy and duplicity) received no further stimulus from outside but continued to evolve along indigenous lines and perhaps in the end might just represent the true face of an acculturated Japanese Christianity: "the Japanese *kakure*, over the space of many years, stripped away all those parts of the religion that they could not embrace, and the teachings of God the Father were gradually replaced by a yearning after a Mother—a yearning which lies at the very heart of Japanese religion."[10]

For Christianity to succeed in Japan then, Endo suggests that at the very least it must be feminized. Indeed, in the hands of the hidden Christians, without the supervision of the European missionaries, and ensconced in remote rural hamlets and fishing villages, the faith instinctively evolved into a form of fertility worship with dedicated saints for field, hearth, and boat. As is known from their Bible and their Christmas Eve ceremony, Mary, the Mother of Christ, assumed a dominant role in both their theology and iconography.[11] The type of Christianity that Endo critiques in both *Silence* and *Deep River* is indeed a stern and masculine Christianity typified by the Counter-Reformation Church brought to both India and the Far East in the sixteenth century and reintroduced once again to Japan in the nineteenth century. Genial individual exceptions had existed, namely among Italian Jesuits—Roberto de Nobili (1557–1656) in India, Matteo Ricci (1552–1610) in China, and Alessandro Valignano (1539–1606) in Japan—each of whom exemplified policies and practices of accommodation to local customs. However, on the whole, the Church, aligned with the powers and institutions of its home countries, was characterized more by conquest and absorption than accommodation for it was not a religion that sought to learn from its counterpart within the framework of mutual dialogue. In addition, this Christianity introduced its own culture wars—Catholic against Protestant—into Asia as well as Central and South America.

Ethnocentric in orientation, this Church is epitomized in *Silence* by the words of the magistrate Inoue's Portuguese interpreter, a resentful former seminarian: "The fathers always ridiculed us. I knew Father Cabral—he had nothing but contempt for everything Japanese. He despised our houses; he despised our language; he despised our food and our customs—and yet he lived in Japan. Even those of us who graduated from the seminary he did not allow to become priests."[12] Encapsulated in the interpreter's words is a sharp critique of the European missionaries which cuts to the problem that sets the novel in motion. Fr. Rodrigues and his Jesuit companion Garrpe travel to Japan at the height of the persecutions to comfort and encourage the underground Christians as much as to investigate the unthinkable rumor that their esteemed mentor, the Jesuit Christovao Ferreira, onetime provincial of the Japanese mission, has apostatized. Through the experiences and reflections of Rodrigues, who is shadowed throughout by Kichijiro, an ambiguous Judas-like character, the novel explores various themes: theodicy (God's apparent "silence"), the nature of faith, and the inevitability of hybridity in a transplanted religion such as Christianity in Japan.

While ministering to the underground Christians, Rodrigues is eventually captured, imprisoned, and made to witness the daily massacre of the Japanese Christians. His faith is challenged by the simplistic belief of these peasants and the bitter irony that he is the cause of death for those who help him. The miserable conditions of their lives also collide with his image of a glorious martyrdom. Rodrigues's first shift in perspective occurs when his captors escort him to a grove in order to witness the martyrdom of three Japanese tied inside rolled mats and ready to be tossed into the sea. With them is his companion Garrpe who can save them if he only apostatizes. But the priest proves unwilling to compromise his faith by trampling on the *fumie*. Faith is depicted here less as a matter of individual conscience than as one with ultimate consequences for others. For Rodrigues, this raises the thorny question of spiritual pride.

When Rodrigues finally encounters Ferreira, his teacher describes his own comparable experience of spiritual blackmail. He, too, could save the lives of five peasants (who had already apostatized) yet remained hanging in the pit alongside him for three days. With the logic of "What would Jesus do?" Ferreira apostatizes in order to save these peasants but also to break the unbearable silence of God in the face of their suffering. This seasoned missionary speaks about Japan in terms of a sapling planted in a mud swamp where the roots rot. He opines that in Japan God has somehow been lost in translation, citing the mistake in Francis Xavier's time of translating "Deus" as "Dainichi" ("the Great Sun," a reference to the Cosmic Buddha).[13]

Faced with this insurmountable cultural conundrum, Ferreira had lost his faith in the mission and was willing to accept the consequence that the Church would consider him a renegade priest, expel him from the mission, and vilify his name in the history of the Church. Nevertheless, the Church and missionary work are something greater than what prelates in cozy offices in Portugal, Rome, or Macao, can really fathom. Ultimately, it is not the princes or popes of the world, but God alone who knows the reasons of each human heart.

Like his teacher, and at Ferreira's urging, Rodrigues also tramples on the *fumie*. Each man is given a Japanese name, a wife, and Japanese dress. Though in form they appear to have apostatized, they have both gained in spiritual depth. Rodrigues especially has been made to admit his own weakness and accept his humanity through the enigmatic presence of Kichijiro, a man who never seems quite able to abandon the priest even after he betrays him multiple times. In Kichijiro, Endo has created a Judas who is a Zelig-like character that offers a parody of the situational ethic often associated with Japan. For Kichijiro assumes whatever identity is necessary at the moment—with Christians he is a Christian, and with Buddhists he is a Buddhist. Whoever or whatever he may be, it is through him that Rodrigues is forced to confront some of his own deepest weaknesses. To some extent, religion had become an idol for Rodrigues, coupled with his desire for a glorious martyrdom and the reputation of being a "saint." More humble than this ambition is the essence of the Christian message—love—whatever form it need assume in each and every situation. Endo will plumb this theme in *Deep River* through the character of Otsu.

In *Deep River* Endo moves the discourse gradually out of any conventional Christian framework through the spiritual trajectory of Otsu's quest for a life dedicated to God, and the novel indicates where such a search would lead. This new and open terrain also depicts Japan at a crucial turning point in its modern history. Since the end of the Pacific War, the U.S. had served as the country's dominant cultural influence with rampant Americanization that undermined Japan's own rich traditions and sense of ethnic identity. But as Japan rose phoenix-like from its defeat to become the world's second largest economy,[14] its global clout freed it from any slavish imitation and the Japanese began to actively explore their own Asian roots in a new spirit of amicability. The strength of the yen also allowed Japanese to travel in great numbers as never before. Given India's status as the birthplace of Buddhism, a religion Japan had embraced since the sixth century, the subcontinent became an attractive tourist destination. It represented much of what Japan had lost as the tour guide Enami explains to his tour group in *Deep River* that they are entering a unique world that Japan once knew but has since forgotten.[15] This world is an enchanted one in the Weberian sense in which religious belief and vitality are both still intact. Endo himself had visited India four times and employs it as the backdrop to this novel for the great Ganges serves as a marvelous Rorschach test for his five characters.

A kind of road novel set in 1984 (the year Indira Gandhi was assassinated), *Deep River* charts the progressive transformation of four major characters (Otsu remains in a class by himself) whose lives converge on a single point—each one is on a personal pilgrimage in search of psychological and emotional healing, purification of the unconscious, a deeper connection with something they cannot define, and meaning in their lives based on a spiritual dimension they sense exists but have not yet experienced. Traveling to India as part of a tour group, each member carrying emotional baggage, these modern-day pilgrim/tourists all hope to find some answer or resolution to the sickness in their souls in a country that Endo here presents as a spiritual superpower. Therefore, the distance and landscape of the outer journey reflects that of the inner emotional and moral journey. It is crucial that the climax for each character occurs on the banks of the Ganges River, described as a maternal river that accepts all living things but also the dead. Though people bathe in and swallow its waters, the river is filthy with corpses and the ashes of other corpses, yet it is nevertheless considered most holy. Pilgrims journey from everywhere in India just to die there.

Endo's characters all undergo a symbolic death at the river and their presumed resurrections will occur some time after we close the book. We never see them but we are allowed to imagine them. For all of these characters—Isobe, Numada, Kiguchi, Mitsuko, and Otsu—loss or death and the mystery it presents, propels each to delve inward and examine the darker side of the soul before they can reemerge transformed. The novel opens with Isobe, a typical Japanese salaryman. Prior to the loss of his wife to incurable and virulent cancer, Endo writes of this man, "he lacked any religious convictions like most Japanese, death to him meant the extinction of everything."[16] Isobe's search begins with the death of his wife and the growing awareness that during the 35 years of their marriage, embarrassed to ever reveal his feelings, he had cheated her of the affection she deserved. His lack of affect extended to his relation with their adopted daughter as well. Isobe is a man who has put off life for a hypothetical future just like the promise of a honeymoon to Spain or Portugal that has to wait until his retirement. Given the premature death of his wife, it never happens at all. But her last words to her husband are, "I'll be reborn somewhere in this world. Look for me … promise."[17] Isobe's search begins then with his wife's death and her puzzling last words that serve as the first chink in his carapace of certainty. Though terribly painful, his loss and loneliness are the only experiences that open him to a state of receptivity in which he can begin to entertain new possibilities about the nature of the universe. He visits his niece in Washington D.C. who happens to be curious about paranormal phenomena. When he leaves, he ends up buying a book by Shirley MacLaine (no doubt the Japanese bestseller, *Out on a Limb*) on reincarnation, and Ian Stevenson's book *Children Who Remember Previous Lives*. Through the character of Isobe, Endo explores New Age spirituality in Japan, its attraction and its limitations, particularly for the psychologically immature that Isobe typifies.

Through a correspondence with a researcher at the University of Virginia School of Medicine, Isobe discovers the name of a girl named Rajini born in a village near Varanasi who claims to have had a past life in Japan. In his attempt to keep his promise to his wife, and quite literally following her words, the now rudderless Isobe travels to India in search of his deceased wife in her next incarnation. But his visit to a given village proves fruitless and his visits to a fortuneteller who extorts money in exchange for more precise information are to no avail. When this search proves to be ever more tenuous, he finally comes to realize the value of his wife. He had wrongly thought that his accomplishments were everything but came to realize too late that he had been an egoist all along. Only in this discovery is he stripped bare. In his confrontation with himself at the Ganges he cries out to the river asking where his wife is. The purity of his confession is accepted, for "the river took in his cry and silently flowed away. But he felt a power of some kind in that silvery silence."[18]

Unlike Isobe, Numada represents not a non-believer at the outset but a pantheist. A famous writer of animal fables for children, he is reminiscent of Anthony de Mello, and, in terms of biography, of Endo himself. He spends his youth in Dalian (Manchuria), experiences the divorce of his parents, and repatriation to Japan. In his boyhood isolation, Numada had learned early to confide his sorrows in his pet dog Blackie who seemed to respond with phrases like "Can't be helped," or "That's what life is all about."[19] Though this was the first animal that taught Numada that it was possible for humans to converse with animals, it became part of a life-long pattern of a deep bond with animals. As an adult, his pet hornbill reminds him of one of the many paintings of clowns by Georges Rouault for whom these buffoons symbolized Christ.

Numada considered all sentient beings to possess an insoluble loneliness. But when he stayed up late nights writing in silence, he and the bird's loneliness made contact. In this communion there was solace. When he was hospitalized for tuberculosis his greatest sorrow was his lack of an animal to whom he could confess his deepest feelings and who would take them all upon himself. Only because of the quality of his relationship with animals was Numada even able to consider the possibility of a God: "he didn't know anything about God, but if God was someone humans could talk to from the heart," then belief was a possibility.[20] To console him, his wife brings a caged myna bird to the hospital. However, when he undergoes his third operation his wife negligently puts the cage on the hospital roof and forgets about him. Although Numada lives, the bird dies. This animal lover is plagued thereafter by the idea of a substitutionary suffering, or that the bird had absorbed his pain fully and died in his place. Numada's birds, Rouault's clowns, the foreigner Gaston, and Otsu are all Christ figures in Endo's novel. Thus, Numada's trip to India is induced by the desire to see the bird sanctuaries. Ultimately, he buys a myna bird there in order to release it, an action of "no marketable value" the narrator reminds us.[21] Releasing animals is actually a fairly common Buddhist practice across Asia, and increasingly in the West. Called *hōjō-e* in Japanese, it acknowledges the mutual sentience and camaraderie of humans and animals, and is meant to liberate the latter whose destiny would otherwise be captivity or a meal on someone's table.

Apropos, the character Kiguchi, a modern-day Japanese industrialist haunted by his past, happens to be a vegetarian, the reason for which is suggested but never made explicit in the novel. During the Pacific War, Kiguchi fought British and Indian troops in the jungles of Burma and survived malaria, starvation, and despair. In a place where every soldier wore a grenade on his belt to take his own life if necessary, Kiguchi walks through a landscape filled with the intermittent sound of grenades detonating. Kiguchi is a Buddhist who during the war has a near-death experience—the vision of an exact replica of himself walking beside him and urging him to walk through this Highway of Death already strewn with Japanese corpses. After the war, he meets again his friend Tsukada who had saved his life in the jungle. Now down and out, Tsukada is an alcoholic haunted by some unspeakable wartime memory that is corroding his soul and driving him to drink. Ultimately Tsukada reveals to his friend how he ate the flesh of one of their comrades, PFC Minamikawa, thinking that it was lizard and even gave some of it to Kiguchi. After the war Tsukada went to meet the wife and child of the man whose flesh he had eaten and is haunted ever after by the eyes of that child. Finally, when Tsukada is in the hospital dying of a liver disease he is visited and comforted daily by an awkward hospital volunteer named Gaston. Gaston, European and Christian, is described as a gangly and good-hearted buffoon. Tsukada expresses dismay at Gaston's belief in God, in terms of a secular position that reveals the fallacy that science must necessarily supplant religion within a unilinear evolutionary scheme, "How can anybody today claim anything so foolish? Why we've got rockets flying to the moon!"[22] But it is Gaston alone who absorbs Tsukada's confession, consoles the man, and evidently absolves him of his corrosive guilt before he dies. When Kiguchi glimpses the tranquil face of his friend he "couldn't help but feel that this peaceful death-mask had been made possible because Gaston had soaked up all the anguish in Tsukada's heart."[23]

Although Kiguchi hates war, his destiny has been bound to it. First he is a soldier in Burma, and later he profits from the business generated from the Korean War that allows the freight company he founded to prosper. As a self-identified Buddhist, Kiguchi wants nothing more than to hold a memorial service for the solace of his dead wartime comrades. This is the reason for his journey to the homeland of the Buddha. On the banks of the Ganges, he will also open his heart to Mitsuko about the cannibalism during the war. Through his act of confession to another, he too purifies his heart and is then able to perform a ceremony chanting the *Amida sutra* for the benefit of those who died decades ago in a Burmese jungle.

Mitsuko herself has come to India in search of Otsu who was a fellow university student in years past. Endo makes it clear that she is of the generation after the student movements of the 1960s without the goals that had moved the rebels of a generation before. She was drawn to Otsu, a devout Catholic at a Catholic university, in order to destroy his faith that she despised. In fact, she and her classmates invite the geeky Otsu out drinking in what becomes a modern-day *efumi* ritual in which she taunts him to dump his God if he wants them to stop forcing him to drink. But Otsu announces the prophetic: "Even if I try to abandon God ... God won't abandon me."[24] When Mitsuko tempts him further by saying she will let him be her boyfriend if he only drops his God, they end up in bed. Although Mitsuko makes love to Otsu, the only joy she feels derives from the hope that she may actually succeed in destroying his faith. What she is actually attacking is the religious hypocrisy that she sees in the Christians in Japan and her sensitivity to the fact that religions are at bottom cultural constructions. Endo describes her feelings as she watches the priest at her university in his white summer robes kneeling at the altar "feeling as if she were looking at some bizarre extraterrestrial."[25] When Otsu tells her about a certain professor's class, she responds, "Isn't he that Catholic priest who does Zen meditation? But in his heart of hearts he's still a European?"[26] This reveals something of the failed attempts of Christian missionaries who borrowed the techniques from Zen but not its spirit. This may actually be the most devious form of cultural sabotage, that of reducing another religious tradition to a technique alone. The other reason Mitsuko deeply resents Christianity is because of its neglect of the feminine side of divinity.

Mitsuko later marries a man from a wealthy family in an arranged marriage but secretly despises him and all people like him who talk excessively of golf and new car models. She is by far the most complex character in the novel. However, she would prefer to be less complicated and to "pass" in the conventional world that surrounds her and become a typical housewife. Although she has no religion, literature becomes her substitute for a spiritual life; she lives through books and has a strong identification with Thérèse of François Mauriac's novel *Thérèse* (1927). Like the protagonist of the novel, Mitsuko is aware of something lurking in the depths of her own heart that she cannot quell. Mauriac's novel opens in court after Thérèse has poisoned her exemplary husband, exactly what Mitsuko would like to do to hers. On Mitsuko's own honeymoon she manages to get away from her husband for a few days and visit Lyon where Otsu has been a seminarian for the past three years. There Otsu confesses that after she jilted him he was lost but that God, the great magician that he is, can turn any situation to the best advantage, "If you hadn't dumped me … I … would not be living this kind of life. … But … I didn't change myself. I was transformed."[27] Although he maintains his faith in God, Otsu is increasingly troubled by the cultural barrier that blocks his full participation as a Christian due to its expression in Western cultural forms and mental frameworks: "The ways of thinking that they've kneaded with their own hands and fashioned to meet the workings of their own hearts … they're ponderous to an Asian like me. I can't blend in with them. And so … every day is hell for me."[28] Otsu perhaps seeks a more Buddhist faith or one not based on an inherent duality in which evil and good are totally separate. He claims that when he returns to Japan he wants to think about a Christianity that better suits the Japanese mind.

By the time Mitsuko sets off for India she is a long way on her journey for she is now a divorced woman and hence no longer living in the "bad faith" of a false marriage. "She no longer wanted imitation love. She wanted real love and nothing less."[29] Once in India, Mitsuko goes in search of Otsu at a Catholic monastery in Varanasi and meets a Caucasian priest (the "western sheriff-priest" as she calls him) at the door who tells her that they take no responsibility for him. She soon comes to understand how far Otsu's search for a true faith has led him from conventional Christianity.

Mitsuko's own liberation begins in the cave temple of Nakshar Bhagavati. As she descends into that sultry dampness, she feels as if she were descending into the depth of her own heart—goddesses with frightening visages wearing crowns of skulls and holding severed heads. They are forces of nature and symbols of both birth and death. Mitsuko's repressed spiritual hunger has been unable to find an outlet in the European forms that she finds full of hypocrisy. But in India, she encounters images of the goddess Chamunda who lives in graveyards, feeds on corpses and, from drooping breasts, still offers milk to children. One of her legs is festering with leprosy, while her stomach is collapsed from hunger, and she is bitten by scorpions. It is an ugly image of a suffering India. Nevertheless, Mitsuko finds "the Asian mother … utterly different from the lofty Holy Mother of Europe."[30] Both Kali, who combines mercy and malevolence, and Chamunda are without hypocrisy. This releases long pent-up energy in Mitsuko.

Finally Mitsuko learns that Otsu is living in a Hindu ashram with *sadhus* since he is no longer acceptable to his Christian brethren. With good reason, Otsu also genuinely fears where God may be leading him. In his little room where he holds a private mass in Latin, he keeps a prayer book, the *Upanishad*, a book by Mother Teresa, and a book of sayings by Mahatma Gandhi. Endo is not suggesting that Otsu is a lost soul but that he is engaged in the actual imitation of Christ that has led him increasingly outside the Church. At the seminary he was amply warned that he had a pantheistic streak lurking in his unconscious mind but as he confides to Mitsuko, "As a Japanese, I can't bear those who ignore the great life force that exists in nature."[31]

Otsu's own experiences reiterate the lesson already learned from Christianity of the sixteenth and seventeenth centuries, namely that many Japanese converts to Christianity possessed a faith that was different from that of the people of Europe since it had mixed with Buddhist elements and the pantheism of Shinto. Yet even in the late twentieth century the words of an upperclassman in Lyon resonate with Cabral's in the seventeenth century. Otsu is told, "If you dislike Europe so much, why don't you leave the church immediately? It is the Christian church in the Christian world that we are set to defend."[32]

Otsu has come to believe that: "God has many different faces. I don't think God exists exclusively in the churches and chapels of Europe. I think he is also among the Jews and the Buddhists and the Hindus."[33] In other words, God transcends the formulations of all religions. While Otsu's superiors thought his mystical approach indicated a rejection of Christ, it was actually an affirmation of his deeply personal faith. Otsu refutes both the European bias and the medieval orientation of the Christians with whom he perpetually finds himself. He has taken to heart the summons to dialogue with other religions voiced by the Second Vatican Council: "I think the real dialogue takes place when you believe that God has many faces, and he exists in all religions."[34] The reason he is a Christian is not because the religion is inherently superior to all others, but simply because he was not brought up in a Buddhist or a Muslim household. The form of religion that a person follows is viewed by Endo as an accident of birth much like his own coerced baptism. However, Otsu also comes to realize that Christianity is hardly the only religion that is parochial. Even the Hindus are exclusive and forbid people of other faiths from entering the cremation grounds. For this reason, Otsu becomes a kind of *kakure kirishitan* who must disguise himself as a Hindu by dressing in a white *dhoti* in order to carry corpses into the cremation grounds.

Conclusion

In *Silence*, Ferreira and Rodrigues are captured, imprisoned, and faced with the same moral dilemma—not to trample on the *fumie* and save themselves, or to trample on the sacred image and save the lives of those Japanese Christians who have been captured and are being tortured. Both, at different times, trample on the *fumie* out of love for others but they will nevertheless have to live with the knowledge that they are outcasts from a Church that will brand them as apostates. In *Deep River*, Endo's final literary testament, he explores various spiritual options in contemporary Japan. Isobe is a secular man susceptible to the pseudo-science of New Age spirituality because he has no religious convictions or tradition of his own. Through Isobe's characterization, Endo explores the limitations of the New Age. While it may keep the mind occupied, it ultimately leads nowhere and often at great expense. Isobe finds himself at a dead end and only after he gives up his spurious spiritual quest does the power of silence descend upon him. Mitsuko's case dramatizes the necessity for the integration of the feminine principle in Japan, which means not only the gentle aspect represented by the Virgin Mary (or the bodhisattva Kannon) but also the dark side represented by the goddesses Chamunda and Kali. Numada and Kiguchi represent Shintoism and Buddhism respectively. For Endo, both of these characters with their profound experience of substitutionary suffering—Numada with Blackie and the myna bird, and Kiguchi through Gaston and others—are not inherently in conflict with Christianity. Substitutionary suffering lies at the heart of Christianity but is also found in Buddhism as well as pantheism, and, as Endo implies, it is universal. Finally, the Christ figure of the novel—Otsu—is a man initially in search of a Japanese Christianity, then an Asian one, and, at last, looks only for God. Although he represents Christ he also exemplifies the Buddhist concept of *upāya*, or skillful means, according to which all religions are ultimately just forms or vehicles.

Otsu is the vehicle through which Mitsuko will come to understand substitutionary suffering. As she descends into the waters of the Ganges dressed in a *sari*, she has a sense of being part of humanity for the first time in her life; she begins to see through all her mistakes and a prayer spontaneously comes to her lips. At this epiphanal moment, Otsu is fatally wounded in trying to protect a mob from attacking a Japanese tourist who has insulted a certain Hindu sensibility by photographing a funeral procession. In this synchronicity, Endo breaks his own silence to affirm the power of a mystical Christ transcendent of any religious tradition.

Notes

1   Bede Griffiths, *Christ in India: Essays Toward Hindu-Christian Dialogue* (New York: Charles Scribner's Sons, 1966), 23.
2   Pope Paul VI, "Declaration on The Relation of the Church to Non-Christian Religions," *Nostra Aetate* (October 28, 1965). http://www.vatican.va/archive/hist_councils/ii_vatican_council/documents/vat-ii_decl_19651028_nostra-aetate_en.html (accessed March 2014).
3   Ibid.
4   Raimon Panikkar, *The Intrareligious Dialogue* (New York: Paulist Press, 1978), xix–xx.
5   "Endo and Johnston Talk of Buddhism and Christianity" (conversation between William Johnston and Shusaku Endo), *America* 171.16 (November 19, 1994): 18–20.
6   Ibid.
7   Shusaku Endo, *Silence*, trans. William Johnston (New York: Taplinger Publishing Company, 1980), 147.
8   Shusaku Endo, "Mothers," in *Stained Glass Elegies: Stories By Shusaku Endo*, trans. Van C. Gessel (New York: New Directions Publishing, 1990), 120.
9   Ibid., 126.
10 Ibid., 135.
11 Christal Whelan, *The Beginning of Heaven and Earth: The Sacred Book of Japan's Hidden Christians* (Honolulu: University of Hawaii Press, 1996).
12 Endo, *Silence,* 87.
13 Endo, *Silence,* 146–50.
14 Figures from the World Bank and IMF for 2013 give the world's top four economies as: 1. America, 2. China, 3. Japan, 4. Germany.
15 Shusaku Endo, *Deep River*, trans. Van C. Gessel (New York: New Directions Books, 1994), 108.
16 Ibid., 22.
17 Ibid., 17.
18 Ibid., 189.
19 Ibid., 73.
20 Ibid., 81.
21 Ibid., 204.
22 Ibid., 99.
23 Ibid., 103.

24 Ibid., 42.
25 Ibid., 45.
26 Ibid., 46.
27 Ibid., 63.
28 Ibid., 65.
29 Ibid., 163.
30 Ibid., 175.
31 Ibid., 118.
32 Ibid., 191.
33 Ibid., 121.
34 Ibid., 122.

8

Agape Unbound in *Silence* and *Deep River*[1]

Elizabeth Cameron Galbraith

Shusaku Endo, who died in 1996, was one of Japan's most renowned novelists. He was also a practicing Roman Catholic. In 1926, when he was three years old, Endo was taken to Manchuria by his parents. When they later divorced, his mother moved back to Japan with her two sons, to live with a sister in Kobe. Following her sister's example, Endo's mother became a fervent, strict observing Catholic and had Endo baptized at the age of 11.[2] Speaking as an adult of his baptism, Endo claimed "I became a Catholic against my will"[3] and spoke of his baptism as an "arranged marriage," or forced union chosen for him by his mother.[4] As he grew older Endo considered alternatives to such enforced Catholicism, including Marxism and even suicide, but he could not quite take off the Catholic suit he had donned at such an early age:

> And anyway, if I were to strip off these ill-fitting clothes, I had nothing to change into. Yes, I had had a go at Marxism and the like, but somehow it didn't appeal. And there was this business of having been handed the faith by my mother, and my attachment to her; it was hardly a noble or ideal business but something that accrued slowly in the heart.[5]

Endo did, however, feel like an alien in Japan during the Second World War. As a Christian he was taught to look to the West as his spiritual homeland, to Europe as Christianity's historical and cultural center, and yet his country was under siege from the West. He felt disloyal and was taunted for his allegiance to the Christian faith.

In 1949 Endo graduated in French literature from Keio University in Tokyo and in 1950 went to the University of Lyon to study French Catholic literature. He spent three years in France, where he was eventually hospitalized for pleurisy. It seems quite plausible that Endo hoped that in France—a country he associated with Christianity—he might feel at home in his faith. On the contrary, his experience with racism from fellow Christians made him feel rejected, and the more he came into contact with European art and culture, the more aware he became that they derived from emotions and a sensibility that remained alien to him. Endo eventually suffered a crisis of faith, occasioned by his sense of European Christianity's foreignness, and this great cultural, religious, and psychological letdown undoubtedly contributed to his severe sickness. Even in his sickbed at the hospital, Endo did not feel consoled by his faith; rather, he longed to escape the oppressive force of European Christianity and return home to Japan.[6]

Soon after returning to Japan in 1953 Endo published his first novellas and in 1955 he assumed the post of Instructor at Sophia University. After publishing two more novels, Endo made a second trip to France in 1960, only to suffer a relapse of pleurisy; he was forced to return to Japan, with an ensuing three years in hospital. During this ten-year period between his first visit to France and the recovery from his second illness, and after a visit to Israel to research the life of Jesus, Endo became preoccupied with the misfit of his European Christian clothing for his Japanese body: "For me Christianity was like a suit of Western clothes that just doesn't fit. I had a hunger for miso soup and Japanese pickles, but they proffered me the butter-rich concoctions of the West; I had an urge to dump it all on the floor."[7] However, rather than throwing off the faith he had inherited from his mother, Endo became determined to fashion or mold his European suit into something more comfortable. "I came to think that I should alter the European suit of clothes my mother had bestowed to me into something Japanese, something that fit me … and somehow I was sure that if the time came when I saw the task was impossible and felt that there was nothing for it but to drop this faith, my mother would forgive me."[8]

Endo's novels from then onwards became preoccupied with precisely the task of retailoring with his own hands the European Christian suit his mother had put on him into a Japanese garment that would fit his Japanese body; and, using characters, plots, and themes to his full advantage, Endo made it very clear how impossible a task that at times appeared to be. Is Christianity so inhospitable to Japanese sensibilities that it is bound to fail in Japan? Is the culture of Japan inhospitable soil for the seed of Christianity? These, among other questions, are raised subtly and oftentimes subversively throughout Endo's fiction.

In some form or other Christianity is, in Endo's view, the center of Western culture, whereas in Japan there is no Christian history, tradition, or cultural heritage. There are also, he believes, three particular Japanese sensibilities, or "insensitivities," which form a barrier to crucial aspects of Christianity. Throughout the novella "Yellow Man" Endo points to the difficulty of making Christians of a people like the Japanese, who struggle with monotheism, are uncomfortable with extreme ways of thinking about evil and good, and are unmoved by the thought of death.[9] Such "insensitivities" which, according to Endo, are the root causes for the failure of Christianity in Japan, are typically understood to be what Endo is alluding to with his now renowned "mudswamp" metaphor in *Silence,* his most celebrated novel.

The Sad, Frail Face of Christ

Set during the seventeenth-century persecution of Christians in Japan, *Silence* relates the experiences of Portuguese Jesuit missionaries, in particular Fr. Rodrigues, who enters Japan illegally to minister to Japanese Christians and to locate his former teacher, Fr. Ferreira, who supposedly had apostatized. A Japanese magistrate, Inoue, is considered a terror to the Christians and apparently devised a brutal method to get Christians to apostatize.[10] Knowing that Japanese Christian peasants honored the Virgin Mary above all, the peasants were required to spit on the crucifix and declare the Holy Mother a whore.[11] Rodrigues is eventually captured by the Japanese authorities, and is informed by Ferreira, his former teacher who had in fact apostatized, that, like a young sapling planted in an inhospitable mudswamp, Christianity is bound to fail in Japan.[12] Later in the novel, Inoue suggests to Rodrigues that Christianity simply cannot put down roots in Japan and that his efforts have been defeated by Japan's mudswamp.[13]

Through the mudswamp motif Endo projects his own "doubts formed during my stay in France as to whether Western culture (not civilization) can ever truly take root when planted in Japan."[14] *Silence* thus portrays Endo's own interior conflict between his Christian self and his Japanese self. The distance between European and Japanese cultures that Endo himself had felt so personally in Paris, "the same sense of distance is evidenced in my novel *Silence*."[15] And yet, as impossible as the challenge at times appears to be, Endo never quite gives up on the hope of reconciling such different cultures, and for the initial source of such reconciliation one need look no further than the very same novel in which the conflict is presented. Endo writes: "At the time of my second illness I slowly realized that Christianity was not simply a European thing. In that suit of Western clothes I began to discern the outline of a kimono. With this realization I began to internalize the faith. I think that fact is visible in *Silence,* the novel I wrote upon being discharged."[16]

While acknowledging deeply challenging differences between European Christianity and Japanese sensibilities Endo provides in *Silence* a vision of Christianity, and in particular of Christ, that is amenable to the Japanese.

We see this vision best through the novel's emphasis on Rodrigues's faith formation. At the outset, Rodrigues believes in the omnipotent and omniscient God of European Christianity. His Christ is a dazzling Christ—the image of a beautiful, glorious victor. Rodrigues notes, however, that the Bible seems strangely silent regarding Christ's physical features.[17] For his part, Rodrigues hopes to be victorious in his mission to Japan but what he experiences contrasts with his glorious expectations. He is constantly faced with the immense suffering of Japanese Christians, and the silence in the midst of their suffering of the almighty God in whom he has such faith. He finds God's silence haunting and begins to question his own faith. His doubts are exacerbated by Ferreira who, once Rodrigues is captured by the Japanese authorities, aids them in their efforts to induce Rodrigues's apostatizing.

Crucial to Rodrigues's own precipitous fall from his strong faith in an omnipotent God is Ferreira's confession that he had apostatized because God did nothing for the suffering Japanese: those Japanese who, when arrested by the Japanese authorities for practicing Christianity, were tortured if they would not renounce their faith. Ferreira also torments Rodrigues spiritually with his claim that if Christ were here, then Christ too would have apostatized, and that Rodrigues should do the same.[18]

In this polarizing of Christ and God, in this questioning of obstinate martyrdom in the face of the suffering of others, and more than anything in this appeal to love, lies the root from which Rodrigues's own apostasy takes hold. In it, however, also lies the crucial transformation in Rodrigues's conception of Christ. Rodrigues begins to envision, not the powerful and dignified beauty of the Christ represented in Western art, but the man who desired to share our pain. The powerful and glorious Christ image instilled in Europe begins to be replaced with the ugly face of Christ, crowned with thorns and thin, outstretched arms. It is a sunken and exhausted face. And yet, behind the outward frailty there is a strength that enables Christ to accept human weakness and come alongside the individual in moments of need. It is this frail Christ, not the almighty God, who in a moment of extreme catharsis pierces the silence that has haunted Rodrigues ever since the commencement of his mission to Japan. Just as he is on the verge of apostatizing by stepping on an image of Christ, Rodrigues, for the first time in the novel, hears the voice of Christ: "Trample! It was to be trampled on by men that I was born into this world!"[19] The ugly, frail, rejected, and sad face of Christ in the *fumie* is not the face of splendor to which Rodrigues had been accustomed, it is not the beautiful, majestic Christ. Yet, this is the Christ who speaks to him: "It was to share men's pain that I carried my cross!"[20] This is a God who is so completely moved by human suffering as to choose to enter into it with us, as Rodrigues later hears Christ claim: "I was not silent. I suffered beside you."[21]

With this epiphany, the seemingly unfathomable gap between European Christianity and Japanese sensibilities has begun to close as Christ may indeed succeed in penetrating the mudswamp of Japan in a manner not available to the European figure of awe and majesty. Convinced that his "Lord is different from the God that is preached in the churches," Rodrigues is now possessed of a faith more real and more profound than that which had inspired him to risk everything in embarking on his mission to Japan. [22] Moreover, he is able to love and serve Christ in a different way from before, and Rodrigues feels that all that has taken place until now has been necessary to bring him to this love.[23] Nor has Rodrigues been defeated by the swamp of Japan as Inoue assumes. In Rodrigues's mental protestation that Christianity is not what Inoue thinks it is, is also to be heard Endo's proclamation that Christ and Christianity can indeed be fashioned by and for Japanese hands.[24] Here it is helpful to quote Endo himself at length:

> *Silence* contains various themes, and it received various interpretations and analyses from the critics. But to me the most meaningful thing in the novel is the change in the hero's image of Christ. The hero, a foreigner, believed in a Jesus of majesty and power, an orderly Jesus who was even governed by order. This was the image conceived by Western artists. The novel's hero brought this image with him to Japan, and from that strong face of Christ he gained courage to evangelize.
>
> After suffering many trials and frustrations, however, he was caught at last and brought before the *Fumie* (picture of Christ which Christians were ordered to step on). Standing there he saw an image of Christ he had never seen before, an image shaped by Japanese hands. It was not the orderly, European, but the worn out face of a Christ suffering as we suffer.[25]

The Sacred Feminine

It is not only the suffering, worn-out image of Christ that makes it distinctly Japanese:

> The image of Christ carved on the *Fumie* was a maternal image, a woman seeking to suffer with her child and to share the child's pain. It is not the paternal image to be found in so much Western art, the face of Christ resplendent with majesty and wearing an expression which

represents the epitome of order and discipline. ... I intended this transformation to be the theme of *Silence*.[26]

This maternal image is arresting, and it requires an explanation. Influenced
by Erich Fromm's account of mother and father religion, Endo claims that
in father religion God is the judge and to be feared, whereas in mother
religion God is as a mother to a bad child: forgiving and suffering with the
child. This crucial distinction between mother and father religion facili-
tated Endo's epiphany as he "began to feel the gulf I had long felt between
Christianity and me was due to the European overemphasis on the paternal
aspect of religion. Christianity seemed distant to us Japanese because the
other aspect, maternal religion, had been grossly neglected from the time
of the early Christian missionaries down to the present."[27] In the "Preface
to the American Edition" of *A Life of Jesus*, which he published after *Silence*,
Endo writes:

> My way of depicting Jesus is rooted in my being a Japanese novelist.
> ... The religious mentality of the Japanese is—just as it was at the time
> when the people accepted Buddhism—responsive to one who suffers
> with us and who allows for our weakness, but their mentality has little
> tolerance for one who judges humans harshly, then punishes them. In
> brief, the Japanese tend to seek in their Gods and Buddhas a warm-
> hearted mother rather than a stern father. With this fact always in mind
> I tried not so much to depict God in the father image that tends to
> characterize Christianity, but rather to depict the kind hearted maternal
> aspect of God revealed to us in the personality of Jesus.[28]

That a Japanese Catholic novelist would identify in Christianity an overly
stern paternal emphasis, an emphasis highlighted in Western Catholic
feminist critiques including those by Elizabeth Johnson in *She Who Is:
The Mystery of God in Feminist Discourse* and Rosemary Radford Ruether
in *Sexism and God-Talk: Toward a Feminist Theology*, is of great interest.
Worthy of note, is the appreciation Endo might have had for the writings of
Julian of Norwich, the fourteenth-century anchoress who in her *Revelations
of Divine Love* repeatedly refers to Jesus as mother, envisions that mother as
suffering with her children, and who finds it almost impossible to justify the
eternal punishment for sins.[29] Instead Julian is overcome with the univer-
salist impression that, despite the magnitude of human sin, "all shall be well
and all manner of things shall be well."[30]

Just as, in an effort to discredit Julian's revelations as heterodox, an early
editor of *Revelations of Divine Love* tried to suggest that Julian's insight
into Jesus as mother was likely little more than the result of her own

experience with a loving mother so it can be argued that Endo's proclivity for the suffering, maternal, and non-judgmental Christ has much to do with his relationship to his own mother.[31] In my view, though, that proclivity likely has as much if not more to do with Endo's affinity for the *kakure* Christians, those Japanese Christians who had disguised their Christian faith throughout the many years of the repression of Christianity in Japan, only to surface again with the opening of Japan to the West. There is evidence to suggest the *kakure* Christians are the most likely candidates for influences that bore fruit in the maternal Christ of *Silence* and for the seeds of a fascinating comparison between Buddhist and Christian religious interpretation. For the *kakure*, Endo tells us in his short story "Mothers,"

> God was a stern paternal figure, and as a child asks its mother to intercede with its father, the *kakure* prayed for the Virgin Mary to intervene on their behalf. Faith in Mary was particularly strong among the *kakure*, and I concluded that their weakness had also prompted them to worship a figure that was a composite of the Holy Mother and Kannon, the Buddhist Goddess of Mercy.[32]

In *Silence* Rodrigues acknowledges his concern that the Japanese Christian peasants sometimes seem to honor the Virgin Mary rather than Christ.[33] And the "composite" of the Virgin Mary and Kannon mentioned above is particularly worthy of note. Kuan-yin, more completely "Kuan-shih-yin" is a translation from Sanskrit of Avalokiteshvara, a figure who perceives or hears the cries of people who suffer from a variety of difficulties. In Japanese Avalokiteshvara is known as "Kannon" or "Kanzeon."

Of perhaps more than passing significance, as Chun-fang Yu documents, is that Kuan-yin, originally male, underwent the most interesting metamorphosis into a female identity in China, where she became a powerful symbol of compassion as the Goddess of Mercy or bodhisattva of compassion.[34] Some have even argued that one of the reasons the *Lotus Sutra* became so popular is because of a close association with Kuan-yin (although Kuan-yin appears in many sutras, the *Lotus Sutra* is the only sutra that includes a significant story about Kuan-yin). Chapter 25 of the *Lotus Sutra* is known as "Kuan-yin's Universal Gate" (a gate in Buddhism is an entrance to the Dharma and a beginning toward awakening). The Bodhisattva Inexhaustible Mind asks, "For what reason does the Bodhisattva Kuan-shih-yin have the name Kuan-shih-yin?" Then Shakyamuni Buddha explains that if anyone who is suffering calls Avalokiteshvara's name with all their heart, they will immediately be heard and will be able to free themselves from suffering.[35] In China in particular many folk stories took shape around Kuan-yin. In one such story Kuan-yin is a Buddhist who through great love and sacrifice during life had earned the right to enter Nirvana after death. However, while standing before the great gates of Paradise she heard a cry of anguish from the earth below. Turning back to earth, she renounced her reward of bliss eternal but in its place found immortality in the hearts of the suffering.

According to Chung-fang Yu, the bodhisattva's increasing feminization in China is the result of indigenous creation and domestication, and one of the main reasons the feminine Kuan-yin appeared may be connected with the anti-feminist stance of the established religions and the overwhelmingly masculine character of those religions of China at the time.[36] Traditions of Kuan-yin made their way from China to Japan and she became known as Kannon, the Buddhist Goddess of Mercy. Interestingly, Endo may be attempting a kind of indigenization and domestication of Jesus for Japan not altogether unlike what had happened to Avalokiteshvara in China.

An acquaintance with Kuan-yin further informs one's reading of *Silence* and may even affect one's study of Christology, if in the crucial apostasy scene in the novel it is possible to find both Christ the maternal suffering savior and a Jesus who, for Endo, has much in common with Kannon. If that is the case, then with the writing of *Silence* Endo has begun to shorten the distance he had formerly sensed between Christianity and himself and in the process discovered a more composite self, one with latent Buddhist, as well as *kakure* Christian Japanese sensibilities. In the next section, I show that the aforementioned distance is finally overcome almost 30 years later in *Deep River*, Endo's final novel, in which the Holy Mother takes central stage.

Suffering Servants

Endo sets *Deep River* in India and for the most significant sections of the novel, at the foot of the Ganges. Though there were presumably numerous reasons for choosing India as the location for this novel, including that it is the birthplace of Buddhism, evidence in the novel suggests theological rationales on Endo's part that connect precisely to the two themes elucidated above: the Christ who suffers as we suffer, and maternal religion. The novel revolves around a group of Japanese tourists, one of whom in particular, Mitsuko, as well as Otsu, a failed seminarian living in India with whom she is obsessed, are of special interest to this study. A cynic, and at times a brutal individual who had earlier in life heartlessly seduced Otsu, Mitsuko both lacks and desperately seeks love. Over the years she and Otsu have maintained a correspondence even though they appear polar opposites in terms of their religious and individual dispositions. She joins the tour to

India once she discovers that Otsu has become a priest and is living and working in Varanasi, the most sacred city of the Ganges.

Before she ever reconnects with Otsu in person, Mitsuko's tour guide introduces her and the other Japanese tourists to the Indian goddesses. Endo's affinity for maternal religion has not diminished in the close to 30 years that separate *Silence* and *Deep River*, though it has taken a significant turn as Endo re-envisions the pure and pristine Holy Mother of the Christian tradition in the same way he had 30 years before re-envisioned the pure and pristine Christ. As Endo has the tour guide suggest:

> The holy mother Mary in Christianity is a symbol of tender maternal love, but the goddesses of India are for the most part called earth-mother goddesses, and while they are gentle deities at times, they are also fearsome beings. There is one goddess in particular, Chamunda, who has taken upon herself all the sufferings of the people of India.[37]

The point of the above remarks, as becomes clear in a series of continuing comparisons throughout the novel, is that the Indian goddesses symbolize all of human existence, the gentle as well as the frightening, including birth as well as death.[38] Whereas one might expect from "goddess" something solely tender, solely maternal, the Indian goddesses give one a window on to the grotesque, including images of Chamunda in which "her breasts droop like those of an old woman," reduced to skin and bones and gasping for breath.[39] The implication is that "she displays all the suffering of the Indian people," that she has "contracted every illness they have suffered through the years."[40] Unlike the Virgin Mary, the suffering goddess of India is not pure and refined, and she wears no fine apparel. Rather she is ugly and worn with age, and she groans under the weight of the suffering she bears.[41] This introduction to the goddesses of India is all important to Mitsuko, for whom Chamunda was utterly different from the "lofty, dignified Holy Mother of Europe."[42] Mitsuko has come to love the India she sees through the river Ganges and the Indian goddesses.[43] Moreover, she feels her heart pierced by the goddess Chamunda in particular, who festers from leprosy, yet nurses children from her drooping breasts, and who groans under the weight of the torments of this life.

For Mitsuko, reflections on Chamunda also bring thoughts of Otsu to mind, and she recalls a biblical text, the fourth of Isaiah's distinctive Servant passages, or Songs (Isa. 53.2–12), which she had once almost miraculously encountered while waiting for him. Pondering Isaiah's "suffering servant," the "image of the goddess Chamunda was superimposed upon that of this man, and the wretched figure of Otsu as she had seen him in Lyon overlapped them both," such that all three blur in dizzying unity.[44]

As with Isaiah's "suffering servant," so with Otsu there is "nothing in his appearance that we should desire him" (Isa. 53.2) and he is "wounded for our transgressions, crushed for our iniquities" (Isa. 53.5) when he is attacked as he attempts to pacify the initiators of violent unrest.[45] Now, the "suffering servant" motif may not have been prevalent in the European face of Christianity to which Endo himself had been exposed in France, but it is in fact deeply biblical, stretching from Isaiah's passage through to the Apostle Paul's kenotic theology (Phil. 2.6–11). Mitsuko's association of the "suffering servant" with Otsu is apt, given that Otsu is a priest who carries figuratively on his shoulders the weight of what it means to suffer with and for others as he ministers to the dead and dying outcastes in Varanasi, India's holy city.[46] Also, Otsu is himself a kind of outcaste from his own tradition, living in a Hindu ashram and wearing Hindu clothing.[47] "Christ himself takes the form of Otsu in this novel. Perhaps I should call it an imitation of Christ, but I have tried to juxtapose the life of Otsu onto that of Christ," Endo explains.[48] *Deep River* clarifies what such Christic imitation entails, when Otsu offers up himself in prayer: "*You carried the cross upon your back and climbed the hill to Golgotha. I now imitate that act. … You carried the sorrows of all men on your back and climbed the hill to Golgotha. I now imitate that act.*"[49] As Otsu empties himself, taking the form of a servant to those whom society has abandoned, Paul's hymn on Jesus's unselfish character, otherwise known as kenotic theology, is borne out (Phil. 2.6–11), even if, at the novel's close, Otsu takes a "sudden turn for the worse," and the reader is left pondering the theological import of Otsu's self-sacrifice.[50]

All things considered, Endo's affinity for the "Christ who suffers as we suffer" has not dissipated in the 30 years that separate *Silence* and *Deep River*, but as is clear in Otsu's characterization, the biblical anchoring of this theology has come to the fore. It would be a mistake, however, to read biblical mooring as Christian retreat from Buddhism and bodhisattva ideals. If anything, in *Deep River* Endo moves both further into and farther beyond both Christianity and Buddhism. Earlier I alluded to three Japanese sensibilities, which according to Endo were the root causes for the failure of Christianity in Japan. They included an aversion for dualistic ways of thinking about good and evil, insensitivity to death, and struggles with monotheism. I think Endo has found the medium, in *Deep River*, through which to cover the distance between Christianity and the Japanese on all three counts, but only by jettisoning religious exclusivity of Christian, Buddhist, or any other kind.

Relatively early in *Deep River* Otsu had proclaimed, "I can't make the clear distinction that these (European) people make between good and evil."[51] India is a country, as unlike Japan as it is unlike Europe, in which purity and defilement, holiness and obscenity, charity and brutality, mingle and coexist. Suffering, illness, and love are intertwined like roots in the goddess Chamunda. Only once he has made suffering as central to the reader's image of Chamunda as it is to the Buddhist dharma does Endo allow another of his characters to exclaim: "I feel that I understand for the first time why Sakyamuni appeared in this land."[52] In the Asian mother, even the dualism between good and evil, or sin, breaks down, just as it does in Buddhism, for which "good and evil are as one."[53]

When in the novel *Silence* the Christ of the *fumie* had invited Rodrigues to apostatize, it was to relieve the suffering of Japanese Christians for the sake of love.[54] In *Deep River*, Otsu speaks of the Ganges as the "river of love," which "flows past, accepting all, rejecting neither the ugliest of men nor the filthiest."[55] In this river "life and death" coexist.[56] Otsu's vocation is centered in love, which in his view had been born in him though his mother's love, itself a portion of divine love, or the "great life force," which is not a being separate from humans, but rather envelops them and all of nature.[57] It is a love that death itself cannot extinguish (Rom. 8.37–9); and as Mitsuko is left to recognize, it is resurrected in the hearts and lives of those who, like Otsu, give rebirth to suffering love in their own lives, just as Kuan-yin found immortality in the hearts of the suffering.[58] Thus, through the Holy Mother Ganges, polluted and sacred at the same time, Endo covers the distance between Christianity and the Japanese insensitivity to death.

Toward the end of *Silence*, Rodrigues became convinced that "my Lord is different from the God that is preached in the churches."[59] Similarly in *Deep River*, Otsu has been "rejected" by his monotheistic Catholic clergy[60] for his pantheism and other heretical beliefs,[61] echoed in claims such as "God has many different faces. I don't think God exists exclusively in the churches and chapels of Europe. I think he is also among the Jews and Buddhists and the Hindus,"[62] and in his fondness for Gandhi's perspective that "there are many different religions, but they are merely various paths leading to the same place."[63] The Holy Mother Ganges is, in the words of Mitsuko, "not just for the Hindus but for everyone."[64] Endo was reading John Hick's *Problems with Religious Pluralism* as he worked on this novel, and Hick's imprint is clear. Just as Endo confessed earlier in his life that, much as he had tried to cast off his Catholic suit he could not do so, so Otsu, despite his burgeoning religious pluralism, finds it impossible to leave the church, because as he admits, "Jesus has me in his grasp."[65]

Mark Williams cautions Endo's interpreters to beware the trap "of reading Endo's texts as theological tracts,"[66] and his caution is laudable. I suspect that like Graham Greene, whom Endo admired and with whom he has been compared, Endo thought of himself as a novelist who happened to be

Catholic rather than as a Catholic novelist.[67] And yet, like Greene's before him, Endo's literary art has the capacity to both unsettle and undergird a reader's theological bearings, thus making hefty and often controversial manna for scholars of religion.

Notes

1   Portions of this chapter first appeared in "Agape and Bodhisattva Ideal in Shusaku Endo's *Silence*," *Dharma World* 33 (2006): 28–34. I am grateful to the editors of this journal for permission to reprint parts of my article.

2   Richard A. Schuchert, "Translator's Preface," in Shusaku Endo, *A Life of Jesus*, trans. Richard A. Schuchert (New York: Paulist Press, 1973), 3.

3   Shusaku Endo, quoted in Philip Yancey, "Japan's Faithful Judas," *Books & Culture* (January/February 1996): 3.

4   Ibid.

5   Shusaku Endo, *Watakushi ni totte Kami to wa* [*What God Means to Me*] (Tokyo: Kobunsha, 1988), 11–12. Unpublished translation courtesy of Professor Paul McGrath, Nagoya Gakuin University, Japan.

6   Ibid., 12.

7   Ibid., 11.

8   Ibid.

9   Shusaku Endo, *White Man/Yellow Man, Two Novellas*, trans. Teruyo Shimizu (New York: Paulist Press, 2014).

10   Shusaku Endo, *Silence*, trans. William Johnston (New York: Taplinger Publishing Company, 1980), 14.

11   Ibid., 56.

12   Ibid., 147.

13   Ibid., 187.

14   Shusaku Endo, "Introduction," in *Foreign Studies*, trans. Mark Williams (London: Peter Owen, 1989), 9.

15   Ibid.

16   Endo, *Watakushi ni totte Kami to wa*, 15.

17   Endo, *Silence*, 22.

18   Ibid., 170.

19   Ibid., 171.

20   Ibid.

21   Ibid., 190.

22   Ibid., 175.

23   Ibid., 191.

24   Ibid., 176.

25   Shusaku Endo, "Anguish of an Alien," *The Japan Christian Quarterly* 40.4 (1974): 181.

26 Ibid.

27 Ibid.

28 Shusaku Endo, "A Preface to the American Edition," in Endo, *A Life of Jesus*, 1.

29 Julian of Norwich, *Revelations of Divine Love* (London: Penguin Books, 1998), 125, 130 (Rev. 52, 54).

30 Ibid., 88, 97 (Rev. 34, 40).

31 Clifton Wolters, "Introduction," in Julian of Norwich, *Revelations of Divine Love* (Baltimore: Penguin Classics, 1966), 38.

32 Shusaku Endo, "Mothers," in *Stained Glass Elegies: Stories by Shusaku Endo*, trans. Van C. Gessel (London: Peter Owen Press, 1984), 129.

33 Endo, *Silence*, 56.

34 Chun-fang Yu, *Kuan-yin: The Chinese Transformation of Avalokitesvara* (New York: Columbia University Press, 2000).

35 See *The Lotus Sutra*, trans. Burton Watson (New York: Columbia University Press, 2003), Chapter 25. I am indebted to Gene Reeves for a commentary on the *Lotus Sutra* he provided me with, as well as for a Dharma talk he gave on Chapter 25 of the *Lotus Sutra* "Kuan-yin's Universal Gate," June 10, 2001.

36 Chun-fang Yu, *Kuan-yin*, 491.

37 Shusaku Endo, *Deep River*, trans. Van C. Gessel, (New York: New Directions, 1994), 31.

38 Traditional or orthodox Catholics do not consider the Virgin Mary a goddess.

39 Endo, *Deep River*, 139.

40 Ibid., 140.

41 Ibid.

42 Ibid., 175.

43 Ibid., 167.

44 Ibid., 175.

45 Ibid., 211.

46 Ibid., 193.

47 Ibid., 163.

48 Shusaku Endo, quoted in Mark Williams, *Endō Shūsaku: A Literature of Reconciliation* (New York: Routledge, 1999), 205; also see *Deep River*, 175.

49 Endo, *Deep River*, 193.

50 Ibid., 216.

51 Ibid., 65.

52 Ibid., 141.

53 Ibid., 200.

54 Endo, *Silence*, 170.

55 Endo, *Deep River*, 185.

56 Ibid., 210.

57 Ibid., 118.

58   Endo, *Deep River,* 215.
59   Endo, *Silence,* 175.
60   Endo, *Deep River,* 163.
61   Ibid.,191.
62   Ibid., 121.
63   Ibid., 191.
64   Ibid., 195.
65   Ibid., 191.
66   Williams, *Endō Shūsaku,* 195.
67   Endo, "A Preface to the American Edition," 1–2.

9

Discerning the Marshland of this World: *Silence* from a Japanese Buddhist Perspective

Dennis Hirota

The lotus does not flourish in the solid earth of lofty plateaus,
but in the muddy ponds of lowland marshes.

Vimalakīrti Sutra[1]

Twenty-five years I've been in Japan. ... I have found a face
different from the one I knew in the past.

Fr. Ferreira, The Golden Country[2]

Japan as Marshland

In the right transept of the Gesù, the Jesuit church in Rome that celebrates the Society's glory, the upheld right hand and forearm of St. Francis Xavier are enshrined in glass, a compelling emblem of the valor and determination with which the seeds of the Christian proclamation were first sown in the alien soil of the Far East. If one seeks in Endō Shūsaku's *Silence* a counter-vailing symbol that manifests the disposition of the newfound terrain, it might be the ordinariness of a children's song of Nagasaki at the time of *Obon*, the late summer festival of lights:

It's a lantern! Yes, it is!
Anyone who throws a stone—the hand will wither away.
It's a lantern! Yes, it is!
Anyone who throws a stone—the hand will wither away.[3]

Obon is the period when the spirits of ancestors descend from the hills to a joyous homecoming in the village for several days. Lanterns are lit in the eaves of houses and carried by children, at times gingerly, to guide the spirits from the gloomy communal burial sites back to the villages. They are lit again in send-off at the time for departure. Although a major Buddhist observance, with services conducted by priests before the home altars where the spirits are presumed to gather, *Obon* harbors traces of a native religiosity, one in which the realm of the dead lies close at hand—in the surrounding hills and mountains—and the world of ordinary experience is an encompassing, unitary realm shared with living beings, the numinous forces of nature, and ancestral *kami*-spirits.

In his works Endō frequently sketches the aural environment of quotidian life as ground bass and counterpoint in scenes of taut personal confrontation with the realities of human existence. Thus, this children's chant occurs three times in *Silence*, framing the scenes of both Fr. Garrpe's drowning and Fr. Rodrigues's apostasy.[4] As the enduring, plaintive backdrop to the passionate agon of each young priest, it manifests a pre-axial or immanental sensibility that continues to underlie life in Japan down to the present, which Fr. Ferreira darkly assesses, "The Japanese to this day have never had the concept of God; and they never will. ... The Japanese do not possess the capacity to think of a God wholly disconnected from the human ... of an existence that transcends the human."[5]

The hand that first planted in Japan what swiftly became a verdant meadow of promising saplings, so that "faith was fragrant like the fresh flowers of the morning,"[6] is venerated in Rome, but *Silence* sets forth an alternative steadfastness, cloaked in Endō's recurrent image of Japan as marshland. Thus, while Rodrigues takes an absolutist stance with regard to religious truth ("If a true doctrine were not true alike in Portugal and Japan we could not call it 'true'"[7]), the magistrate Inoue asserts the primacy of context and substitutes the botanical metaphor: "A tree which flourishes in one kind of soil may wither if the soil is changed."[8] Religious awareness in Japan, it intimates, cannot be divorced from the primordial wellsprings of the life of its people. It is not that Christian teachings can be weighed on some reasoned scale of persuasiveness together with native beliefs. If Christian propagation of "the kingdom of God" is the sowing of a doctrine of sheer transcendence, then Japan is an impervious "swamp" in which such seedlings cannot take hold. Western religion is inevitably defeated, not by suppression, but by the all-transfiguring ambiance of the country itself.

In *Silence*, the metaphor of the swamp is first employed by Ferreira, the accomplished theologian who has become unable to accept either the rift in the understanding of the Japanese, who have bent Christian symbols to their own predilections—"twisted and changed our God"[9]—or the challenge presented by God's "silence" amid the excruciating suffering and fervent prayers of those very Christians. It has, however, also been adopted by Inoue, and perhaps even has its origins with the notorious persecutor. The order of appearance in the novel is significant. For Ferreira, the image of Japan as mudswamp forms part of the argument for apostasy that he makes to Rodrigues; for Inoue, it encapsulates an attempt to come to terms with his own success in defeating the missionaries. In *The Golden Country*, the play produced the same year as the publication of *Silence*, Endō depicts Ferreira's own prior apostasy. There, it is Inoue who remains torn, wounded by the temperament of his countrymen and the power of the "swampland" of Japan to alter the faith of the Christians.

This chapter explores Endō's perception of the "marshland of Japan." It proceeds by seeking to locate his delineation of a Christianity transformed by native sensibilities in the hybrid space between two modalities of religious outlook. On the one hand is Endō's view of Western Christianity, portrayed at the beginning of the novel in the staunch conviction and confidence of the young missionaries who occupy center stage. On the other hand is his perspective on Japanese Buddhist tradition, which was originally, like Christianity, what is commonly termed a "system of thought introduced from outside" (*gairai shisō*). It may be said, however, that Mahayana Buddhism in Japan possessed the fundamental insight and capacity to become acclimated to the local ethos. Through a long process of indigenization, it has absorbed and reconstituted deep-rooted attitudes of the native religiosity. Thus, Western Christianity and Japanese Buddhism are not merely rival doctrinal stances, but embody disparate modes of religious awareness. It is this that enables the kinds of complexity and ambiguity—perhaps aptly characterized by the marshland imagery—that *Silence* harbors. We must begin, however, by considering the background of Endō's interreligious comparison.

Moral Weakness and Salvation

Near the close of *Silence*, Inoue relates to Rodrigues a conversation he has previously had with a Christian priest:

> I once asked a Christian padre like yourself, "How do the compassion of the Buddha and the compassion of the Christian Deus differ? The Buddha's compassion that sentient beings cling to in their own inexorable weakness—this is what is taught as salvation in Japan."
>
> But the padre clearly declared: "The salvation that Christians speak of is different. Christian salvation is not just to rely on Deus, it must be accompanied by the strength of spirit (*kokoro no tsuyosa*) that the believer safeguards to the very limits of his powers (*chikara no kagiri*)."

"In that case, Padre, the Christian teaching has after all gradually been deformed within this mudswamp called Japan."[10]

In *The Golden Country*, where this exchange is related to Ferreira instead, Inoue's account of the answer he received is even more emphatic:

> Once, when I was young, I asked a Christian padre like yourself: In Japan, too, there is the compassion of Amida, just as there is the compassion of the Christian Deus. We sentient beings, in our utter weakness, rely on Amida's compassion. This is what is taught as salvation in Japan.
>
> But then the padre clearly declared: "The compassion of the Christian Deus is different. ... Christian salvation is not merely relying on the compassion of God. A person must struggle to the end, to the very limits of his powers, so that his strength of spirit and the compassion of Deus intermingle as one. This is what Christians speak of as salvation."[11]

In both *Silence* and *The Golden Country*, this dialogue is placed after the priest-interlocutor has already "fallen" or been "turned" about (*korobu*). Thus, Inoue's reminiscence is not presented as part of his strategy to precipitate apostasy. Rather, it harbors candid reflection on the apparent failure of Christian propagation in Japan and what that might imply regarding the temperament of the Japanese. In *Silence*, Inoue concludes the conversation:

> "The Christianity you brought to Japan has changed its form and has become a strange thing," said the Lord of Chikugo as he heaved a sigh from the depths of his bosom. "Japan is that kind of country; it can't be helped. Yes, father ..."
>
> The magistrate's sigh was genuine, and his voice was filled with painful resignation.[12]

Christianity appears to demand of adherents a firm resolve and a "spirit of indomitable courage,"[13] the heroism that is commemorated in the ornate, marbled walls of the Gesu and that Rodrigues desires to attribute to Ferreira at the beginning of *Silence*. In Japan, however, Christianity has been imperceptibly transmuted into something now bizarre and unrecognizable (*etai no shirenu*). The country's penchant for such alteration presents a hopeless (*dō ni mo naranu*) situation for the Western religion. But the samurai Inoue is pained at being compelled to recognize the inability of the Japanese people to assert the personal moral fiber that Christianity seems to cultivate and to demand as the counterpart of divine love. Here we have the crux of the problem Endō perceives in Western Christianity's encounter with Japanese religious reflection. To be sure, exhortation to moral strength may nurture the believer's character, and genuine faith may make one strong. Thus

Kichijiro's question early in the novel harbors a faint echo of Job's: "Why has Deus Sama given us this trial? We have done no wrong."[14] But can divine compassion demand greater courage than one is capable of? In Endō's view, the Japanese inevitably shift the perspective to this intensely personal query and ask: What of the weak? Or as Kichijiro cries out, in a question that would never cross Job's mind, "I was born weak. One who is weak at heart cannot die a martyr. What am I to do?"[15]

Christianity and Shin Buddhism

The question Endō poses concerning two disparate modes of apprehending compassion is not, of course, merely academic. In the semi-autobiographical story "Unzen" (1965), which translator Van C. Gessel calls "a preliminary sketch for the character of Kichijirō,"[16] the writer researching the martyrs tortured on the mountain is himself described:

> He was more than adequately aware of his own spiritual slovenliness and pusillanimity. He was certain that an unspannable gulf separated him from the ancient martyrs of Nagasaki, Edo and Unzen. ... Suguro diligently searched the Christian histories for someone like himself.[17]

It was largely through the imaginative search for a figure who mirrored his own concerns as a Japanese Christian—a Christian with an Asian outlook—that Endō developed the character of Kichijiro. At the same time, he saw that Kichijiro's question has lain at the heart of Japanese Buddhism.

In the dialogue quoted above, Inoue uses the name "Amida" Buddha, the Buddha of "Immeasurable Light and Life," whose vow as a bodhisattva is to bring all sentient beings to awakening by enabling them to attain the realm of his enlightenment, the Pure Land. It is clear from Inoue's reference as well as other Buddhist terminology that the comparison he undertakes is with Japanese Pure Land Buddhism, specifically the prominent Shin Buddhist tradition (Jōdo Shinshū) stemming from the medieval thinker Shinran (1173–1263). This is also confirmed by Endō's explicit references in his essays. Shinran, after being exiled from the capital in a persecution of the Pure Land teaching, spent several decades in propagation among people of the countryside, and he was familiar with the urgent question Kichijiro raises:

> When people first begin to hear of Amida Buddha's Vow of compassion, they wonder, having become thoroughly aware of the karmic evil in their hearts and minds, how they will ever attain birth as they are. To

such people we teach that since we are possessed of blind passions, the Buddha receives us without judging whether our hearts are good or bad.[18]

The early Jesuits themselves quickly discerned a resemblance in salvific structure and narrative between Pure Land Buddhism and Christianity. At the height of its success, the Jesuit missionary effort in Japan was directly supervised by the Superior Allessandro Valignano (1539–1606), Visitor of Missions to the Far East. He is attributed with shifting a formerly rigid policy of European imposition toward an accommodating adaptation of native dress and social manner. He appears early in *Silence* in Macao, where, misunderstanding the circumstances of his priests' apostasy in Japan, he cautions Rodrigues about "the savagery of Inoue ... who is indeed a terror for the Christians."[19]

Historically, Valignano is recognized as an astute observer of Japanese social and cultural practices. While another Jesuit missionary, Fr. Luis Frois, systematically cataloged Japanese customs in terms of European manner and values turned completely upside down, Valignano perceived in Shin Buddhism a distinctly familiar religiosity:

The very same doctrine [as Luther's] has been bestowed by the devil upon the Japanese heathendom. Nothing is changed except the name of the person in whom they believe and trust.[20]

It is as though Satan, through the propagation of self-indulgent protestant attitudes, has gained a head start in the race for the souls of the Japanese. We should note, however, that the subtle difference between Christian and Pure Land attitudes highlighted by Endō in Inoue's dialogue was not overlooked by the nineteenth-century Protestant missionaries. Even while sympathetic to the striking similarities in doctrine and institutional practice with Shin Buddhism, they too perceived a fundamental dissonance with Japanese Pure Land Buddhist religiosity.

One of the most insightful, though polemical, comparative accounts of Shin Buddhism from a Christian perspective is that of theologian Karl Barth in a long note in *Church Dogmatics*. Out of his own theological concerns with the problem of religious truth, Barth actively searched among the religious traditions of the world for one with doctrinal elements similar to those of Christianity. This was not in order to confirm Christian doctrine, but rather to demonstrate that the truth of Christianity could not rest on any merely human determination of religious truth. Nevertheless, he was astonished by the extent and depth of the resemblances found in Shin. Quoting words of Shinran, "Since even the good person is saved, it goes without saying that so is the evil person," he catalogs a number of shared motifs, including "representative satisfaction" and self-awareness of evil.[21] At the same time, he insists on four elemental differences in attitude:

> (1) The starting point of the Pure Land (Jōdo) movement was … the popular wish for an easier and simpler path to salvation; but one could hardly say of Luther or Calvin that they too began from exactly there. Accordingly, (2) among the ideas of Pure Land Buddhism in parallel to those of the Reformation one fails to find any doctrine of a law of Amida, or of his holiness, or his wrath; … as a result his redemption of man lacks drama, lacks the character of a real solution to a real problem. It appears, therefore, (3) that the Pure Land antithesis to cultic and moral works-righteousness also lacks that stress on a struggle for the honour of God against human willfulness and arrogance. … (4) Pure Land religion, along with the rest of Buddhism, thus stands or falls with the inward power and validity of the passionate human desire for a redemption through dissolution, for entry into Nirvana, to which the 'Pure Land', to be reached by faith alone, is only the forecourt. … In Jōdo religion this goal of human desire, and not Amida or faith in him, is the real governing and determining force.[22]

I quote at length here because each of these closely intertwined points of Pure Land Buddhism's difference—roots in the quest for an accessible path, absence of divine wrath, release from the self-contradiction of struggle against willfulness, and the faith-relationship as merely secondary—is also crucial for Endō in articulating the breach between European Christianity and Japanese sensibilities. In indicating a rupture in Japan with conventional Western values and judgments, each point lends itself to characterization by the mudswamp image. They also, however, indicate loci at which Endō discerns the potential for the bridging of Christianity and Japanese perceptions through subtle shifts of religious outlook and attitude. Let us consider them in relation to Endō's depictions of religious awareness in *Silence*.

"Let Us Go to Paraiso Temple … That Distant Temple!"

The notion of a spontaneously realized path to a realm of bliss that Barth mentions is central to Endō's depiction of the unassuming, stoic faith of the Japanese villagers. ("Paradise Temple" [*paraiso-dera*] in their hymn may have called to mind a glorified image of the familiar Buddhist temple [*tera*] in the hills above the village.) Endō identifies the physical characteristics of the peasants ("decaying eye," "stench of fish") to emphasize their station in society and the oppressive conditions of their lives. They first appear to Rodrigues as being like "ignorant beasts," unaware of their fate.[23] His impression, like Barth's of Pure Land Buddhism, is that of a simplistic faith of the uneducated. Inoue, in *The Golden Country*, presents a similar view from the opposite perspective, and reveals how the notion of effortlessness becomes an aspect of Endō's swamp imagery:

> The swamp [of Japan] too has its good qualities. If you will only give yourself over to it, you'll eventually grow accustomed to the comfortable warmth. ... The doctrine of Christ is like a flame. ... It sets a man on fire. But the tepid warmth of Japan will eventually nurture gentle sleep.[24]

Pure Land Buddhism did indeed spread in Japan during the medieval period as a religion of the common people, who for the first time were introduced to a form of Buddhism available to them and not legally restricted as ritual practices for the aristocracy. Thus Shinran advises his followers in the countryside, recalling the words of his teacher:

> Simply achieve your birth, firmly avoiding all scholarly debate. I recall hearing the late Master Hōnen say, "Persons of the Pure Land path attain birth in the Pure Land by becoming their foolish selves." Moreover, I remember him smile and say, as he watched humble people of no intellectual pretensions coming to visit him, "Without doubt their birth is settled."[25]

It should be understood, however, that while the Pure Land tradition has found its model practitioners among the ordinary people rather than the social or religious elites, its purported ease and simplicity are more often than not hard won. Rodrigues's perception of the Christian peasants is, of course, condescending and misguided, and his prejudices are exposed to all in his mistaking the victims' groans from the pit for snoring. While the peasants express a naïve faith in the attainment of a mythic "*paraiso*" in the afterlife, just as they might a mythic Pure Land, that in itself seems insufficient to account for their unobtrusive courage. In "Unzen," the writer in the narrative ponders the strength of the martyrs: "Why had they all been so indomitable?"[26]

Endō's focal interest, however, lies with those transfixed by this question— not with the faithful able to persevere in their resolve, but with the weak who succumbed and apostatized, who, as he states in another story, "had abandoned their religious beliefs because of the fear of death and the infirmities of their flesh."[27] In this, he comes quite near the probing self-awareness that animates the Japanese Pure Land path and that is expressed by Shinran.

When, at the age of 35, Shinran was stripped of his priesthood and exiled from the capital in a persecution of the Pure Land teaching, he adopted the name "Gutoku" ("foolish/stubble-haired"), which he used for the remainder of his life. At the time, *toku* ("stubble-haired") was a derogatory term for a dissolute priest who violated his precepts. Underlying this choice of name, however, is not a sense that the Pure Land path is for the uneducated or incapable, but rather a notion of radical equality rooted in a religious grasp of the nature of human existence itself. Nishida Kitarō explains:

> "Gutoku" not only gives clear expression to Shinran's character, but further is a profession of the Shin teaching and a marker pointing to the fundamental nature of religion itself. Among human beings, some are wise, some foolish; some are virtuous and some not. But however great it may be, human wisdom is human wisdom, human virtue human virtue. ... Yet when a person, once undergoing a complete turnabout, abandons this wisdom and this virtue, he or she can attain new wisdom, take on new virtue, and enter into new life. This is the living marrow of religion.[28]

In Shin tradition, it has been people of the countryside who have been able to "experience deeply what it is to be 'foolish/stubble-haired,'"[29] all attachment to their own abilities and genuine goodness having fallen away in insight into the inherent distortions of one's perceptions and the obduracy of one's self-attachments.

The affirmation of an "easy path" to religious attainment may appear lax and undemanding from the viewpoint of Western Christianity, but for Shinran, it is also, paradoxically, "the most difficult of all things difficult."[30] In Nishida's words, it demands that a person "once let go from the cliff's ledge and come back to life after perishing," so that "only the person who has been able to experience deeply what it is to be 'foolish/stubble-haired' can know genuine wisdom and virtue."[31]

Further, the falling away of attachments to one's own powers—what Nishida expresses as a "letting go"—is concomitant with the arising of a penetrating self-awareness. Shinran manifests such self-reflection in his writings, for example, when he exclaims in his major work, "How grievous it is that I, Gutoku Shinran, am sinking in an immense ocean of desires and attachments and am lost in vast mountains of fame and advantage. ... How ugly it is! How wretched!"[32] Endō appears to have absorbed such strains of Pure Land religiosity, which have become thoroughly ingrained in Japanese society. Thus, *Silence* traces the radical shift in Rodrigues's imitation of Christ, in which he is inexorably moved from youthful ideals of heroism and self-sacrifice to the falling away of an elitist spirituality. It is at that point of existential pain that he is enabled to hear the voice of Christ.

Paternal and Maternal Religion

Barth points out quite accurately that in Shin Buddhism, it is impossible "to find any doctrine of a law of Amida, or of his holiness, or his wrath."[33] A fearful awe is not an emotion practitioners possess when they say Amida Buddha's Name, and an Amida of anger is unimaginable. In his comparisons of Christianity and Shin Buddhism, Endō casts Barth's contrast in terms of gender. He states, for example, quoting the same words of Shinran that Barth does in *Church Dogmatics*:

> "Since even the good person is saved, it goes without saying that the evil person is." These well-known words [of Shinran] mean, simply put, that it is the person full of faults who is dear to Amida. In other words, Amida is not the father who judges and punishes, but a motherly presence that seeks to help the errant child.[34]

In his essays, Endō returns again and again to the notion of the Japanese religious awareness as maternally oriented in nature, more inclined to cherish a mother's loving acceptance of one's weaknesses than to strive to shoulder the stern demands of a moralistic code.

> A strict "paternal religion" that expresses wrath at human weakness, judges and punishes it, is not suited to the Japanese. The Japanese inevitably seek a gentle "maternal religion" that is understanding toward their weakness, that forgives it and on occasion suffers together with them.[35]

Despite the Orientalist overtones, surely the feminine and maternal that Endō finds congenial to the Japanese outlook lie at the heart of the "marshland" or "swamp" imagery that pervades *Silence* as well as other writings. They enable the notion, voiced by Inoue and elaborated by Ferreira, of Christianity's failed transplantation, and of its cause as a failure of human determination among the very populace that has embraced it. For those two, individual purposiveness and resolve are absent in the Japanese, having been stifled by an all-embracing, non-discriminate life-force. Wholesale compassion works to deflate the personal endeavor to transcend.

To begin, it should be noted that the basic contrast Endō indicates can, and indeed in Japan has been, drawn without rigid reference to gender. Although Amida Buddha is normally referred to in masculine terms,

Shinran also states, "Sakyamuni and Amida are our father and our mother, full of love and compassion for us."[36] Further: "When sentient beings think on Amida Buddha just as a child thinks of its mother, they indeed behold the Honored One, who is never distant."[37] Pure Land Buddhists refer to Amida as "*oya-sama*," or "parent," which may be said to be gender-neutral, but in nuance is rather gender-inclusive, "our loving parent." In *Silence*, the early Japanese Christians employ the same term "*oya*" ("Our Parent") for God in the Lord's Prayer, as when the peasant voices are heard from their cell in evening prayer.[38] This is, perhaps, part of Endō's preparation for the adaptation in Rodrigues's own apprehension of Christ, shifting from the majestic object of aspiration to the face exhausted from sharing the weight of human suffering but suffused with loving acceptance. At present, standard translations of the Lord's Prayer employ the common word *chichi*, "father."

Already in 1911, even while employing patriarchal Judeo-Christian allusion, Nishida is able to convey the gender-inclusive conception of *oya-sama*:

> Japanese Pure Land Buddhism (Shin Buddhism) is ... religion that has taken the foolish person and the evil person for its true occasion. Christianity, which developed from Judaism, is likewise an other-power religion centered upon love, but within it the concept of righteousness is still strong and there is a certain disposition to condemn evil. Shin Buddhism, however, differs from this in being religion of absolute love, absolute Other Power. Like the father who welcomes home his prodigal son in the parable, so, however foolish a person, however evil, Amida Buddha welcomes him or her into the Pure Land, saying, "It is for you alone that I have broken my body and ground my bones to dust."[39]

We find here a message remarkably similar to that which Rodrigues ultimately hears, the words that for him break the perplexing silence of the divine.

We see, therefore, that although Endō tends to frame his comparative reflections in terms of gender, this does not necessarily arise directly from native perceptions. Endō's own biography—as treated explicitly in such pieces as his story "Mothers" (1969), published only a few years after *Silence*—may account in important ways for his grasp of the "maternal" nature of Japanese religiosity. In addition, he sought to understand the religiosity of the early Christians in Japan through visiting modern "hidden Christians" (*kakure*), who survived through concealing their religious practices, and appears to have discovered confirmation of his view in a maternal Madonna figure—in native guise—used as an altar image. As Rodrigues states in *Silence*, "The peasants sometimes seem to honor Mary rather than Christ."[40]

Endō's reliance on gender appears to arise in part from his effort to negotiate the impassable rift between Christian imagery of personhood and the more nebulous, fluid apprehension of the real in Japan. Japanese Buddhists have sensed a resonance between the Christian concept of *kenosis*, by which the divine assumes existence in the world in order to take on the suffering of human beings. In its motif of salvific manifestation, it resonates with Buddhist notions of formless reality or inconceivable dharma-body appearing as form accommodated to human apprehension. But as we have seen, Pure Land Buddhism maintains a fluidity that undercuts the gender determinations required by a fully personal conception of the divine. This pervasive, nondiscriminative fluidity also may contribute to Endō's image of Japan as marshland.

The Drama of Religious Life

Barth further asserts that Japanese Pure Land Buddhism "lacks that stress on a struggle for the honour of God" found in Christian tradition. Here he lays forth a central theme found in *Silence*, which relates precisely the antitheses of righteous struggle: Rodrigues's relinquishment of the drama he has imagined as his imitation of Christ, and Kichijiro's obsessive reenactments of betrayal and repentance. As Nishida states in "Gutoku Shinran," the attitude in Japanese Pure Land Buddhism is that, "When concerned with the actualities of the spirit, great and heroic figures and ordinary men and women are one."[41] Religious life in Japan ultimately turns, not on resolutely upholding one's relationship with the divine, but on letting go of all pride in one's own spiritual capacities. It is for this reason that in Endō's Japanese Christian context of a personal bond with the divine, the personhood of divinity takes maternal and not paternal form. Rodrigues's long journey is toward release from the self-attachment that drives his priestly sense of duty and his heroic appropriation of the passion of Christ. It is at that point of relinquishment that Christ's accepting voice and visage are apprehended.

Nishida further comments that, unlike Japanese Pure Land Buddhism, in Christian thinking, "the concept of righteousness is still strong."[42] He attributes this to its Judaic roots. The philosopher and intellectual historian Charles Taylor, however, has pointed out that there was also "a turn in Latin Christendom" toward emphasis on "defining and applying codes of conduct."[43] "The attempt was always to make people over as more perfect practicing Christians, through articulating codes and inculcating disciplines. Until the Christian life became more and more identified with these codes and disciplines."[44] The force of such an emphasis appears salient in the thinking of the Jesuit missionaries in Endō's depiction and intensifies the efficacy of the *fumie* test.

Shinran's treatment of good and evil runs directly counter to such discourse. This is because for him, as for Buddhist tradition more generally, evil is not fundamentally transgression or disobedience. Rather, it signifies any action that does not move one toward the attainment of enlightenment, for then it can only lead to further existence in birth-and-death, compulsively driven by ego-attachments rooted deep in the unconscious. Moreover, in Shinran's view, it is impossible to break one's clinging to a falsely conceived self from within the stance of the self. He therefore characterizes the ineluctable quality of the human condition:

> Human beings are such that, maddened by the passions of greed, we desire to possess; maddened by the passions of anger, we hate that which should not be hated, seeking to go against the law of cause-and-effect; led astray by the passions of ignorance, we do what should not even be thought.[45]

Shinran employs such metaphors as madness, drunkenness, or being poisoned to characterize the life of ignorance, driven by afflicting passions. Nevertheless, as practitioners engage the teaching,

> they reflect on and grow deeply aware of the karmic evil of their actions and of their hearts and minds. ... To such people we teach that because we are beings possessed of afflicting passions, the Buddha receives us *without judging whether our hearts are good or bad.*[46]

We see here that, in place of wrath, divine judgment, and the will to accord with God's will, the Buddha's compassion awakens human beings to the nature of their own conditioned existence. It is in this way that self-awareness of human finitude and incapacity becomes possible, and that persons are enabled to act with that awareness without reifying it as their own courage or resolve. In Shinran's expression, compassion arises in one's existence "naturally" or "spontaneously" (*jinen ni*), unwilled and without calculation. Thus he goes on:

> Formerly you were drunk with the wine of ignorance and had a liking only for the three poisons of greed, anger, and folly, but since you have begun to hear the Buddha's Vow you have gradually awakened from the drunkenness of ignorance, gradually rejected the three poisons.[47]

Thus, to hear the Buddha's message in this way is to undergo a transformation. It is said that thereupon "gentle-heartedness and forbearance arise in one naturally, by the working of the Buddha's compassion."[48] Shinran states that there is "a change in the heart that had been bad and in the deep warmth for friends and fellow-practicers."[49] Even with regard to those who persecute the teaching and prohibit one's saying the Name of Amida (*nembutsu*), "without bearing any ill will toward such persons, you should keep in mind the thought that, saying the nembutsu, you are to help them."[50]

Speaking of the awareness of good and evil in the Buddhist sense arising out of his own hearing of the Buddha's message, Shinran states:

> I know nothing at all of good or evil. For if I could know thoroughly, as Amida Buddha knows, that an act was good, then I would know good. If I could know thoroughly, as the Buddha knows, that an act was evil, then I would know evil. But with a foolish being full of blind passions, in this fleeting world—this burning house—all matters without exception are empty and false, totally without truth and sincerity. The nembutsu alone is true and real.[51]

In place of the human struggle to avoid sin and in all acts accord with the will of God, we see in Shinran the falling away of self-will and the spontaneous enactment of compassionate action. Endō, sensing in Japanese tradition a disruption of the orderly demarcations embedded in the Western Christian perspective, seeks to negotiate a position between the incommensurate modes of awareness. He does this in the character of Kichijiro.

At the beginning of *Silence*, together with Rodrigues, we recoil from the very physical presence of Kichijiro, drunken or seasick, and from his furtive glances and obsequiousness. Later, again like Rodrigues half amused and half disgusted, we see him swagger about the Christian villages. And yet, as the novel progresses, Kichijiro ceaselessly follows Rodrigues and they draw inexorably closer, until they come together as apostates. In the end, as we see in the "Appendix," Kichijiro becomes Rodrigues's attendant. He remains under suspicion, however: "On searching his pocket ..., there was found in the amulet-case he wore hung from his neck an image ... with St. Paul and St. Peter on one side and Xavier and an angel on the other."[52]

For Shinran, the transformative hearing of the Buddha's compassionate working is decisive, occurring once and thereafter deepening in the practitioner. A disciple writes:

> For the person of wholehearted single practice of the nembutsu, change of heart and mind *occurs only once*. ... Even when our thought and deeds are evil, if we thereby turn all the more deeply to the power of the Vow, gentle-heartedness and forbearance will surely arise in us through its spontaneous working.[53]

Shinran employs an alchemical metaphor of transmutation: "We, who are like bits of tile and rubble, are turned into gold," grasped by the light of the Buddha's wisdom-compassion.[54] That is, being illumined as it is to our self-awareness, "all our past, present, and future evil … without being nullified or eradicated, is made into the highest good," that which moves us toward awakening.[55] For Endō, Japanese Buddhism shows that salvation must embrace the weak and not only the strong—those who lapse into evil inseparably from those who would uphold good. But because he understands evil by Christian definition as sin against God, and thus fundamentally as betrayal, the commission must be followed by repentance, atonement, and reestablishment of personal relationship.

The drama of finite, corruptible human life for Endō, therefore, is not lineal but cyclic, and cannot unfold the decisive transformation, while remaining ordinary, that Shinran speaks of as arising in a single "thought-moment" of genuine entrusting. We see in the figure of Kichijiro the recurrence of a terrified betrayal of his faith and his fellow Christians together with a dogged stalking of Rodrigues, unable either to overcome his weakness or to break off his precarious allegiance. In the end, we are brought to see this in Rodrigues himself, pressed ever harder to denounce his religion. It is in this way that Endō stakes out a middle ground between divergent Western Christian and Japanese Buddhist modalities of perception.

The Nature of Human Existence

There is a dimension of thought that underlies the divergences we have considered—between the gendered and formless conceptions of reality, or the absoluteness and situatedness of moral values—involving the understanding of self or mind. Barth asserts that ultimate fulfillment in the Pure Land path, as in all forms of Buddhism, lies in the dissolution of self, not in a relation to Amida or an afterlife in the realm of Amida's enlightenment. Again, Barth's point is both accurate and insightful, as far as it goes. The Pure Land path is not a simple promise of paradise for the illiterate. Thus, notions of the self as ungraspable, as well as the real, are entwined in Endō's marshland metaphor.

We may turn to an essay by the philosopher Nishitani Keiji for a concise statement of the views in question. To begin, there is our conventional, commonsense view of mind:

> Ordinarily we think of ourselves as *having* a mind, or that there is a mind *within* us. When the mind is thought of as the unity of various

faculties ... then the self becomes that which *possesses* these faculties. ...
[T]he self is the vantage point from which all things come to be seen.[56]

Because this understanding of mind identifies it with the self and places it at
the center from which the surrounding world is grasped, Nishitani calls this
the "self's self-centered mode of being."[57] Here, the self stands as the transcendent subject, which views all things as its objects.

Although the self-centered view of the self is the prevalent modern
understanding, Nishitani points out that another conception has also been
widely held historically:

> In contrast to viewing the mind from the vantage point of one's "self,"
> the mind is seen from the vantage point of the "world." ... From this
> viewpoint, that which is seen as the faculties the self "possesses" within
> it, ... can also be seen as something which extends throughout the world
> and has universality. ... From this perspective, ... human beings are
> individuations of the great "mind" extending throughout the world.[58]

This is not a self-centric, but "world-centric" vantage point, the perspective
from the all-pervasive "cosmic mind or life."

There are two points of interest in relation to Endō's work. First, according
to Nishitani, "The two ways of viewing the mind [mind as world-pervasive
and mind as self-centric] have been inseparably preserved throughout
Buddhism."[59] It is not that the views are opposing and mutually exclusive;
rather, both can be maintained simultaneously. This is, in fact, the case with
Shinran, who states:

> Tathagata [reality, nirvana, the uncreated, suchness, etc.] pervades the
> countless worlds; it fills the hearts and minds of the ocean of all beings.
> Thus, plants, trees, and land all attain Buddhahood. Since it is with this
> heart and mind of all sentient beings that they entrust themselves to the
> Vow of [Amida], this entrusting is none other than Buddha-nature.[60]

The mind of the Pure Land practitioner is possessed of false discrimination
and afflicting passions, but at the same time is pervaded by enlightened
wisdom-compassion, which manifests itself as the entrusting of oneself to
Amida's Vow. This is not an individual's resolute faith, but an awareness that
arises from beyond the self.

The second point is that by contrast, Christian influence has underpinned
the modern Western view of the self-centric mind:

> [E]ver since Christianity became dominant, the main axis of thought in
> the West has to this day been the egocentric way. In Christian teaching
> God has personal existence, as expressed by the biblical proclamation, "I

am that I am." ... [B]oth where sin obtains and where love obtains, God and human beings equally are assumed to exist in the mode of self-being expressed, "I am."[61]

According to Nishitani, the understanding of mind in the Christian West has been closely bound to the understanding of the relationship between God and human beings as a personal one between wholly discrete selves.

The contrast between the Christian and the Buddhist views of mind—the first self-centric and the second a fusion of both self- and world-centric perspectives—is noteworthy for our considerations here because qualities of the latter appear to enter into Endō's exploration of an understanding of Christian faith in the milieu of Japan as marshland. The long-suffering resignation of the Christian peasants depicted in *Silence* holds an impenetrability for Endō, and in "Mothers" the narrator notes:

> I can't help feeling that the faithful in those days, rather than deciding individually whether to die for the faith or to apostatize, were instead bowing to the will of the entire community. ... That, I felt, was the fundamental distinction between Japanese Christian martyrdoms and the martyrs in foreign lands.[62]

This emphasis on a "sense of community, based on blood relationships,"[63] is not a merely sociological explanation. The narrator is drawn to modern *kakure* "hidden Christians" by the perception that, "because they are the offspring of apostates ... they live out their lives, consumed by remorse and dark guilt and shame."[64] There are unknowable, unconscious forces that move from beyond the individual awareness and shape us more powerfully than we imagine.

Significantly, aspects of a world-centric view appear in Endō's treatment of a myna bird in the story "A Forty-Year-Old Man" (1964). Suguro, about to undergo a serious operation, confesses to the bird his moral helplessness ("I couldn't help what happened. ... It wasn't a sin. It was just something that happened"[65]) and also his realization of the consequences of past wrong actions: "One ripple has expanded into two, and two ripples have grown into three. Everyone is covering up for everyone else."[66] The bird listens silently, like a priest in confessional. In the end, however, the bird dies during the operation and recovery, as though in place of the patient. Suguro goes to see the cage: "There was a smell to the deserted cage. It was the smell of the bird, of course, but the smell of Suguro's own life was also a part of it."[67] The importance for Endō of this motif of the shared, karmic life of a bird as companion and substitute in death for a sick man is seen in his adoption of it in his last novel, *Deep River*, as well.

It is the insight into the close interwovenness of life and the inter-subjective awareness supported by the world-centric view of mind that enables Endō to explore the questions of human weakness and Christian salvation that he takes up in *Silence*. While the moral weakness of Kichijiro is a personal matter of the man as an individual in the Western view, the question that Endō raises inverts Job's challenge: not, Why do I suffer when I am righteous?, but, Why must I be abandoned because I am weak? The question concerning the role of Judas, the archetypical enactor of betrayal, and why Jesus accepts his sin, is similar. Shinran states:

> When I consider deeply the Vow of Amida, which arose from five kalpas of profound thought, I realize that it was entirely for the sake of myself alone! Then how I am filled with gratitude for the Primal Vow, in which Amida resolved to save me, though I am burdened with such heavy karma.[68]

Near the close of *Silence*, Rodrigues again hears the voice of Christ: "I understand your pain and your suffering. It is for that reason that I am here."[69] It enables him to become free of self-attachments and to share his joy with Kichijiro: "There are neither the strong nor the weak. Can anyone say that the weak do not suffer more than the strong?"[70] Divine compassion does not judge. Further, Christ's words enable an insight close to Shinran's intuition in the passage above that Amida's compassion is finally free of judgment, wholly "for the sake of myself alone." Rodrigues is brought to the realization that "he was not betraying his Lord. He loved him now in a different way from before. *Everything that had taken place until now had been necessary to bring him to this love.*"[71]

Notes

1   *Taishō shinshū Daizōkyō* 14, Takakusu Junjirō et al., eds. (Tokyo: Taishō Issaikyō Kankōkai, 1924–34), 549b.

2   Shusaku Endo, *The Golden Country*, trans. Francis Mathy (North Clarendon, VT: Tuttle Publishing, 2003), 125.

3   My translation, Endō Shūsaku, *Chinmoku* (Tokyo: Shinchōsha bunko, 2003), 201. See also Shusaku Endo, *Silence*, trans. William Johnston (Tokyo: Sophia University & Charles E. Tuttle, 1969), 208, 218, 272.

4   This song is similarly employed in *The Golden Country*, where it frames the apostasy of Ferreira. See the opening stage directions and Inoue's reference (Endō Shūsaku, *Bara no yakata, Ōgon no kuni* [*House amid roses; The golden country*], Tokyo: Shinchōsha, 1969), 17, and also the stage directions

for Act III, scene 4, immediately following the apostasy in the play but set a year later (197), where the words of the song are indicated.

5   Endō, *Chinmoku*, 236; Endo, *Silence*, 241; translation modified.

6   Endō, *Chinmoku*, 237.

7   Ibid., 179.

8   Ibid.

9   Ibid., 239.

10 Ibid., 288–9, translation mine; see also Endo, *Silence*, 293.

11 Endo, *Golden Country*, 126; Endō; Ōgon no kuni, 207; translation modified.

12 Endo, *Silence*, 294.

13 Ibid., 19.

14 Ibid., 95.

15 Ibid., 259.

16 Shusaku Endo, *Stained Glass Elegies*, trans. Van C. Gessel (New York: New Directions, 1984), 7.

17 Ibid., 98.

18 Dennis Hirota et al., trans. and ed., *The Collected Works of Shinran* I (Kyoto: Honpa Hongwanji, 1997), 553.

19 Ibid., 35.

20 Allessandro Valignano, *Historia del Principio y Progresso de la Compania de Jesus en las Indias Orientales (1542–64)*, translated in George Elison, *Deus Destroyed* (Cambridge, MA: Harvard University Press, 1973), 43.

21 Shinran's statement is from a record of his spoken words, *Tannishō*. Regarding Barth's comparison, see my comments in Dennis Hirota, ed., *Towards a Contemporary Understanding of Pure Land Buddhism* (Albany: State University of New York Press, 2000), 35–7.

22 Karl Barth, in Garrett Green, trans., *On Religion: The Revelation of God as the Sublimation of Religion* (London: T&T Clark, 2006), 104. See also *Church Dogmatics* 1, 2 (Edinburgh, T&T Clark, 1961), 342.

23 Endo, *Silence*, 135.

24 Endo, *The Golden Country*, 127.

25 *The Collected Works of Shinran* I, 531.

26 Endo, *Stained Glass Elegies*, 98.

27 Ibid., 127.

28 See my article, "Nishida's 'Gutoku Shinran,'" *The Eastern Buddhist* 28.2 (Autumn 1995): 242.

29 Ibid., 243.

30 *The Collected Works of Shinran* I, 70.

31 Ibid., 243.

32 Ibid., 125.

33 Barth, *On Religion*, 104.

34 Endō Shūsaku, "Iesu ni atta onna-tachi" (The Women Who Encountered Jesus), in Yamaori Tetsuo, ed., *Kami to watakushi: jinsei no shinjitsu o*

motomete [God and myself: In search of the truth of human life] (Tokyo: Asahi Shinbun Shuppan, 2000), 226.

35 Ibid., 227.
36 *The Collected Works of Shinran* I, 380.
37 Ibid., 357.
38 Endo, *Silence,* 171; Endō, *Chinmoku,* 163.
39 "Nishida's 'Gutoku Shinran,'" 243–4.
40 Endo, *Silence,* 98.
41 "Nishida's 'Gutoku Shinran,'" 243.
42 Ibid., 243–4.
43 "The Perils of Moralism," in Charles Taylor, *Dilemmas and Connections: Selected Essays* (Cambridge, MA: Harvard University Press, 2011), 347.
44 Ibid., 351.
45 *The Collected Works of Shinran* I, 550.
46 Ibid., 553; translation modified.
47 Ibid.
48 *Tannishō* §16. See *The Collected Works of Shinran* I, 676.
49 Ibid., 551.
50 Ibid., 563–4.
51 *Tannishō,* "Postscript," Ibid., 679.
52 Endo, *Silence,* 301.
53 *Tannishō* §16, *The Collected Works of Shinran* I, 675–6.
54 *The Collected Works of Shinran* I, 459–60.
55 Ibid., 453.
56 Nishitani Keiji, "The Standpoint of Zen," trans. John C. Maraldo, *The Eastern Buddhist,* new series 17:1 (1984): 13.
57 Ibid., 13.
58 Ibid., 13–14.
59 Ibid., 16.
60 *The Collected Works of Shinran* I, 461.
61 Nishitani, "Standpoint of Zen," 15, translation modified.
62 Endo, *Stained Glass Elegies,* 115–16.
63 Ibid., 115.
64 Ibid., 126.
65 Ibid., 23.
66 Ibid., 23.
67 Ibid., 27.
68 *Tannishō,* "Postscript," *The Collected Works of Shinran* I, 679.
69 Endo, *Silence,* 297.
70 Ibid., 297–8.
71 Ibid., 298.

10

A Buddhist Reading of the Blue Eyes of Jesus in *Silence*

Mark W. Dennis

"In my opinion one of the finest novels of our time."[1]

Graham Greene

This chapter interprets Shusaku Endo's novel *Silence* through the lens of Buddhist thought, focusing first on the story and then on the text, the story's "vehicle." Both sections draw from an observation made by my co-editor Darren J. N. Middleton whose chapter in this volume compares the fiction of Shusaku Endo and Graham Greene. In describing his own efforts to understand their work, Middleton borrows the image of the pilot fish from the literary critic George Steiner, who states that the function of the critic is to act like the "pilot fish, those strange tiny creatures, which go out in front of the real thing, the great shark or the great whale, warning, saying to the people, 'It's coming.'"[2] But Middleton wonders what precisely is the "real thing" in Greene's or Endo's work, asking "What signifies the 'it' that is 'coming'?"[3] Uncertain about the referents of these terms, he concludes that the fiction of both novelists "opens out to many readings and diverse meanings—to those who construe it humanistically, as locating the enormous within the everyday, and to those, like me, who read it theologically, as gesturing toward Transcendence. No, I am not sure of the 'real thing' in Endo's and Greene's work. But I suspect that reading defies stasis."[4]

Indeed, Endo's work, especially *Silence*, has been a natural subject for theological interpretation since the story of the novel's protagonist, Fr. Sebastian Rodrigues, raises compelling questions about transcendence and other Christian teachings on faith and suffering, apostasy and martyrdom. Rodrigues travels to Japan to search for his mentor and minister to the nascent Japanese Christian community during an era of brutal repression of the faith. He arrives in the Japanese islands with the expectation of a glorious martyrdom and a faith firmed by an imagined Christ, whose beautiful face and blue eyes appear repeatedly in his mind's eye, serving not only as the fount and guarantor of meaning and action, but also as a symbol of the oppositions that inform his view of the "Oriental other." For example, the beautiful blue-eyed face of Christ imagined by Rodrigues contrasts starkly with the yellow "Japanese" eyes of Kichijiro, an ugly Judas-like figure who ultimately betrays the priest.

But in his direct encounter with the embodied and suffering Kichijiro, Rodrigues comes to see this miserable man not simply as an instrumentality for attaining glory and a singular salvation, but also comes to see his suffering, and the intense suffering of the *kakure*, as the very fount of meaning and activity. Indeed, this face-to-face encounter with the "other" forces Rodrigues to question the nature of this faith, redefine his understanding of martyrdom, and reimagine the face of Christ. This transformation offers a point of departure for engaging in the first half of this chapter in one possible "Buddhistic" reading of the story as it brings up the Buddhist teaching on suffering: that is, desire—whether for wealth, fame, or a glorious martyrdom—leads inevitably to suffering, and the path of the bodhisattva to freedom lies not in turning away from the humanity in the face of the other, but in transcending these base desires.

But Middleton's comments about the "real thing" (hereafter, *real thing*) raise other questions about Endo's text of the sort commonly taken up by Buddhist thinkers. Nāgasena, for example, would share Middleton's uncertainty about this phrase since it suggests the existence of some singular and stable thing. Indeed, Nāgasena engages in a well-known dialogue with King Milinda about such *real things* in which he uses the king's chariot—one sort of vehicle—to illustrate the Buddhist teachings of emptiness and interdependence. That is, because any thing—whether a chariot, a person, or a text—lacks an unchanging foundation or identity, it exists only in dependence on other things. To initiate their investigation of Milinda's chariot, Nāgasena declares: "This chariot is a mere sound. But what is the real chariot?"[5]

In the second part of this chapter, we will frame our inquiry into Endo's text—the story's "vehicle"—by recasting Nāgasena's statement to read, "*Silence* is a mere sound. But what is the *real Silence*?" Drawing on Nāgasena's model, we will consider the relationships and functions of the text's parts: how they depend on each other and other things, and how they can influence a reader's perception of the text's meaning and value. This Buddhistic approach to the study of things, which resonates with post-structuralist thought, focuses on change and interdependence over stasis and singularity, and highlights the ambiguity of language, whether we use it to represent a wooden chariot to convey a king or a wooden cross to crucify a messiah, whether it appears in a story about a seventeenth-century Jesuit priest who imagines the face of that messiah to be beautiful and blue-eyed.

Part I: Endo's Story

The Buddhist Path to Freedom from Suffering

To address the first set of questions about Endo's story, we begin with key elements of the Buddha's life and teaching. We consider first his decision, as Prince Siddhārtha, to abandon his wife and newborn son Rāhula ("The Fetter"), and set out on a spiritual quest, seeking to understand the human suffering he had seen outside his cloistered palace walls. Indeed, that quest was precipitated by these so-called "passing sights": the faces of suffering associated with sickness, old age, and death. These sights destabilized the prince's worldview and led him to engage in extreme ascetic practices that he ultimately abandoned. He then sat beneath a banyan tree—the *bodhi*, or "wisdom," tree—determined to attain freedom from suffering. During his meditation he withstood the assaults of Māra, or "Death," who represents the range of negative human emotions, including the "three poisons" of greed, hatred, and delusion. But Siddhārtha remained steadfast in his meditative absorption, finally realizing the truth, or "dharma," about human suffering. In so doing he had become the Buddha, the "Awakened One."

The dharma he discovered included four truths that explain the causes of suffering and put forth a path leading to its extinction. These truths—the four noble truths—assert that human existence is inevitably filled with *duḥkha*, which points not only to suffering but also to other unpleasant physical and emotional states, such as unsatisfactoriness, difficulty, anguish, and discomfort. In turn, *duḥkha* is caused by *trishna* (*tṛṣṇā*), literally "thirst," but translated variously as desire, clinging, and attachment. But *trishna* points, more accurately, to human craving—craving for all sorts of tangible and intangible things. Each of these things—whether seen to be real or fake, beautiful or ugly—lacks a substantial, unchanging core, and so is described as *śūnyatā*—that is, "empty" of inherent existence. Thus, despite our attempts to cling to people, stuff, or ideas, none can offer any sort of permanent satisfaction since each, having come into existence, must eventually, and inevitably, disappear.

This lack of a substantial, unchanging core also holds true for the perceived self, which Buddhists see as the mental projection of a fictitious unity that masks our selflessness (*anātman*) and interdependence. Indeed, these three qualities—suffering, impermanence, and selflessness—are known as the "three marks of existence." Even so, we assiduously pursue the pleasurable while avoiding the painful, thoughtlessly becoming consumed with all manner of craving. Many sorts of craving are obvious in their appearance and effects: the relentless pursuit of power, wealth, or fame; the desire for physical pleasure and beauty; or an unquenchable thirst for things that intoxicate the mind, whether alcohol or absolute truth claims. But Buddhist literature makes clear how such craving, whether obvious or subtle, distorts our thinking and behavior by reinforcing the false sense of an enduring and independent self, which obscures our interdependence and can blind us to the suffering of others.

For example, India's Prince Ajātaśatru, consumed by the lust for power, jailed—and, in some versions of the story, murdered—his father, King Bimbisāra, to usurp the throne, while Angulimāla is notorious in these sources as a serial killer who wore the severed fingers of his victims around his neck, but turned to the path of non-violence when the Buddha made him understand the suffering he had caused. The destructiveness of *trishna* is also depicted in Hermann Hesse's novel *Siddhartha,* a creative retelling of the Buddha's story in which each character represents some form of human craving and endures its attendant suffering: one craves wealth, another beauty and sensual pleasure, and yet a third craves a definitive teaching of an absolute truth.

Whether one craves power like Ajātaśatru, or has become intoxicated by substances or ideologies, as is true for the two central characters of *Silence,* suffering inevitably follows. To attain freedom from such suffering, we must reduce our cravings and reverse the tendency to put the self first while increasing our compassion for others. The model for this process of self-emptying and compassion appears in the *Jātaka Tales,* parables about the Buddha's previous lives. These didactic tales recount his lives as a bodhisattva, a "wisdom being," who progressed on the path toward enlightenment by selflessly putting the suffering of others first, whether by sacrificing his body to feed a hungry tigress and her cubs, or by giving away the things he valued most. Indeed, the *Vessantara Jātaka* recounts how the bodhisattva, having accumulated good karma over many lifetimes, was reborn as Prince Vessantara, who accrued great merit by giving away such precious things, such as his auspicious rain-making elephant to another kingdom suffering from drought, his son and daughter to a greedy Brahmin priest—even his wife Maddi. After Vessantara died, the bodhisattva took his final birth as Siddhārtha, the one who would free himself from suffering by abandoning even the most subtle cravings of the self.

Over time, the *Lotus-sūtra* and other texts put forth the bodhisattva as the ideal of the self-proclaimed Mahāyāna, or "Great Vehicle," traditions found mainly to the north and east of the Buddha's original dispensation. Vowing to postpone final liberation until all sentient beings have attained *nirvana* (*nirvāṇa*), the state free from suffering, the bodhisattva emulates the Buddha's renunciation of the self and compassionate decision to return to the world to teach others the path to freedom. To this end, the bodhisattva follows a set of ethical precepts, or "perfections," which promote selfless, compassionate behavior, such as *dāna*, or "giving," as seen in Vessantara's generosity. The bodhisattva also avoids selfish behavior and toxic substances, vowing to refrain from clouding the mind with alcohol or uncompromising ideologies, never thinking that any single form of knowledge—even the Buddha's teachings—represents changeless, absolute truth, and seeks it instead in the suffering face of the other. Indeed, the ubiquity of suffering— the first of the four noble truths—becomes the fount of meaning and activity for the bodhisattva, who vows to act with the benefit of others always in mind, not only avoiding actions that create *duḥkha* but also never turning away from it. This behavior emulates the example of the Buddha, who had faced the suffering of others in whatever form it appeared—whether in the pitiable face of Kisa Gotami, a young mother overcome with grief at the death of her child, or in the suffering wrought by violent behavior like that of the serial killer Angulimāla.

Suffering in *Silence*

In a similar way, Fr. Rodrigues, the protagonist of *Silence*, confronts varied faces of suffering that serve for him as "passing sights" and which lead him to reimagine the meaning of martyrdom and the authentic teachings of Jesus. Indeed, craving, violence, and intense suffering fill Endo's story. As the novel begins, Rodrigues sets out for Japan from his cloistered Portuguese seminary—a comfortable world of accepted ideas and public favor. Clear in intention and resolute in faith, his sense of good and evil is crisp and neat like the well-trimmed beard he remembers of his mentor, Fr. Christovao Ferreira. He sails east to search for Ferreira, whose letters about the Jesuit mission's success in Japan had abruptly stopped, and to minister to the *kakure*, the hidden Christian community. Arriving on the Japanese islands with the help of the duplicitous Kichijiro, the priest immediately confronts callousness and violence, witnessing the torture and martyrdom of the simple and fearless *kakure*, who, possessing an unshakable faith, refuse to apostatize by treading on the *fumie*. These Christians suffered greatly at the hands of the brutal military leader Inoue, who devised techniques of torture to expurgate the foreign faith from the hearts of the converts. Their suffering serves then as one of the "passing sights" for Fr. Rodrigues.

Angered by the silence of God in the face of this wanton suffering, the priest buoys his spirits by clinging tightly to the face of Christ—at first a beautiful, blue-eyed face made all the more striking by the colorless and drab terrain and by a group of hostile and faceless Buddhist priests. Christ's beauty also contrasts starkly with the ugly face and yellow "Japanese" eyes of Kichijiro, a richly despicable character who guides the priest from Macao to the Japanese islands and plays the role, well-known in the Christian story, of the betrayer. But his character can also be interpreted through the lens of the Buddhist teachings on craving and suffering. Lying repeatedly and drinking heavily, his thirst for alcohol is matched only by his desperate craving for self-preservation, blinding him to the suffering of others, even his own family's. Our revulsion at this miserable, cowardly man mounts as we read of his selfishness displayed in acts small and significant: he defecates in a hut built for travelers but also defiles the sacred bonds of family. Displaying none of the priest's religious conviction, Kichijiro vacillates and hides his Christian faith, saving himself by trampling more than once upon Christ's face to signal his apostasy. But he then watches from a distance as his family are martyred for refusing to do the same. Although Kichijiro boasts to the *kakure* villagers that it was he who had guided the priest to them, he quickly turns and betrays Rodrigues for a few silver pieces. And yet this miserable man appears before the priest again and again, even after this betrayal, begging for forgiveness and absolution while bemoaning his own weakness in the face of danger.

As an ugly, Judas-like figure, Kichijiro represents the antithesis of the beautiful face and blue eyes of Jesus the priest imagines—an image of the messiah filtered through the lens of the priest's Portuguese self. Kichijiro's weakness and opportunistic faith contrast, moreover, with the clarity and resolution of the priest, who arrives on the Japanese islands with the missionary's religious zeal and ideological certainty. Rodrigues carries with him the desire for a glorious martyrdom, a subtle sort of clinging to the self that privileges the salvation of his own soul—an exaltation of self that is precisely the opposite of the bodhisattva's path to freedom from suffering. The priest, intoxicated with the *holy spirit*, holds fast to a set of clear-cut truths and binaries that motivate his actions and color his perception of Kichijiro; indeed, Rodrigues dismisses his alterity, viewing Kichijiro as the "other"—an inversion of the qualities of his idealized Christ who is beautiful, white, and blue-eyed. In contrast, Kichijiro is described by the priest as having crafty "Japanese" eyes—yellow and drunken eyes that appeared dark and dead. And yet, as the priest reflects on the effects of his missionary work, he comes to recognize in the face of Kichijiro a powerful form of suffering, which thus serves as another "passing sight" that forces Rodrigues to reimagine the authentic teachings of Jesus.

Just as Fr. Rodrigues condemns Kichijiro's cowardice and weakness, so too he judges the apparent weakness of his mentor whom he finally meets in prison. Ferreira reveals that the rumors were true—he had trampled upon the face of Christ. His act was motivated not by weakness or cowardice, he tells his student; rather, it was done out of compassion, meant to alleviate the suffering of the *kakure* who were being tortured. By waving his hand to signal his apostasy, their physical suffering had ceased and their precious Christian lives had been spared. His decision was thus a selfless act of true faith that, while condemned by Church officials, expressed the authentic teachings of that man who had suffered greatly for all of humanity. Although immediately critical of his mentor, Rodrigues soon faces the same dilemma. And in his direct encounter with the incredible suffering of the *kakure*, he looks to the still silent image of Christ thrust before his feet, and sees a dirty and stained image, not the beautiful, blue-eyed face of Christ he had imagined again and again in his mind's eye. It is this suffering and exhausted face that implores him to trample on the very thing the priest had held sacred and holy.[6] We read that the priest places his foot down, dawn breaks, and in the distance the cock crows.

Jeff Keuss, one of this volume's contributors, writes, "The image of Jesus that had appeared to Father Rodrigues numerous times is that of a transcendent, static heroic Jesus. Gradually, though, as Rodrigues's resolve to maintain this image of Christ as true faith [fails], causing the death of many Japanese as a result—the face of Jesus begins to change into one marked by human suffering."[7] He adds, "From that point on, the novel uses words like suffering, uneasy, exhausted, and ugly to describe the face of Jesus," descriptions that highlight the centrality of suffering to Endo's story and echo the range of *duḥkha's* meanings described above.[8]

In this way, the face of Christ takes on those very features that Rodrigues had used to describe the face of Kichijiro, thereby dissolving the binary between self and other, between the idealized and the embodied. That face serves then as another "passing sight" for the priest, who comes to see the suffering in all these faces—the *kakure*, Kichijiro, and Jesus—as the authentic fount of meaning and action. In confronting these varied faces of *duḥkha*, Rodrigues must resolve the tension between clinging tightly to the sweet and intoxicating ideology of an absolute truth and dealing compassionately with the immediacy of suffering which that truth seems utterly incapable of alleviating. This collision of abstraction and embodiment occurs not in the comfort of the seminary, but in an unfamiliar place where actual human flesh and bone, not homilies and abstractions, were being torn apart. Indeed, as the face of Christ takes on the features of the ugly and loathsome Kichijiro, Rodrigues must confront what William Cavanaugh describes as the "paradox of the cross": to love the poor and dispossessed, even the despicable and evil.[9] By witnessing the suffering in the face of the beautiful and transcendent made ugly and low, moreover, Rodrigues reimagines the meaning of martyrdom itself. Cavanaugh argues,

> In effect, *Silence* asks if there is only one kind of martyrdom. Could one sacrifice not only one's body, but one's very moral integrity for the sake of others? ... But Endo suggests that a deeper martyrdom may await Rodrigues—the death of his very self as a Christian and as a moral person. This suggests that the standard concept of heroic virtue is radically effaced by the logic of God's kenosis, by God's self-emptying to take the form of a slave, as Paul puts it in Philippians. In *Silence*, Endo provocatively pushes basic Christian logic, already paradoxical, to a more extreme conclusion. If it is true, as many Christian martyrs have affirmed, that for the Christian, the body is as nothing when compared to the eternity of the soul, then is the crucifixion of the soul a martyrdom which makes other martyrdoms pale in comparison?[10]

These descriptions—"the death of his very self," "kenosis," and "self-emptying"—resonate with the Buddhist teaching of selflessness and bring into relief the distinct motivations of Kichijiro and the priest. That is, while Kichijiro apostatizes to save himself and causes others to suffer, the priest does so to end their suffering, regardless of the personal cost. By performing such a selfless act, Rodrigues, like Vessantara, offers of himself that which is most precious—what he believes to be the salvation of his eternal soul. He thereby shifts the locus of activity from a self-seeking martyrdom to this utter abandonment of self. As we have seen in the *Jātaka Tales*, ultimate freedom comes, paradoxically, in precisely this radical effacing of the self and privileging the suffering of the "other."

If told in a Buddhist land more than a millennium earlier and many miles to the west, such a story of self-denial might appear in the pages of the *avadāna* ("noble deeds") literature, Buddhist parables about the meritorious acts of Buddhist sages. These texts offer, to borrow Thomas J. J. Altizer's phrase, the "parabolic enactment" of the Buddha's "perfections" recounted in the *Jātaka Tales*, which illuminate the tradition's teachings of selflessness and compassion. By trampling upon the suffering face of Christ, the priest gives up the intoxication of a fixed ideology and reimagines the face of Jesus and his authentic teachings—what Altizer calls his "contemporary and apocalyptic presence."[11] In describing the changing face of Christ, Jeff Keuss refers to Altizer's statement that entering

> this parabolic enactment through the medium of literature is to reverse every image of Jesus we have known if we are to be open to his

contemporary and apocalyptic presence. Just such a reversal has continually occurred in the Christian imagination, a reversal not only of
given images of Jesus, but also, and even thereby, a reversal of all given
Christian images of God.[12]

Such a reversal of received tradition is described in Buddhism as "going
against the stream," which suggests the need to remain vigilant in keeping
the Dharma vital and relevant, but also to reverse our common way of
viewing ourselves and those things we construe as other. That is, we are to
shift our angle of critical vision so we see the things of the world not as fixed
structures and stable identities, but as dynamic and interdependent relationships and networks of meaning, whether we imagine the face of Christ or
the cross used to crucify him, whether we analyze the chariot of an ancient
Indian king or the text of a modern Japanese novelist.

Part II: Text as "Vehicle"

A Buddhist view of *"Real Things"*

The impulse to question static structures and singular interpretations
informs Middleton's comments above about the *real thing*. Those comments
highlight the interpretive variation we find across readers of a text like
Silence, or the collected works of a single author, whether Endo, Greene,
or Nikos Kazantzakis. As suggested above, moreover, we can use the interpretive techniques of Buddhism to identify other sorts of variation in *Silence*
that complicate any efforts to discover the *real thing* and that highlight the
dynamic interdependence of text, author, and reader.

We begin with the *Questions of King Milinda*, a text that records a conversation about the Buddha's teachings between the Buddhist monk Nāgasena
(no dates) and King Milinda (d. 130 BCE). During their wide-ranging
conversation, Nāgasena asks the king about the chariot that had brought
him to their meeting. The monk wonders if they can find the chariot in its
various parts, asserting, "Just a mere sound is this 'chariot'. But what is the
real chariot?"[13] After an extended dialogue, the king realizes that it is only
"in dependence on the pole, the axle, the wheels, the framework, the flag-
staff, etc., there takes place this denomination 'chariot', this designation, this
conceptual term, a current appellation and a mere name."[14]

In this way, Nāgasena had taught the king how inanimate things like
a chariot lack an unchanging and essential core, which precludes their
discovery of the "real chariot." Even so, Nāgasena would argue not that

the material object conventionally designated "chariot" cannot physically transport the king, but that our understanding of his chariot, or any other apparently singular and selfsame thing, shifts when we observe that it is an aggregation of parts that depends on other things. Indeed, Nāgasena's simple query of the king represents the sort of question commonly raised in Buddhist epistemology that we can apply to a chariot, a person, or a text. In the case of an inanimate thing, this deconstructive approach calls for us to investigate its constituent parts: how those parts relate to each other and to other things, and how each functions for that thing's range of potential uses and users. This approach also requires us to consider that thing's alternative ways of appearing in the world, its "modes of existence," and, in turn, each mode's constituent parts and potential range of uses and users. In this way, our perception of that thing—for instance, the parts needed to perform a particular function, its quality and utility, or its meaning and value—will vary depending on the mode in which we engage it and the purpose for which we use it.

For example, if we conceive the central function of the chariot to be simple physical transport, then the axles and wheels are crucial but the flag-staff is not; thus, when viewed through the lens of its most basic "transport-function," a chariot without a flag-staff would still be seen as a chariot. Indeed, the flag-staff is likely an addition, serving as the receptacle for a flag used as a decoration in a procession or as a signal to allies and enemies in battle. But even if King Milinda used the chariot for this common function, he could do so in different ways depending on whether he travels into battle, to his audience with Nāgasena, or along the boulevard in a royal procession to celebrate victory with his wife and grandson. In each case, the king may ride in the chariot wearing different clothing and be accompanied by different people; he may also travel at different speeds for different periods of time. His chariot may be altered for each occasion by adding or subtracting armor, cushions, or a flag. But his grandson, young and mischievous, may understand "riding" quite differently from his stodgy grandfather, refusing to sit quietly in his seat with his feet on the floor and back straight as his grandfather implores him. He may ride instead on the chariot's roof or hold on to the back of the chariot so he is pulled along through a muddy area. Despite this range of potential appearances and methods of riding, we connect each to the thing we designate "chariot."

But the chariot could be used in other ways not limited to physical transport, however conceived. It could be used for the storage of grain or wine, as a barrier to block the road, or a fort for his grandchildren's play. Its parts might be disassembled and used to create other things. After a battle or an accident the chariot could be broken apart and its metal used to fashion a sword or to construct a *stūpa*, while its wood could be used for kindling or to make the paper used to record the king's conversation with a Buddhist monk. But even if the material object was dismantled, that chariot can also remain in the world as an image, idea, and a spoken or written word: it could be reproduced in a painting, remembered in the Buddhist canon, or used as an example in a twenty-first-century chapter about a Japanese novel. Although none of these modes of existence is capable of physical transport, we naturally associate each with the word "chariot" and each is capable of producing particular sorts of actions and effects. Whether appearing in a material or abstract mode, moreover, the chariot also exists in dependence on other things: builders and buyers; the battlefield, art market, and publishing industry; and the properties of metal, cloth, and wood.

Endo's Text as "Vehicle"

Nāgasena's analysis of Milinda's chariot offers us a useful model for investigating Endo's text, the story's "vehicle." An obvious function of the text is to transmit that story, which was the subject of the previous section. Endo's text, appearing in the material form of a book, depends on its parts, which include words, images, and that material form, but also other external things—booksellers and readers, literary prizes and scholarly reviews, and the price of ink and paper. When viewed through the lens of the "story-function," Endo's words—his descriptions of the characters and their actions, the states of silence and suffering, and the changing face of Jesus, for instance—are crucial, while other parts, such as the cover, copyright information, introduction, and publicity blurbs, serve as supplements like the flag-staff of Milinda's chariot.

But Endo's text exists not only as a book written in Japanese; rather, it has also been translated into English, and thus can be read in two languages, each with unique grammar, syntax, and systems of representation. Unlike the essential parts of Milinda's chariot, however, the words of the text—whether appearing in Japanese or English—can be removed and used in other texts, like this one, without damaging the "original"; similarly, those words can be reproduced or recast in Steven Dietz's play and Martin Scorsese's film—two other modes of existence for Endo's text. Each of these alternative English-language modes is titled "*Silence*" and each has a particular interdependent—temporal, semantic, and productive—relationship to Endo's Japanese text but also has its own parts and range of uses, users, and potential effects. If we return to the vehicle metaphor, we could then say that the English translation represents the same "vehicle"—a written text presented in the form of a book—which is intended for a distinct linguistic audience, while its adaptation for stage and screen represents and transmits the text through different "vehicles," each with its own ways of producing meaning, barriers to entry (linguistic, educational, monetary), and so on, which are still capable, however, of performing the story-function.

"Reading" *Silence*

If we consider first William Johnston's English translation, we can imagine various types of readers, readings, and uses; for example, while Middleton and I have read the novel multiple times, most of our students will do so only once. My first reading of the novel was for an East Asian history course I taught at Gustavus Adolphus College, a liberal arts college in southern Minnesota, in which the novel served mainly to facilitate discussion of the effects of Christian missionary activity on local converts, focusing on the Shimabara Rebellion. But at Texas Christian University, where I currently teach, I have used *Silence* in a World Religions course that focuses on the climactic scene, asking students to use Slavoj Žižek's notion of the "authentic act" to argue, from their perspectives on Christian notions of martyrdom, whether Fr. Rodrigues's decision to step on the *fumie* should be viewed as such an act.[15] That is, does it reflect the true face of Christ? But I also ask them to consider the authentic act through the lens of Buddhist and post-structuralist thought, and thus to think about the epistemic entailments of the implied question: "Who is the *real* Jesus?"

Even though I have framed and mediated *Silence* for my students in this way, they naturally engage and understand it in different ways. For them, the novel serves as a course requirement, and so some may see it as an obstacle to a good grade and to completing a course that is part of the university's core curriculum. Although most of my students will read it just once, they will do so in different ways: one, engrossed by the story, could read it slowly and thoughtfully from cover to cover. A Disciple of Christ—TCU's Christian denomination—perhaps she discusses it at length with her roommate and recommends the novel to her mother, just as I did after my brother, a teacher of East Asian history, had recommended it to me. Another student could read only what his friend or the previous owner highlighted in the book, while a third might read the first few chapters and then online summaries. And in a future semester, another student, young and mischievous, may "read" it by watching Martin Scorsese's film, and may recommend that her younger brother, also a TCU student, save time and money by doing the same.

Indeed, once the studio releases Scorsese's adaptation of *Silence*, the public will be able to see the film before reading the text, and many, like our hypothetical student, will probably never read it. I have never read Nikos

Kazantzakis's *The Last Temptation of Christ* but have, as a fan of Scorsese's work, seen his adaptation of the text. But if asked, I could participate in key activities related to the "story-function" since I have engaged in a form of reading Kazantzakis's text—not the *book*—if we understand "reading" and "text" in their broader senses. That is, we can "read" music, someone's face, or oracle bones to divine the future, and a "text" is any thing that can be "read," whether Endo's *Silence*, a street sign, fashion trends, or a work of art, a film, or a play.[16]

In this way, moreover, a version of what Jerome Bruner calls the "virtual text" exists in my mind that has been filtered through the film's cinematography, music, and casting—the actors Willem Dafoe as Jesus and Harvey Keitel as Judas, for instance.[17] We can imagine similar scenarios when Scorsese's *Silence* is released that illustrate the complex and interdependent relationship between Endo's Japanese language text and its adaptations; for example, a Japanese fan of Scorsese might view the English language film— adapted by Jay Cocks for the screen presumably based on William Johnston's English translation—with Japanese dubbing. We could also imagine an American fan, perhaps the student noted above, watching the film but never reading William Johnston's translation. Having done so, she might be able to write a paper, pass a quiz, and engage in class conversation about *Silence*, and has thus "read" the text in the same way I have "read" *The Last Temptation of Christ*. Like me, moreover, these and other fans would create in their minds a virtual text, and could certainly appreciate, if well written, directed, and acted, the sniveling and debauched Kichijiro, or the wrenching decision of Rodrigues to step upon the face of Christ—the silence finally broken. That *silence*—a single word that is essential to the story—can be represented in Scorsese's film in a quite different way from the 1980 English translation, where it appears to readers as a word on a page. As such, this single word *silence*, however it is represented, is crucial to how we interpret, or "read," the text in any of these modes.

Nāgasena would argue that "silence," as a word, lacks a stable and discrete referent, and so, like all words, serves as a useful but limited tool—a "skillful means"—for representing any sort of thing. Indeed, to counteract our tendency to essentialize words and their referents, Buddhist authors and teachers will deploy distinctive linguistic techniques—the poetic *haiku* and paradoxical *kōan*, for instance—to remind us of the emptiness and interdependence of any animate or inanimate thing, whether Nāgasena or Kichijiro, a chariot or cross, suffering or silence.

In this way, we can recast Nāgasena's statement about Milinda's chariot to read, "This '*Silence*' is a mere sound. But what is the *real Silence*?" This substitution offers us a paradoxical, *kōan*-like, statement highlighting the ambiguity of its key terms: silence, sound, and real. For example, the English word *silence* can be read in silence or out loud, thereby producing a sound that means its opposite. And just as *chariot* is an English word translated from Pali, silence is the English translation of the Japanese word "*chinmoku*" (沈黙), a Japanese compound *kanji*, or "Chinese character," which produces meaning differently from the letters of the alphabet used to represent English words since a single *kanji*, unlike a single letter, often has multiple pronunciations and meanings. And *silence*, which can function in English as a noun or a verb, appears outside the text, serving as a title for the English translation, Dietz's play, and Scorsese's film. But the ambiguity of this single word multiplies when we consider it also points in the novel to a condition that readers could construe as the silence of the *kakure,* the faceless and oppressive Buddhist priests, or of God. But even the last possibility could be taken as the silence of God experienced by Fr. Rodrigues, who believes God to be real, or as conceived by Nietzsche who would argue that because "God is dead," silence is the only possible "sound." As such, a reader who considers just the simple, one-word title of all three English-language modes is faced immediately with a range of possible meanings if he or she were to ponder our question about the "real *Silence*."

Silence as *Text* and *Work*

The deconstructive analytical techniques and "linguistic turn" of Nietzsche and his successors resonate with elements of Buddhist epistemology since these thinkers reject the existence of any such unchanging and *real thing*, and seek, like Nāgasena, to destabilize common ways of seeing, refusing to cede absolute generative authority to a creator or founding figure, nor to privilege the "original" form of a teaching or a text. For example, in his studies of authors and texts, Roland Barthes distinguishes the "work" (hereafter, *work*) from the "text" (hereafter, *text*): the former preserves and transmits the words of an author, like Endo, in the familiar form of a book, a material object bound by a front and back cover. Indeed, its very materiality suggests that it is a singular and *real thing* like a wooden chariot or cross, as does its title, which can appear as a simple referent in a library's online catalog or in a course listing. The syllabus for my World Religions course includes a simple reference: "Shusaku Endo, *Silence* (New York: Taplinger Publishing Company, 1980)." This reference suggests to my students a discrete thing apart that they can easily identify on a bookshelf and distinguish from other things that together constitute what Nāgasena might describe as its "non-*Silence*": Endo's other novels, the works of Graham Greene, and even King Milinda's chariot.

The *work* is thus fixed and closed, and, until the creation of digital texts, subject to the material limitations of writing, printing, and book making. In describing the *work*, Barthes invokes a passage from the Gospel of Mark: "The work does not upset monistic philosophies, for which plurality is evil. Thus, when it is compared with the work, the text might well take as its motto the words of the man possessed by devils: 'My name is legion, for we are many' (Mk. 5:9)."[18] As this passage suggests, the *text* is multi-vocal and dynamic, opening out to the multiple readings of *Silence* found in this anthology and elsewhere. Never complete nor fully and finally understood, *Silence*, as a *text*, can be viewed as an "activity" whose metaphor is the "network," an image that resonates with the interdependence of things expressed in Nāgasena's analysis of Milinda's chariot, but also with his deconstructive analysis of the perceived "self" (hereafter, *self*). Indeed, we can draw from that analysis to investigate the *selves* of those figures who appear in varied relationships to the *text* in all its modes.

Buddhist Views of *Self*

To this end, we return to Nāgasena's dialogue with King Milinda. In their conversation, Nāgasena uses the king's chariot to teach him how the principles of emptiness and interdependence apply not only to inanimate things like a chariot, but also to what we perceive as a stable and enduring *self*, asking the king about where they can find the "real Nāgasena." Here the monk commends the king's insight stating,

> Your Majesty has spoken well about the chariot. It is just so with me. In dependence on the thirty-two parts of the body and the five Skandhas, there takes place this denomination 'Nagasena', this designation, this conceptual term, a current appellation and a mere name. In ultimate reality, however, this person cannot be apprehended.[19]

In this way, what we take to be a stable and enduring *self* is a fictitious unity that we hypostatize as an unbroken subjective continuity; that is, the perceived *self* coalesces as an aggregation of things each of which exists only in dependence on other things, and so Buddhists describe it as *anātman*, or "selflessness." The designation "Nāgasena" thus points to an apparently singular but constantly shifting admixture of the body's 32 parts that constitute *rūpa*, or "form." *Rūpa* is one of the five *skandhas*, or "aggregates," which also include sensation, perception, volition, and consciousness.

And like Milinda's chariot, "Nāgasena" can appear in words and images, each of which has a particular relationship to the previously embodied and living person. Although these modes of existence cannot physically converse with us about the Buddha-Dharma, his words can do so, as is the case here, through the teachings they record in his name; he thus appears to us in the same discursive realm in which we, as readers, encounter Rodrigues, Kichijiro, and Jesus. Indeed, these characters from Endo's story, lacking consciousness and thus internally generated agency, are, like the Nāgasena presented here, highly dependent on others: for Endo the author to create and present them, and for readers to interpret their actions. But the logic of Nāgasena's teaching of *anātman* can help us investigate not only the diverse *selves* of these characters, who, as key parts of the text, inhabit the imagined world of *Silence,* but also to think about the *self* as it relates to Endo, the creator of that world, and to his diverse readers whom he invites in to explore this world.

The *Real* Kichijiro

For example, we have seen that Kichijiro can be interpreted Buddhistically as the face of raw suffering and a "passing sight" for Fr. Rodrigues, but also, through a Christian lens, as the betrayer. As the betrayer—a sort of *avatar* of Judas—Kichijiro represents a temporal duality since he appears as a fictional character set in one historical time—seventeenth-century Japan—while his act of betrayal points to a previous time and place. Indeed, the complexity of Kichijiro's *self,* his interdependent richness, is reflected in an ambiguous Japanese name that is lost, however, in the English translation in which "Kichijiro" appears as the transliteration of this proper name, written in Endo's Japanese in *katakana* as キチジロー. *Katakana* is one of two Japanese syllabaries used, among other purposes, to render non-Chinese foreign terms phonetically—signaling that a referent may be outside and other. Japanese names, presented surname first, are generally written in *kanji*: for example, Endō Shūsaku, the author's name, which we address below, appears in Japanese editions of the novel as 遠藤 (Endō) 周作 (Shūsaku).

Thus, the use of *katakana* for Kichijiro's name could be interpreted to mean that it is, in some way, distinct or unusual. Moreover, since Kichijiro is written in *katakana,* and thus lacks the logographic element of the *kanji,* it has a greater degree of ambiguity because it could point to a number of homophones. Even so, it would likely appear to readers of the Japanese *text* who consider its range of possible meanings as the combination of *kichi* キ チ and *jirō* ジロー, since *jirō* is a common suffix for male names—often appearing as the compound *kanji* 次郎—which means the "second son" or "next son." As such, a reader of the Japanese *text* who considers the name's meaning might take *kichi* to represent the *kanji* 吉, meaning "auspicious," "lucky," or "fortunate," and thus render his name as the "Second Son of

Auspiciousness." If understood in this way, our reader could interpret it ironically: "Auspicious indeed!" Or, maybe, having dissolved the binary between the face of Christ and Kichijiro, another reader may see this choice to suggest that we must see the face of Christ in those whom society has shunned, whether the impoverished and dispossessed, or the debased and wicked. And yet another reader may wonder if Endo gives Kichijiro a familiar sounding Japanese name rendered in *katakana* to signal the duality of his fictional and historical *selves*, his familiarity and otherness. However interpreted, this range of potential meanings is foreclosed to most English-speaking readers; indeed, for my students, who often struggle with unfamiliar Japanese or Chinese names, this figure represents a different sort of alterity. And while Kichijiro and the other characters are essential "parts" of the *text* when viewed as a vehicle, functioning like the chariot's wheels or axles, other parts are additions that are not essential to the story-function.

The Paratext of *Silence*

Those parts that have been added to the Taplinger version of *Silence* are what Gérard Genette refers to as "paratext," the functional equivalent of the chariot's flag-staff. Indeed, many written texts, when appearing as a book, contain such paratextual material: linguistic and artistic additions, such as a title, cover, introduction, blurbs, and so on. These sorts of supplements enable a *text* to become a book and offer readers a doorway into the *text's* world as a zone of "transition," but they also mediate the *text*, making it a zone of "transaction."[20] To illustrate the paratext's potential "transactional" influence on readers, Genette asks us to imagine how we would read James Joyce's *Ulysses* without the title and other such paratextual materials, a question that highlights, much like our chariot example, the interdependent relationships and functions of *its* parts.

In a similar way, we can continue our investigation of *Silence's* parts by considering how we might read *it* stripped of all such material. What if, for example, William Johnston's English translation lacked the title and the image of a crucified Christ on the front cover, or lacked blurbs by Graham Greene and others on the back cover? Or, what if it bore a different title, such as the *Scent of a Sunny Place* (*Hinata no nioi*) as Endo had considered, or, *Suffering!*, *Apostasy!*, or *Kichijiro: The Betrayer*? To consider these scenarios, and thus better understand the function of the paratext, we can compare, as an example, the covers of the 1981 Shinchōsha Japanese version and the 1980 Taplinger English translation.

A reader who looks at the cover of that Japanese version of Endo's *text* will see, written in *kanji*, the title *Chinmoku* 沈黙 and the author's full name,

Endō Shūsaku 遠藤周作, accompanied by a photograph of the sun about to peek out from behind some clouds. Seeing just the cover, our reader would have no basis for associating the title with the crucifixion and the suffering Christ—indeed, unless our reader knew Endo to be a famous Catholic novelist, the only obvious visual cue to the contents would be this scene, which naturally does not suggest the story's intense cruelty and suffering. But a reader of the Taplinger translation will see something quite different. That reader will find instead "*Silence*," the translated title, and the author's trans-literated name, "Shusaku Endo," at the top right of the front cover, pairing a familiar English word with what is likely an unfamiliar name. Below these words our reader finds a red, hand-drawn image of a crucified Jesus—his head slumping down and to his right, thereby obscuring the beautiful face and blue eyes imagined by Fr. Rodrigues. But this gray cross is oddly shaped, drawn as the second of the two *kanji* that appear in *Chinmoku* 沈黙—thus our reader, and most native English-speaking readers, would find an unrecognizable symbol depicting Jesus crucified not on the traditional wooden cross, but on some similarly shaped thing that gestures toward a mysterious otherness.

While these two covers serve as a zone of transition into the *text*, they are also transactional: that is, although they present the same story in different languages, they frame it in different ways. While the former pairs the *kanji Chinmoku* with a photograph of the sky, thus foregrounding a natural scene that belies the colorless and drab environment experienced by Fr. Rodrigues, the latter combines *Silence* with a drawing of Jesus in a state of intense suffering, highlighting a central character, whom Rodrigues constantly imagines, and theme in the story. And while both photographs and drawings represent moments in time, we often see the former, although open to manipulation, as a snapshot of "reality" itself, while we recognize that an artist can easily alter her work to create more realistic or abstract effects, easily combining anachronistic and other incongruous elements, such as an image of Jesus crucified on a Chinese character, or, as is common in Buddhist thought, horns on a rabbit.

If we focus on just the image of the crucified Jesus, we can also imagine multiple interpretive possibilities: perhaps the artist depicts Jesus on such an unusual cross to point to the crucifixion as a historical event in time while also gesturing toward its transcendence—a central element of the "theological" reading suggested by Middleton. Maybe the artist obscures the face of Jesus to hide his pain, or to enable the reader to imagine his own image of the messiah—a possibility with which we conclude this chapter. However interpreted, the English language cover presents to readers familiar with even the most basic elements of the life of Jesus, the impression that this is, unlike the impression given by the Japanese cover, a Christian story.

This sense would be reinforced by reading some of the blurbs that appear on the back cover of the 1980 Taplinger edition, which describe, for example, a "Portuguese priest ... [and] the fearful persecution of the small Christian community," "theological quandaries," "Western mode of religion," and "men of faith in a faith-denying situation."[21] And an excerpted review from *America* states, "The Calvary of Father Rodrigues is so brilliantly brought before us that even if no such person ever actually existed, he lives now. ... This is the best book on a Christian theme I have read for years."[22] As seen above, moreover, Graham Greene, well-known as a Catholic novelist, writes of *Silence*: "In my opinion one of the finest novels of our time."[23] These and other such blurbs offer descriptions of the *text* and its author—best, brilliant, finest, foremost, masterpiece, perfect, powerful, major talent, profoundly moving—that bolster the perceived value of *Silence* and influence a reader's sense of what lies inside. And like the English translation's cover art, these comments are not part of Endo's "original" Japanese *text*; they serve, rather, as supplements, without which his words, whether in Japanese or English, could still perform the "story-function." Another blurb states, "Shusaku Endo is Japan's foremost novelist, and *Silence* is generally regarded to be his masterpiece."[24] The linguistic structure—an explicit or implied "to be"— imparts to this and the two previous statements an ontological certainty that naturally reinforces the apparent singularity of the *text* and its author. And so, as with the chariot and Nāgasena, and with *Silence* and Kichijiro, we can ask, Who is the "real" Endo?

Endo the *Author*

Roland Barthes, whose work we noted above, distinguishes two types of authorial *selves:* the "scriptor" and the "author." For *Silence,* the former represents the historical Endo who, some chapterists note, was influenced by a complicated relationship with Catholicism, the experience of racism while living in France, and prolonged bouts of serious illness. It was Endo, as *scriptor*, who was interviewed by Van Gessel and who now lies buried at Huchu Cemetery in Fuchu City, a pilgrimage site visited by Middleton and other scholars and fans of the author.

But the name of the man who was interviewed by Gessel and who lies buried in Fuchu City lives on with *Chinmoku/Silence* and his other works. This latter *self*, what Barthes calls the *author*, represents an evolving discursive figure who serves as a sort of character in his novel whose signature is neither paternal nor privileged as the source of definitive interpretation. Instead, there is a reversal wherein the *text's* reception affects the life rather than the life affecting the *text*.

In "What is an Author?," Michel Foucault offers another perspective on the authorial *self*, arguing that the author's name does not refer "purely and simply to a real individual since it can give rise simultaneously to several selves, to several subjects—positions that can be occupied by different classes of individuals."[25] The author's name thus possesses a "paradoxical singularity," a quality that emerges, in part, from the ambiguity common to all proper names that we explored above in considering the names "Nāgasena" and "Kichijiro." But Foucault argues that there are also significant differences between the names of an individual person and an author since "the links between the proper name and the individual named and between the author's name and what it names are not isomorphic and do not function in the same way."[26] He offers the following as an example:

> If, for example, Pierre Dupont does not have blue eyes, or was not born in Paris, or is not a doctor, the name Pierre Dupont will still always refer to the same person; such things do not modify the link of designation. The problems raised by the author's name are much more complex, however. If I discover that Shakespeare was not born in the house that we visit today, this is a modification which, obviously, will not alter the functioning of the author's name. But if we proved that Shakespeare did not write those sonnets which pass for his, that would constitute a significant change and affect the manner in which the author's name functions. If we proved that Shakespeare wrote Bacon's *Organon* by showing that the same author wrote both the works of Bacon and those of Shakespeare, that would be a third type of change which would entirely modify the functioning of the author's name. The author's name is not, therefore, just a proper name like the rest.[27]

In this way, the name of an *author*, whether Aristotle or Shakespeare, Greene or Endo, possesses the "author-function," which distinguishes it from other proper names, like Kichijiro, Rodrigues, and Pierre Dupont, but also from other similar sorts of discourses, such as the writer of one of the blurbs examined above, a scholarly chapter like those in this anthology, or a book review, a private letter, or an advertisement.

As we have done with *things* and *selves,* we should focus then on the functions, appearances, and dependencies of Endo's name rather than affording it an absolute generative authority. The proper name we find on the English translation's cover, Scorsese's film, and Dietz's play paired with *Silence* points then not to a singular and stable *self*, but possesses instead multiple and evolving descriptions that affect how "readers" interpret and value the *text*, in whichever mode they engage it. For instance, over the reception history of *Silence*, Endo's name has come to include, Japanese Catholic novelist, wearer of ill-fitting Catholic suit, Tanizaki prize-winner, friend of Graham Greene, subject of scholarly study, and now, author favored by Martin Scorsese. These and many other such descriptions suggest the complexity and interdependence of Endo's authorial *self*: how, for example, the functioning of his name, as an author, depends on human relationships and activities, which include not only Endo's friendship with Graham Greene, as Gessel's and Middleton's chapters note, and self-reflection on his Christian upbringing, but also the activities and perceptions of others: the reviews of "pilot fish" and the blurbs of experts, marketing strategies, scholarly anthologies, literary prizes, but also, as we have seen, the translation of *Silence* into English and its adaptation for stage and screen. To borrow Foucault's language, if we discover that Endo was born on March 27 instead of March 26, this modification would not "alter the functioning of the author's name," while the publication of John Updike's 1980 review of *Silence* in *The New Yorker* clearly did so, as Van C. Gessel argues in this volume, as will the release of Scorsese's film. Indeed, as a "great whale" swimming freely in the ocean of film, Scorsese will, through his adaptation of *Silence*, bring Endo's name to the lips of many more people—perhaps by a factor of tens, if not hundreds, of thousands—than any scholarly study, and his film will alter the *text*'s modes of existence. Indeed, Updike's review and Scorsese's film are just two ways in which Endo's text has been recognized as a valuable piece of literature, an evaluation echoed in our title's use of "classic novel."

A Buddhist View on *Silence* as the *Real Thing*

This chapter began with Middleton's recognition of the interpretive variation we inevitably find across readers of a *text*, whether *Silence*, *The Last Temptation of Christ*, or the sonnets of Shakespeare. In *Contingencies of Value*, Barbara H. Smith considers the factors that lead to such variation across readers of the sonnets, but also describes how her evaluation of the individual sonnets has varied significantly as she, a single reader, has reread them. In her first chapter, titled "Fixed Marks and Variable Constancies: a Parable of Value," she thus argues that their meaning and value are "contingent," depending on a shifting set of personal and other factors, and so, "like all value, literary value is not the property of an object or of a subject, but, rather, the product of the dynamics of a system."[28]

Although that system naturally includes experts like her trained in Shakespeare's work—those who interpret and evaluate the sonnets as a "canonical" audience under canonical conditions—it also includes many other sorts of readers who engage them in other modes and use them for other purposes. This diverse group of readers—possessing distinct social positions, linguistic skills, educational levels, types of embodiment, and so on—can access and engage the sonnets in many ways: for instance, as a few words in conversation or on t-shirts that reproduce passages from the sonnets, but also in film, theater, comic books, or Wikipedia pages. Some of these "readers" may only know the sonnets exist but have little or no idea what they say, but will likely recognize their value simply because of their association with Shakespeare's name.

In a similar way, I have used Buddhist and post-structuralist thought to show the potential variation in the way "readers" can engage and interpret Endo's *text* because of their linguistic skills, religious background, and so on. And like Smith's experience with multiple readings of the sonnets, my appreciation of *Silence* has evolved, as I have, for varied purposes, returned to the *text* again and again. For me, it has served not only as a course reading and a subject of scholarship, but also as a source of entertainment and spiritual reflection, a source of friendship and community. And while my academic training in Buddhist Studies, Japanese literature, and post-structuralist thought has naturally influenced my interpretation of *Silence,* it has also evolved through my ongoing engagement with the *text* through workshops and presentations, discussion and writing, and through co-editing this anthology.

These activities have occurred mainly in the religion departments of Gustavus Adolphus College and Texas Christian University—two Protestant-affiliated institutions where I have discussed the *text* with students and colleagues whose worldviews have been shaped in some way by the figure of Jesus and the Christian teachings that have been transmitted in his name. Although not trained academically in Christian history or thought, I have also brought to these readings a set of ideas about Christian traditions, especially Catholicism. I encountered Christian teachings at a young age: my mother's family are Catholics, I occasionally went to church, attended confirmation class, and worked in my teens at the rectory of the Blessed Sacrament Church affiliated with the Dominican order. My family and the Dominican fathers sparked an early interest in the life of St. Francis of Assisi and other Catholic saints and in Christian-themed films such as "Jesus Christ Superstar" and "The Last Temptation of Christ."

As one reader of *Silence,* my perception of the *text's* meaning and value is thus complex and shifting, depending on those who populate the various communities that have been crucial to my intellectual and spiritual development. Indeed, in an attempt to recognize in writing this interdependence,

I have structured this chapter as an imagined dialogue with my friend and co-editor who has helped shape my understanding of *Silence*, which we both recognize, in our own ways, as a "classic novel" that is worthy of study and reflection, but also worthy of the public's attention and recognition. But I have also tried to instantiate interdependence by recognizing the work of other contributors to this volume, who offer their own readings of the climactic scene, the significance of Kichijiro, and the face of Christ. Their divergent readings suggest the elusiveness of the "great shark," and thus the difficulties of our discovering the *real thing.*

While this interdependent and dialogic approach to reading, interpretation, and writing naturally highlights my connections to these individuals and communities, it is also meant to disperse the locus of what appears as a singular interpretive agency—shifting it away from the persuasive ontological force we naturally impute to an individual's name and, more broadly, to words themselves. Through the lens of Buddhist thought, although these words can be taken as my words, in important ways they are not mine since they emerge only through my dependence on the ideas and compassion of my teachers and colleagues, family and friends.

This Buddhistic approach to interpretation, which focuses on the dynamism and multivalence of *things* and *selves,* calls us to remain open to alternative ways of reading and engaging a *text*, the interpretive equivalent of "riding" through the mud or atop the roof, even if we are middle-aged and our mischievousness is purely aspirational. This openness to other possibilities—the so-called Beginner's Mind of Zen—can reveal to us elements within a *text* hidden from us by our academic training and expertise. Indeed, this chapter—which views *Silence* through the lens of Buddhist ideas on suffering, emptiness, and interdependence—shows how Endo's *text,* framed for its English-speaking audience as a Christian story, transcends that context.

The Blue Eyes of Jesus

In this way, the chapter illustrates an observation of Charles Hallisey, a scholar of Buddhism, who, in drawing from the work of Hans-Georg Gadamer, reminds us that "the texts we interpret always fundamentally precede and exceed us and that 'performing' this is crucial to how we come to know Buddhist texts."[29] And so if we limit our "epistemological performances" by seeking only to put a text in its context, we limit "what it might say that transcends that context."[30] This observation appears in an article reflecting on a series of workshops that brought together scholars of Womanist and Buddhist thought; those workshops were conceived by Hallisey and my

TCU colleague Melanie Harris, a scholar of Womanism with whom I have not discussed *Silence* at length, but who has, nonetheless, influenced my reading of it. She and Hallisey designed those workshops to promote this sort of interdependent, communal reading, and so to explore the benefits of applying such divergent angles of critical vision and reading practices to Buddhist texts, including the story of Ajātaśatru, described above.

In the workshop that I attended, after discussing the king's story in small groups, Arisika Razak, a professor of Women's Spirituality at the California Institute of Integral Studies (but also an African American healer, ritualist, spiritual dancer, and midwife), stood before the group and *re-presented* the story of Ajātaśatru from the perspective of his mother, Queen Vaidehi, who had become distraught by her son's imprisonment and ill-treatment of her husband. Swaying gently from side-to-side as her arms and hands moved rhythmically up and down, Razak offered the group an extemporaneous and poetic narration of Vaidehi's plight, thereby "breathing life" into a woman from another place and time whose suffering was at once unique but also ubiquitous, as states Buddhism's first noble truth. For me, Razak's "epistemo-logical performance"—offered to our community of readers through what Buddhists refer to as "body, speech, and mind"—was the most memorable interpretive practice of the workshop because it reminded me how a *text* that I knew well as a scholar of Buddhism had meanings and potential modes of engagement hidden from me by my training in a particular form of "reading."

Indeed, the word "apocalypse," which appears in Altizer's phrase, "contem-porary and apocalyptic presence," points broadly to the revelation of things hidden from view, like the face of Christ on the cover of the Taplinger edition of *Silence*. By engaging in this sort of interdependent "reading" of the *text*, as we do in the present volume, each of us can discover things that lie hidden in Endo's wonderful but excruciating story, whether we focus on the scene of Rodrigues's apostasy, the duplicity and raw suffering of Kichijiro, or the face of Christ—at first, a beautiful, blue-eyed face that becomes ugly and exhausted as the priest witnesses the many faces of suffering as "passing sights."

The varied interpretations of that face found in this volume and elsewhere lead us back to Nāgasena's questions of King Milinda, which we can alter to read, This 'Christ' is a mere sound. Who is the *real* Christ? From the perspective of Buddhist thought, this question, and all the other "real" questions posed above, is ill-formed, leading us to reify that which is, in time and over time, dynamic and interdependent. Here, the ambiguity of "real" emerges because *it* can point to the historical Christ, a man whose physical appearance is lacking in the canonical Gospels—a gap in the record noted by Endo and by his character Rodrigues. This lack of a physical description of Jesus, the intervention of some two millennia, and the transmission of Christian teachings across many cultures have led to his appearing in literature and art, film and theater with a bewildering array of faces and features, some with blue eyes, others with black skin. But "real" can also suggest that which is "authentic," whether Rodrigues's decision to step on the *fumie* believing that his act authentically represented the true face of Christ, or the value readers find in Endo's novel. This second meaning would seem to resonate with Altizer's Christology wherein, instead of seeking to recover the facial features, eye color, and other biographical details of the historical Jesus, we are better served by exploring the dependencies, functions, and appearances of that man through the lens of what we could call the "founder function." This reversal of our angle of critical vision leads us to focus on how, in any time, that appearance has shifted so that it is relevant and inspiring to those living in the present. Such a reversal creates a paradoxically vibrant space for the legitimacy of the maternal face of Christ so important to the Japanese, as suggested in this volume by Dennis Hirota and Van C. Gessel. To make this point, Gessel quotes Leith Morton:

> Endō ... has repeatedly linked his vision of Christ with images that strike a deep resonance from Japanese tradition. ... In Endō's fictions we apprehend a grand dream, a dream of a Japanese Christ, more feminine than masculine, a Christ reminding us more of a Mother than a Father. Such a dream may frighten us or fascinate us, but its source surely derives from the same desire that rests within us, within all people, a desire profoundly spiritual that looks to the divine, to the good.[31]

Fascinated by this and other such dreams, I am grateful the artist hid the face of Jesus on the cover of the Taplinger edition, thereby not privileging one of these many faces over another. Each of us can use our imagination to bring forth our own image, whether a beautiful and blue-eyed face, a maternal Japanese Christ, or some other image. For example, in *Speaking of Faith,* Krista Tippett describes her experience with Ted, a young boy she and her husband met at a summer youth camp in Philadelphia, writing, "Ted's face remains the face of Christ for me: nine years old, black, delightful, heart-breaking, his smile a pure gift."[32]

Like my reading of *Silence,* my "reading" of that man's face has evolved over time. At Ted's age, I would likely have imagined the delicate features of Ted Neeley who played the title role in "Jesus Christ Superstar"—a film I saw multiple times and whose music I still know by heart. But when I have pictured that man while writing this chapter I have imagined not only the broken down face of intense suffering Fr. Rodrigues confronts in the *fumie,* but also a laughing Jesus in a black-and-white print that I received

as a gift from my aunt. In contrast to Neeley's delicate features, I also have
seen the rugged, craggy features and blue eyes of Willem Dafoe in Scorsese's
adaptation of *The Last Temptation of Christ*. Having read and studied
Silence, I also imagine a feminine Christ with features not unlike those of
the bodhisattva Kannon discussed in this volume by Elizabeth Cameron
Galbraith and Jeff Keuss. Since attending the Womanist-Buddhist workshop
and reflecting here upon Altizer's notion of the "contemporary and apocalyptic presence," I also see the face of a black man. All these images, which
clearly cannot accurately represent the Christ of history, coalesce under one
paradoxically singular name, "Jesus Christ."

Even though neither Middleton nor I can get a firm hold of the *real
thing* in *Silence*, we were motivated to edit this volume because we agree
with Greene's assessment that it is "one of the finest novels of our time." I
do so because it brings us back, again and again, to the faces of the suffering
"other" in its many guises—the very fount of meaning and compassionate
action on the Buddhist path. And while Endo brilliantly and painfully
reveals to us the suffering in the faces of Kichijiro, Rodrigues, and the *kakure,*
this is especially true of the one Endo describes in beautiful simplicity as *ano
hito,* "that man."

Notes

1   Shusaku Endo, *Silence,* trans. William Johnston (New York: Taplinger
    Publishing Company, 1980, outside back cover).
2   See Darren J. N. Middleton's chapter in the present volume.
3   Ibid.
4   Ibid.
5   "Nagasena on No-Self," *The Questions of King Milinda,* quoted in *Indian
    Religions: A Historical Reader of Spiritual Expression and Experience,* ed.
    Peter Heehs (New York: New York University Press, 2002), 128.
6   In this volume, Mark Bosco, Kevin Doak, and Van Gessel all note the
    problem with William Johnston's translation of this crucial passage, which
    reads in Endo's Japanese as *fumu ga ii*. Rather than using the imperative—
    "Trample! Trample!"—Johnston would have been more accurate to have
    rendered the passage, as Bosco suggests, "You may trample. I allow you to
    trample."
7   Jeff Keuss, "The Lenten Face of Christ in Shusaku Endo's *Silence* and *Life of
    Jesus,*" *The Expository Times* 118.6 (2007): 274.
8   Ibid.
9   William T. Cavanaugh, "The God of *Silence*: Shusaku Endo's Reading of the
    Passion," *Commonweal* 125.5 (March 1998): 12.

10 Ibid.

11 Thomas J. J. Altizer, *The Contemporary Jesus* (Albany: State University of New York Press, 1997), quoted in Keuss, "The Lenten Face," 277.

12 Ibid.

13 *The Questions of King Milinda,* 128.

14 Ibid.

15 Gustavus Adolphus is affiliated with the Evangelical Lutheran Church in America (ELCA), while TCU is affiliated with the Christian Church (Disciples of Christ). For another perspective on teaching the novel in a Christian setting, see John Kaltner's chapter in this volume, which describes his experience teaching *Silence* at Rhodes College, a liberal arts college affiliated with the Presbyterian Church (USA).

16 Unwittingly, my point forms part of the thesis of Darren J. N. Middleton's edited volume on the novel *and* the film. See Darren J. N. Middleton, ed., *Scandalizing Jesus?: Kazantzakis's The Last Temptation of Christ Fifty Years On* (New York and London: Continuum, 2005).

17 This usage represents an expansion of Bruner's notion of the "virtual text." See Jerome Bruner, *Actual Minds, Possible Worlds* (Cambridge, MA: Harvard University Press, 1986).

18 Roland Barthes, "From Work to Text," *The Rustle of Language,* trans. Richard Howard (New York: Hill and Wang, 1984), 60.

19 *The Questions of King Milinda,* 128.

20 Gérard Genette, *Paratexts: Thresholds of Interpretation,* trans. Jane E. Lewin with foreword by Richard Macksey (Cambridge: Cambridge University Press, 1997), 7.

21 Endo, *Silence,* outside back cover.

22 Ibid.

23 Ibid.

24 Ibid.

25 Michel Foucault, "What is an Author?," *Modern Criticism and Theory: A Reader*, ed. David Lodge (Essex: Longman House, 1988), 205.

26 Ibid.

27 Ibid., 201.

28 Barbara Herrnstein Smith, *Contingencies of Value: Alternative Perspectives for Critical Theory* (Cambridge, MA: Harvard University Press, 1988), 15.

29 Charles Hallisey, "'It Not the Only One': Womanist Resources for Reflection in Buddhist Studies," *Buddhist-Christian Studies* 32 (2012): 75.

30 Hallisey, "It Not the Only One," 75–6.

31 Leith Morton, "The Image of Christ in the Fiction of Endō Shūsaku," *Working Papers in Japanese Studies* 8. (Melbourne: Japanese Studies Centre, 1994): 13.

32 Krista Tippett, *Speaking of Faith: Why Religion Matters—and How to Talk About It* (New York: Penguin Books, 2008), 115.

Part Three

Endo's Theology

11

Literature as *Dōhansha* in *Silence*

Jeff Keuss

This chapter offers a phenomenological and theological exploration of Endō Shūsaku's work as missionary literature. *Silence* changes the face of Christ to counteract Western missionary efforts to sublimate Japanese notions of the Sacred through the propagation of essentialist Christian doctrines.[1] Central to this interpretation of *Silence* will be the Japanese notion of *dōhansha*, or "companion."[2] Indeed, *Silence* exemplifies Endō's poetics as a form of literary rebellion that offers a true *companion* for engaging and maintaining the fluidity of such Japanese notions of the sacred in the face of missionary attempts to dominate and control the person of Christ. To prevent Japanese literature from succumbing to these missionary efforts to control indigenous culture and local sensibilities of the sacred, Endō releases the sacred into the poetics of *Silence* through what I will explore as "textual *dōhansha*"— that is, as a constant companion of the text that *suffers* with the reader, therein offering a poetics of Christ fully realized beyond received doctrinal formulations.

By reading *Silence* through the lens of textual *dōhansha*, we, as readers, are forced to challenge and reconstitute our notions of the subject and the sacred as Endō's literary moves bring us into what Heidegger would term "clearing" in relation to the fictive space as a pathway to truth. In his account of true writing that seeks truth, Heidegger said that his project was "an *on-the-way* in the field of paths for the changing questioning of the manifold question of Being."[3] This metaphor of being on "the field of paths" is an apt one for readers of Endo's *Silence* who might become frustrated with the destabilizing images of Christ offered in the novel and the lack of definitive dogmatic resolve. As seen in his idea of *die Lichtung des Seins*, or "the clearing of Being," Heidegger draws from colloquial German (*eine Lichtung*), which is the sense of a forest clearing made to allow light to shine upon Being (*Sein*).[4] When one undertakes the task of walking through the woods, there is a way through, even though the paths are not defined or mapped. As Heidegger saw that only by walking amid the uncharted woods would a path be made evident, so it is that readers of *Silence* see the way of Christ that is found in fiction and faith that arises only after being *on-the-way* and where, akin to the road to Emmaus account of Christ appearing mysteriously yet prophetically alongside the travelers in Lk. 24, the Christ companion is one who suffers with us and is seen and heard anew. Mark Williams sees this as a theme throughout Endō's fiction: "Here is Christ, the companion (*dōhansha*) figure so prominent in the author's work, a being who, resolved not to look down in judgment, chooses rather to share in the individual's pain and anguish as his 'companion.'"[5]

If we take the notion of *dōhansha* not merely as a plot point embodied in Christ's image, but in the entirety of Endō's fiction, four angles of critical vision illustrate the author's poetics. First, textual *dōhansha* reveals a "rupturing" of conceptions and tropes that serve as analogs to the multivalent *pharmakon* of Jacques Derrida's thought, wherein this single Greek term can mean both "poison" and "cure." As I argue elsewhere, this rupture in relation to the person and work of Jesus Christ has always been crucial to the Christian faith's confessional heritage.[6] Indeed, works such as *Silence* will continue to arise to bring forth a "poetic apotheosis," which is a freeing of form for the sake of establishing a greater intimacy with the sacred. Because the nature of God is beyond category and ultimate description, forms that seek to render God visible and tangible inevitably become ruptured, are opened anew, and then leave the community of readers grasping for yet another means of locating God in our midst. This apotheosis reveals a sort of *heresy* of dogmatic formulations of Christianity, and it also highlights the limits of an essentialized formalism by showing how many credal practices, though useful as guides for the faithful, can foreclose access to God's *in-breaking* into reality. Second, textual *dōhansha* as seen in Endō's poetics calls forth what Japanese psychoanalyst Doi Takeo terms *amae*, or deep abiding dependence.[7] Drawing from the five relationships of Confucianism (ruler-subject, parent-child, husband-wife, older brother-younger brother, and friend-friend), Doi uses *amae* to deconstruct the subject-object distinction and to argue for an interpersonal and reciprocal intimacy in which the subject relinquishes a degree of control. We will see how Endō reanimates *amae* in *Silence* by exploring how such a deep dependence subverts the novel's obvious binaries and hierarchies so that only mutuality and deep intimacy remain.

Third, by viewing *Silence* through textual *dōhansha* we can reconcile apparently contradictory signs of the sacred in Endō's reimaging of Christ through the lens of the hidden Christians. That reconciliation is evident in the Japanese fusing of religious sensibilities of Christianity and Buddhism through the integration of the Mary and Kannon feminine archetypes. As

Endō demonstrates through his portrayal of the hidden Christians, we find in hidden places a willingness to forgo clear and rigid distinctions in favor of encounter and intimacy beyond categorical imperatives. Lastly, Endō allows the fictive space to remain unresolved, and thus the sacred comes to the reader as the unnamed in a hospitable repose of the text as true companion. Herein suffering and pain simultaneously bind and release reader and text in a form of true companionship, or textual *dōhansha*.

The Space of Fiction as *dōhansha*

Writing in his essay "Is Nothing Sacred," Salman Rushdie upholds fiction's tendency toward polysemy.

> Between religion and literature ... there is a linguistically based dispute. But it is not a dispute of simple opposites. Because whereas religion seeks to privilege one language above all others, one set of values above all others, one text above all others, the novel has always been about the way in which different languages, values and narratives quarrel, and about the shifting relations between them, which are relations of power. The novel does not seek to establish a privileged language, but it insists upon the freedom to portray and analyze the struggle between the different contestants for such privileges.[8]

Likewise, Endō's *Silence* operates on numerous levels. As a work of historical fiction, it reimagines the experiences of Fr. Sebastian Rodrigues, the seventeenth-century Portuguese Jesuit priest, who travels to Tokugawa Japan. Yet what is seen in a deeper reading of the text is that it offers what Rushdie describes as the "freedom to portray and analyze the struggle between the different contestants" in the task of meaning-making *vis-à-vis* the phenomenological and theological fluidity of imaging the face of Christ. Endō locates the theme of the novel in the transformation of the face of Jesus, not the transformation of the characters, stating, "To me the most meaningful thing in the novel (*Silence*) is the change in the hero's image of Christ."[9] The image of Jesus that had appeared to Rodrigues numerous times is that of a transcendent, static, and stoic Jesus; however, as Rodrigues resolves to maintain this image of Christ, causing the death of many Japanese as a result, the face of Jesus begins to change into one marked by human suffering.[10]

For Endō, the dynamic nature of Christ is seen most clearly in attempts by a dominant culture to sublimate the freedom of the sacred by imposing a static and essentialized image; such attempts to control ultimately render the divine invisible amid human suffering. Endō makes this point clearly in the preface to the American edition of *A Life of Jesus*, stating that, "the religious mentality of the Japanese is—just as it was at the time when the people accepted Buddhism—responsive to one who 'suffers with us' and who 'allows for our weakness,' but their mentality has little tolerance for any kind of transcendent being who judges humans harshly, then punishes them."[11] It is only by recollecting the treatment of human suffering through the maternal aspect of Japanese Buddhism that a reader of *Silence* can truly grasp the dislocation and rupture present in the sacred, Endo states: "In brief, the Japanese tend to seek in their gods and buddhas a warm-hearted mother rather than a stern father. With this fact always in mind, I tried not so much to depict God in the father-image that tends to characterize Christianity, but rather to depict the kind-hearted maternal aspect of God revealed to us in the personality of Jesus."[12] In this way, rather than offering a distant and completely transcendent figuring of Christ, Endō's maternal Jesus resonates with the Japanese notion of *dōhansha* as the constant companion. Here, Christ is not the sole property of the indigenous and missionary communities exclusively, but, as true companion, a figure of the marginalized who shares in their pain and anguish.

Pain as the *furoshiki* of God—Kitamori's *Theology of the Pain of God*

The notion of *dōhansha* appears in Endō's work at the intersection of the subject and the sacred, wherein there is the mutuality of "suffering with" as companions. Indeed, Endō's understanding of suffering was influenced by the Japanese theologian Kazoh Kitamori's seminal *Theology of the Pain of God* (1946).[13] Here, the central theme of pain and suffering is a plumbline by which to measure and understand Japanese lived experience after World War II. Kitamori draws from seemingly disparate cultural and religious resources. In particular, he frames God through the work of the Kyoto School philosopher Hajime Tanabe who sought a Buddhist synthesis of opposites—a kind of unity out of duality.[14] In Tanabe's thought, such unity is forged out of duality by acknowledging the reality of pain and suffering that permeates all human existence—a central tenet of Buddhism. This overarching theme of suffering as a hermeneutic through which to understand the unifying totality yet irreconcilable expanses of God in relation to humanity is what

Kitamori refers to as a *"furoshiki* theology." A *furoshiki* is a piece of cloth used by Japanese students to wrap up their books and by homemakers to pack the goods they buy in shops. The *furoshiki* image is useful for understanding Kitamori's theology, which emphasizes how God envelops and, therefore, shares in creation's pain. Pain and suffering are the *furoshiki* that brings together the opposites inherent in a theology of the cross that seeks to hold together the struggle between God's love and God's wrath, caused by our sinfulness.

In Kitamori's theology, pain penetrates God's being when the crucified Christ invokes Psalm 22's opening line concerning divine abandonment. This commingling of human tragedy with divine compassion enables God to overcome wrath and forgive sinners through the act of Emmanuel, or "God with us." This nearness and intimacy of God through pain and suffering is a central critique that Kitamori levels against both Barthian theology and liberal Protestantism. Kitamori argues that Karl Barth has, by stressing God's transcendence and distance from sin, offered a "totally Other" God that ultimately lacks the very content of the Word of God made flesh as the full incarnation that includes all of humanity, including pain and suffering. In a similar vein, Kitamori criticizes liberal Protestant theology because it focuses too much on God's love as a comfort without the cost of suffering. By wrapping the disparate and potentially divisive aspects of humanity in the *furoshiki,* Kitamori hopes to offer a compassionate and human response of God to our deepest humanity, which is found in our greatest moments of weakness and humiliation. Where Kitamori offers a formal theological explication of *furoshiki* theology, Endō's fiction informally wraps pain and suffering. *Silence* not only embraces as *furoshiki,* but the text opens and binds intimately with the reader as a companion—the *dōhansha.* In light of this metaphorical elaboration of *furoshiki,* Endō frames the subject and sacred as textual *dōhansha* in his fiction, echoing Derrida's early literary work as "rupture."

The Movement of Rupture

In explaining rupture, Derrida argues that true literature finds its voice through the distinction between true identity and metaphor since identity ultimately exists only in the "difference" between meaning and the label placed upon it. When Western Christian missionaries first heard counter-narratives to the church's doctrines, there was anxiety about the meaning of key theological signifiers, such as "Jesus." In response, missionary institutions worked to control the indigenous reinterpretation of these signifiers—efforts that represent, in Derrida's thought, a key point of rupture.[15] Once we begin to recognize that the structure of any given sign is merely a structure, and nothing else, a rupture *can* occur. When people believe that the structure is something *other* than a structure, they have chosen form over meaning; or, in the case of missionary efforts, the protection of their cultural norms rather than recognizing the deep meaning and liberative possibilities of the sacred in their unfamiliar circumstances.

In a more contemporary vein, one could see this clash of opposites as part of what media critic Hal Foster describes as "a shift in conception from reality as an effect of representation to the real as a thing of trauma."[16] In this reading, the "real" lies beyond critique as "the traumatic," and is thus beyond categorization and language. This conceptual shift enables us to see *with* reality, not merely to construct *a* reality to be seen. By developing such a *poetics of Jesus* as rupture, the unconditioned meaning of *Jesus* through "the shattering of form" is revealed—an image that is rarely seen in biblical criticism and fiction.

Any assertion of identity based on a signifier like "Jesus" reveals form as both metaphor and metonym; as such, the deep meaning one seeks through form and content may differ from that which is suggested by either the metaphor or the metonym. Thus, the very face we may seek—that face which gives us the location and name of God—is not then to be found. The face we *do* figure, as Derrida reminds us, "is neither the face of God nor the figure of man: it is their resemblance. A resemblance which, however, we must think before, or without, the assistance of the Same."[17] We who seek this "face" are in the space between

> the same and the other, which is not a difference or a relation among others, has no meaning in the infinite … this horizon is not the horizon of the infinitely other, but of a reign in which the difference between the same and the other, *differánce*, would no longer be valid, that is, of a reign in which peace itself will no longer have meaning.[18]

The grand irony for Endō enabling the text to remain as authentic *dōhansha* is that it is in the text as pure silence that we, along with the characters, experience the height and depth of the "voice" of God that is more dynamic than the printed "word" upon the page. As Fr. Rodrigues reflects

> If God does not exist, how can man endure the monotony of the sea and its cruel lack of emotion? (But supposing … of course, supposing, I mean.) From the deepest core of my being yet another voice made itself heard in a whisper. Supposing God does not exist. …

This was a frightening fancy. If he does not exist, how absurd the whole thing becomes ... Plucking the grass as I went along I chewed it with my teeth, suppressing these thoughts that rose nauseatingly in my throat. I knew well, of course, that the greatest sin against God was despair; but the silence of God was something I could not fathom.[19]

This clash of opposites, which includes the collapsing of the beautifully grotesque, the maternal Christ, and the silent voice into one image is what Thomas J. J. Altizer describes as true Christology's essential character. A true Christology brings us to an apocalypse where everything we have known must be reevaluated in totality, including our very lives and the world that sustains them. The clash of opposites is

> a full coming together of total opposites, the opposites of total ending and total beginning, and the totally old world or aeon and a totally new aeon or world ... a *coincidentia oppositorum* is at the very centre of the Christian epic, as is a calling forth and voyage into an apoca-lyptic totality, and (the Christian) epic totality is an apocalyptic totality if only because it embodies such a radical and total transformation. Here, this transformation is deepest in envisioning the depths of the Godhead itself, depths that are apocalyptic depths, and hence depths unveiling a new Godhead only by bringing an old Godhead to an end.[20]

To enter this parabolic enactment through literature is to reverse every image of Jesus we have known if we are to be open to his contemporary and apocalyptic presence. This reversal has continually occurred in the Christian imagination, a reversal not only of given images of Jesus, but also, and even thereby, a reversal of all given Christian images of God.[21] When we read Endō's poetics as *dōhansha*, the constant suffering companion as the text of fiction announces such a reversal of every image in an apocalyptic present. Through the act of writing a vulnerable poetics, which subverts and makes strange the Christian savior in the pages of *Silence*, Endō offers a *via media* between the Scylla of dogmatism and essentialist theological rhetoric and the Charybdis of speculative fiction that seeks only to retell a "life of Jesus" as the human face divine. Endō's rupture of poetics with the refrain "trample trample!" destabilizes preconceived images of Christ and awakens within the reader new possibilities imbued with deep meaning. This is what "true fiction" represents, namely, the "attempt, apparently doomed to failure and abandoned by our time, to identify subject and object, to reconcile man and nature, consciousness and unconsciousness by poetry which is 'the first and last of all knowledge.'"[22] For missionaries, this attempt is often bound up in merely retelling the life story of Christ handed down to them without question or imagination. Yet the person and work of Jesus the Christ cannot be essentialized and diminished so readily. At the center of these attempts to reconcile "man and nature, consciousness and unconsciousness by poetry"[23] was a desire to ground and stabilize the historical Jesus of Nazareth, often with ruinous results. Consider how Friederich Schleiermacher's *Christmas Eve Celebrations* (1806) and *The Christian Faith* (1821–2)[24] led him to conceive of Jesus as an archetype of authentic humanity in relation to God without honest conversation with the Church's apostolic past—emotion stripped of the flesh of history.[25]

Whether speaking of the living Christ theologically or poetically, Jesus is a difficult protagonist to render in any genre. As Barth noted, "Jesus of Nazareth fits extremely badly into theology. ... The historical in religion, the objective element, the Lord Jesus is a problem child (*Sorgenkind*) to the theologian, a problem child that ought throughout to be accorded respect and that somehow does receive respect, but a problem child nonetheless."[26] Post-structuralist biblical scholars like Stephen D. Moore have taken up Jesus as *Sorgenkind* to see whether writing itself, as an act of incarnation, reflects the spirit of Jesus. As Plato states rather resolutely in *Phaedrus*,

> once a thing is put into writing, the composition drifts all over the place, getting into the hands not only of those who understand it, but equally of those who have no business with it; it doesn't know how to address the right people, and not address the wrong. And when it is ill-treated and unfairly abused it always needs its parent to come to its help.[27]

The struggle to figure the Christ through various means and media represents a continual search for not only the *content* of the figure in question (what makes up and makes possible this union of human and sacred), but ultimately the *form* within which this figuring is shown and understood. John McIntyre, in his Warfield Lectures delivered at Princeton Theological Seminary, begins his discussion of christology and christocentrism by employing a term not typically used in doctrinal discourse, or to put it more directly, *shape*. As McIntyre states, "if we were asked to give in a summary form the distinguishing characteristic of Protestant theology in our time, many of us would reply that it is its *christocentric* quality which claims this title. And the evidence would be convincing."[28] He surmises:

> It is by this time clear, then, that christology has come to exercise in theology a range of functions for which it was not originally designed: in this range we find exegetical, expository and hermeneutical as well as

normative and critical elements ... classical christology has come under severe strain in these new settings in which it has of late found itself and a crisis has begun to develop which can only be resolved by a radical reassessment of the basic *shape* of this central doctrine of the Christian faith as today expressed.[29]

McIntyre notes that there is indeed a continual search for the basic *shape* of this central doctrine of the Christian faith that is the nature of Christ, which goes back to the very foundations of the Church itself.

Amae—the Blurring of Object and Subject through Intimate Companionship

The movement of rupture by the textual *dōhansha* as the constant suffering companion carries the reader into a relationship of dependence with the text; this relationship ultimately blurs the lines between subject and object in keeping with Doi Takeo's notion of *amae*. Doi describes what he sees in the Japanese structure of deep dependence as something misunderstood and at times reviled by Westerners who value individuality and separateness above all else. *Amae* means that the Japanese seek relationships that allow them to rely upon others; in whatever social situation, there is always somebody with whom they enjoy a level of symbiotic responsibility of sympathy and help. This relationship is overtly hierarchical in keeping with the Confucian structure of relationships. Doi argues that hierarchical *amae* relationships imply a certain blurring between object and subject, and are mainly governed by emotional, not rational, standards.

In *Silence*, *amae* brings forth the deconstruction of mediating hierarchy and formalism, thereby leaving the pure presence of relationship and companionship that lies beyond subject/object binaries. This movement is most clearly explicated at the end of the novel where the image of Jesus is joined with the totality of Jesus in the stomping upon the *fumie*. This collapsing of image and content into a single action is what is at stake in Doi's notion of *amae*, which is forged in symbiotic intimacy and the blurring of distinctiveness rather than the hierarchical sense of relationship. This reimagining of *amae* impresses upon readers the importance of analyzing the novel in light of a heightened level of intimacy; it is a mode of reading that will disturb those who make absolute pronouncements about Jesus based on an imagined objective mandate. Indeed, some may regard this sort of reading, wherein the immanence of such a volatile Christ of silence, to be heretical.

Companionship as the Fusing of Compassion—
Mary and *Kannon*

Jean Higgins[30] notes that the history of the *kakure*, which is a central plot point for Endō in *Silence*, offers readers the fusing of religious sensibilities in a multivalent compassion that can be found in the Christian and Buddhist female archetypes of Mary, the Mother of Jesus, and Kannon, the Bodhisattva of Compassion.[31] The former is a historical figure whose importance has more to do with the religious needs and sensibilities of believers, filling a deep-felt human need for the feminine element in a religious tradition that is markedly masculine in its conception of divinity and in its ritual and organizational functioning. The many places of pilgrimage dedicated to her throughout the world bear witness to her devotees and numerous are the miracles ascribed to her intercession. The Bodhisattva Kannon is held to be non-historical; her vocation thus transcends historical time and becomes something for the ages. This legendary figure appears first under the name of Avalokitesvara, a male bodhisattva, in India. In the journey east along the Silk Road, however, diverse religious sensibilities transformed the bodhisattva so that in East Asian traditions Avalokitesvara is generally, but not exclusively, revered as female. In Tibet she is known as the gentle female Tara, in Vietnam as Quan-ân, in China as Guanyin, in Korea as Kwanüm, and in Japan as Kannon. Much loved by the Japanese people as the compassionate "Hearer of Cries," Kannon is considered "one of the most popular of all bodhisattvas."[32] Stories of miracles ascribed to her are legion and pilgrimages to famous Kannon images have been popular for many centuries. Both Mary and Kannon, the predominant feminine figures of Roman Catholic Christianity and Japanese Buddhism, played a major role in sustaining and inspiring a group of persecuted Christian believers addressed by Endō in *Silence* as the *kakure kirishitan*. These Japanese Christians underwent severe persecution in the late sixteenth century and were forced into apostasy or hiding during the reign of the Tokugawa shoguns (1603–1867). Under threat of discovery and death, all trace of Christian faith had to be removed from their lives and homes. They complied with the regulation externally, putting away images of Mary, the Mother of Mercy, and replacing them with those of the compassionate Kannon. Whatever the direction of their meditations before these images, their prayers were apparently heard. These outwardly Buddhists survived and so did their beloved Christian images. In some secret places and hallowed caves Jesus and Mary lay hidden from the persecuting authorities. Such secrecy enabled the *kakure kirishitan* to be creative as well as subversive. The novel makes clear that some Kannon figures had a secret opening at the back where hidden inside was a Christian image or medal which became the key apostasy marker for Fr. Rodrigues. Kannon images appeared among the *kakure kirishitan* showing the Buddhist goddess of mercy depicted as a mother with child in her arms. Turning to Kannon for assistance in their persecuted position, the hidden Christians continued the practice of their faith for over two centuries. As the generations went by, Kannon and Mary, the Mother of Christ, fused into one to become *Maria-Kannon*.

As missionaries met this fused image of *Maria-Kannon*, there emerged a dogmatic need to tear apart this dynamic *amae* of intimacy and companionship. Endō does not share this dogmatic appetite. His *Silence* offers abundant life in relation to Jesus as a true fiction that is neither reduced nor foreclosed.[33] By having Fr. Rodrigues stomp on the *fumie*, Endō releases the reader from fixed signs and symbols and into God's mystery. In novels like *Silence*, Endō and other fiction writers find that it is in the act of writing and reading itself that the figure whom many missionaries and some biblical critics sought to stabilize found new life. As Stephen D. Moore aptly puts it,

> As writing, Jesus must contend with invisible forces other than demons. As writing, he must be delivered up to powers other than the Jewish and Roman authorities. This force, this power, is the reader. Temma F. Berg asks: "Who is the reader?" She replies: "The reader is legion ['for we are many' – Mark 5:9]. And to give oneself to readers, to allow strange others the power of breathing life into you, is to deliver yourself into the unknown. It is to take the greatest chance of all, the risk of annihilation, of death." But if to write is to run the risk of death, it is also to seize the chance of a life after death (undead, the author lives on in his or her tome). Although Mark condemns Jesus to death by making him write, Mark *as* writing also offers him a body to live on in.[34]

Naming and Unnaming

Moore's reflection on writing and reading leads us to the fourth movement of textual *dōhansha* evident in Endō's work, one that moves fiction into the space of true companionship. Here, the act of apophasis and unnaming for the sake of longing as real presence becomes realized. In keeping with the apophatic tradition, Endō's Christ is unnamed in trampling, in elusiveness, in being found and lost repeatedly, and is only heard in silence and found silent in the attempts to name.

The mystical theologian Pseudo-Dionysius claims that to name God is to acknowledge that God is before us as no other being; in both the naming and unnaming of the divine, God will "transcend existence,"[35] and "although [God] is the cause of everything, [God] is not a thing since [God] transcends all things."[36] The divine cause of created reality is not in itself a being among beings, and divinity will continually escape and evade naming. While God cannot be fully named, God can indeed be known in unnaming through acknowledging the limited nature of language and its labels, where naming both points to and away from those whom we truly love and desire. As Bernard McGinn puts it, "all things both reveal and conceal God. The 'dissimilar similarity' that constitutes every created manifestation of God is both a similarity to be affirmed and a dissimilarity to be denied."[37] Created in and through God's ecstatic outpouring of God's self into the cosmos, beings manifest this divinely transcendent cause through the employment of naming. The danger is to hold tightly to these names and the theologies that support them, which, acting as a bridge for our lives, are meant to disclose God. Hans Urs von Balthasar writes, "Things are both like God and unlike him, but God is not like things."[38] In this way, we must deconstruct as well as construct names and theologies in order to be released into the possibility of a deep encounter with the Signifier. Pseudo-Dionysius states:

> Since it is the Cause of all beings, we should posit and ascribe to it all the affirmations we make in regard to beings [*kataphasis*], and, more appropriately, we should negate all these affirmations, since it surpasses all being [*apophasis*]. Now, we should not conclude that the negations are simply the opposites of the affirmations, but rather that the cause of all is considerably prior to this, beyond privations, beyond every denial, beyond every assertion.[39]

Von Balthasar declares that in the kataphatic mode of theology, emphasis is placed on the "manifestation of the unmanifest."[40] As immanent to all creation, God "has the name of everything that is"[41] and "the theologians praise it by every name."[42] Grounded in the causal activity that relates God to each and every being, the naming of God involves an infinite proliferation of names drawn from all creation, including things we would not ordinarily expect to be suited to God—such as "stone," "worm," and even "silence," in the case of Endō. As Pseudo-Dionysius reminds us "[God] is superior to them all because he precedes them and is transcendentally above them. Therefore every attribute may be predicated of him and yet he is not any one thing."[43] This negative theology harmonizes with Fr. Ferreira's remarks at the novel's close:

> "When you [missionaries] first came to this country churches were built everywhere, faith was fragrant like the fresh flowers of the morning, and

many Japanese vied with one another to receive baptism like the Jews who gathered at the Jordan.

And supposing the God whom those Japanese believed in was not the God of Christian teaching..." Ferreira murmured these words slowly, the smile of pity still lingering on his lips ...

"The Japanese are not able to think of God completely divorced from man; the Japanese cannot think of an existence that transcends the human. ... The Japanese imagine a beautiful, exalted man—and this they call God. They call by the name of God something which has the same kind of existence as man. But that is not the Church's God."[44]

Endō challenges the tendency to overname or "undername" God, and by doing so to move us as readers to acknowledge that such attempts at capturing God in a name may result in our downfall. In this way, Endō offers freedom to call upon God without having to arrive at a definitive name. This grand challenge enables us to see and hear the names that we invoke and thus the limited nature we impose. The apocalyptic nature of unnaming comes with the deconstruction of preconceived notions of God; here, we must release the names we have previously employed in favor of the unknown and perhaps unknowable, as when Rodrigues contemplates the *fumie* and decides to trample upon it.[45] In concert with the earlier discussion of Doi's *amae* as the collapsing of subject and object into a totality of presence, Endō places the reader in a destabilized text wherein locating and naming God becomes a challenge. Perhaps this is the crowning theological achievement of *Silence*: showing how God supersedes naming. As Heidegger states, "Wherever theology comes up, the god has been on the run for quite a while."[46] Expressed differently, Being and the Sacred vanish when a figured god, a highest being, is delimited by text and considered to be the most powerful thing in a great chain of beings. *The questioning after* the Being of all beings is the task of poetic writing, and such questioning is that which Endō's *Silence* offers us as true companionship.[47]

This is where literature is theology and theology is literature, and both ultimately fail in choosing to figure Being and the Sacred amid images, metaphors, and tropes—language that belongs to the realm of ontotheology and thus to the oblivion of Being and the Sacred. With Endō's textual *dōhansha* we are called into a space of rupturing, a place of blurring where the subject and the object, the sacred and the profane merge and intimately embrace. It is with an embrace and a covering of something akin to *furoshiki* as the linen-thin wrapping of faith that acknowledges our unity with God and humanity in our suffering; this unity provides for a deep sense of interconnection and dependence as *amae*. It is in this movement that we can also release our need to dominate and control the names of God, to desacralize the names and theologies that bind and constrict the divine and walk away once and for all from the need to establish, dominate, and manage. Where Jesus tells his followers in the post-resurrection accounts that only in his leaving will his ministry be fulfilled, so too must we understand that the true missionary is one who walks away and relinquishes all need for control in order that the God we so blithely invoke can at last become present in our absence as well.

Notes

1   While much has been written in literary criticism about Endō Shūsaku's various novels, this chapter builds on such work and explores the phenomenological and theological aspects of Endo's work, especially *Silence*.

2   This notion of *dōhansha* is explored in Kawashima Hidekazu, *Endō Shūsaku ai no dōhansha* 77 (Osaka: Izumi Shoin, 1993), which was published in Japanese, as well as in Mark B. Williams, *Endō Shūsaku: A Literature of Reconciliation* (London: Routledge, 1999).

3   Cited by Dorothea Frede in "The Question of Being: Heidegger's Project," in ed. Charles B. Guignon, *The Cambridge Companion to Heidegger* 2nd edn. (Cambridge: Cambridge University Press, 2006), 42.

4   Cited in David Farrell Krell ed., *Basic Writings of Martin Heidegger* (London: Routledge, 1996), 441–2.

5   Williams, *A Literature of Reconciliation*, 122.

6   See Jeffrey F. Keuss, *A Poetics of Jesus: The search for Christ through nineteenth century literature* (Burlington, VT: Ashgate, 2002), and *Freedom of the Self: Kenosis, Cultural Identity and Mission at the Crossroads* (Eugene, OR: Pickwick, 2010).

7   Doi Takeo, *The Anatomy of Dependence* (New York: Kodansha USA, 1999).

8   Salman Rushdie, "Is Nothing Sacred?" *Granta* 31 (Spring 1990): 102–3.

9   Cited by Philip Yancey, "Japan's Faithful Judas: Shusaku Endo's struggle to give his faith a Japanese Soul," in *Books & Culture* (January–February, 1996): 3, 6–7.

10 See Jeff Keuss, "The Lenten Face of Christ in Shusaku Endo's *Silence* and *Life of Jesus*," *The Expository Times* 118.6 (2007): 273–9.

11 Shusaku Endo, *A Life of Jesus*, trans. Robert Schuchert (New York: Paulist Press, 1978), 1.

12 Ibid.

13 Kazoh Kitamori, *Theology of the Pain of God* (Eugene, Oregon: Wipf and Stock, 2005).

14 Hajime Tanabe, *Philosophy as Metanoetics*, trans. Takeuchi Yoshinori (Berkeley, CA: University of California Press, 1986).

15 Jacques Derrida, *Writing and Difference* (London: Routledge Press, 1978), 280.

16 Hal Foster, *The Return of the Real* (Boston: MIT Press, 1996), 146. Foster maintains that this idea of *trauma* is central to critical theory after postmodernity (168): "Across artistic, theoretical, and popular cultures (in Soho, at Yale, on *Oprah*) there is a tendency to redefine experience, individual and historical, in terms of trauma … Here is indeed a traumatic subject, and it has absolute authority, for one cannot challenge the trauma of another: one can only believe it, even identify with it, or not."

17 Jacques Derrida, *Writing and Difference*, 109.

18 Ibid., 129.

19 Shusaku Endo, *Silence,* trans. William Johnston (New York: Taplinger Publishing, 1980), 68–9.

20 For additional details on Altizer see Keuss, "The Lenten Face of Christ," 276–7. Also see Thomas J. J. Altizer, *The Contemporary Jesus* (Albany: State University of New York Press, 1997), xiv–v, xxiii.

21 I think Altizer is an instructive interlocutor for reading Endō's overturning of the entrenched images of Christ and seeing the path of true devotion as more of an apocalyptic rather than dogmatic turn. See Altizer, *The Contemporary Jesus*, xxv.

22 René Welleck, "Romanticism Re-examined," in Stephen G. Nichols, ed., *Concepts of Criticism* (New Haven: Yale University Press, 1963), 221.

23 Ibid., 222.

24 Pelikan states that Schleiermacher's lectures marked the first in the modern University to "lecture publicly on the topic of the life of Jesus" and "making this the subject of academic lectures at the University of Berlin five times between 1819 and 1832, although the book to come out of student notes on the lectures did not appear until 1864." See Jaroslav Pelikan, *Jesus Through the Centuries* (New York: Harper and Row, 1985), 195.

25 Writing in *The Christian Faith*, Friedrich Schleiermacher says, "The archetype (*Urbild*) must have become completely historical … and each historical moment of this individual must be born within the archetypal." Cited in Pelikan, *Jesus Through the Centuries,* 195.

26 Cited in Keuss, *Poetics of Jesus,* 10.

27 Plato, *Phaedrus*, in *The Collected Dialogues of Plato*, ed. Edith Hamilton (Princeton: Princeton University Press, 1961), 275.

28 John McIntyre, *The Shape Of Christology* (London: SCM Press, 1966), 9.

29 Ibid., 11.

30 Jean Higgins, "Maria-Kannon of the *Kakure*," *Dialogue & Alliance* 12.1 (Spring/Summer 1998): 5–20.

31 Kannon is the Japanese name for Avalokiteshvara (Sanskrit) the

companion of Amitabha (Sanskrit)/Amida (Japanese), a bliss body emanation of Buddha who resides in the Western paradise of Sukhavati.

32 Higgins, "Maria-Kannon of the *Kakure*," 16.

33 Here I am alluding to John 10.10.

34 Stephen D. Moore, *Mark and Luke in Poststructuralist Perspectives: Jesus Begins to Write* (New Haven: Yale University Press, 1992), 17–18.

35 Pseudo-Dionysius, "Divine Names," in *Pseudo-Dionysius: The Complete Works*, trans. Paul Rorem (New York: Paulist Press, 1987), 587.

36 Ibid., 593.

37 Bernard McGinn, *The Foundations of Mysticism* (New York: Crossroad Press, 1992), 174.

38 Hans Urs von Balthasar, *The Glory of the Lord: A Theological Aesthetics* 2 (New York: Crossroad, 1982), 168.

39 Pseudo-Dionysius, *The Mystical Theology* in *Pseudo-Dionysius: The Complete Works*, 1000.

40 Von Balthasar, *The Glory of the Lord*, 164.

41 Pseudo-Dionysius, *The Mystical Theology*, 596.

42 Ibid.

43 Ibid., 824.

44 Endo, *Silence*, 147, 150.

45 The seminal scene of apostasy in *Silence* comes in the apocalyptic encounter with the *fumie* at the end of Chapter 8 (171).

46 Cited in a paper by Martin Schäfer, "The Sacred: A Figureless Figure: On Heidegger," presented at the Conference on Theology and Criticism at Johns Hopkins University, March 4–7, 1999.

47 Ibid.

12

Is Abjection a Virtue?: *Silence* and the Trauma of Apostasy

Dennis Washburn

Every day, Jesus humbles Himself just as He did when He came from His heavenly throne into the Virgin's womb; every day He comes to us and lets us see Him in abjection, when He descends from the bosom of the Father into the hands of the priest at the altar.

St. Francis of Assisi

… man, in his philosophical inquiry, is faced again and again with the experience that reality is unfathomable and Being is mystery—an experience, it is true, which urges him not so much to communication as to silence. But it would not be the silence of resignation, and still less of despair. It would be the silence of reverence.

Joseph Pieper[1]

The moment of crisis that Endō Shūsaku's novel *Silence* builds to and falls away from is a coerced renunciation of belief and identity. In this particular instance, apostasy is publicly confirmed by the ritual trampling of a *fumie* (literally, "a picture for stepping on") bearing an image of the face of Jesus. When the apostate, a Jesuit priest, hesitates, trembling from mental anguish, he is offered reassurance by the Japanese interpreter: "… What do formalities matter? … You only have to go through the exterior form of trampling."[2] Then, at the moment the priest raises his foot, he hears the face on the *fumie* speaking to him: "It is all right to trample on me. More than anyone else I understand the ache in your foot. It is all right to trample. I was born into this world in order to be stepped on by people like you."[3]

This priest, Sebastian Rodrigues, is a fictional Portuguese Jesuit modeled on the real-life apostate Giuseppe Chiara (1602–85). His character is developed in the opening four chapters, a first-person epistolary narrative that focuses on the priest's inner turmoil with regard to his mission—a struggle between his confident faith, courage and pride on one side, and his doubts about and occasional feelings of disgust toward the people he has come to serve on the other. This psychological struggle sets the stage for his apostasy and reveals the full extent of the spiritual and psychic ruptures caused by the decision to step on the *fumie*.

The feelings of shame and guilt that haunt Rodrigues after his apostasy are made apparent in the narrative through his attempts to justify and redeem himself by re-inscribing his personal story onto the larger narrative of Christ's life. In the closing chapter of *Silence* Rodrigues admits that he has renounced the Church as an institution, but he insists that deep inside he has not renounced his faith, that he has achieved a more self-reflective, critical consciousness that permits a new understanding of the nature of faith.

Like any accomplished work of literary art, the achievement of *Silence* (*Chinmoku*, 1966) is that the story of Rodrigues's apostasy invites and sustains multiple interpretations. As a historical novel, it has been praised in Japan and abroad for its vivid, compelling representation of political authority in early Tokugawa society, the origins of the Hidden Christians, and the tensions created by the first direct contact between Japanese and European cultures. As a meditation on moral choice, the narrative's treatment of the problem of God's silence in the face of evil presents a crucial, vexing theological issue that had special political, secular significance for many Japanese readers who lived through the postwar period, when debates about personal responsibility and complicity in war crimes and coercive state violence raged. As a reflection on the question of the compatibility, or translatability, of values across cultures—specifically, the issue of whether a religion such as Christianity can find a place in Japan—*Silence* had particular resonance for a readership dealing with rapid cultural change and wrestling with the consequences of defeat and occupation. While some lamented the collapse of the old order, others blamed the disruptions of postwar society on Japan's apparent failure to modernize its ethical outlook and the standards for justifying belief in values.[4]

These readings each emphasize a significant element in the narrative, but in mentioning a few of the many possible critical approaches to *Silence* at the outset of this essay, I do not mean to signal agreement or disagreement with them or to privilege one particular reading over the other. Each of them reflects the application of a particular "readerly" framework that in its own way opens up the text and reveals its complexity, while at the same time revealing the limits of any interpretive scheme. Nevertheless, these multiple readings are, in a very real sense, part of the textual history of the novel—not just the "history" that Endō chronicles, but the accumulation of meta-textual meanings created by the postwar milieu in which he wrote.

Thus, readers who are not as familiar with Japanese history and culture must at least consider these approaches in order to come to a more complete and sensitive engagement with *Silence*.

One way to account for them, to give them coherence and see how they mutually engage and overlap, is to consider the way the novel's meanings emerge out of Endō's stylistics, which is distinguished by two major features. The first is a complex structure created by the use of multi-vocal, multi-perspective narration. The second is the novel's narrow focus as a character study. At the risk of oversimplifying the work, at its core is a description of the transformation of the moral dispositions of an individual who, when placed in extreme circumstances, is forced to behave in ways contradictory to the very modes of thought and feeling that ground his self-conception and identity.

Even the most accurate and sensitive of historical novels leave anachronistic traces of the process of their composition, and in the case of *Silence* these are apparent in the way in which the formal apparatus of the modern novel is used to represent Rodrigues's narrative of self-identity. There are radical historical differences in discursive practice between the story Rodrigues tells about himself and how that story is used as a rhetorical component of Endō's novel. Up to the moment of his apostasy, Rodrigues's self-narrative is orthodox in its religious orientation, exterior in its perspective, and idealistic in its narrative mode. In contrast, the narrative of *Silence* is, as a matter of discursive practice, heterodox with regard to religious views. It employs highly interiorized perspectives, and its primary mode is realistic and, in its use of multi-vocal narrative, heteroglossic. These differences in discursive practice are revealed in the intentionally complicated, concentric structure of the narrative, which shifts perspective from the first-person accounts of Rodrigues's four letters to the third-person account of his imprisonment, apostasy, and later life. This perspective is in turn framed by the "historically objective," detached voice created by the Prologue at the beginning and by the "official" records contained in the Appendix. The lack of a single authoritative voice complicates the "facts" of history, making it much more difficult to judge Rodrigues's action with any degree of moral certitude.

Within this complex narrative structure, Endō tightly focuses on the disposition of his main character, especially the perspective and state of mind of an individual in crisis, to further amplify the sense of indeterminacy concerning moral judgments of the behavior of the protagonist. As the story unfolds, Rodrigues is initially in control of his own narrative, which he interprets and gives coherence to by constantly reading his own life as an analog of the story of Jesus Christ. Once he is captured, however, the loss of control is indicated in rhetorical terms by the switch to a third-person narration in the second half of the work. The crisis of apostasy that follows is triggered by the realization on the part of the protagonist, the priest Rodrigues, that the people whose souls he is committed to saving may not be capable of truly understanding the teachings of the Church. His doubts about the loss of control of his beliefs arise when he encounters cultural differences that create what he takes to be an unbridgeable chasm between Western and Japanese values.

In one of his early letters Rodrigues notes with unease that many of the Japanese Christians he meets are more interested in obtaining the icons of the religion as magic talismans than in studying the doctrines.[5] After he is betrayed by his guide, Kichijirō, his captors play upon his nagging doubts to devastating effect. They torture and execute Japanese Christians, but do not harm him despite his protests that he alone should be punished. They have no intention of allowing him to complete his own narrative and write himself into the book of Christian lore by attaining the glory of martyrdom. Instead they give him the opportunity to show "Christian" mercy and love by sacrificing his own identity to save Japanese adherents, who do not really understand the foreign religion anyway.

The force of this argument becomes overwhelming when Christovao Ferreira (1580–1650) is brought in to make the case for apostasy. Endō's decision to use the historical figure of Ferreira in this context is not simply a gesture toward historical veracity. It is a shrewd rhetorical device that creates sympathy for Rodrigues (and complicates our judgment of him) by showing the kind of psychological pressure that would make apostasy not just plausible, but understandable. When Ferreira insists that Christianity cannot take root in Japan, Rodrigues protests that that is only because the roots are torn up. Ferreira responds without emotion, like an automaton: "This country is a more terrible swamp than you can imagine. Whenever you plant a sapling in this swamp the roots begin to rot; the leaves grow yellow and wither. And we have planted the sapling of Christianity in this swamp."[6]

As might be expected under the circumstances, Ferreira comes across as a duplicitous tempter, since the reader knows little about him at this point other than that he is an apostate. However, the depiction of Rodrigues is hardly more trustworthy. Because he is not being tortured, he knows nothing of the suffering he talks about, and thus he comes across as either naïve or hypocritical. He attempts to parry Ferreira's seductive argument by pointing out the peasants who are being tortured in his presence will know the reward of "eternal joy" as recompense for their sufferings. Ferreira leaps on his response, accusing Rodrigues of self-deception, of disguising his own weakness behind beautiful sounding platitudes. When Rodrigues, who is puzzled and unsure in the face of this accusation, demands to know why his belief in the salvation of the Japanese who are dying for their faith is a weakness, Ferreira answers that it is because the priest puts himself and his own salvation above those who are suffering, refusing to save them out of fear of betraying the Church. He then adds the most crucial statement in the narrative: "You dread to be the dregs of the Church, like me."[7] At that moment Ferreira's voice weakens, as if he were remembering the anguish of his own apostasy, and for a moment he seems to show genuine empathy: "On that cold, black night I, too, was as you are now. And yet is your way of acting love? A priest ought to live in imitation of Christ. If Christ were here …"[8]

Ferreira's argument could be viewed in strictly doctrinal terms as an accusation that Rodrigues is being prideful and lacking the virtue of humility necessary for salvation. At the same time, he is also striking at Rodrigues's pride by calling him cowardly, by claiming that he is afraid of self-abjection. The psychological force of this statement is devastating because it takes advantage of the very character traits that not only drove Rodrigues to undertake his mission, but also fueled his sense of unease. At this moment in the story, the literary skill Endō has brought to his depiction of Rodrigues becomes apparent. The apostasy comes to seem inevitable not simply as a matter of historical fact, but as the result of the accumulative affective power of the portrait of the protagonist's moral dispositions.

The question of motive as a dramatic element creates a serious complication for how we interpret the nature of Rodrigues's apostasy. Since the story is based on a historical incident, Rodrigues's motives and his change in consciousness in the fictional world of the narrative have to be givens. Questions about the truthfulness of the account, or of the sincerity of motives, are thus not really relevant to an analysis of the work. After all, the minimal expectation a reader brings to a work of historical fiction, apart from its "facticity," is that it be plausible. Unlike historical narratives, however, there is no expectation that a work of fiction is obliged to take into account the contingency of events. Thus, the heuristic value of a novel—most especially a work of historical fiction—does not lie in its presentation of facts, but rather in its making explicit the way we talk about things, how we understand the world in narrative terms, and, through that understanding, how we come to knowledge.

Real-life facts in *Silence* should be read as just another rhetorical element, though that does not in any way diminish their significance. Indeed, the historical grounding of the novel helps establish multiple contexts for examining the questions it raises concerning the trauma of apostasy and its aftermath. Was Rodrigues's apostasy a denial of faith, or was it the perfect exemplification of Christian virtue? What constitutes Christian virtue? Rodrigues puts this question to himself early in the novel, when, disquieted by what he sees as errors in the religious beliefs of Japanese converts and disgusted by the abject nature of the peasants to whom he ministers, he attempts to justify his work to himself: "Christ did not die for the good and beautiful. It is easy enough to die for the good and beautiful; the hard thing is to die for the miserable and corrupt—this is the realization that came home to me acutely at that time."[9]

Rodrigues's attitude reveals both pride and good will, and as such he comes across as simultaneously admirable and condescending. However, his view of Christ as abject is a recurring element in the New Testament story that he desperately wants to identify with. Is he abasing himself in making this observation? Has he already conditioned himself to accept Ferreira's argument? To put the matter more succinctly, in Rodrigues's moral universe, is abjection a virtue?

It may be difficult to respond to this question by recourse to our own contemporary values; and in this regard the issue of the translatability of values and beliefs, which plays such an important role in the novel, is relevant to our consideration of it. The possibility that moral or religious concepts are not universal, that they may not always cross cultural borders, has profound implications for religious faith in particular and for moral judgments more generally.

Rodrigues wrestles with the problem of translating and transcultural understanding early in his mission. At one point Kichijirō, the weak-willed, filthy, untrustworthy guide whom the priest considers his own Judas, asks what evil the Japanese believers committed to have brought such suffering on themselves. In one of his letters, Rodrigues mulls over the problem and cannot escape the uncomfortable fact of the silence of God: "… in the face of this terrible and merciless sacrifice offered up to Him, God has remained silent. This was the problem that lay behind the plaintive question of Kichijirō."[10]

Precisely because of the profound challenge posed by the problem of God's silence in the face of evil, Ferreira's belief in the untranslatability of cultures, which he explains through the metaphor of Japan as swamp, carries such force. He asserts that the swamp of Japan so alters the essential nature of Christian doctrine that the God worshiped by converts to Catholicism is not the God of the Church. He tells Rodrigues that "What the Japanese of that time believed in was not our God. It was their own gods. For a long time we failed to realize this and believed that they had become Christians."[11]

In considering the translatability (or commensurability) of belief systems within the context of this work, the reader has to consider the important historical role that virtue ethics played in both Catholic ideology and Japanese society at the time the story unfolds. Humility, abjection, or renunciation would seem to be eminently translatable as social and religious values, but were they considered virtues within the dominant forms of ethical discourse in seventeenth-century Japan? More important, if abjection or humility results only in silence, that is, in a failure to reach communion with God, does it have any ethical significance at all?

Examining the role of virtue ethics in the religious discourse by which the reader is asked to judge the events of *Silence* may prove helpful as a way to pull together the various literary, religious, and cultural strands and meanings of the novel. In general, aretaic ethics, as opposed to duty-based or consequentialist systems of moral thought, attempts to ground belief in moral values and strictures by following examples of good and righteous behavior. What matters as much if not more than rules or outcomes in justifying belief in certain values is the cultivation of a disposition to do the right things. By considering Rodrigues's apostasy within the context of the virtue ethics that guided his worldview, the question as to whether he did the right thing can be reframed. Did he do the right thing *as a Catholic priest*?

It is somewhat strange to think of abjection as a virtue. The more normal term for the virtue in Catholic teaching (as manipulated by Ferreira) is humility. Taking up the style of analysis employed by Aristotle in the *Nichomachean Ethics*, Thomas Aquinas defined humility as the proper mean situated between the vices of pride at one extreme and too great an obsequiousness, or abjection of the self, at the other. In the Thomistic account of Christian virtues, then, abjection was considered an excess of humility and thus destructive of moral character, since an individual must have a proper understanding of his or her own worth. Otherwise, humility would be false. However, any self-assessment has to be made in the context of one's unworthiness in the eyes of God and of service to Christ.

Despite the authority of Aquinas in establishing the ethical system of Christian virtues, there was and continues to be a slightly different view of abjection that effectively equates it with humility, and takes it to be the true descriptor of the notion of Christhood. As the epigraph from St. Francis of Assisi makes clear, abjection is a visceral, bodily abasement that suggests the infinite extent to which Christ lowered himself by becoming man. In St. Francis's view, given the greatness of the humiliation and suffering Jesus endured (not to mention that he offers his body and blood to us as a purifying sacrifice), abjection is a virtue that Christians should aspire to cultivate.

It is important to note that a similar view of abjection is presented by St. Francis de Sales in his 1609 treatise, *Introduction to the Devout Life*, a work that enjoyed wide circulation and would have certainly been known to the historical figures that Endō draws upon in composing his novel. St.

Francis de Sales discusses abjection as a virtue at some length in Part 3, note 6 of his *Introduction*. He explicitly urges his readers to rejoice in their own abjection, claiming that in Latin the term is essentially a synonym for humility. Despite the word's etymology, however, he argues that there is a difference between humility and abjection. He takes abjection as the poverty, vileness, and littleness in human nature that is given no heed, whereas humility implies a real knowledge and voluntary recognition of that abjection (here he is more or less following Aquinas). Still, he goes further than Aquinas and seems to echo Assisi by arguing that the highest point of humility is not merely acknowledging one's abjection, but taking pleasure in it. Moreover, abjection does not point to lack of character or courage, but is motivated by a desire to give all glory to God and to esteem others more highly than one's self.

This notion of abjection is not a call to quiescence, or to total abasement that results in inaction. When confronting evil, all Christians are called upon to at least try to overcome it. In addition, abjection is not something that should necessarily be chosen, but accepted as God's choice—a point, it should be noted, that has clear implications for our understanding of Rodrigues's justification for apostasy. For St. Francis de Sales, when a choice is forced upon an individual, the greatest abjection is preferable in that it is most contrary to an individual's personal inclinations.

The Christian notion of abjection as a virtue was thus well established within the religious discourse that historical figures like Chiara and Ferreira would have been intimately familiar with. However, the fact that the fictional Ferreira in *Silence* is shown making use of abjection as the justification for renouncing Christian faith suggests the problematic nature of the term and of its use within the discourse of virtue ethics.

A good illustration of the troubling ambiguity of the concept of abjection as a mark of divinity is provided by Jorge Luis Borges's intriguing, dryly ironic short story, "Three Versions of Judas." Borges's narrator assumes an archly detached, scholarly tone to relate the story of Nils Runeberg, a theologian who lived in the early part of the twentieth century. Runeberg's work leads him to propose a heretical view of the nature of Christ. Since God is in all things perfect, Runeberg's thesis runs, he would have been perfectly abject when he lowered himself to the status of man for the redemption of mankind: " ... we may conjecture that His sacrifice was perfect, not invalidated or attenuated by any omission. To limit what He underwent to the agony of one afternoon on the cross is blasphemous."[12]

On the basis of this argument, Runeberg ends up concluding that "He could have been Alexander or Pythagoras or Rurik or Jesus; He chose the vilest destiny of all: He was Judas."[13] When no one accepts the beautiful, terrible logic of his argument, Runeberg concludes (being the academic he is) that God has ordained indifference to his discovery so that the secret truth would not get out. This realization drives Runeberg mad: "Drunk with insomnia and vertiginous dialectic, Nils Runeberg wandered through the streets of Malmö begging at the top of his voice that he be granted the grace of joining his Redeemer in Hell."[14]

Although Borges's story is obviously different in tone and conception from a work like *Silence*, bringing it into comparison with Endō's novel helps illustrate the nature of the dilemma that arises when we attempt to judge whether or not Rodrigues's embrace of abjection is a virtue that actually justifies his apostasy. There is, after all, some precedent within Christian ethics that would allow an understanding and acceptance of Rodrigues's turn. Yet, as is made explicitly clear in Borges's story (and implicitly so in *Silence*), the reader must be wary of the motives of characters and narrators in all literary fictions, even those based on historical facts. Ferreira's appeal to abjection as living in imitation of Christ can and should be read as just another story that can be told, as nothing more than beautiful words that possess no more truth than Rodrigues's own story that the suffering of the Japanese martyrs is justified on the grounds that eternal life and joy awaits them. If self-abjection *is* a Christian virtue, it must at least be acknowledged to be a paradoxical one.

Given the various ethical, religious, and historical discourses that Endō drew upon to serve the literary aims of his character study, it may be helpful to consider one more view of abjection that examines the concept through a more contemporary psychological lens. Julia Kristeva developed the idea of the abject as something that is rejected by or disturbs social reason—the communal consensus that underpins social order. The abject, in other words, is located outside the symbolic order, and being forced to confront it is traumatic and leads to the kind of revulsion that one feels in the presence of filth, waste, or death—that is, to anything that was once a subject but has been cast out of the world.

Kristeva develops her definition of abjection as part of a larger project, a psychoanalytical analysis of horror in which she argues that abjection is done to exclude or separate from the maternal (that is, that which created us) in order to construct an identity. Paradoxically, ritual contact with the abject is often used as a way to exclude it, and for that reason Kristeva relates (but does not identify) her notion of the abject with the feeling of the uncanny that arises when encountering something that seems at once familiar and disturbingly alien. Feelings of disgust and revulsion are associated with the abject (usually as reasons for casting it out), but it is not simply the unclean or unhygienic that cause abjection. Rather it arises from what disturbs identity, system, order. What does not respect borders, positions, rules. The in-between, the ambiguous, the composite. The traitor, the liar, the criminal with a good conscience, the shameless rapist, the killer who claims he is a savior. ... Any crime, because it draws attention to the fragility of the law, is abject, but premeditated crime, cunning murder, hypocritical revenge are even more so because they heighten the display of such fragility. He who denies morality is not abject; there can be grandeur in amorality and even in crime that flaunts its disrespect for the law—rebellious, liberating, and suicidal crime. Abjection, on the other hand, is immoral, sinister, scheming, and shady: a terror that dissembles, a hatred that smiles, a passion that uses the body for barter instead of inflaming it, a debtor who sells you up, a friend who stabs you.[15]

I have cited Kristeva at length in part because her catalog of the possible causes of the psychological state of abjection corresponds strikingly to certain elements of Endō's narrative of the traumas that befell his protagonist and led to the self-abjection of apostasy. More important, Kristeva goes on to cite the example of Christian mystics who saw the abject not as something to be cast away, but as a state of being that moved toward pure spirituality. She notes that the mystic's embrace of the abject is often a source of ecstasy and a way toward a closer communication, or communion, with the divine. She points to St. Francis of Assisi's treatment of lepers, to whom he not only provided alms, but also bathed and, famously, kissed on the mouth. She also mentions Angela of Foligno, who believed that to set oneself up as evil was a way to abolish evil in oneself, and that abjection, a source of evil mingled with sin was, paradoxically, a requisite for any reconciliation between body and spirit.

When taken on their own apart from her larger agenda, Kristeva's observations on Christian mystics are helpful in understanding how abjection could function as a form of reconciliation, communication, and consolation. This conception of the abject is present in an important scene that gives us insight into Rodrigues's mind when he is imprisoned, but just prior to his apostasy. He is visited by Kichijirō, who has come seeking absolution despite having betrayed the priest to the authorities: "Kichijirō shifted and shuffled. The stench of his filth and sweat was wafted toward the priest. Could it be possible that Christ loved and searched after this dirtiest of men? In evil there remained that strength and beauty of evil; but this Kichijirō was not even worthy to be called evil."[16]

Suppressing his disgust, Rodrigues performs the ritual of absolution, which, it seems, would indicate that he has reached some form of reconciliation, that he has reached a holy state of self-abjection, and yet that narrative makes it clear that in terms of his inner disposition he is not sanctified. As he lies in bed, he mulls over the stories of how Jesus sought out the ragged and the dirty, and he repeats to himself the idea that true love means accepting humanity even when "wasted like rags and tatters. Theoretically the priest knew all this; but still he could not forgive Kichijirō."[17]

Though the novel is primarily concerned with the nature of religious belief, Rodrigues's self-abjection also carries with it the weight of the history of European encounters with radically other cultures, belief systems, and political practices. These encounters transformed Western cultures, shaping how they conceived their place and identity in the world. The consciousness of difference that Europeans experienced as a result of their contact with what they saw as the unfamiliar, uncanny, and abject was disruptive in that it made visible the ways in which the institutions and practices that defined Western cultures and identities were constructed and justified. The challenge to claims of timeless and universal values posed by the recognition of relative difference led, as often as not, to chauvinistic reaffirmations of long-held beliefs, but the effort to resist, control, or subjugate non-Western cultures is itself evidence of the impact that other cultures had on the consciousness of European identities.

In this regard, then, the self-abjection depicted in *Silence* is the outcome of both a struggle with the meaning of religious faith and a clash of cultures. Within these psychological and social contexts, Rodrigues's self-justification (another form of abjection) may be thought of as a way for him to transform his apostasy into a type of conversion, expressed as an ongoing negotiation between competing narratives of his (Christian) identity. An analysis of the experience of self-abjection/apostasy as conversion must therefore account not only for the historical facts of such an experience, which would include observable changes in beliefs, outlooks, and practices, but also for the habits of thought and processes of composition revealed by the discursive and ritual practices of conversion narratives. Endō's novel reveals in the play of its words the transformations of both internal character and external narrative of identity that make conversion possible, suggesting that conversion is in some measure a venture in poetics.

Since Rodrigues tries so hard to map his own life experiences onto the story of Jesus, tying his identity to an idealized narrative, it is no stretch to read his apostasy as a narrative of conversion. Of course, the best-known and most exemplary Christian narrative of conversion is the story of Saul, which is generally understood as an instance of a sudden, blinding conversion. Yet what is striking about this account is that Saul's conversion is not so sudden after all—at least it is not instantaneous. It is certainly precipitated by an unexpected divine visitation that brings on the crisis of Saul's blindness. But the actual conversion takes place several days later when Ananias explains the full implications of the blinding light. Only after Saul understands the meaning of the story of Christ—a story backed up with the proof provided by the miraculous restoration of his sight—can he accept its truth, re-inscribe his own life story, and create his new, true identity as Paul.

Silence explicitly embraces several key elements of the model of conversion provided by the story of Saul/Paul. One is the ecstatic, hallucinatory quality of the moment of turning, which is recounted in the passage cited at the beginning of this essay. Another is the emphasis on the interior disposition, or state of mind, of the convert as the determining factor in the experience, a narrative element that again corresponds to the emphasis on the protagonist's character and the judgment of his actions according the standards set by the ethical system of Christian virtue. Both of these elements are crucial in creating the ambiguous depiction of the process of Rodrigues's self-abjection/conversion. He experiences a miraculous encounter with the divine, the voice of Jesus, which both encourages and justifies his apostasy. But the actual conversion of Rodrigues, that is, the turn to a new, more personal (Protestant?) form of belief in God, takes place only after the process of reflection has allowed him to come to terms with his actions. The story he tells himself does not provide the comfort of justification, but rather initiates a change in identity that situates his own abjection in a new narrative of redemption.

This reading of the stories of Paul and of Rodrigues suggests that conversion may be described as a rewriting of identity, a narrative process that ends with the humbling consciousness that a change has taken place. Without such self-awareness—the consciousness of difference that is constitutive of the protagonist's new identity—conversion cannot be an operative description. The changed consciousness that emerges from the rewriting, however, is not just an inner affect, but the result of the process of translating the values and practices that previously structured the inner narrative of an individual's life into a narrative more in line with the values and practices of the new community of the apostate/convert.

This view of the process of conversion is supported by Robert Hefner, who argues that the "necessary feature of religious conversion ... is not a systematic reorganization of personal meanings" but a recalibration of the understanding of self-identity through the adoption of practices and beliefs seen as more true.[18] Because conversion implies at an analytic minimum "the acceptance of a new locus of self-definition,"[19] Hefner argues for a balanced view that situates the dispositions of individuals within the disciplining authorities established by a range of social, religious, and political institutions. Conversion is better described within an analytical framework that recognizes that identity develops from ongoing and deeply contingent social-psychological interactions.[20]

The model of conversion as a creative interaction of social and personal narratives more accurately describes the nature of the conversion recounted in *Silence*. For it brings us back to the suggestion above that conversion is an ongoing process involving some sort of negotiation between competing narratives of identity—a process that arises when an individual is forced to adjust to a new set of personal and social conditions. Talal Asad, following Karl Morrison, sees this view as especially appealing because it takes conversion as a subject of analysis rather than as an analytical tool: "… it would be better to say that in studying conversion, one was dealing with the narratives by which people apprehended and described a radical change in the significance of their lives. Sometimes these narratives employ the notion of divine intervention; at other times the notion of a secular teleology."[21]

Morrison, for his part, takes the notion of conversion *as narrative* even further. Though he remains alive to the various possibilities of experience that the term conversion holds out to us, he argues that the conversion experience of an individual is essentially inaccessible to others because of the mediating force of text. His point is not to dismiss "the entire literature of conversion as without historical reliability. It is to establish the study of conversion as a venture in poetics, for texts witness to processes of composition and to habits of thought at work in them more than to the dramatic events that the texts portray. *Processes and habits are historical too.*"[22]

Morrison's insight helps explain how *Silence*, which is rhetorically and historically constrained by the need to replicate the essential arc of Christian narrative, can provide a representation of the phenomenon of conversion that is not culturally bound. The depiction of conversion experience in *Silence* is compelling and sophisticated not, as mentioned above, because of the novel's emphasis on historical factuality, but because the novel represents in the manner of its composition—its discursive practices—the social and psychological processes that enable self-abjection and conversion.

Rodrigues at first stubbornly resists Ferreira's blandishments, clinging to the notion that the Christian God and the teachings of the Church are universal and transcendent. But Ferreira counters with the observation that notions of transcendence are completely alien to Japanese culture and cannot be translated. From that point of view Rodrigues's stubborn refusal to apostatize and save the Japanese who are being persecuted is not heroic but selfish and immoral. Ferreira urges him to live in imitation of Christ, saying, "Surely Christ would have apostatized for them."[23]

It is this final appeal that turns the priest. Rodrigues later learns, in a bitterly ironic twist, that his earlier assessment of the situation—that Japan was not a "swamp" and that the Church's mission in Japan was failing because the authorities would not allow it to flourish—was correct. Near the end of the novel, during an audience with the Lord of Chikugo, Rodrigues once more hears Japan described as a swamp, but the Lord of Chikugo makes it plain that his intent was to cut the roots of the Church through the example of the priest. This revelation furthers clouds the meaning of the priest's story. Should we take this comment to mean that conversion is possible, that the Church can be translated to Japan if not suppressed? Did Rodrigues apostatize in vain?

The novel effectively leaves this question unanswered. Near the end of the main narrative, right before the official records that appear as an Appendix, the priest is visited once more by Kichijirō, who admits his acts of betrayal to the faith. Still, Kichijirō seeks to excuse himself by complaining that his abject nature puts a greater burden on him than the burden carried by martyrs who were strong enough to resist apostasy. His remarks strike a deep chord with Rodrigues, who immediately recalls the moment of his own apostasy when the voice of Christ spoke to him, assuring him it was all right to trample on the image. Rodrigues at last engages that voice in a dialogue:

> "Lord, I resented your constant silence."
> "I was not silent. I suffered beside you."
> "But you told Judas to go away: What thou dost do quickly. What happened to Judas?"
> "I did not say that. Just as I told you to step on the image, so I told Judas to do what he was going to do. For Judas was in anguish as you are now."[24]

The priest justifies his decision by again repeating that even though he was betraying the Church, his changed conception of his love for God meant that he was not betraying Christ, that his behavior was in accord with the virtue of true humility. Through self-abjection and the mystical, incomprehensible joy he experienced when he stepped on the *fumie*, he had reached communion and final identification with Christ.

Still, this resolution is ambiguous at best; and that ambiguity is reinforced by the story of Rodrigues's final years, which are recounted in the officer's journal that ends the text. Rodrigues's attitudes and evident weaknesses are so striking in this impersonal account because the discursive practices that determine the way Rodrigues authored his own story are in the end subordinated to the discursive practices that characterize the novel as a whole. If the outcome of Rodrigues's apostasy is that it converts him to a consciousness of heterodox identity, it is because his story is literally translated into, and disciplined by, the discursive practices not of his religion, but of the modern novel.

In a larger sense, Rodrigues's turn may be read as a microcosm for an important element of the history of Japan's earliest direct encounter with Europe. As noted above, the contact with radically other cultures was deeply transformative of modern Western societies.[25] Yet *Silence* is not a simple allegory of the turmoil and violence of colonial encounters. Rodrigues's apostasy and its aftermath are not played out on the cultural ground that gave rise to his mission. Instead, he has to rationalize his actions and beliefs, to search for some understanding of the meaning of his life, in a foreign land. He is doubly alienated. Isolated both physically and spiritually, he is stripped of the autonomy and power typical of the relationship between Western colonizers and the lands they subjugated.

We learn in the final part of the novel—the account of the officer guarding the priest's residence—that Rodrigues was forced to undergo a kind of absolute conversion after his apostasy. That is, he is forced to turn Japanese, to go native in the most basic, abject sense of the term. Rodrigues is given a Japanese name, Okada San'emon, is married to a Japanese woman, and is put in charge of a household. He lives on for 30 years in that residence. Although this final document routinely notes official suspicions of Christian-related activity by San'emon and one of his attendants, Kichijirō, they are reported as having denied the charges, while another man, Hitotsubashi Matabe, is evidently tortured and executed for the crime. This incident reinforces the mystery of the priest's apostasy by hinting at a private faith publicly subordinated by coercion and personal weakness. When San'emon dies his conversion is completed by the ritual conferral of a posthumous Buddhist name: Nyūsen Jōshin Shinshi.

The way in which Endō structures the closing of the narrative reinforces both the sense of historical distance and the mystery of Rodrigues's conversion. His choice suspends *Silence* at a point where entirely different interpretations of the meaning and rationale of Rodrigues's actions are possible. The title of the novel itself announces that distance and mystery to the reader. *Chinmoku* (沈黙), suggests not just an absence of noise, or a state of quiescence, but a deliberate decision not to speak up. The sense of deliberate silence is made clear during Ferreira's interrogation of Rodrigues, when the priest is forced to confront the fact that God has not intervened to save the Japanese who are being tortured; and that sense is driven home in the dialogue between Rodrigues and Jesus.

The significance of silence in this novel, with its implication of moral failure to speak up in the face of evil, or to act as an exemplar, had special

poignancy for many Japanese readers (regardless of their religious affili-
ation) in the postwar era. It is hard even now to read Rodrigues's story
without thinking of the forced political conversions, *tenkō*, of the 1930s and
1940s. Like Rodrigues, those who underwent the experience of *tenkō* had
to confront the constructed nature of their new identities, to experience a
rupture between inner attitudes and beliefs and outward, socially sanctioned
practices. Accused of collaboration, they suffered a humiliation and self-
abnegation that created a spiritual and historical rupture of identity and
selfhood that had been largely defined by values defined within an older
discourse of virtue ethics.

The historical grounding of *Silence* is thus a crucial rhetorical element in
that, as noted above, it establishes multiple perspectives that make it difficult
to render a moral judgment about Rodrigues's apostasy and the virtue of
abjection with any certainty. The same multiplicity of perspectives and voices
also makes it impossible to read the novel as a simple allegory of *tenkō* or
of colonial history, since such interpretations do nothing to clear away the
lingering mystery at the heart of the priest's turn. This mystery remains in the
narrative as a profound silence, or void. This silence stands in for a kind of
reverence that hesitates to judge and that points to the stillness that allowed
the Hidden Christians to survive in Japan for more than two centuries. At
the same time, this silence is the rhetorical means by which Endō marks out
the irreducible and irreconcilable conflict between Rodrigues's pre-modern
Catholic self, represented by his religious beliefs and practices, and his
modern consciousness, represented by the discursive practices of the novel.
The silence Rodrigues experiences is a textual *aporia*. It is a marker of what
cannot be translated or reconciled; it is a textual supplement that functions
poetically to describe the complex dynamics of abjection as both Christian
virtue and as trauma.

Notes

1   Josef Pieper, *The Silence of St. Thomas* (Chicago: Regnery, 1957), 38.
2   Shusaku Endo, *Silence*, trans. William Johnston (New York: Taplinger
    Publishing, 1980), 171. The Japanese version I used in preparing this essay
    comes from *Endō Shūsaku shū, Shinchō Nihon bungaku*, vol. 56 (Tokyo:
    Shinchōsha, 1987).
3   Endo, *Silence*, 171.
4   An example of this sort of explanation of Japan's modern predicament is
    provided by the work of the influential intellectual historian Maruyama
    Masao, especially his short treatise *Nihon no shisō* [*Japanese thought*],

which was published in 1961 by Iwanami Shoten. Even though *Silence* is a historical novel, it is important to note here the moral and political debates that dominated Japan during the period of the novel's composition, for these debates certainly influenced the literary conception of the work.

5   Endo, *Silence*, 45.
6   Ibid., 147.
7   Ibid., 169.
8   Ibid.
9   Ibid., 38.
10 Ibid., 55.
11 Ibid., 147.
12 Jorge Luis Borges, *Labyrinths* (New York: New Directions, 1964), 98.
13 Ibid., 99.
14 Ibid., 100.
15 Julia Kristeva, *Powers of Horror: An Essay on Abjection*, trans. Leon S. Roudiez (New York: Columbia University Press, 1982), 4.
16 Endo, *Silence*, 115.
17 Ibid., 116.
18 Robert Hefner, "Introduction: World Building and the Rationality of Conversion," in *Conversion to Christianity*, ed. Robert Hefner (Berkeley: University of California Press, 1993), 17.
19 Ibid.
20 Ibid., 26.
21 Talal Asad, "Comments on Conversion," in *Conversions to Modernities*, ed. Peter van der Veer (New York: Routledge, 1996), 266.
22 Karl F. Morrison, *Conversion and Text* (Charlottesville, VA: University Press of Virginia, 1992), 144. My italics. Morrison's insistence that there is little to differentiate interpretive strategies of historical fiction from straight fiction is too sweeping to accept at face value. As noted above, readers of historical fiction bring certain expectations concerning factuality and contingency that are not present in either "straight" history or fiction.
23 Endo, *Silence*, 169.
24 Ibid., 190.
25 Stephen Greenblatt, *Marvelous Possessions: The Wonder of the New World* (Chicago: University of Chicago Press, 1991), 23–5.

13

"And Like the Sea God was Silent": Multivalent Water Imagery in *Silence*

Frances McCormack

The organic imagery of Shusaku Endo's *Silence* is dominated by the motif of water, from the rain that drenches the parched earth to the wearisome sea-crossings that mirror the spiritual journey of Fr. Rodrigues. In the Christian tradition, and in the New Testament in particular, water is a symbol of faith and grace, from the cleansing of sin in baptism to the quenching of spiritual thirst promised by Christ as the fountain of life. The motif of water in *Silence*, however, is far more ambiguous: not only does it provide relief from the oppressive heat, but it also serves as a site of torture and death. In this way, it echoes the moral and spiritual ambiguities of the novel. This chapter will analyze the way in which Endo's multivalent employment of the motif of water problematizes interpretation and adds a richness of theological nuance to the text. It is not my intention to examine this imagery through an ecocritical lens, but to explore how images of water in *Silence* shape the narrative by drawing on a wealth of theological imagery. This analysis will later consider the motif of tears and the monastic doctrine of compunction to which they relate, evoking a reconsideration of the character of Rodrigues.

The *Penguin Dictionary of Symbols* lists three main symbolic interpretations of water in ancient traditions: 1) a source of life; 2) a vehicle of cleansing; and 3) a center of regeneration.[1] However, "like all symbols, water can be regarded from two diametrically opposite points of view which are not, despite this, irreconcilable, and this ambivalence occurs at all levels. Water is the source both of life and of death, is creator and destroyer."[2] The duality of the imagery of water as both creator and destroyer is, perhaps, most evident in the Psalms. In Ps. 68,[3] for example, water is clearly a destructive force from which the psalmist entreats to be saved:

> Save me, O God: for the waters are come in even unto my soul. I stick
> fast in the mire of the deep: and there is no sure standing. I am come

into the depth of the sea: and a tempest hath overwhelmed me. ... Draw
me out of the mire, that I may not stick fast: deliver me from them that
hate me, and out of the deep waters. Let not the tempest of water drown
me, nor the deep swallow me up: and let not the pit shut her mouth on
me.[4]

Elsewhere in the Psalms, this destructive force is calmed only by God's
intervention:

If it had not been that the Lord was with us, let Israel now say: ...
perhaps the waters had swallowed us up. Our soul hath passed through
a torrent: perhaps our soul hath passed through a water insupportable.[5]

Water frequently functions as an instrument of God's judgment: the Flood
narrative of Gen. 6–9, and the drowning of the Egyptians in the Red Sea
(Exod. 13.17–14.2), for instance, clearly delineate those who are in God's
favor and those who are to be punished. The pericope of Water from the
Rock (Exod. 17.1–7), by which God gives sustenance to the Israelites,
is repeated throughout the Old Testament,[6] recalling God's favor of the
Israelites and his covenant with them.

At other points in the Psalms, water is a source of spiritual restoration
and refreshment: "As the hart panteth after the fountains of water: so my soul
panteth after thee, O God. My soul hath thirsted after the strong living God.
... My tears have been my bread day and night. ..."[7] Sometimes, too, it is a
symbol of spiritual purity: "I will wash my hands among the innocent; and
will compass thy altar, O Lord."[8] This motif of water of the Spirit is particularly prevalent in the New Testament. In the Gospel of John, for instance,
water is equated with life, which is portrayed as a blessing that follows from
faith in Christ. In John 4.13–14, Jesus tells the Samaritan woman that anyone
who drinks of him will never thirst: "Whosoever drinketh of this water shall
thirst again; but he that shall drink of the water that I will give him shall
not thirst for ever. But the water that I will give him shall become in him a
fountain of water, springing up into life everlasting." The Gospel of John is
abundant in images of water; Christ turns water into wine at the wedding in
Cana (Jn 2.1–10), walks on the troubled sea (Jn 6.17–19), and washes the feet
of his disciples as a sign of humility (Jn 13.12–17). The symbol of water in
this Gospel therefore represents the development of faith, rebirth in Christ,
and cleansing of sin.[9]

Water in the Bible is, therefore, generally a boon to the faithful: it is a
reward for their faith; it is a sign of cleansing and renewal; it is a relief from
thirst and drought; it is a punishment for the enemy. In *Silence*, however,
water is often an unwelcome element. Although Rodrigues himself employs

the theological symbolism of water—"In this desert from which missionaries and priests had been expelled the only one who could give the water of life to this island tonight was myself"[10]—he wavers in his faith in God's Providence, interpreting God's silence as abandonment, thereby rejecting those signs traditionally seen as symbols of God's presence and favor. Christopher Link writes that: "Endo's 'mudswamp Japan' [must] be understood as a metaphor for the psyche, especially that part of the soul that in any individual resists the paradoxes of Christianity as unassimilable or, if assimilated, as somehow disingenuous, problematic or suspect."[11] As I shall demonstrate below, the metaphor of a mudswamp with its failure to embrace the paradoxes of Christianity, is a metaphor not only for the Japanese, but for Rodrigues himself.

The rainy season of Rodrigues's Japan brings but little relief from the oppressive heat, and contributes to the sense of futility that the reader suspects will underlie his mission:

> Yesterday rain again. Of course this rain is no more than a herald of the heat that follows. But all day long it makes a melancholy sound as it falls in the thicket which surrounds our hut. ... Seeing nothing but rain and more rain, a feeling like anger rises up within our breasts. How much longer is this life to continue?[12]

In fact, while mists and gentle rain are signs of God's beneficence in the Bible,[13] a downpour of rain is frequently associated with God's punishment—more specifically, punishment for sin and for lack of faith.[14] Rodrigues notes "what a gloomy pest this rain is—a pest that destroys everything both on the surface and at the root."[15] Later in the novel, a debate will rage about the failure of Christianity to take hold in Japan; both Inoue and Fr. Ferreira attribute this to Japan being a metaphysical swamp. Ferreira insists that: "This country is a more terrible swamp than you can imagine. Whenever you plant a sapling in this swamp the roots begin to rot; the leaves grow yellow and wither. And we have planted the sapling of Christianity in this swamp."[16] Endo himself attributed the failure of Christianity to flourish in Japan to a lack of metaphysical concord between the two traditions, writing the following in an undergraduate essay: "there is in the Japanese sensibility something that is incapable of receiving Christianity ... a threefold insensitivity: an insensitivity to God, an insensitivity to sin, and an insensitivity to death."[17] Rodrigues, however, asserts that Christianity has "penetrated this territory like water flowing onto dry earth,"[18] and insists that the failure of his mission is due to his own struggle with his faith: "My struggle was with Christianity in my own heart."[19] Nonetheless, the rain-drenched landscape and the vast black sea are ever present in those parts of the novel narrated by

Rodrigues, leading the reader to wonder whether they symbolize an outward projection of that narrator's interior state or whether the reader is meant to interpret them as a lack of awareness and rejection of those gifts of faith that theologians have for so long celebrated.

Water provides mere bodily refreshment in the novel; it does not provide sustenance for the soul. Frequently Rodrigues experiences thirst, and frequently he meditates upon Christ on the cross as he is offered gall (translated by William Johnston in the present edition of the novel as "vinegar") to quench his thirst. While Matthew (27.34, 48) and Jn (19.28–30) present this pericope without censure of the soldiers, Luke reads it as a mocking gesture (23.36). Mark states that the wine offered was mixed with myrrh, perhaps as an anaesthetic to ease suffering. Rodrigues, however, reads the gesture in terms of his own suffering, and interprets the offering as a sign of scorn and mockery:

> Grasping my staff and moving on, I found that the dryness in my throat was even more unbearable, and now I realized only too clearly that the wretch had deliberately made me eat the dried fish. I recalled the words of the Gospel how Christ had said, "I thirst"; and one of the soldiers put a sponge full of vinegar on hyssop and held it to his mouth.[20]

In fact, Rodrigues frequently makes a correlation between water and God's absence, thereby overturning one of the key theological symbols of spiritual fulfillment. Meditating on the martyrdom of Mokichi and Ichizo, he notes

> now there arose up within my heart quite suddenly the sound of the roaring sea. … The sound of those waves that echoed in the dark like a muffled drum; the sound of those waves all night long as they broke meaninglessly, receded and then broke against the shore. This was the sea that relentlessly washed the dead bodies of Mokichi and Ichizo, the sea that swallowed them up, the sea that, after their death, stretched out endlessly with unchanging expressions. And like the sea God was silent. His silence continued.[21]

Rodrigues is therefore heedless of the symbolic possibility of grace in the water that surrounds him—and, by implication, in the grace to be found in the trials that are sent his way—and it is this discordance between his desire for glorious martyrdom and his inability to find God among the darkness, the storms, and the pitiful peasant faces that leads him to reject for so long the possibility of mercy that will, perhaps, be his eventual redemption.

Rodrigues is clearly far from suited to his undertaking; his sacerdotal focus is on sacrament and rite rather than priestly duty. Although, his view of the importance of his mission cannot be underestimated—"I thrilled with joy as I listened to the solemn voice of Garrpe as he recited the baptismal prayers. This is a happiness that only a missionary priest in a foreign land can relish."[22]—his optimism is quickly tempered by the rigors of this mission and by the trials that he faces both from within and from without. Writing on the protagonist's crisis of faith, William T. Cavanaugh notes that Rodrigues's lack of empathy for his potential congregation is at the root of his doubts:

> Rodrigues's growing doubts stand against the backdrop of the enduring faith of the peasants. However, rather than soothe his doubts, Rodrigues finds the simple faith of the peasants a further irritant. The more the peasants seem to suffer for their faith, the more Rodrigues seems to recoil from the whole missionary enterprise. Against his will, he begins to struggle with the idea that faith is a mere escape from reality; worse, he is haunted by the dim awareness that the suffering of the peasants is increased because of his own presence. And much worse still, their faith now appears as a cruel burden laid on them by a God who refuses to speak.[23]

This lack of empathy is most evident in those passages in the novel treating baptism:

> They come to my house one after another, completely ignoring the ban on Christianity. I baptize the children and hear the confessions of the adults. Even when I keep going all day long I don't get through them all. They remind me of an army marching through the parched desert and then arriving at an oasis of water—this is the way they come to me, thirsty and longing for refreshment. The crumbling farm house that I use for a chapel is jammed tight with their bodies, and so they confess their sins, their mouths close to my ear and emitting a stench that almost makes me vomit.[24]

Water imagery in the novel therefore often functions as a reminder of Rodrigues's increasing dissociation from God, from his mission, from his congregation and from himself. Central to this type of imagery is Endo's depiction of the sea. Whether echoing Rodrigues's psycho-emotional state, foreshadowing events to come, or being the subject of pathetic fallacy and acquiring human attributes, the sea is a powerful force in *Silence*. Writing on Gabriel García Márquez, Clementina Adams notes: "The special, peculiar flavor of this writer's fictional world results from the unique blending of sociocultural ambiance, personal feelings and recollections, and extreme and powerful climatological factors whose junction is both mimetic and symbolic."[25] Likewise, Endo's use of water imagery takes on resonances both mimetic and symbolic: the sea is a reminder of distance, both spiritual and geographical; it is a portent of impending disruption; it is a mirror of psychic states; it is an ever-present theological symbol; it is unfamiliar and precarious.

In the Old Testament, the sea is unknown, and therefore feared. The Hebrew word used in Genesis to refer to the sea is תְּהוֹם (tehom, "the deep," "the abyss"). It was from the Deep that Noah was afflicted by flood, and it was the Deep that Moses parted to allow the Israelites to pass out of Egypt; it is the Deep that God will parch to make a path for his people on Judgment Day: "And the Lord shall lay waste the tongue of the sea of Egypt, and shall lift up his hand over the river in the strength of his spirit: and he shall strike it in the seven streams, so that men may pass through it in their shoes."[26] Similarly, for Rodrigues, the sea is unpredictable, unknowable, foreign: "All around me is the black sea; it is impossible to tell where the blackness of the night begins. I cannot see whether there are islands around me."[27] As the novel progresses and Rodrigues's crisis of faith begins to manifest itself, the unknowability of the sea becomes a vehicle in the metaphor for the priest's doubt in God's presence: "So he prayed. But the sea remained cold, and the darkness maintained its silence. All that could be heard was the monotonous dull sound of the oars again and again."[28] Here, Rodrigues's seemingly unanswered prayer is juxtaposed with the repetitive, wearisome sound of the oars, and the silence, darkness and coldness of the sea with God's apparent absence.

While water imagery—rain, rivers, fountains, and so on—frequently stands for God's grace in spiritual and theological writings, the sea is far more ambiguous. Frequently, the sea represents God's power and, more specifically, his judgment:

> The story of the Flood, the drowning of the Egyptians in the Red Sea, and the general fear of the sea and deep waters expressed by the psalmist (18:16; 32:6; 46:3; 69:1ff., *etc.*) indicate that water could in Yahweh's hands be an instrument of judgment, although at the same time there was the thought of salvation through danger for the faithful people of God (*cf.* Is. 43:2; 59:19).[29]

The sea of the Bible is a site of trial and ordeal, something to be vanquished or tamed, but through such ordeal a possible site of redemption. Günther Bornkamm writes on the pericope of the stilling of the storm in Matthew 8.23–7, which reads as follows in the Douay-Rheims version:

> And when he entered into the boat the disciples followed him. And behold a great tempest arose in the sea, so that the boat was covered with waves; but he was asleep. And they came to him, and awaked him,

saying: Lord, save us, we perish. And Jesus saith to them: Why are you fearful, O ye of little faith? Then rising up, he commanded the winds, and the sea; and there came a great calm. But the men wondered, saying: What manner of man is this, for the winds and the sea obey him?[30]

Bornkamm argues that the evangelist's alteration of the story as it appears in Mark and Luke is

> a description of the dangers against which Jesus warns anyone who overthoughtlessly presses to become a disciple. At the same time it shows him as one who … is able to reward the sacrifice of abandoning earthly ties. The story becomes a kerygmatic paradigm of the danger and glory of discipleship.[31]

This idea of the "danger and glory of discipleship" permeates *Silence*. Storm imagery repeats throughout the novel, and the relentless rain is more a portent of doom than a relief from the oppressive heat. When the missionaries set out from port at Macao, Garrpe and Rodrigues offer thanks to God for the good weather. It is not long, however, before a storm breaks out at sea:

> But now it was dead of night and the only thing possible was to abandon our ship to the wind and the waves. Meanwhile in the front of the ship a great rift was opened and the water began to pour in. For almost the whole night long we worked at stuffing cloth into the rift and bailing out the water.[32]

At many points throughout the novel, the vessels in which Rodrigues sails are beset by bad weather. Paul Minear, writing on metaphor of ships and boats in the New Testament, asks:

> Is there is an intended analogy between the boat in the storm and the church in the world? Or again, the story of Jesus walking on the waves to a boatload of disciples who were frantically fighting at night against a contrary wind ([Matthew] Ch. 14:22–27). Does this reflect the helplessness and the fears of a church left alone by its master to carry on its difficult mission? And does the boat-church analogy appear again in the postcrucifixion fishing of the disciples (John 21:8)? If this association of church and boat were certain, we might discern allusions elsewhere, as, for example, in those varied occasions when Mark pictures Jesus as teaching the crowds from a boat (Mark 4:1).[33]

In light of this metaphor, then, the stormy and troubled sea voyages reflect the precariousness not only of Catholicism in Japan but also of Rodrigues's own vocation.

A useful point of access to the sea imagery in *Silence* is the medieval tradition of *peregrinatio pro amore Dei*: a pilgrimage for the love of God.[34] Dorothy Whitelock provides a wealth of examples from insular sources about various *peregrini* who abandoned themselves in currachs (or coracles: small, rudderless wickerwork boats, propelled by paddles), putting their faith in providence, noting that the drive for voluntary exile is in imitation of Matthew 19.29: "And every one that hath left house or brethren or sisters or father or mother or wife or children or lands, for my name's sake, shall receive an hundredfold and shall possess life everlasting." Richard Marsden notes a central paradox in the practice of *peregrinatio*: that the harshness of the journey makes it all the more compelling.

> Seafaring is a wretched business—as the speaker has firmly persuaded us with his own "true story"—and *therefore* ... he must embrace it all the more. The more uncompromisingly realistic the opening account of seafaring, the more disturbing—and therefore effective— the paradox.[35]

This tradition of *peregrinatio* is, perhaps, hinted at by Endo in *Silence*, when Rodrigues reflects on the saints who had crossed the sea before him, putting their trust in God to lead them safely to shore:

> Sometimes he would open his eyes, and always he could hear the sound of the oars in the water. ... "Lord, may Thy will be done," he murmured, as though in his sleep. But even though his halting words seemed to resemble those of so many saints who had entrusted their all to the providence of God, he felt that his were different.[36]

The theme of exile is clearly present in *Silence*. Rodrigues, too, has forsaken the familiarity and kinship of home to embark on his mission. The concept of exile is starkly drawn when he meditates on the work of St. Francis Xavier and the other Jesuit missionaries who made the arduous journey to attempt to plant the seed of Christianity in Japan. Endo's Prologue, in fact, depicts this correlation between exile and the vagaries of the sea with the narrative of the expulsion of the missionaries from Japan in 1614:

> Reports from the missionaries tell of how on the 6th and 7th October of this same year, seventy priests, both Japanese and foreign, were herded together at Kibachi in Kyushu and forced to board five junks bound for Macao and Manila. Then they sailed into exile. It was rainy that day, and the sea was grey and stormy as the ships drenched by rain made their way out of the harbor, passed beside the promontory and disappeared beyond the horizon.[37]

In Endo's terms, though, exile is from the missionary endeavor, rather than toward it: the homeland is where the seeds of faith are to be sown, and the exile of the missionaries is away from their ministry. Elsewhere, though, Rodrigues depicts the journey *toward* his mission as a sort of exile, and clearly in opposition to the sense of homecoming that awaited the missionaries before him:

> How many missionaries had crossed over to this island on a tiny boat just as I had done! And yet how different were their circumstances from mine! When they came to Japan, fortune smiled gaily upon their every venture. Everywhere was safe for them; they found houses in which they could rest at ease and Christians who welcomed them with open arms.[38]

The sea therefore comes to be a reminder of Rodrigues's distance from his native land:

> Never again would he cross the leaden sea to return to his native land. When in Portugal he had thought that to become a missionary was to come to belong to that country. He had intended to go to Japan and to lead the same life as the Japanese Christians. Whatever about that, now it was indeed so. He had received the Japanese name Okada San'emon; he had become a Japanese. ... Fate had given him everything he could wish for, had given it to him in this cynical way.[39]

Unlike those seafarers in the tradition of the *peregrinatio*, his journey is not driven by penitence, but rather by a desire to discover the truth about the alleged apostasy of Ferreira. Like those *peregrini*, though, the harshness of the journey is a test of faith. At first, Rodrigues's belief in Providence is strong, and the sea is merely an obstacle to be overcome with God's aid:

> Until this day there was no sign of land, no trace of an island. The grey sky stretched out endlessly and sometimes the rays of the sun struck to the ship so feebly as to be heavy on the eyelids. Overcome with depression we just kept our eyes fixed on the cold sea where the teeth of the waves flashed like white buds. But God did not abandon us.[40]

Later in the novel, though, the sea becomes menacing and increasingly dark, and onto it is projected Rodrigues's wavering faith in God's providence:

> The sea and the land were silent as death; only the dull sound of the waves lapping against the boat broke the silence of the night. Why have you abandoned us so completely?, he prayed in a weak voice. ... Have you just remained silent like the darkness that surrounds me? ... There is a limit to our endurance. Give us no more suffering. ... So he prayed.

But the sea remained cold, and the darkness maintained its stubborn silence. All that could be heard was the monotonous dull sound of the oars again and again.[41]

The sea itself therefore takes on a wealth of interpretive valences, reflecting the precariousness of the displaced Church, the isolation of missionary work, the tenuousness of Rodrigues's faith in providence, and the terror of God's absence.

Water from God can be a punishment, a blessing, or an ordeal. There is, however, one more motif of water that is central to scripture, as well as to classical and patristic theology—the motif of tears. Affective devotion encouraged meditation on the sufferings of Christ, and was thought to lead to a deeper faith. Stephen Shoemaker writes: "pious reflection turned to contemplate, with increasing fervour, the excruciating pains endured by Christ in the crucifixion, inviting the faithful to share mentally in the torment and sorrow."[42] One particular aspect of this affectivity of religious experience, compunction, was considered to be particularly efficacious in strengthening the individual's relationship with God. Depicted most frequently in the outward manifestation of tears, compunction was seen by Church Fathers as a charism by which, through a pricking of the heart, the individual may come to a more profound experience of faith. As Sandra McEntire, in her book-length study on the topic writes:

> compunction is a grace, gratuitously given, with which the beneficiary must cooperate. … tears are the exterior expression of the greater activity, prayer between the individual and God. The grace of tears is never sought for its own sake, but as the abiding sign of the deep interior sorrow one feels before the greatness and mercy of God. The interior attitude is expressed in the outward sign of tears; both tears and compunction are elements of grace being given.[43]

The doctrine of compunction has its roots in Scripture, in the New Testament in particular, where a personal and emotive mode of devotion is emphasized in the relationship between the incarnate God and his followers. Central to this tradition is the story of the infamous public sinner who washed Christ's feet with her tears.[44] The Scriptures are full of images of people weeping out of regret for their sins, or in humility before the mercy of God and his promise of salvation. In Isaiah, for instance, tears figure prominently as an outward sign of inward devotion. God replies to the weeping of Ezechias with the following words: "I have heard thy prayer, and I have seen thy tears."[45] The repeated exhortation that we "harden not our hearts"[46] is central to the doctrine; the softening of the hardened heart is enacted through *gratia lacrymarum*—the grace of tears—and many writers on compunction figure the softened heart that weeps for repentance to be sign of God's grace. Richard of St. Victor, the twelfth-century French mystical theologian, emphasizes that compunctive tears can melt the most hardened of hearts, opening its pores to virtue. Tears, therefore, spring from a hardened heart, and further soften the heart allowing God's grace to enter:

> Therefore I think that there is need … more for inner compunction than profound investigation; more for sighs than arguments; more for frequent lamentations than an abundance of argumentations. However, we know that nothing so purifies the innermost places of the heart and nothing so renews the purity of the mind; nothing so drives away the clouds of ambiguity; nothing leads better or more quickly to serenity of heart than true contrition of soul, than deep and innermost compunction of soul.[47]

Chromatius distinguishes between tears of compunction and all other forms of weeping: "What mourning must be understood by us as healthy? Surely not that which is born of the loss of things, nor from the loss of dear ones, nor from the loss of earthly dignities, all things which will not hurt a man who has been made poor in spirit."[48] Tears of compunction are, when in response to loss, directed toward spiritual rather than material deprivation: the fear of salvation lost, or the awareness of the proximity of death and final judgment, for example. Irénée Hausherr asserts, however, that not all compunctive tears are those of sadness. She adds to the prospect of salvation lost and the certainty of death and judgment the individual's daily faults, brotherly love ("mourning for salvation that has been lost, either by oneself or others"), and pure love of God.[49] On this point, Gregory the Great distinguishes between compunction of fear and compunction of love, the former being an inferior precursor to the latter.[50] Among the concepts associated with compunction in the Christian tradition, then, are pity for one's fellow man, a hunger for God's presence, and a sense of grief at the human condition.

The doctrine of compunction underpins so much of the theology of Endo's novel, as Rodrigues's faith shifts from jubilant to affective, and as the image of Christ as king is replaced by images from the Passion. In fact, it seems that Rodrigues's psycho-spiritual turmoil is born from the lack of affectivity in his characterization of Christ:

> From childhood the face of Christ had been for him the fulfillment of his every dream and ideal. The face of Christ as it preached to the crowd the Sermon on the Mount. The face of Christ as he passed over the Lake

of Galilee at dusk. Even in its moments of terrible torture this face had never lost its beauty. Those soft, clear eyes which pierced to the very core of a man's being were now fixed upon him. The face that could do no wrong, utter no word of insult. When the vision of this face came before him, fear and trembling seemed to vanish like the tiny ripples that are quietly sucked up by the sand of the sea-shore.[51]

The humanity of Christ—his suffering and his sorrow—seems to dawn on Rodrigues only gradually. At last, it is his ability to conceive of the affective image of Christ that allows him to trample the *fumie* and to save the Christians from their death:

Before him is the ugly face of Christ, crowned with thorns and the thin, outstretched arms. Eyes dimmed and confused the priest silently looks down at the face which he now meets for the first time since coming to this country. ... With saddened glance he stares intently at the man in the centre of the *fumie*, worn down and hollow with the constant trampling. A tear is about to fall from his eye.[52]

Writing on what he refers to as the "soteriology of ugliness" in Endo, Christopher Link asserts that

If [Graham] Greene has been moved, to some degree, simply by the essential degraded human condition itself, then Endo seems rather more emphatically to insist upon the primacy of the image of Christ—that is, on the saving power of the ugly, defeated Christ, the man of sorrows— and therefore, upon the specifically Christological redemption of that same degraded human situation.[53]

Only upon meditation on the image of the suffering Christ, only through this affective piety, does Rodrigues come to understand the nature of his ordeals, the apparent silence of God, and the true import of his missionary work. One may read Endo's depiction of the crowing cock at the moment of Rodrigues's apostasy as an indictment of the priest's actions—a comparison with Peter's betrayal of Christ. At this moment of the text, however, Rodrigues acknowl- edges the centrality of the Passion to theodicy and faith, and the affectivity of his devotion serves as a vindication of his actions.

Although Rodrigues does eventually experience compunction, it does not come easily to him. This is most evident in his attitude to Kichijiro. He alternates between pity and contempt for the fisherman,[54] perhaps because, as the omniscient narrator notes, his pity has been devoid of love: "His pity for them had been overwhelming; but pity was not action. It was not love. Pity, like passion, was no more than a kind of instinct."[55] Whether Rodrigues learns to love his fellow man is never made clear, but his love for Christ leads him to a development of compunction that actualizes his pity and cements it as a powerful force in his redemption. On looking at Ferreira, Rodrigues "simply felt his breast swell with the pity one feels for a living being that has lost its life and spirit."[56] Even late in the novel, however, but before his trampling of the *fumie*, Rodrigues lacks compunction in his dealings with Kichijiro:

> Yes, he had whispered the words of absolution for Kichijiro; but this prayer had not come from the depths of his heart. He had simply recited the words out of a sense of priestly duty. That was why they lay heavy on his tongue like the residue of bitter food.... Even though he no longer entertained emotions of hatred and anger, he could not erase from his memory the feeling of contempt.[57]

Kichijiro himself is frequently compunctive, crying out in a tearful voice for absolution,[58] and bewailing his betrayal of the priest. Yet Rodrigues himself is conscious of the lack in his own experience of compunction, and this consciousness paradoxically brings compunction to him:

> Our Lord had searched out the ragged and the dirty. ... Anyone could be attracted by the beautiful and the charming. But could such attraction be called love? True love was to accept humanity when wasted like rags and tatters. ... Once again near his face came the face of Christ, wet with tears. When the gentle eyes looked straight into his, the priest was filled with shame.[59]

Water is instrumental in the development of Rodrigues's compunction, bringing to him images of Christ's Passion and moving him to affective contemplation of how his own sufferings echo those of Christ:

> Resting his head on the hard floor and listening to the sound of the rain, the priest thought of a man who had been put on trial like himself. ... The rays of the dawn stretched out beyond the Dead Sea bathing the mountain range in golden white, the brook Cedron babbled on, ever giving forth its fresh sound. ... This emaciated man was his perfect ideal. His eyes, like those of every victim, were filled with sorrowful resignation as he looked reproachfully at the crowd that ridiculed and spat at him ... this case was just like his own. He had been sold by Kichijiro as Christ had been sold by Judas; and like Christ he was now being judged by the powerful ones of this world. Yes, his fate and that of Christ were quite alike; and at this thought on that rainy night a tingling sensation of joy welled up within his breast. ... On the other hand, he had tasted

none of the physical suffering that Christ had known; and this thought made him uneasy.[60]

It is specifically his meditation upon the image of the suffering Christ—a meditation entered into through his own suffering—that enacts compunction in Rodrigues. This compunction is not grounded in the fear of his own possible torture and death, but in the love that he feels is not present in his epistemological scheme. He experiences the compunction of love that Gregory the Great insists to be a superior form of compunction:

> 'Women of Jerusalem, weep not for me but for yourselves and for your children. For the day will come...' These words came up in his mind. Many centuries ago, that man tasted with his dried and swollen tongue all the suffering that I now endure, he reflected. And this sense of suffering shared softly eased his mind and heart more than the sweetest water.
> 　　'Pange lingua...' He felt the tears streaming down his cheeks. 'Bella premunt hostilia, da robur fer auxilium.'[61]

Rodrigues vacillates between compunction and lack of compassion, between celebrating the relief provided by the rain to bewailing its relentlessness, between marveling at the vast unknowability of the sea to feeling an acute sense of abandonment in an unfamiliar land, both spiritual and geographical. Like Ferreira, he remains an imperfect model of sacerdotal stoicism and piety—a "bad priest," as Christopher Link puts it. But as Brett Dewey writes,

> There is a place for weakness and forgiveness in the community. Endo shows us that the church is made of redeemed Peters and Judases; it is a broken community whose triumph is in the shared suffering with God. The "Appendix" suggests that Rodrigues has taught Kichijiro, who in turn is teaching others, about the veneration of saints and the order of the Church.[62]

Endo presents us with a soteriology of ugliness, "a theological aesthetic of sin and suffering";[63] he creates a protagonist who should be exemplary, but who misreads conventional Christian symbols and thereby displays an ambivalent faith; he portrays in Rodrigues a sort-of-Christ who becomes a sort-of-Judas, and allows Kichijiro, the traitor, to become central to the promulgation and continuance of Christianity in the region; he allows Rodrigues to experience compunction through bewailing his lack thereof. But Endo's theodicy insists that Judas "was no more than the unfortunate puppet for the glory of the drama which was the life and death of Christ,"[64] and his novel, filled as it is with flawed characters, and saturated as it is by ambiguous biblical imagery, testifies to the paradox at the heart of Endo's writing: God speaks loudest in his silence.

Notes

1   "Water," in *The Penguin Dictionary of Symbols*, ed. Jean Chevalier and Alain Gheerbrant, trans. John Buchanan-Brown (Harmondsworth: Penguin, 1994), 1081.

2   Ibid.

3   In citing the Psalms, I have used the numbering of the Septuagint and the Vulgate.

4   Psalms 68.2–3; 15–16, *The Holy Bible: Douay Version* (London: Catholic Truth Society, 1956). All quotations from the Bible are taken from this edition unless otherwise indicated.

5   Psalms 123.1–5.

6   Numbers 20.1–13; Ps. 78.15–16, 20; 105.41; 114.8; Isa. 43.20; 48.21.

7   Psalms 41.1–4.

8   Psalms 25.6.

9   See, for example, Myung Kwan Noh and Andy Baek, *Water in the Gospel of John: Finding Christ through Water* (Bloomington, IN: Xlibris, 2011); Craig R. Koester, *Symbolism in the Fourth Gospel: Meaning, Mystery, Community*, 2nd edn (Minneapolis, MN: Fortress, 2003).

10 Shusaku Endo, *Silence*, trans. William Johnston (London: Peter Owen, 2009), 60–1.

11 Christopher A. Link, "Bad Priests and the Valor of Pity: Shusaku Endo and Graham Greene on the Paradoxes of Christian Virtue," *Logos* 15.4 (Fall, 2012): 77.

12 Endo, *Silence*, 118.

13 Levictus 26.3; Deut. 11.11; 33.13; Ps. 72.6–7.

14 Genesis; Exodus 9.17–35.

15 Endo, *Silence*, 99.

16 Ibid., 237.

17 Endo Shusaku, "The gods and God," quoted in, and translated by, Francis Mathy, "Shusaku Endo: Japanese Catholic Novelist," *Thought: A Review of Culture and Idea* 42 (Winter, 1967): 593.

18 Endo, *Silence*, 61.

19 Ibid., 292.

20 Ibid., 129–30.

21 Ibid., 116–17.

22 Ibid., 70.

23 William T. Cavanaugh, "The God of *Silence*: Shusaku Endo's Reading of the Passion," *Commonweal* 10 (March, 1998): 10.

24 Endo, *Silence*, 77.
25 Clementina R. Adams, "The Endless Rains of Death and Desolation in García Márquez's Short Stories," in *Climate in Literature: Reflections of Environment*, eds Janet Pérez and Wendell M. Aycock (Lubbock, TX: Texas Tech University Press, 1995), 71.
26 Isaiah 11.15.
27 Endo, *Silence*, 106–7.
28 Ibid., 157.
29 J. B. Taylor, "Water," in *The Illustrated Bible Dictionary*, ed. J. D. Douglas, rev. edn, 3 vols (Leicester: Inter-Varsity Press, 1980, 1994), 1632.
30 Matthew 8.23–7.
31 Günther Bornkamm, "The Stilling of the Storm in Matthew," in *Tradition and Interpretation in Matthew*, ed. G. Bornkamm, G. Barth, and H. J. Held (Philadelphia, PA: The Westminster Press, 1963), 57.
32 Endo, *Silence*, 49–50.
33 Paul Sevier Minear, *Images of the Church in the New Testament* (Philadelphia, PA: Westminster John Knox Press, 1960), 33.
34 Dorothy Whitelock, "The Interpretation of *The Seafarer*," in *Early Cultures of Northwest Europe*, C. Fox and B. Dickens, eds (Cambridge: Cambridge University Press, 1950), 261–72.
35 Richard Marsden, *The Cambridge Old English Reader* (Cambridge: Cambridge University Press, 2004), 7.
36 Endo, *Silence*, 157.
37 Ibid., 20.
38 Ibid., 108–9.
39 Ibid., 294–5.
40 Ibid., 52.
41 Ibid., 159.
42 Stephen J. Shoemaker, "Mary at the Cross, East and West: Maternal Compassion and Affective Piety in the Earliest *Life of the Virgin* and the High Middle Ages," *Journal of Theological Studies* 62.2 (2011): 571.
43 Sandra McEntire, *The Doctrine of Compunction in Medieval England: Holy Tears* (New York: Edwin Mellen, 1990), 55.
44 Luke 7.37–38.
45 Isaiah 38.5.
46 Hebrews 3.7–19 and Ps. 95.8.
47 Richard of St. Victor, *The Mystical Ark*, in *The Twelve Patriarchs; The Mystical Ark; Book Three of the Trinity*, ed. and trans. Grover Zinn (New York: Paulist Press, 1979), 265.
48 Chromatius, *Corpus Christianorum: Series Latina* (Turnhout, Belgium: Brepols), 1953ff. Cited and translated in McEntire, *Holy Tears*, 35.
49 Irénée Hausherr, *Penthos: The Doctrine of Compunction in the Christian East*, trans. Anselm Hufstader (Kalamazoo, MI: Cistercian Publications, 1982), 26–52; quotation from 41.

50   Gregory the Great, *Dialogi*, in *Patrologia Cursus Completus: Series Latina*, ed. Jacques-Paul Migne, 221 vols. (Paris, 1844–64), 3, caput XXXIV; cited in, and translated by, McEntire, *Holy Tears*, 50–1.

51   Endo, *Silence*, 170.

52   Ibid., 270–1.

53   Christopher Link, "Bad Priests," 90–1.

54   Endo, *Silence*, 131.

55   Ibid., 219.

56   Ibid., 235.

57   Ibid., 260.

58   Ibid., 258.

59   Ibid., 189.

60   Ibid., 202–3.

61   Ibid., 164.

62   Brett Dewey, "Suffering the Patient Victory of God: Shusaku Endo and the Lessons of a Japanese Catholic," *Quodlibet Journal* 6.1 (January–March, 2004), http://www.quodlibet.net/articles/dewey-endo.shtml (accessed May 8, 2014).

63   Link, "Bad Priests," 88.

64   Endo, *Silence*, 128.

14

Laughter Out of Place: Risibility as Resistance and Hidden Transcript in *Silence*

Jacqueline Bussie

In the historical fiction novel *Silence*, Shusaku Endo plumbs the plight of Japanese Christians during the early seventeenth century, an era in the nation's history when practicing Christianity was a crime punishable by death. Though the novel is a tragic tale about torture, apostasy, fear, doubt, martyrdom, and betrayal, the oppressed characters within its pages repeatedly exhibit the same incongruous behavior: they laugh in the face of their own suffering. Inexplicably, the scholarly literature on the novel virtually ignores the meaning of this fascinating yet dislocated and unanticipated risibility. This chapter, however, fills this unacceptable gap in critical inquiry by answering the following questions. Why are these characters—martyrs, apostates, impoverished peasants, and imprisoned priests—laughing? What does it mean for a person of faith to laugh at the horrible, or to laugh while she is suffering? How does Endo's work help Christian thought elucidate the theological and ethical significance of the laughter of the oppressed as well as a nuanced understanding of a theology of the cross? Weaving through answers to these questions, this chapter concludes that laughter functions as an invaluable ethical and theological mode of resistance, a manifestation of the hidden transcript constructed by the persecuted in the face of negativity that has ruptured language and traditional belief. In particular, Endo's novel reveals that the laughter of the oppressed not only protests evil and unmasks the limits of theodicy, but also deconstructs the dominant consciousness.

In the brilliant book, *Domination and the Arts of Resistance: Hidden Transcripts*, social scientist James C. Scott contrasts what he terms the public, official dominant transcript of power relations with the hidden offstage transcript. Explains Scott:

> If we think, in schematic terms, of public transcript as comprising a
> domain of material appropriation (for example, of labor, grain, taxes),

a domain of public mastery and subordination (for example, rituals of hierarchy, deference, speech, punishment, and humiliation), and finally a domain of ideological justification for inequalities (for example, the public religious and political worldview of the dominant elite), then we may perhaps think of the hidden transcript as comprising the offstage responses and rejoinders to that public transcript. It is, if you will, the portion of an acrimonious dialogue that domination has driven off the immediate stage.[1]

Scott uses the term "hidden transcript" to describe the rich, driven-underground political life of oppressed, persecuted groups and their everyday alternative discourse and counterhegemonic acts of resistance. For example, during the gruesome era of slavery in the United States, a slave by day might exhibit polite obsequiousness to the master (public transcript), but under the cover of darkness, sing nightly of revenge and freedom in the created hush arbor of slave religion (hidden transcript). Scott describes the hidden transcript as the aggregate of commonplace prosaic forms of resistance such as poaching, squatting, folk religion, foot-dragging, folktales of revenge (for example, Brer Rabbit), "disguised discourses of dignity," gossip, rumor, and the "creation of autonomous social space for assertion of dignity."[2] He continues, "The hidden transcript is, for this reason, the privileged site for non-hegemonic, contrapuntal, dissident, subversive discourse."[3]

Fascinatingly, Scott does not include laughter on his list, and yet I would argue that laughter is one of the most crucial elements of the hidden transcript of resistance buried in the oppressed's repertoire, used above all for reclaiming their dignity and deconstructing the dominant consciousness.[4] *Silence* makes this point clear. But before turning to Endo's specific reimagining of how the laughter of the oppressed revolutionizes theological reflection, we must first acquire a general understanding of traditional Christianity's interpretations of laughter. Against such a backdrop, the laughter in Endo's unique and controversial novel—and its profound theological ramifications—can be better perceived, as if in bas relief.

To speak candidly, in mainstream Christian theology—in Christianity's dominant, public transcript—laughter has an abysmal reputation. Those theologians like myself longing for historical interpretations of laughter beyond antipathy or ambivalence come up empty-handed. We are completely unable, if restricted to using only resources from the theological tradition, to interpret the strange laughter Endo shares in his reconstructed hidden transcript of the interior lives of tortured apostates and persecuted Christians.

Though many contemporary Christians may find such history counter to their lived experience of laughter, the fact remains that the church's most respected voices, from Augustine on down through the modern period, interpret laughter *vis-à-vis* Christianity, the church, and God, as an insidious plebeian behavior that seeks to undermine ecclesiastical authority and doctrine. Church father St. Augustine denounces laughter in one of his sermons, "Human beings laugh and weep, and it is a matter for weeping that they laugh."[5] Hugo of St. Victor shockingly identifies laughter with pure evil, "Joy may be good or evil, depending on its source, but laughter is in every respect evil."[6] Church father Basil anathematizes laughter as negation of an appropriate attitude of Christian righteousness and seriousness, "The Christian … ought not to speak evil, to do violence. … He ought not to indulge in jesting; he ought not to laugh nor even to suffer laugh-makers,"[7] while Tertullian censures laughter as demonic, "Laugh at what you will, but let them [the demons] laugh with you!"[8] St. Benedict extrudes laughter from the life of holiness, decreeing in the Benedictine Rule that risibility incites *hubris* rather than humility, "We absolutely condemn in all places any vulgarity and gossip and talk leading to laughter. … for it is written: 'Only a fool raises his voice in laughter.' The eleventh step of humility is that a monk speaks gently and without laughter."[9] St. John of Chrysostom, Bishop of Constantinople, excoriates laughter by appealing to the fact that in the scriptures, Christ never laughs:

> Nothing so unites and bonds to God as such tears. … If you also weep such tears, you have become a follower of your Lord. For he too wept. … And this indeed one may often see him do, but nowhere laugh nor smile even a little; no one at least of the evangelists mentions this. … That is why Christ says so much to us about mourning, and blesses those who mourn, and calls those who laugh wretched.[10]

And finally, even the modern Reinhold Niebuhr, from whom one might expect more nuanced ethical thought, reprehends laughter as an inappropriate response to threats to life's meaninglessness, claiming (in stark contrast to Endo's laughing apostate priest) that we never laugh at "things that affect us essentially," or at "ultimate incongruities of existence which threaten the very meaning of our life."[11] One historian of religions summarizes laughter's historical evaluation best when he concludes, "From the beginning, the church stood in firm opposition to laughter. After all, lowly peasants just might learn to … organize and launch their own scoffing attacks. Scornful laughter could turn every peasant into a self-styled vigilante."[12]

Yet, Scott would remind us that all of this is the dominant, public transcript of laughter. A chasmic disconnect emerges between ordinary Christians in their lives of laughter and tears, and these assessments of laughter's value in the life of faith. Everyone quoted above who condemns laughter as deleterious and un-Christian expounds from the dizzyingly powerful heights of ecclesiastical authority. But what of those, to use Dietrich Bonhoeffer's phrase, who do not look down from the top rung but instead live life "from below"? How is laughter used and understood from the perspective of those who suffer and are persecuted precisely for their refusal to accept the dominant transcript as their own—in the case of *Silence*, minority Christians who refuse to accept the dominant majority religion of Buddhism?

Endo, in *Silence*, is interested in going down so deep into the hidden transcript, that we can claim that he explores the depths of the hidden hidden transcript. Contrary perhaps to our expectations, Endo spends considerably more time and attention reconstructing not the hidden transcript of the resistance of the Christian martyr-peasants such as Mokichi and Ichizo, but instead that of the apostates, in particular the peasant Kichijiro and the fallen priest Fr. Rodrigues. Of course the martyrs' stories are a crucial part of the hidden transcript of the oppressed Christians in Japan, but theirs is a story that—though fragmented—will proudly be made public and be told and re-told by the church. The apostates' stories, on the other hand, are so hidden and far removed from the public official transcript, that even the church cannot claim knowledge of them, and moreover, out of shame, would not retell such tales even if it did have access to them. Thus, by choosing to focus the novel primarily on the fallen apostates Kichijiro and Rodrigues, Endo attempts to unmask a double hiddenness, a story behind a story, or better, as I will argue, a theology of the cross hidden *sub contrario* behind a dominant (and tragically flawed in Endo's view) public transcript of a theology of glory.

Endo believes we have much to learn from the untold stories of apostates whose interior life and struggles never made it into the annals of author-itative history. Rather than hastily condemning the apostates like the ecclesial authorities, Endo in his work instead sympathetically portrays the complexity of the apostate's situation—"the unrecorded despair and ignominy endured by those who, for whatever reason, ultimately succumbed to torture, both physical and psychological, and went through the ritual of *efumi* (treading on the crucifix), that most public act of apostasy."[13] Endo says that *Silence* imagines answers to questions that pursued him upon seeing a *fumie* (historical painting of Christ) in a Nagasaki museum: "1) If I had lived in that period of history, would I have stepped on the *fumie*? 2) What did those who stepped on the *fumie* feel? 3) What kind of people trod on the *fumie*?"[14] These comments reveal that Endo recognizes the existence of the hidden transcript and seeks to reconstruct it.

So, what can theology learn from the theology of laughter embodied by Endo's laughing apostate priest, who not only trod on the *fumie*, but laughs repeatedly—contra Niebuhr—at those very incongruities of his existence that most painfully threaten the meaning of his entire vocation? Why are both he and the apostate peasant Kichijiro frequently laughing throughout the narrative? And how does their laughter function as a form of resistance to oppression, despair, evil, terror, and the dichotomous thought that is the cornerstone of the dominant consciousness?

When Rodrigues embarks for Japan, his optimism abounds about his "great mission," and he comments, "Never have I felt so deeply how meaningful is the life of a priest. These Japanese Christians are like a ship lost in a storm without a chart."[15] Rodrigues finds meaning and purpose—and no doubt a hint of superiority—in his perceived vocation as the lost peasants' "chart." In his first letter, Rodrigues writes that he contemplates the face of Christ and finds it to be one of "encouragement"; "It is a face filled with vigor and strength. I feel great love for that face. I am fascinated by the face of Christ just like a man fascinated by the face of his Beloved."[16] At this early moment in the narrative prior to an encounter with radical evil, Rodrigues believes unquestioningly in divine Providence and in his status as Christ's beloved. As a person of privilege and stature, he also upholds the classic snappy (dominant transcript) theodicy that everything that happens in the world is according to God's omnipotent will and plan. Commenting on the fate of an unfortunate missionary who is unable to continue on to Japan because of illness, Rodrigues decrees with cavalier flourish, "Alas, I feel no inclination to write about Santa Marta. God did not grant to our poor companion the joy of being restored to health. But everything that God does is for the best."[17] At another early moment in the narrative, Rodrigues once again affirms God's unquestionable wisdom and absolute ultimate control over human affairs, "God bestows upon man a better fate than human knowledge could possibly think of or devise. ... Perhaps God in his omnipotence will make all things well."[18] Already here Endo lays the groundwork for the reader to think the unthinkable alongside of Rodrigues, "But what if God does not make things well? What kind of God is that, and how can one love such a God?"

Indeed, when Rodrigues's piety eventually crashes headlong into radical evil in the form of the soul-chilling systematic murder and torture of the Christian peasants and his own complicity in their suffering, his facile everything-God-does-is-for-the-best theodicy shatters under pressure like a hot glass filled with ice water. Consider for example the following passage:

> I do not believe that God has given us this trial to no purpose. I know that the day will come when we will clearly understand why this perse-cution with all its sufferings has been bestowed upon us—for everything

that Our Lord does is for our good. And yet, even as I write these words I feel the oppressive weight in my heart of those last stammering words of Kichijiro … : "Why has Deus Sama imposed this suffering upon us?" … I suppose I should simply cast from my mind these meaningless words of the coward; yet why does his plaintive voice pierce my breast with all the pain of a sharp needle? Why has our Lord imposed this torture? … The silence of God. … In the face of this terrible and merciless sacrifice offered up to Him, God has remained silent. This was the problem that lay behind the plaintive question of Kichijiro.[19]

In this important passage, Rodrigues's shopworn, fallback theodicy begins to fissure as he becomes increasingly troubled by God's ostensible apathy and silence. Notably, nearly each fissure is accompanied by a salvo of laughter, exposing traditional theological discourse as not only inadequate, but shattered by the encounter with radical evil. Though Rodrigues does not laugh in the above passage, these troubling theological reflections scaffold the shocking laughter that Rodrigues emits a few pages later upon witnessing the ghastly death of Mokichi and Ichizo by water torture—the first martyrdom the priest has ever witnessed. Reflecting on the fact that unlike his priest-predecessors who lived as the samurais' darlings and brought joy to the peasants, he is dressed in a dead peasant-martyr's clothing and "has brought disaster'" to the very people he came to help; Rodrigues comments, "I looked out into the darkness and clasping my knees I laughed softly."[20]

Scholars, as well as sufferers, of trauma have long explained that an encounter with radical evil or radical suffering ruptures language. Think of the most horrible thing that has ever happened to you in your life; are you able to communicate with perfect precision your experience of horror and pain to someone else, using mere words? In Endo's novel, nearly all of the oppressed characters exhibit this rupture of language. For example, when Rodrigues questions the peasant apostate Kichijiro, who witnessed the public execution of his non-apostate entire family, about death by water torture, Kichijiro starts to speak, but "his face became distorted, then suddenly he lapsed into silence."[21] For the rest of the novel, Kichijiro never directly speaks of the murder of his family, much in the same way that Rodrigues's predecessor in apostasy, Fr. Ferreira, never talks to Rodrigues about the pain of his own apostasy or life-long imprisonment.

Holocaust scholars like Susan Shapiro refer to this phenomenological reality as the crisis of representation. Observes Shapiro:

How can one express or convey the experience of a radically negating event that shatters the very conventions of speech and discourse without employing those conventions and, thereby, already domesticating that radical negativity? How can one tell about an event that negates and shatters our assumptions about order (including ... conceptions of God) ... in discourse, the main function of which is the ordering of human experience?

One ... [must] testify ... to the impossibility of fully, actually telling.[22]

So, how does one write a book about a historical horror such as the genocide of Japanese Christians, and at the same time testify to the impossibility of fully recounting the hidden transcript of the persecuted's lives? Endo uses laughter to achieve this end. Early in the tale, Rodrigues tries to interrogate Kichijiro about his faith and his story, but Kichijiro laughs rather than bares his soul, "He has the most fawning, obsequious laugh you could possibly imagine. It leaves a bad taste in our mouths."[23] Because Rodrigues himself is not yet among the oppressed, and has not encountered radical evil, he does not understand Kichijiro's incongruous laughter as in any way appropriate to the situation. Once, however, Rodrigues finds himself no longer one of the dominant but instead, just like Kichijiro, one who hides like a vagabond from his oppressors in the mountains, Rodrigues's own laughter echoes the peasant's, "When I reflected on my own condition a strange desire to laugh rose up within my heart."[24]

Much like tears, but with more of a spirit of protest against the evil that has been endured, laughter in *Silence* functions as a placeholder that says: beyond this point language cannot go. Evil ruptures rational discourse and renders it—laughably, we might say—inadequate. In a world where evil has become banal and commonplace, laughter interrupts this banality, re-naming evil as absurd and contrary to the way the world can and should be. By insisting on absurdity rather than acceptability, the oppressed's laughter protests evil. When Rodrigues first meets his captors and they ask him to apostatize, he laughs in their face. "And supposing I refuse?" the priest replies quietly, laughing all the time. "Then you'll kill me I suppose."[25]

Philosopher Kenneth Surin, writing on the Holocaust, helps us recognize that the problem of evil presents a peculiar dilemma to the person of faith—that is, the narrative of faith collides with the narrative of negativity, but neither cancels the other out. Thus the person of faith must live a life of paradox, replete with dialectical tension. Explains Surin:

The narrative of faith collides with the narrative of its negation, but neither achieves an ascendancy over the other. ... The testimony of its witnesses speaks for both these seemingly irreconcilable moments, moments which must nevertheless be simultaneously affirmed. To safeguard the possibility of truth it is necessary to hold the one moment as the necessary dialectical negation or counterpoise of the other. The testimony of affirmation needs to be 'ruptured' by its counterpart testimony of negation, and vice versa.[26]

I would elaborate upon Surin and say that for Christians who confront evil, the narrative of the promises of the gospel and God's love collide with the narrative(s) of their personal suffering and the world's horrors. In the case of *Silence*, lofty promises of God's presence and accompaniment collide with the raw lived experience of God's absence and silence.

As I have described at length in my book *The Laughter of the Oppressed*,[27] what Surin fails to remark in his otherwise brilliant analysis is that rational discourse cannot achieve what Surin rightly names is necessary for the person of faith who suffers. Language cannot hold two irreconcilable narratives together in the one moment, nor can it claim two things at once that are mutually contradictory. Surin does not propose any *concrete means by which the real-life person of faith survives the collision of narratives with both narratives still in play*. But where Surin's analysis stops, mine begins. For I contend that laughter steps in where language fails and does what it cannot. Laughter is the real-life means many people use to survive the collision of narratives without giving in to atheism on the one hand or Pollyannaism on the other. Laughter is the "language" of paradox—or better, our human supra-linguistic response to paradox.

A paradox is defined as a statement that is seemingly contradictory or against common sense, but that may be nonetheless true. Paradoxes make us laugh, then, because language—rational discourse—cannot express the seeming irrationality of simultaneous belief in two contradictory truths. Laughter, in other words, signals that the person who is laughing allows the dialectical tension between two opposites to stand unresolved in the one moment. I would argue that in the situation of evil, what a believer yearns to express are two things at once, both of which ostensibly negate one another. Namely, in colloquial terms, that, God is good and life can be horror. God is all-powerful and yet horrible shit happens. Surely these are absurd claims. Yet Endo's work suggests that theology fails the everyday believer if it does not recognize that the juxtaposition of these contradictory claims is the daily struggle of faith for so many suffering people of faith throughout the course of history, especially those whose experience can only be found through attention to the hidden transcript.

When narratives collide, then, people laugh. As Rodrigues develops as a character and takes his own place among the lowest of the low, he laughs precisely at those crucial moments when he can no longer ignore the messy collision of negativity and faith. Often these paradoxical points in the text are signaled to the reader by Rodrigues's repeated use of the watchword phrase "and yet." The following passage is an excellent case in point:

> And yet... and yet... if that man [Christ] was love itself, why had he rejected Judas in the end? ... Had he been cast aside to sink down into eternal darkness? Even as a seminarian and a priest, such doubts had arisen in his mind like dirty bubbles that rise to the surface of water in a swamp. And in such moments he tried to think of these bubbles as things that soiled the purity of his faith. But now they came upon him with a persistence that was irresistible. Shaking his head, he heaved a sigh. The Last Judgment would come. It was not given to man to understand all the mysteries of the Scriptures. Yet he wanted to know; he wanted to find out. ... The priest sat down on the floor soaked with urine, and like an idiot he laughed.[28]

Another moment in which we witness the collision of narratives occurs right after the peasants Mokichi and Ichizo's gruesome slow death by torture.

> Supposing God does not exist. ... If he does not exist, how absurd the whole thing becomes. What an absurd drama become the lives of Mokichi and Ichizo, bound to the stake and washed by the waves. ... Myself, too, wandering here over the desolate mountains—what an absurd situation! ... "The Lord preserved the just man when godless folk were perishing all around him." ... Surely he [God] should speak but a word for the Christians.[29]

Here Rodrigues juxtaposes the scriptural promise of God's "preservation of the just man" (narrative of faith) with the lived reality of God's silence in the face of Mokichi and Ichizo's water-torture death (narrative of negativity). A few seconds later, Rodrigues returns to the relative safety of his hut, only to find that a passerby (Kichijiro, ironically) has left a pile of excrement inside it. Rodrigues is enraged and reflects, "But the situation had its ludicrous side, too; and I burst out laughing."[30] Quite literally in this scene, Rodrigues laughs at the unexpected intrusion of feces into the center of his life's home.

In light of my earlier comments about the collision of narratives, we would do well to read the excrement passage as a metaphor. What is evil, after all, if not an irreconcilable dung-heap of waste, found incomprehensibly at the center of this otherwise heartbreakingly beautiful world we call home? The evil persecution that has caused the immense suffering of the peasants is a pile of shit that has been dropped by life into the center of Rodrigues's triumphal theology, as captured in the peasant Kichijiro's nagging unanswerable question that rises up from the depths of all oppressed peoples' experience, "Why has Deus Sama imposed this suffering upon us?"[31] How does the believer claim that, on the one hand, God is love and perfect power, and on the other—horrible shit can happen, even to those who love God? Surely this is preposterous.

Rodrigues cannot let go of God, which, to use Surin's terms, would be tantamount to allowing the narrative of negativity to achieve ascendancy, just as ignoring Kichijiro's cries of "Why does God impose such suffering upon us?" and not allowing this difficult question to enter his theological landscape would be to allow the narrative of faith to achieve ascendancy. Instead of either of these paths, Rodrigues laughs, a sign that he is clinging to the absurd reality of the validity of both narratives, rather than jettisoning either. Laughter, which embraces the both-and, signifies a rejection of the either/or and its scaffold of platitudinous theodicean clichés. Yet both Rodrigues and Kichijiro want—indeed, struggle—to believe that both narratives' claims are equally true; neither of them wants to discount the reality of hope or the reality of the suffering that renders hope such a dire necessity.

The men's laughter thus constantly underscores the limits of the facile dominant transcript theodicy—a rational justification for evil—and its shortcomings. Their laughter shows a grappling with the problem of evil and the love of God, but refuses to let the tension resolve into a discursive explanation. Their laughter lets the question of why stand, but lets it stand as a protest before God, rather than just ending the relationship with God and becoming a genuine apostate. Though both men are forced into public apostasy (dominant transcript), they are still believers in secret (hidden transcript). They thus incarnate a paradox in their very selfhood, for they have become believing apostates.

Their strange laughter, then, is perhaps best understood as the hallmark of a protest theodicy in the style of theologian John Roth, for it summons God to greater compassion and active presence in human lives. As Roth notes, "A protesting theodicy. ... supposes that human life is always under siege ... yet the human prospect is not hopeless. ... That prospect can be enhanced to the degree that the widespread experience of despair is turned on itself to yield the spirit of dissent ... God's promises call for protests."[32] From inside his prison cell, Rodrigues listens to the sound of the peasants being tortured by hanging upside down over a pit of excrement and screams, "Stop! Stop! Lord, it is now that you should break the silence. You must not remain silent. Prove that you are justice, that you are goodness, that you are love ... He had been able to thrust the terrible doubt far from the threshold of his mind. But now it was different. Why was God continually silent while those groaning voices go on?"[33] The priest's laughter expresses both his refusal to domesticate the negativity he encounters as well as his concomitant revision of his previous theology to include a more tragic theology, one that does not hasten to sweep the pain of the world's least-of-these under the worn-thin rug of "God's will."[34]

Another phrase we might use to better understand Rodrigues's theological transformation that laughter helps him to express would be the phrase from Martin Luther, *theologia crucis*—a theology of the cross. Luther believed that the church in his own day exploited the peasants, ignored the cries of the suffering poor, and had become triumphalistic, imperious, and elite. Luther termed this a "theology of glory" and believed the church had lost touch with its true foundation, the crucified Christ of the gospels. Swollen with money, power, and pride, the church allowed the glory of the resurrection to eclipse the scandal of the crucifixion. In the early pages of *Silence*, Rodrigues manifests a theology of glory; he prides himself on being a salvific "chart" for the "lost" and "ignorant" Japanese Christians, and condemns Ferreira's and Kichijiro's apostasy as pure weakness and a sign of unbelief, "Faith could not turn a man into such a coward ... Men are born into two categories: the strong and the weak, the saints and the commonplace, the heroes and those who respect them."[35] With regard to Ferreira, he adds, "For a long time he had felt almost no hatred for Ferreira, nothing but the pity a superior person feels for the wretched."[36]

The theology of glory is, to use other terms, the dominant transcript. According to the facile logic of the dominant consciousness that seeks to constantly justify its privilege, the world is divided into either/or categories, and moral and theological ambiguity do not exist as everyone gets exactly what they deserve. Observes Rodrigues, "He had come to this country to lay down his life for other men, but instead of that the Japanese were laying down their lives one by one for him. ... According to the doctrine he had learned until now, it was possible to pass judgement on certain actions distinguishing right from wrong and good from evil."[37] Fascinatingly in step with Rodrigues's thoughts, Max Weber argues that the dominant religious ideology serves only to justify the privileged majority's dominance and good fortune. The privileged person wants to believe that "he has earned his good fortune, in contrast to the unfortunate one who must equally have earned his misfortune. ... What the privileged classes require of religion ... is this psychological reassurance of legitimacy."[38] Rodrigues's own experience of oppression shatters this ideology. Explains feminist theologian Deanna Thompson,

> Luther's theology of the cross ... narrates a public corporate story about an alternative to a glory theology that creates a fictitious universe where ecclesial, theological, and monastic institutions come to practice a

theology of human power, majesty, and achievement. ... Jesus Christ's death on the cross tells us that appearances ultimately deceive. ... Precisely where God is least likely to be—in the shameful event of the Cross—there God is, hidden in the suffering.[39]

Rodrigues himself starkly juxtaposes the majestic, fictitious universe of a theology of glory with the world of the theology of the cross after he witnesses his first martyrdom, "I had long read about martyrdom in the lives of the saints—how the souls of the martyrs had gone home to heaven, ... how the angels had blown trumpets. This was the splendid martyrdom in my dreams. But the martyrdom of the Japanese Christians I now describe to you was no such glorious thing. What a miserable and painful business it was! ... The sea which killed them surges on uncannily—in silence."[40]

In numerous passages like this in *Silence*, Rodrigues's laughter symbolizes the inbreaking of a theology of the cross into his previously held theology of glory. Throughout the narrative, prior to his own forced apostasy, Rodrigues imagines the fictitious face of Christ as beautiful and encouraging, strong and majestic—clearly the Christ of a theology of glory. But at two crucial moments in the text, just as Thompson predicts, Rodrigues discovers the authentic face of the Christ of a theology of the cross in a place where he least expects to find Christ at all, and laughs both times. The first occurs right after the death of Mokichi and Ichizo:

> There reflected in the water was a tired, hollow face. I don't know why, but at that moment I thought of the face of yet another man. This was the face of a crucified man. ... They portrayed his face—the most pure, the most beautiful that has claimed the prayers of man. ... No doubt his real face was more beautiful than anything they have envisaged. Yet the face reflected in the pool of rainwater was heavy with mud and with stubble; it was thin and dirty, it was the face of a haunted man filled with uneasiness and exhaustion. Do you realize that in such circumstances a man may suddenly be seized with a fit of laughing? I thrust my face down to the water, twisted my lips like a madman, rolled my eyes and kept grimacing and making ludicrous faces in the water. Why did I do such a crazy thing? Why? Why?[41]

In this watery mirror, Rodrigues for the first time sees the face of the authentic suffering Christ hidden in his own suffering face.

The second occurs at the moment when Rodrigues is faced with the unexpected (non-)choice of either apostasy or the death of three peasants in the pit. Rodrigues decides to trample on the *fumie* because in a complete reversal of expectations, rather than seeing this as a betrayal, Christ tells him to trample, stating that it was to be trampled on by human beings that he came into this world. The priest realizes to his utter astonishment that such an act of emptying himself to the point of humiliation is exactly what the crucified Christ would have done. Rodrigues looks at the *fumie* at his feet, and the Christ he sees there is the Christ of a *theologia crucis*—weak, "ugly," "crowned with thorns," "sunken and utterly exhausted" and "worn down and hollow with constant trampling."[42] In that moment, Rodrigues realizes that Christ himself was considered an apostate, a viewpoint that Endo unambiguously asserts also in his non-fiction.[43]

Ironically, in becoming an apostate himself, Rodrigues has become more of a Christ-follower than he ever was, for he emulates Christ's *kenosis* and undergoes complete rejection. Writes Endo elsewhere, "A person begins to be a follower of Jesus only by accepting himself the risk of becoming one of the powerless people in the visible world."[44] Christ does not reign in glory, Rodrigues discovers, Christ is a co-sufferer with humanity, "'Lord, I resented your silence.' 'I was not silent. I suffered beside you.'"[45] Laughter marks the beautiful denouement when the *theologia crucis* at last supplants the *theologia gloriae* in Rodrigues, "I bear no grudge against you! I am only laughing at man's fate. My faith in you is different from what it was, but I love you still."[46]

When Rodrigues's oppressors claim that he was defeated by the swamp of Japan that cannot embrace western Christianity, Rodrigues insists contrariwise that his own theology of glory, and not Japan, was the problem all along. "Gradually he had come to realize it was against his own faith that he had fought. But he could scarcely expect the Lord of Chikugo to understand a thing like that."[47] Those in the corridors of power like the Lord of Chikugo who have not lived life from below, experienced feelings of God-forsakenness, or listened to the cries of those who have, cannot grasp the *theologia crucis*. But a theologian of the cross understands that what the world conceives of as uselessness and weakness—traits such as mercy, compassion, and forgiveness of those who blatantly betray us—Christ reveals paradoxically to be the heartbeat of strength in the eyes of God. Until Rodrigues's own apostasy, he is egocentrically obsessed with his own usefulness, but he does not realize that he has confused usefulness with privilege, with being the one always in the position to help others, "Yes, to be useful to others, to help others, this was the one wish and the only dream of one who had dedicated himself to the priesthood. The solitude of the priestly life was only when one was useless to others."[48]

In the intriguing novel *Wonderful Fool*, Endo uses the phrase "a useless tree" to describe the narrative's blatant Christ figure.[49] *Silence*, too, in its *theologia crucis* portrays Christ as a useless tree. Though the uncomfortable allusion may be lost on a Western audience, I believe Endo borrows this metaphor from the fourth-century Chinese tale of Chuang Tzu entitled, "The Useless Tree." (Fascinatingly, this story was a favorite of another Catholic writer as well—Thomas Merton, who retells it in his book *The Way of Chuang Tzu*.) Chuang Tzu's thought is often credited with having had a tremendous influence on the Zen Buddhism of Endo's own Japanese culture. In the tale "The Useless Tree," a sage sees an enormous tree on a hill. The sap is bitter, the leaves are too fragile to be woven into mats, and the roots are too gnarled to make baskets. The sage then realizes, "'This, indeed, is a tree good for nothing! That is why it has reached so great an age! ... We all know the advantage of being useful, but only this tree knows the advantage of being useless!' The wise man sat in the shade of that great tree for the rest of the day, ... happily contemplating his own uselessness."[50] The Christ of a theology of the cross may appear useless to the power-engorged, but the least among us—notably those whom our society also misconceives of as useless—comprehend that only in his arms can the comforting shade of redignification and restoration be found. God values us for our very being, not for our doing.

Endo explicates in his theological essays that Japanese culture, which is deeply influenced by Buddhism and its teachings of human compassion not *deus ex machina*, cannot stomach a theology-of-glory God, "The religious mentality of the Japanese is—just as it was at the time when the people accepted Buddhism—responsive to one who 'suffers with us' and who 'allows for our weakness,' but their mentality has little tolerance for any kind of transcendent being who judges humans harshly, then punishes them."[51] Endo himself cannot accept such a view of God either, "In writing *Silence* I felt as though I had buried the distance I had formerly sensed between Christianity and myself. In short, that represents a change from Christianity as a paternal religion to Christianity as a maternal religion. The male image of Christ that the hero started out with is transformed into a female image. ... The image of Christ carved on the *fumie* in silence is a maternal image, a woman seeking to suffer with her child and share her child's pain."[52] In a theology of the cross, Christ is a co-sufferer who stands alongside the oppressed and is their *kenotic* redeemer.

Explains theologian of the cross Mary Solberg, "A theologian of the cross is someone who has been struck ... by what God reveals on the cross: namely, God's own self. Sent reeling, the theologian ... glimpses ... that his or her expectations and categories—even the words to articulate who this is on the bloody cross, what is going on here, or anything else one could call reliable human knowledge—have been upended, reversed, short-circuited."[53] When Rodrigues becomes an authentic theologian of the cross, every category of his thought is upended, "Christianity is not what you take it to be ...! The priest wanted to shout this out ... but ... no matter what he said no one would ever understand his present feelings."[54] Rejected as a fallen priest by the church who does not have a category of the believing apostate, which Rodrigues has arguably become, Rodrigues gives words to the hidden transcript of his both-and reality, "'What do you understand? You superiors in Macao, you in Europe!' He wanted to stand face-to-face with them in the darkness and speak in his own defense. 'You live a carefree life of tranquility and security, in a place where there is no storm and no torture—it is there that you carry on your apostolate!'"[55] Rodrigues grasps at last that his once avowed theology of glory rejects the scriptural claim of strength through weakness and fails to take seriously the experience of radical evil (the storm) or the suffering of the poor (the torture).

As Solberg predicts, other reversals abound. Ferreira, to whom Rodrigues once felt infinitely superior, now becomes Rodrigues's "inseparable twin."[56] The theology of the cross shatters either/or dichotomous thought and incarnates the both-and; concludes Rodrigues on the last page of the text just prior to forgiving Kichijiro's sins, "There are neither the strong nor the weak."[57] No longer is Kichijiro the weak coward and he the proud priest, "I wonder if there's any difference between Kichijiro and myself. And yet, rather than this *I know that my Lord is different from the god that is preached in the churches.*"[58] To Rodrigues, the God of a theology of glory does not even seem like the same God as the God he experiences when he becomes one of the world's despised.

This collision of narratives between Rodrigues's newfound theology of the cross—the hidden transcript theology of the oppressed faithful—and his previously held theology of glory—the dominant theology upheld by the privileged in the church—makes Rodrigues laugh out loud. When Rodrigues, the once privileged priest, literally becomes a peasant as he is forced by the authorities to take the name, wife, and life of one, we read, "He had become a Japanese. Okada San'emon! He laughed in a low voice as he uttered the name."[59] Such laughter is perfectly in keeping with the philosophical incongruity theory of laughter proposed by Arthur Schopenhauer. Explains Schopenhauer, "The phenomenon of laughter always signifies the sudden apprehension of incongruity between such a conception and the real object thought under it, thus between the abstract and concrete objects of apprehension. The greater and more unexpected, in the apprehension of the laugher, the incongruity is, the more violent will be his laughter."[60] Laughter functions as an apposite supra-linguistic expression of a theology of the cross because a theology of the cross itself bespeaks paradox, resists language, and results from an incongruous collision of narratives.

In conclusion, *Silence* helps us rediscover the hidden transcript of subversive resistance practiced every day by those who live under persecution and tyranny. In the spaces between the words of this transcript, laughter rings out like a summons to an alternative consciousness. Such incongruous and unexpected laughter from oppressed people of faith protests evil, resists the forces of dominant glory-theologies, and takes the unanswered question of human suffering as seriously as it takes hope and redemption. Contemplating the commingled tragedy and beauty of life, Jack Gilbert in the poem "A Brief for the Defense," writes, "The poor women at the fountain are laughing together/There is laughter/everyday in the terrible streets of Calcutta,/ ... We must have the stubbornness to accept our gladness in the ruthless furnace of this world/ ... We must admit there will be music despite everything."[61] And readers of Endo might add: we must admit there will be laughter despite everything.

Notes

1 James C. Scott, *Domination and the Arts of Resistance: Hidden Transcripts* (New Haven: Yale University Press, 1990), 111.

2 Ibid., 198.

3 Ibid., 25.

4 Scott does mention jokes as a form of the hidden transcript, but only in passing and without analysis. In any case, this chapter is not concerned with laughter at the humorous, but with laughter at the horrible, a theme utterly untouched by Scott.

5 Josef Kuschel, *Laughter: A Theological Reflection* (New York: Continuum, 1994), 45.

6 Barry Sanders, *Sudden Glory: Laughter as Subversive History* (Boston: Beacon, 1995) 128–9.

7 Ibid., 128.

8 Ingvild Soelid Gilhus, *Laughing Gods, Weeping Virgins: Laughter in the History of Religions* (New York: Routledge, 1997) 57.

9 Timothy Fry, ed., *The Rule of St. Benedict in English* (Collegeville, MN: Liturgical Press, 1982) 31, 37.

10 Kuschel, *Laughter*, 46–7.

11 Reinhold Niebuhr, "Humor and Faith," in *Holy Laughter*, ed. Conrad Hyers (New York: Seabury Press, 1969) 135.

12 Sanders, *Sudden Glory*, 70.

13 Mark Williams, *Endō Shūsaku: A Literature of Reconciliation* (New York: Routledge, 1999), 106.

14 Ibid., 106.

15 Shusaku Endo, *Silence*, trans. William Johnston (New York: Taplinger Publishing Company, 1980), 26, 31.
16 Ibid., 21.
17 Ibid., 22.
18 Ibid., 19.
19 Ibid., 54–5.
20 Ibid., 63.
21 Ibid., 17.
22 Susan Shapiro, "Hearing the Testimony of Radical Negation," *Concilium* 175 (1984): 3–10.
23 Endo, *Silence*, 25.
24 Ibid., 66.
25 Ibid., 85.
26 Kenneth Surin, "Taking Suffering Seriously," *The Problem of Evil: Selected Readings*, ed. Michael L. Peterson (Notre Dame: Indiana University Press, 1992), 344.
27 Jacqueline A. Bussie, *The Laughter of the Oppressed: Ethical and Theological Resistance in Wiesel, Morrison, and Endo* (New York: T&T Clark, 2007).
28 Endo, *Silence*, 164–5.
29 Ibid., 68–9.
30 Ibid., 70.
31 Ibid., 54.
32 John K. Roth, "A Theodicy of Protest," in *Encountering Evil: Live Options in Theodicy*, ed. Stephen Davis (Atlanta: John Knox Press, 1981), 15, 17.
33 Endo, *Silence*, 168.
34 The helpful term "tragic theology" comes from Larry D. Bouchard, *Tragic Method and Tragic Theology: Evil in Contemporary Drama and Religious Thought* (University Park, PA: Penn State University Press, 1989).
35 Endo, *Silence*, 24, 77.
36 Ibid., 130.
37 Ibid., 132.
38 Quoted in Scott, *Domination*, 68.
39 Deanna A. Thompson, "Becoming a Feminist Theologian of the Cross," in *Cross Examinations: Readings on the Meaning of the Cross Today*, ed. Marit Trelstad (Minneapolis: Augsburg Press, 2006), 78–9.
40 Endo, *Silence*, 60–1.
41 Ibid., 67–8.
42 Ibid., 170–1, 175.
43 See Shusaku Endo, *A Life of Jesus*, trans. Richard A Schuchert (New York: Paulist Press, 1973), 92. "His enemies considered Jesus not only a false prophet but also an apostate."
44 Ibid., 145.
45 Ibid., 190.
46 Ibid., 189.

47 Ibid., 186.

48 Ibid., 143–4.

49 Shusaku Endo, *Wonderful Fool* (London: Peter Owen Publishers, 2000), 172. "He might even be called a saint … But to be a saint or a man of too good a nature in today's pragmatic world, with everyone out to get the other fellow, was equivalent to being a fool, wasn't it? At least, to a young girl like Tomoe, Gaston … was just a huge, inert, useless tree. Yes, a big useless tree."

50 Quoted in Belden C. Lane, "Merton as Zen Clown," *Theology Today* 46.3 (October 1989): 256–68.

51 Endo, *A Life of Jesus*, 1.

52 Quoted in Williams, 123–4.

53 Mary M. Solberg, "All That Matters: What an Epistemology of the Cross is Good For," in *Cross Examinations: Readings on the Meaning of the Cross Today*, ed. Marit Trelstad (Minneapolis: Augsburg Press, 2006), 140.

54 Endo, *Silence*, 187.

55 Ibid., 175.

56 Ibid., 177.

57 Ibid., 191.

58 Ibid., 175. (italics mine)

59 Ibid., 189.

60 John Morreal, *The Philosophy of Laughter and Humor* (Albany: SUNY Press, 1987), 54–5.

61 Jack Gilbert, "A Brief for the Defense," The Poetry Center at Smith College. http://www.smith.edu/poetrycenter/poets/abrief.html (accessed on May 8, 2014).

Part Four

Teaching *Silence*

15

Silence in the Classroom[1]

John Kaltner

I first encountered *Silence* many years ago as a student when I was introduced to it by a professor with whom I was taking a tutorial course.[2] Our conversations about the novel left a profound and indelible impression on me as we dissected the many theological, ethical, and cultural issues it raises. That course was one of the high points of my education, and as I look back on my student years, *Silence* was clearly one of the most influential and memorable books I read during that time of my life.

In the years since, having slid over to the professor's chair, I have had the opportunity to use *Silence* on many occasions in my own teaching in an undergraduate setting.[3] This chapter describes some of my experiences using the novel as a pedagogical tool to identify and explore questions of meaning and value for students. I will do this by treating four scenes in the book that I have found to be particularly effective in generating and sustaining discussion and debate among them. In the process, I will offer some comments on the plot, characterization, and other literary features of the novel that make it such an accessible and fertile resource for both teachers and students. The essay also describes an assortment of questions, conversation starters, and assignments I have developed over the years that are meant to encourage students to explore the richness and relevance of Endo's masterpiece.[4]

Scene One: The Executions of Mokichi and Ichizo

The passage describing the executions of the two Christians Mokichi and Ichizo at the hands of the Japanese authorities is an important one for a couple of reasons. Prior to this point in the novel the danger of professing Christianity is acknowledged, but it is still a somewhat abstract and theoretical notion. In this scene that danger becomes real and tangible. The martyrdom of the two men is a graphic illustration of the risk involved in following the faith, and it is a disturbing reminder of the consequences a Christian might suffer if he or she were to be discovered. It is also an important scene because, in its aftermath, Fr. Rodrigues ponders the silence of God for the first time, a theme that will continue to surface throughout the remainder of the novel. God's silence is actually first mentioned a few pages earlier in the context of Rodrigues's response to a question posed by Kichijiro, but the priest does not reflect upon it in any depth. This scene therefore introduces key components into the narrative, and so it merits careful consideration and analysis.

Something students often note about the scene is that, unlike the next one to be considered, it is a first-person account. This gives it a sense of immediacy as the events are focalized through the character of Rodrigues and the reader observes the executions from his perspective. At the same time, students often point out that Rodrigues is not physically present on the beach where Mokichi and Ichizo meet their fate, but he is watching from the relative safety of the hut he shares with his Jesuit comrade Fr. Garrpe. The physical distance between Rodrigues and the Japanese martyrs creates a corresponding metaphorical space between them that one student has described as a "credibility gap" that injects a sense of irony into the scene. The Japanese literally put their lives on the line in the name of their faith, but the one whose life should be most committed to that faith can only watch from afar and does not participate in their extreme act of commitment.

As he does elsewhere in the narrative, Rodrigues reads christological meaning into what he observes by interpreting the executions within the context of Jesus's life and teachings. Consequently, the trees on which the martyrs are tied are cruciform in shape for him, and when those being tortured are presented with *sake* to drink he is reminded of the vinegar offered to Jesus at his crucifixion. This encourages the reader to understand the deaths within the framework of Christian faith and to see them as examples of that most noble form of passing, martyrdom. The priest struggles to view the deaths of Mokichi and Ichizo in this way, however, because they do not match his idealized vision of what martyrdom should be. The disconnect between the idea of a thing and the thing itself is a common theme in the novel, and it is a topic that can generate much discussion in the classroom. "I had long read about martyrdom in the lives of the saints—how the souls of the martyrs had gone home to Heaven, how they had been filled with glory in Paradise, how the angels had blown trumpets. This was the splendid martyrdom I had often seen in my dreams. But the martyrdom of the Japanese Christians I now describe to you was no such glorious thing. What a miserable and painful business it was!"[5] Rodrigues's words here mark the first of a series of realizations that he comes to throughout the book that his preconceptions and prior assumptions do not match the reality he is experiencing, and they provide an excellent opportunity to discuss with students this same phenomenon as it relates to their own lives. In a writing assignment meant to facilitate such a conversation I have asked students to first describe an experience they have had in which a belief they held was challenged by a reality they encountered and then to answer several questions: Why did this happen? What effect did it have on you? What lessons can you (and Rodrigues) take away from this experience?

Another assignment related to this scene that has proved effective entails asking students to pay attention to Endo's use of repetition, in particular on the level of vocabulary. Are there any words, or related sets of words, that appear with a high degree of frequency? With a close reading it quickly becomes apparent that terms associated with the sea or water are commonly found throughout the passage. In fact, in this relatively brief section such words are found more than 30 times and they are used in reference to the sea itself, water, rain, the tide, waves, the shore, and tears. When asked why there is such a high concentration of water-related terminology in the scene, students often associate this with Rodrigues's musings at the end of the passage in which he equates the silence of the sea with the silence of God. He makes the connection as he asks himself, "What do I want to say? I myself do not quite understand. Only that today, when for the glory of God Mokichi and Ichizo moaned, suffered and died, I cannot bear the monotonous sound of the dark sea gnawing at the shore. Behind the depressing silence of the sea, the silence of God … the feeling that while men raise their voices in anguish God remains with folded arms, silent."[6]

As noted above, this is the first time in the novel that Rodrigues reflects on God's silence. The use by the translator of an ellipsis immediately after the phrase "the silence of God" is an effective way of underscoring the deity's reticence, a pregnant pause that delays the narrative flow and creates a gap in which the divine silence is intensified. Similarly, the image of a wordless God with arms folded reinforces this sense and is in stark contrast to the description of the two Japanese martyrs with arms outstretched, singing a hymn celebrating their journey to paradise.

In discussing Rodrigues's words, students often remark that his description of the sea as silent is odd in light of the references he makes to its noisiness. In the passage quoted above he mentions the "monotonous sound of the dark sea gnawing at the shore," and elsewhere in the scene he refers to the "monotonous roar" of the waves,[7] the "sound of the waves,"[8] the "sound of the rain,"[9] and the sea surging on uncannily "in silence."[10] Anyone who has spent time standing on the shore before a raging body of water knows that, despite the seeming contradiction, the sea can be silent and noisy at the same time. This might be what Endo is trying to convey through his use of the adjective "monotonous." At times, the sea's sound can be so loud, ongoing, and unvaried that it seems to be no sound at all. It seems to be silence, although it is not silence. Only when there is a break in the noise does one realize how close monotony and silence can be to one another.

When this paradox is pointed out to them, students begin to think about the silence of God in a new way. Perhaps the point Endo is trying to make is that, like the sea, God is simultaneously "noisy" and silent. Because of his assumptions regarding martyrdom and faith in general, Rodrigues expects God to speak in a certain manner. When that does not occur, he believes that God is silent. He will learn later in the novel that God is not silent, but is in fact speaking in a way Rodrigues does not anticipate because it goes against his mistaken understanding of how God should speak. He is incapable of hearing the sound of God's voice because it takes a form he does not expect—it takes on the quality of a "monotonous roar" that he assumes is silence.[11] This once again highlights how our preconceptions can sometimes be misconceptions.

This scene inevitably raises a host of questions in students' minds, and I often ask them to try to articulate them. Some are theological: Why does God let innocent people suffer? Does Rodrigues question God's existence? Is God really silent? Others are more personal: What assumptions are my beliefs based on? What should I do if those assumptions are challenged? Should I have doubts about what I believe? Would I be able to do what Mokichi and Ichizo did? I remind them that some of these questions will take a lifetime to answer, and for some the answers will likely never come. Nonetheless, there is a great benefit to knowing what questions to ask, even if the answers remain a mystery.

Scene Two: The Deaths of Garrpe and the Three Japanese Christians

This second scene of martyrdom shares some key elements with the previous one, but it extends and develops those themes in a way that pushes the narrative into important new directions. It begins with Rodrigues's learning that Garrpe has been captured, and as the events unfold he watches in horror as his Jesuit companion and three Japanese Christians he met previously are put to death. In one of the most memorable passages in the novel, mats are rolled around the bodies of the Japanese with their heads protruding so they resemble "basket worms," and they are rowed out to sea where they are pushed from the boat.[12] As they sink under the surface, Garrpe meets the same watery fate when he attempts to swim to their rescue. The first task I assign to students is to identify and discuss the most significant similarities and differences between this scene and the earlier one.

The surface similarities with the previous scene are obvious since both describe martyrdoms in the water that Rodrigues observes from a distance. But students are quick to point out some key differences between the two passages. The scene involving Mokichi and Ichizo is told in the first person from Rodrigues's perspective, while this one is a third-person account. This slight shift has the effect of magnifying Rodrigues's onlooker status as the distance between him and the events he is witnessing is enhanced in the reader's mind. As a result, the "credibility gap" mentioned earlier is now more apparent and operative because Rodrigues is further removed from a scene depicting a supreme act of faith that he himself should be participating in. The presence of his colleague Garrpe, who fills a role that should also be played by Rodrigues, reinforces this sense for the reader. At the same time, Rodrigues is not watching the events unfold from the relative safety of his hut, as in the first scene. He, too, is a prisoner, and he is being forced by his captors to witness the deaths of his friends. This creates a degree of sympathy for his character and raises ominous questions about what awaits him.

The many references to the sea and water are another obvious similarity between the two scenes that students call attention to, and some have noted that sometimes the passages have shared vocabulary. This can be seen, for example, in the description that "the sluggish waters made the same monotonous sound as they gnawed at the shore."[13] The close connection between the sea and God is a theme first mentioned in the previous scene, and it continues to be explored in this one. Just prior to it, as Rodrigues waits to be taken to the place where Garrpe and the three Japanese will die, he repeats the correlation. "The sea was silent as if exhausted; and God, too, continued to be silent."[14] One astute student has proposed an interpretation that brings together the God/sea connection and the two martyrdom scenes. She noted that the description of Garrpe's head bobbing up and down in the water recalls the depiction of Mokichi and Ichizo disappearing and reappearing as the tide comes in and the waves cover them. In both cases all the martyrs are completely submerged by the sea, and this student has suggested that this may be a way of symbolizing that they have been engulfed in or embraced by God for their acts of faith.

Another similarity sometimes pointed out by students is that here, as in the previous scene, Rodrigues continues to struggle with how his circumstances challenge what he has been taught to believe. As he watches the Japanese lay down their lives for their beliefs, he notes that they are doing the very thing that he himself came to Japan to do. This calls into question his sense of self and his reason for being there. In the same way, he realizes that if Garrpe obeys the Japanese officials' order to recant his faith, then he will be doing two things, one of which would be in line with everything he believes and the other would go against all he stands for. How can that one act both save the Japanese Christians and lead to Garrpe's damnation? These musings on Rodrigues's part can trigger a host of questions and issues about a range of topics like doubt, faith, commitment, and purpose that often lead to fascinating classroom discussion.

This is related to a significant dimension of the scene—the dramatic tension is considerably heightened due to Garrpe's presence. No longer a hidden observer from the security of his hut, the Portuguese Jesuit Garrpe is now an active participant whose behavior and decisions will have a momentous impact on the outcome. The three Japanese Christians have already trampled on the *fumie* and have renounced their faith, outwardly at least. But this is not enough to save them. The authorities insist that Garrpe must apostatize as well in order for the Japanese to be spared. Will he, or won't he?

As noted above, this situation puts in sharp relief the contrast between Garrpe and Rodrigues, the one experiencing firsthand the ramifications and consequences of their decision to come to Japan as the other watches helplessly from the sidelines. As students read this scene I ask them to analyze and interpret how Endo characterizes Rodrigues as he observes his companion wrestling with the choice that confronts the latter. Many students point out that it is actually a choice that confronts both Jesuits because Rodrigues personalizes Garrpe's dilemma and makes it his own. "I would apostatize. I would apostatize. The words rose up even to his throat, but clenching his teeth he tried to stop himself from uttering the words aloud."[15] His thoughts will prove prophetic, of course, because apostatize is precisely what Rodrigues will go on to do at the end of the novel when he finds himself in a similar situation. But he is not quite there yet. Students are struck by Rodrigues's inability to articulate his thoughts here as he seals his lips to choke off his words. Earlier in the scene he "shouts out the words in his heart," closes his eyes and literally turns his back on his fellow Jesuit in an attempt to avoid facing the painful reality.[16] Rodrigues knows what should be done, what must be done, but he is incapable of articulating that knowledge publicly and plainly. Some students have commented on the poignancy and ambiguity of Rodrigues's very next thought. "You are silent. Even in this moment are you silent?"[17] To whom is he speaking, to God or to himself? If the latter, then he is chastising himself for his cowardice and inability to proclaim aloud what needs to be said. If he is speaking to God, then students have suggested that there is a powerful irony at work here since Rodrigues is complaining about God's silence while he himself is the one who suppresses his speech and lacks a voice. It could be that God is speaking loudly through the monotonous sound of the sea while Rodrigues is the mute, wordless one.

The details of this scene allow the class to explore important questions related to morality and the choices people make. Both Garrpe and Rodrigues find themselves in difficult situations that test their mettle and challenge long-held beliefs about right and wrong. There is a level of ambiguity regarding both characters, and this is what makes them such rich objects of discussion in the classroom. As noted above, it is unclear if Rodrigues is rebuking himself or God for being silent. Similarly, does his inability to speak his mind suggest that he is still wavering on the question of whether or not he would apostatize? Regarding Garrpe, he is placed in the impossible position of having to recant his faith to save those to whom that faith has brought him. Something that students and other readers often miss is that the novel is unclear as to whether or not Garrpe *does* apostatize in a futile attempt to rescue the three Japanese Christians. When he plunges into the water he repeats something over and over again that gets fainter as the waves wash over him, but his actual words are never reported to the reader. Does he or doesn't he apostatize?

As a way of getting at some of these issues I ask students to write an essay in which they discuss one of the two characters in terms of the choices he confronts and the implications of those choices. I also ask them to clear up the ambiguity by suggesting what choice the character eventually makes. Does Rodrigues speak to God or to himself? Does Garrpe renounce his faith or not? The final part of the assignment asks students to relate this scene to the contemporary world, either in relation to some social issue that is not easy to resolve or in relation to some personal experience they have had in which, like Garrpe and Rodrigues, they have had to make a difficult choice fraught with ambiguity. In our discussions of those essays I am always struck by how the distance between the real world of the twenty-first century and the fictional world of seventeenth-century Japan disappears.

Scene Three: Rodrigues's Encounter with Ferreira

Although he does not make an appearance until relatively late, the character of Ferreira looms large behind the scene throughout the novel. He is a complex figure whose presence/absence instills a not insignificant amount of anticipation and expectation into the narrative. As their mentor and a missionary trailblazer to Japan, the older man functions as a role model and inspiration for Rodrigues and the younger Jesuits. At the same time, his rumored apostasy and fall from grace have tarnished his reputation and diminished him in their eyes. Several times the Japanese authorities remind Rodrigues of Ferreira's presence in the country, and on at least one occasion he believes a reunion with his former teacher is imminent only to have his hopes dashed. Despite its delay, the reader knows that such a meeting is inevitable. As one student has put it, "Until the end I wasn't sure if Rodrigues would trample on the *fumie*, but there was never a doubt in my mind that he would meet up again with Ferreira."

The long-anticipated encounter finally takes place in Chapter Seven when Rodrigues is brought to a temple where Ferreira is now residing. It is a scene charged with tension and drama. With his knees shaking, Rodrigues expectantly looks on as Ferreira enters the room dressed in Japanese garb with downcast eyes, walking behind an old monk. He eagerly waits to hear the first words that will pass from his old spiritual director's lips, but is met instead with… silence. The quiet continues until Rodrigues can no longer stand it and he clumsily blurts out, "Please … say … something … If you have any pity for me … please … say … something."[18] When asked to comment on how the scene begins, students note the obvious parallels to previous passages in which the theme of silence is a central motif. Just as he struggles with the silence of the sea and the silence of God, here Rodrigues is uncomfortable with the lack of communication from Ferreira. Some have suggested that, given his larger-than-life status in Rodrigues's eyes, perhaps Ferreira plays a God-like role for him. His words—"If you have pity for me, please say something"—could have been uttered at earlier points in the story when he felt frustrated by divine silence.

Some students have remarked that, in a subtle way, this scene continues the theme of Rodrigues having difficulty coming to terms with a present reality that does not meet his own expectations. This is seen when he realizes that what he most wants to say to him is that he is surprised Ferreira has shaved off his beard. The now clean-shaven Ferreira does not fit the image that Rodrigues has had of him during the years since they last saw one another. It is a relatively minor element in the story, but it indirectly reinforces the characterization of Rodrigues as someone who has a hard time accepting things that undermine his preconceptions. Just as with the martyrdoms of Mokichi, Ichizo, and Garrpe and the issues they raised about faith and mission, Rodrigues's long-held belief about Ferreira's appearance is being challenged. If Ferreira is meant to be a God-like figure in this scene, as some students have proposed, then this introduces a theological element into Rodrigues's seemingly insignificant comment about Ferreira's beard.

Related to this is the fact that his lack of a beard renders Ferreira visually less Christ-like, and he can no longer be associated with the bearded "face of a man," an allusion to Christ that Rodrigues sees and reflects upon throughout the novel. In effect, his beardlessness is symbolic of Ferreira's rejection of his faith and is a marker that he is no longer a priest who can act *in persona Christi*.

Another somewhat minor aspect of this scene that some students have called attention to is Ferreira's work translating a book on astronomy. As he explains this activity to Rodrigues, Ferreira repeatedly reminds him that through this work he is making a significant contribution to the Japanese people by increasing their level of scientific knowledge. Students have detected in his remarks evidence of Ferreira's insecurity regarding his usefulness to society and his desire to convince his former student that he is, despite appearances to the contrary, still engaged in scholarly work. Some have also pointed out an ironic dimension to Ferreira's new profession in that the former Jesuit whose job it was to instruct the Japanese about heaven and how to get to it has now been reduced to teaching them about what the heavens are made of.

But astronomy is not the only topic Ferreira has been writing on these days. As the conversation unfolds, Rodrigues learns that his former mentor is also busy at work composing a refutation of Christianity for the Japanese authorities. When Rodrigues replies that he considers this to be a form of torture, the comment elicits an unexpected response from Ferreira. "Suddenly, as Ferreira tried to turn his face away, the priest saw a white tear glistening in his eye. The black Japanese kimono! The chestnut hair bound back in Japanese style! The name: Sawano Chuan! And yet this man is still alive! Lord, you are still silent. You still maintain your deep silence in a life like this!"[19] Rodrigues's response to Ferreira's tear is important on a couple of levels. First of all, it continues the theme of God's silence that runs like a thread throughout the novel, and the close connection between water and God seen in earlier passages is subtly echoed. Here it is the silent tear of Ferreira, not the monotonous roar of the sea, that causes Rodrigues to ponder the silence of God. Of more interest to students has been the critique of Japanese culture and society that is implied in Rodrigues's reaction to Ferreira's tear. The latter's clothing, hairstyle, and name might be Japanese, but deep down he is still "alive." For some students, this suggests that to be Japanese is to be dead or something less than fully alive. It is a sentiment that privileges the West and denigrates all things non-Western as inferior, imperfect, and incapable of sustaining life. This is an idea that is found in several passages earlier in the novel, but it is here in the showdown between Ferreira and Rodrigues that it is expressed in its fullest form.[20]

Prior to this scene, Japan is referred to as "a remote country at the periphery of the world," "a desolate and abandoned land," "a barren island,"[21] and the Japanese people are described as "wandering bewildered in the darkness," a people who never previously knew human warmth, "who work and live and die like beasts."[22] Such characterizations reflect the Catholic Church's attitude throughout much of its history toward those places and peoples to whom missionaries were sent in order to bring the "true faith." As a product of his time Ferreira shares this view, and in his conversation with Rodrigues he argues that because of the unreceptive nature of Japan and its people any missionary effort is bound to fail. "This country is a swamp. In time you will come to see that for yourself. This country is a more terrible swamp than you can imagine. Whenever you plant a sapling in this swamp the roots begin to rot; the leaves grow yellow and wither. And we have planted the sapling of Christianity in this swamp."[23] He goes on to say that the Japanese people never actually embraced the Christian faith, but they changed and molded it to fit their own understanding of God and religion. In a memorable image, Ferreira compares the Christian God in Japan to a butterfly caught in a spider's web—it has become a skeleton and only God's exterior form remains. Rodrigues refutes this idea and espouses the view common at the time (and sometimes in our own) that "Christianity and the Church are truths that transcend all countries and territories."[24]

Because it remains relevant for our own time, this exchange between Rodrigues and Ferreira touches many nerves for students, and it has led to some lively and heated classroom discussions. There are many ways to unpack the issues and questions it raises. Sometimes, I have had individual students or groups of students take on the role of either Rodrigues or Ferreira and engage in a debate with one another over the following questions: Should a religion be brought from one place to another? What are the pros and cons of mission work? How should followers of different faiths interact and engage with one another? What should be done when religions make competing truth claims?[25]

It is also interesting to consider the novel in light of the context in which it was written. It first appeared in the mid-1960s, soon after the close of the Second Vatican Council. That gathering of Catholic leaders led to a dramatic change in the Church's dogma and practice in many areas, including some that relate to *Silence* such as attitudes toward non-Christians, mission work, and enculturation of the gospel in non-Christian settings. One way of exploring this that I have found to be effective entails having students read excerpts from the Vatican II document *Nostra Aetate*, the Declaration on the Relation of the Church to Non-Christian Religions, and then offer some thoughts on how the novel would be different if the characters had been operating out of a mindset informed by this theology. Imagine, for example, what Rodrigues's and Ferreira's attitudes toward Japanese religion and culture would have been in light of these words from the second paragraph of *Nostra Aetate* regarding other faiths: "The Catholic Church rejects nothing that is true and holy in these religions. She regards with sincere reverence those ways of conduct and of life, those precepts and teachings which, though differing in many aspects from the ones she holds and sets forth, nonetheless often reflect a ray of that truth which enlightens all people."[26]

Scene Four: Rodrigues Tramples on the *Fumie*

This scene echoes the previous one in that it describes a face-off between Ferreira and Rodrigues, only this time Ferreira is the more vocal and assertive of the two. The roles have been reversed as it is Rodrigues, rather than Ferreira, who is reluctant to speak when the episode opens. When asked to parse the dynamics of the scene, some students have suggested that Ferreira appears to have resumed his role as Rodrigues's teacher as he draws upon his own experience in a similar situation to instruct the younger man about how he should act. Rodrigues is at first a reluctant student who is not convinced by Ferreira's logic and argument, but by the end of the scene he has been persuaded to do the unthinkable and he tramples on the *fumie*.

Rodrigues is initially hesitant because he continues to operate out of a mistaken mindset. After having noted how in each of the three previous scenes Rodrigues has had a hard time letting go of his long-held beliefs when they do not fit the reality he is facing, students are quick to see the same tendency present here. Rodrigues continues to misread things and he holds wrong assumptions about what he is experiencing. Sometimes this occurs on the level of his senses, as when he thinks he hears snoring in an adjacent cell when it is actually the moans of Japanese Christians who will continue to be tortured unless he apostatizes. Elsewhere his misperception has more profound consequences that cause him to reevaluate his own identity and sense of self. The realization that these are fellow Christians who are being tormented for their faith cuts Rodrigues to the core and challenges his self-understanding. "He had believed in his pride that he alone in this night was sharing in the suffering of that man. But here just beside him were people who were sharing in that suffering much more than he."[27] As he journeys through this long dark night of the soul with his old mentor Ferreira as his companion and guide, Rodrigues gradually comes to realize at the light of day that many of his presuppositions—about the Japanese, God, Jesus, and himself—have been wrong, and so he tramples.

A question I always pose to students asks them to explain what it is that causes Rodrigues to put his foot to the *fumie*. What lessons has he learned from his teacher Ferreira that enables him to go against all his values and step on the image of Jesus? Many of them point to Ferreira's observation that "prayer does nothing to alleviate suffering" as a significant comment that completely reorients Rodrigues's thinking.[28] Throughout the novel, Rodrigues prays and appeals to God whenever he feels overwhelmed by divine silence. He begs and pleads with the deity to intervene and relieve human misery, and he is met with the same stony silence each time. Ferreira's statement that prayer does not alleviate suffering is validated repeatedly after Rodrigues's arrival in Japan.

So if prayer is not the solution, what is Rodrigues to do? Some students have proposed that the answer is literally right in front of him, or at least at his fingertips. Some years earlier, when he occupied the same cell, Ferreira had scratched on the wall the words *laudate eum*, a Latin phrase meaning "Praise him." He now asks Rodrigues to grope in the darkness until he finds the words, and to trace out the letters with his fingers, something Rodrigues has already done prior to Ferreira's arrival. On one level, this seems strange coming from a man who believes that prayer is pointless in the face of suffering. But, as students have noted, prayer is only one form of praise, and sometimes it may not be the best form for a given situation. Rodrigues seems to acknowledge this in an earlier scene when, from another jail cell, he witnesses the martyrdom of a Christian referred to as "the one-eyed man."[29] In frustration and confusion Rodrigues exclaims, "Lord, do not abandon me any more! Do not abandon me in this mysterious way! Is this prayer? For a long time I have believed that prayer is uttered to praise and glorify you; but when I speak to you it seems as though I only blaspheme."[30] Here, Ferreira is urging Rodrigues to praise God not through words and supplications, but by means of his actions. He is to let his deeds do the talking and, just as Ferreira himself did, trample on the *fumie* for the sake of the Japanese Christians. What finally convinces him is Ferreira's reminder that, if he had been in the same situation, Jesus would have acted, not prayed. "Certainly Christ would have apostatized for them."[31]

With this one act Rodrigues simultaneously violates his priestly duties and lives out the gospel message. He has been emptying himself of delusions and preconceptions throughout the novel, and he now goes all the way with a step of his foot that paradoxically puts him on the road to both his vilification and his renewal. Students are usually struck by this scene that describes Rodrigues performing what Ferreira refers to as "the most painful act of love that has ever been performed."[32] As he gazes at the image of Jesus and prepares to trample, Rodrigues meets this face for the first time since he entered Japan. Students are often surprised by this unexpected comment because on at least eight other occasions in the novel Rodrigues refers to the face of Christ, and in a number of those places he actually conjures Jesus's face in his mind.[33] It is a familiar face that offers him comfort and strength in times of difficulty, a face he has known well since he was a student in Portugal. And yet he now believes he is seeing it for the first time. For many students, this is the moment that signals Rodrigues's transformation is now complete. He realizes that his understanding of Jesus has been inaccurate or incomplete, and that he has created his own personal portrait of Christ just as the Japanese people have drawn upon their prior religious traditions to shape their view of God and Christianity. [34]

The evolution of Rodrigues's character, as he gradually divests himself of longstanding views and attitudes that do not stand up under the scrutiny of his experiences, is something that resonates with students who are being exposed to things new and unfamiliar during their college years. On one level, *Silence* is a story about one person's struggle to change and adapt as he confronts a world that is bigger and more complex than he thought it was. This is precisely where many students find themselves at this point in their lives, and so Rodrigues is a valuable prism through which they can talk about and reflect upon their own circumstances. One way I try to get at this is by asking students whether Rodrigues's life speaks to them today, despite his being a fictional character from a different time and place. In our discussions it is always clear to me that the Portuguese Jesuit is a paradigm of growth and change whose story remains relevant.[35]

But it is also a story that was originally written in a language other than English, and I always remind students of this easily forgotten fact. When we read something in translation, we are always on the outside looking in and we are at the mercy of the translator. No translation is perfect, and even if the text cannot be read in its original language, then the reader must keep in mind that the translator's decisions do not always reflect the intent of the author. One place this can be seen in *Silence* is in the final scene discussed here. As Rodrigues prepares to step on the *fumie* Jesus finally breaks the silence and says, in William Johnston's translation, "Trample! Trample! I more than anyone know of the pain in your foot. Trample!" Some scholars have questioned the accuracy of this translation with its three grammatically imperative forms.[36] The Japanese original conveys a softer tone that gives permission to Rodrigues to trample rather than commanding him to do so. Some have suggested that it is a maternal-like appeal that presents Jesus and God in the role of a mother.[37] This is a significant difference, and I have had some fascinating discussions with students exploring the impact it has on the meaning of the scene, which in turn have raised broader issues about the acts of reading and interpretation.

There are, of course, many other scenes in the novel that are pedagogically useful and worth discussing with students. I have chosen these four because they are the ones that typically have generated the most conversation since they address themes of interest and relevance for modern readers. Almost 50 years after its publication, Endo's work remains a popular classroom resource. When I informally survey students, they always list the novel among the two or three best readings they encounter in our three-semester "Plato-to-NATO" Western civilization course. That explains why there is never silence when discussing *Silence*.

Notes

1 I wish to express my gratitude to Isabel Buonopane, my student research assistant at Rhodes College. The many lengthy and enjoyable conversations we had about the novel, in particular the four scenes discussed here, helped inform and give shape to this chapter.

2 The instructor of that course was Rev. John Kaserow, MM of the Maryknoll School of Theology, and I remain indebted to him for introducing me to the novel.

3 Most of my experience teaching the novel has been in the course "The Search for Values in the Light of Western History and Religion," also known as "Search," at Rhodes College.

4 Very little has been written on *Silence* and pedagogy. The only discussion of the topic I have found is the brief treatment in Mark Roncace and Patrick Gray, eds., *Teaching the Bible through Popular Culture and the Arts* (Atlanta: Society of Biblical Literature), 298–9.

5 Shusaku Endo, *Silence*, trans. William Johnston (New York: Taplinger Publishing Company, 1980), 60. All quotations from the novel in this essay are taken from this edition.

6 Ibid., 61.

7 Ibid., 58

8 Ibid., 59.

9 Ibid.

10 Ibid., 60.

11 Ibid., 58.

12 Ibid., 132.

13 Ibid.

14 Ibid., 130.

15 Ibid., 133–4.

16 Ibid., 133.

17 Ibid.

18 Ibid., 142.

19 Ibid., 145.

20 For a fine discussion of issues related to religion and culture in *Silence* and other novels by Endo, see John T. Netland, "From Resistance to *Kenosis*: Reconciling Cultural Difference in the Fiction of Endo Shusaku," *Christianity and Literature* 48.2 (1999): 177–94. An analysis that approaches the topic from the perspective of aesthetics and theology is found in Sean Somers, "Passion Plays by Proxy: The Paschal Face as Interculturality in the Works of Endō Shūsaku and Mishima Yukio," in Holly Faith Nelson, Lynn R. Szabo, and Jens Zimmerman, eds., *Through a Glass Darkly: Suffering, the Sacred, and the Sublime in Literature and Theory* (Waterloo, Ontario: Wilfred Laurier University Press, 2010), 329–46.

21 Endo, *Silence*, 7, 29, 138.

22 Ibid., 31–2, 43.

23 Ibid., 147.

24 Ibid., 150.

25 Endo struggled with some of these questions in his own life as he reflected on what he called "the gulf between the Japanese on the one hand and Christianity and Europe on the other." His reflections on the topic are found in Shusaku Endo, "The Anguish of an Alien," *The Japanese Christian Quarterly* 40 (1974): 179–85.

26 For online access, see: http://www.vatican.va/archive/hist_councils/ii_vatican_council/documents/vat-ii_decl_19651028_nostra-aetate_en.html (accessed March 2014).

27 *Silence*, 167.

28 Ibid., 169.

29 Ibid., 117–19.

30 Ibid., 119.

31 Ibid., 169.

32 Ibid., 170.

33 In *Silence*, references are made to the face of Jesus on pages 43–4, 67, 103, 106, 116, 137, 159, and 161.

34 Endo himself stated that Rodrigues's changing image of Jesus is the most meaningful aspect of the novel. See Endo, "The Anguish of an Alien," 181, and Jeff Keuss, "The Lenten Face of Christ in Shusaku Endo's *Silence* and *Life of Jesus*," *The Expository Times* 118.6 (2007): 274. The shift in Rodrigues's view of Jesus is also discussed in Hitoshi Sano, "The Transformation of Father Rodrigues in Shusaku Endo's *Silence*," *Christianity and Literature* 48.2 (1999): 171–3.

35 For an analysis of the transformation of Rodrigues's character throughout the novel see Mark B. Williams, *Endō Shūsaku: A Literature of Reconciliation* (London and New York: Routledge, 1999), 105–29.

36 This issue is discussed in Van C. Gessel, "Hearing God in *Silence:* The Fiction of Endo Shusaku," *Christianity and Literature* 48.2 (1999): 159–61. See also, Junko Endo, "Reflections on Shusaku Endo and *Silence, Christianity and Literature* 48.2 (1999): 145–6.

37 Endo maintained that in *Silence* he was emphasizing the maternal side of Christianity. He discusses his thoughts on the difference between paternal and maternal religion in Shusaku Endo, "Concerning the Novel 'Silence'," *The Japanese Christian Quarterly* 36.2 (1970): 102–3, and "The Anguish of an Alien," 181.

Part Five

Later Adaptations

16

Silence, a Play ("Chinmoku")

a play by Steven Dietz
adapted from the novel by Shusaku Endo

Cast of Characters

(6 Japanese, 4 American; pairings indicate actor doubling)

Kichijiro ... a Japanese peasant

Inoue ... a Japanese magistrate

Interpreter ... a bi-lingual
  Japanese man, employed
  by Inoue
Matabe ... a Japanese peasant
Fourth Figure
Sailor

Mokichi ... a Japanese peasant
Japanese Official
Figure One
Sailor
Guard One
Prisoner
Peasant Man
Bonze
Man Hanging in the Pit

Monica ... a Japanese peasant
Figure Two
Concubine
Voice of Christ [in Japanese]
Japanese Wife

Ichizo ... a Japanese peasant
Figure Three
Sailor
Samurai
Oarsman
Guard Two
Prison Guard
Prisoner

Rodrigues ... a Jesuit priest

Garrpe ... a Jesuit priest
  Voice of Christ [in English]

Valignano ... a Superior in the
  Catholic church

Ferreira ... an apostate priest,
  Rodrigues' former teacher

Time and Place

1637.
Lisbon, Portugal. Macao, China.
And, most prominently, the coastal region of southern Japan -- near Nagasaki.

Setting

A large, open playing space which will be transformed into a variety of locales. Minimal scenic pieces. The primary transformation of the stage will be done through lighting.

This draft calls for one specific scenic element: a raised upstage area which will be referred to as "THE HILLSIDE." The main requirement of this area is the ability to feature images in SILHOUETTE -- sometimes accomplished solely through lighting, and other times in conjunction with a large billowy piece of WHITE FABRIC in front of the image. This draft also calls for PROJECTIONS upon this fabric. Above all, quick, unseen access to this area is paramount.

Note on Language

All underlined text will be translated and spoken in Japanese.

Historical Overview

Catholic missionary work in Japan -- which had been fostered by the Jesuit priest, Francis Xavier, among others -- came to an official end in 1587 when Hideyoshi, a feudal ruler, announced the prohibition of Christianity. Missionaries were expelled from the country, though some -- such as Christovao Ferreira -- remained behind, continuing their mission in secret. The Shogun's fear of Western religion stemmed, in part, from the belief that foreign powers (Spain, Portugal, Holland, England) wishing to expand their domain would often send first, their missionaries; then, their merchants; and, finally, their soldiers. Following the Shimabara rebellion of 1637, nearly all foreign commerce was halted as well. Japan was to remain a "closed country" for the next two hundred years.

From 1627 to 1858, all residents of Nagasaki (as well as other parts of Japan) were required by law to trample on the *fumie* once a year -- to prove that they were not Christians.

The *Fumie*

The *fumie* is a holy image -- often a depiction of Jesus on the cross, or the Virgin Mary holding her Child. It was usually made of a thin piece of bronze, attached to a flat wooden board about eight inches square.

Suspected Christians were forced to "trample" on this image -- that is, to place their foot down upon it for a moment, as evidence that they had rejected the Church and its teachings.

Act One

"Today I have the impression that the sea is made of all the tears in the world."

-- Albert Camus

(**Lisbon. Portugal. Early 1600s.**
MUSIC: **"Gloria 'ad Modum Tubae'"** The music, rich in grandeur, fills the theatre as lights reveal ---

A PRIEST, standing, seeming to loom over all around him. He wears beautiful flowing robes, a rosary attached to his belt. This is **FERREIRA**. MUSIC CONTINUES, as **FERREIRA** extends his arm, gesturing off stage, and ---

A YOUNG PRIEST, in simple garb, head bowed, walks slowly toward **FERREIRA**. He stops, kneeling at **FERREIRA**'s feet. This is **RODRIGUES**.

FERREIRA looks down at **RODRIGUES**. He offers **RODRIGUES** holy communion -- first the "HOST," then the chalice of WINE. When this is complete, **FERREIRA** begins to give the benediction. As he is making the sign of the cross ---

A HUGE SUN appears, filling the upstage wall.

FERREIRA turns and sees the SUN. Then he gestures for **RODRIGUES** to stand. **FERREIRA** removes the ROSARY from around his own belt and gives it to **RODRIGUES**. He holds his shoulders for a moment, affection-ately. Then, **FERREIRA** turns and moves away towards the SUN.

He stops. He turns and faces the audience. He lifts his arm up in front of him, as though about to deliver the benediction, as ---

MUSIC CRESCENDOS, and ---
The SUN glows hot and red and full, and then, suddenly -- ABRUPT SILENCE, as ---
Lights isolate **FERREIRA**, in front of the SUN, and reveal ---

Macao, China. 1637. **VALIGNANO**, holding a LETTER. With him is a young priest, **GARRPE**. **RODRIGUES** continues to look at **FERREIRA**.)

VALIGNANO   Word has arrived from the church in Rome. Father Christovao Ferreira has apostatized.

(The LIGHT on FERREIRA SNAPS OUT.
Silence. **RODRIGUES** turns to **VALIGNANO**.)

RODRIGUES   Impossible.

VALIGNANO   Despite the expulsion of all missionaries from Japan, Father Ferreira stayed and continued his priesthood -- in secret -- for many years. In doing so, he became a beacon of hope for all Portuguese priests, to the entire Jesuit order. But, while held captive in Nagasaki, he has renounced his faith.

RODRIGUES   It could never happen.

VALIGNANO   Father Rodrigues ---

RODRIGUES   Not Ferreira. Anyone but him.

GARRPE   With respect, Father: Was he tortured? Was he tricked? Were his words corrupted to suit the authorities?

VALIGNANO   Father Ferreira was your teacher, wasn't he?

RODRIGUES   Both of us. Both Garrpe and myself.

(**VALIGNANO** approaches **RODRIGUES**, puts his hand on his shoulder.)

VALIGNANO   Send him, then, not your questions -- for we will never know why. We will never know why he chose to betray his faith.

(The SOUND of a BELL TOLLING in the distance.)

Instead, as his student, and as a priest whose faith is still strong, send him your prayers.

(**RODRIGUES** stares at **VALIGNANO**, then extends his hand. **VALIGNANO** hands him the letter from Rome.)

You've traveled a great distance from Portugal, but you'll have a home here in China. The mission in Macao is strong. It will offer you safety.

GARRPE   And what of our ship? We were told you could secure a ship that would take us to Japan.

VALIGNANO   There will be no more priests in Japan, I'm afraid. Ferreira was the last. And with his failure, the church in Japan has died.

GARRPE   But you yourself said there are Christians -- hundreds, perhaps thousands of them, carrying the mantle of faith in secret -- throughout the country.

VALIGNANO   Brother Garrpe ---

GARRPE   We cannot simply abandon them ---

VALIGNANO   The flame in Japan is extinguished ---

GARRPE   Among the priesthood, yes, but not among the people ---

VALIGNANO   We will direct our work elsewhere.

GARRPE   But Father, we have studied the language, we've traveled for months to ---

VALIGNANO   My decision is made.

(Silence. **RODRIGUES** holds the letter from Rome.)

RODRIGUES   Is he alive?

VALIGNANO   No one knows.

RODRIGUES   We must find out.

VALIGNANO   I implore you ---

GARRPE   As Jesuits, we have taken a vow. We are committed to carry out whatever his Holiness demands of us, without hesitation or excuse, in whatsoever country he may send us to, whether among the faithful, the infidels, the heretics ---

VALIGNANO   I am aware of our vows ---

GARRPE   The church in Rome has decreed ---

VALIGNANO   The church in Rome knows nothing of Japan.

GARRPE   And Japan, it seems, too little of Rome. That is why we've crossed two oceans to be here. To keep the holy flame alive -- the word of our Lord God, brought to the Japanese people by the priests before us. And if we abandon this cause – the lives of those priests, their struggles, even their glorious martyrdoms were surely in vain.

VALIGNANO   There is now, in Nagasaki, a new magistrate.

(**A SILHOUETTE ON THE HILLSIDE:** INOUE, slowly washing his hands in a large BOWL which sits in front of him.)

His name is Inoue. He is more ruthless than any we have faced. He has made himself the architect of Christian persecution in Japan.

RODRIGUES   But why? What threat does the Church pose to him?

VALIGNANO   Inoue suspects that if our priests gain a foothold in Japan … they will be followed by our merchants; and, in time, by our soldiers.

(**VALIGNANO** stares at them, then holds up another piece of paper, as --- The SILHOUETTE FADES AWAY.)

Here is the Shogun's latest announcement.

(Opposite, a JAPANESE OFFICIAL shoves a MAN onstage, kicking him from behind, beating him. The MAN wears filthy rags. He holds a WOODEN SIGN which is attached to a stake. This is **KICHIJIRO**.)

[**Reminder: All underlined text will be translated and spoken in Japanese.**]

JAPANESE OFFICIAL   "The Christian faith has been prohibited for many years."

VALIGNANO   (reads) "The Christian faith has been prohibited for many years. All suspicious persons are to be reported to the authorities. The following sums shall be paid in reward:

(As Valignano speaks, the **OFFICIAL** yells something to **KICHIJIRO** -- prompting him to pick up a stone and begin pounding the sign into the ground during the following announcement. The **OFFICIAL** addresses a gathered [unseen] crowd. Written on the sign -- in Japanese -- is the information being announced.)

JAPANESE OFFICIAL   For informing on a Priest -- 300 pieces of silver.

VALIGNANO   (overlapping slightly throughout …) "For informing on a Priest -- 300 pieces of silver.

JAPANESE OFFICIAL   For informing on a Brother -- 200 pieces of silver.

VALIGNANO   "For informing on a Brother -- 200 pieces of silver.

JAPANESE OFFICIAL   For informing on an Apostate who has returned to the faith -- 200 pieces of silver.

VALIGNANO   "For informing on an Apostate who has returned to the faith -- 200 pieces of silver.

JAPANESE OFFICIAL   For informing on a lay Christian -- 100 pieces of silver.

(**KICHIJIRO** has finished pounding the sign. The **OFFICIAL** tosses him a pathetic piece of dried FISH -- then leaves.

KICHIJIRO bows to the **OFFICIAL** -- thanking him, many times -- then curls up on the ground near the sign and hungrily devours the fish, like a starved animal.)

VALIGNANO   (still reading, during the above action) "Even though the informer himself is a Christian, he shall be paid the due reward. Anyone found sheltering such outlawed persons will bring severe punishment upon not only himself, but his family, his neighbors, and his entire village."

(**VALIGNANO** lowers the paper and looks to **RODRIGUES** and **GARRPE**, awaiting their answer. They stare back at him.)

Brothers, you are young and headstrong. Your faith is loud within you. But, let it not blind you to the facts: Ferreira is lost to us. We must accept that.

RODRIGUES   With respect, Father: Who was your teacher? The man who first led you to the Church?

(**VALIGNANO** stares at him, saying nothing.)

Are you not still in his debt? As we are to Ferreira? And, if that man were lost -- if he were alone and abandoned -- could you stay here and do nothing?

VALIGNANO   It is Ferreira who has abandoned the Church.

RODRIGUES   If so, let us be certain of it. Let us find him and be certain.

(Silence. **VALIGNANO** continues to stare at **RODRIGUES**.)

Please, Father. Grant us this one chance.

(Silence. **VALIGNANO** speaks more quietly now.)

VALIGNANO   I am charged with providing for the safety of our priests in Asia. If you make this trip, I have no way of protecting you.

RODRIGUES   Pray for us. That will suffice.

(**VALIGNANO** looks at him for a long moment, then at **GARRPE**, then quietly relents, saying ---)

VALIGNANO   You will have the prayers of us all.

(A CRASH OF DRUMS is heard, and lights isolate: **Kichijiro.** Having finished his food, he stands and begins to run his fingers over the words carved on the sign, speaking quietly to himself ...)

KICHIJIRO   Padré ... Mio Padré ... <u>forgive me</u> ...

(KICHIJIRO collapses onto the sign, breathing heavily. He holds the sign, tightly, crying quietly ...)

<u>Forgive me.</u>

(He rushes off, as lights isolate: **RODRIGUES**.)

RODRIGUES   Pax Christi. Praise be to Christ.

My dear brothers, today I have wonderful news: A ship has been found to take us to Japan. Macao is the center of Chinese trade with Japan -- and this morning we were granted passage on a Chinese junk bound for Nagasaki.

One need remains: We must find a Japanese to be our guide. Someone here in Macao who wishes to return home. To protect us, and lead us to the Christians hiding in Japan. Without this person, our trip cannot happen. For weeks we asked the Chinese merchants and sailors if they knew of such a Japanese in Macao. They knew of no one.

(**GARRPE** rushes on.)

GARRPE   Brother, come quickly.

RODRIGUES   What is it?

GARRPE   Good news.

(**GARRPE** moves off. **RODRIGUES** turns to the audience.)

RODRIGUES   And then I saw him -- the first Japanese I ever met in my life.

(**A Dock, in Macao. KICHIJIRO** is sitting in the dirt, surrounded by empty SAKE bottles. Drinking. Wrapped around his shoulders and falling to the ground is a large, weathered FISHING NET. **GARRPE** is near him. **RODRIGUES** stands at a distance.)

KICHIJIRO   (a frightened, drunken paranoia) <u>I am Kichijiro. I am a fisherman in Goto. My people are there ...</u>

GARRPE   (to **RODRIGUES**) He told me he'll help us. His name is Kichijiro. He's a fisherman from the Goto islands ---

KICHIJIRO   (overlapping) <u>Yes. I am Kichijiro. Take me back. I beg of you ...</u>

RODRIGUES   Brother, this man can't be our guide. Look at him. We can't depend on him to take us to safety in Japan ---

GARRPE   He is our only chance. The Chinese say he hid away on a boat and arrived here. Now, he wants to return.

RODRIGUES   Why did he leave Japan?

GARRPE   No one knows.

KICHIJIRO   Please help me. I am frightened here. I need to go home ...

(**GARRPE** grabs the bottle of *sake* away from **KICHIJIRO**. **KICHIJIRO** responds like a wounded dog, begging, pleading.)

I will help you. I will take you there. Please don't leave me here ...

RODRIGUES   (to **GARRPE**) Is he a Christian?

GARRPE   (to **KICHIJIRO**) Are you a Christian?

(**KICHIJIRO** stares at GARRPE, terrified.)

Pax Christi.

(**KICHIJIRO** continues to stare, tightening himself into a ball. **GARRPE** removes the large CRUCIFIX from his robe and holds it in front of **KICHIJIRO**'S face.)

GARRPE   Ave Maris Stella, Dei Mater alma, Atque semper virgo, Felix coeli porta.

(**KICHIJIRO** begins crying and whipping himself with ROPE from the fishing net. During the following, **RODRIGUES** steps in and grabs him ---)

RODRIGUES   We must have a guide ---

GARRPE   (trying his best to interpret, to **KICHIJIRO**) A guide ---

RODRIGUES   To help us find the Christians hiding in Japan, to administer to them ---

GARRPE   Hidden Christians ---

RODRIGUES   It's no use. The man is a drunkard. We're wasting our time ---

GARRPE   (overlapping, still to **KICHIJIRO**) To perform baptisms -- hear confessions -- confessions -- we will hear confessions ---

(**KICHIJIRO** suddenly looks up at **GARRPE**, serious.)

KICHIJIRO   Confession?

GARRPE   Confession -- YES.

(**KICHIJIRO** quickly bows his head, repeating softly ---)

KICHIJIRO   Confession! Confession -- confession -- confession ---

GARRPE   (to **RODRIGUES**) He understands us, he will be of use ---

RODRIGUES   Brother, listen to me ---

KICHIJIRO   (desperately) I … must … go … home.

(**RODRIGUES** looks at **GARRPE**. **GARRPE** replaces his CRUCIFIX.)

GARRPE   The boat is leaving. We've no choice.

KICHIJIRO   (pats his own chest, pleading) Kichijiro … GUIDE.

GARRPE   (taking **KICHIJIRO**'S hands in his)

To Japan.

(**KICHIJIRO** smiles, as ---
GARRPE rushes off, leaving **RODRIGUES** alone with **KICHIJIRO**.

KICHIJIRO sees the **ROSARY** -- from Ferreira -- which
RODRIGUES wears. He touches the rosary, gently, tentatively. **RODRIGUES**
stares at him, intently.
As **KICHIJIRO** respectfully lowers the rosary back down, **RODRIGUES**
begins to turn and leave, but ---

KICHIJIRO -- giving a sort of animal grunt -- grabs the ROSARY with force, stopping **RODRIGUES**. Standoff. The men's faces are inches apart. **KICHIJIRO** emits his quick, fawning laugh. Then, suddenly ---)

KICHIJIRO   Mio Padré.

(--- **KICHIJIRO** gives **RODRIGUES** a quick KISS on the cheek. He lets go of the rosary, grabs his bottle of sake, and rushes off.

RODRIGUES stands alone, in stunned silence. Finally, he completes his letter. As he does so, lights reveal ---

The Ship to Japan. FOUR SAILORS carry on a series of WOODEN CRATES. The crates define "the Ship." DISTANT LIGHTNING. ROLLING THUNDER.)

RODRIGUES   And so we embark, a drunken and cowardly stranger as our guide. I must continue to remind myself what Father Ferreira taught us: That our Lord, too, entrusted his destiny to the most untrustworthy of men.

(The SOUND of WATER lapping against the ship, GULLS circling.)

The Chinese sailors, while loading the ship, came for our belongings. But, we have none. We bring no luggage to Japan but our own hearts.

(A HUGE CRACK OF THUNDER/FLASH OF LIGHTNING fills the theatre. The stage darkens, ominously, as the STORM ARRIVES. The LOUD SOUND of WIND, RAIN and THUNDER.

KICHIJIRO curls into a ball, weeping, bleeding.

RODRIGUES and **GARRPE** take shelter near one of the crates, holding on tightly. They shout over the RAGING STORM. **RODRIGUES** is the more terrified of the two.)

GARRPE   DON'T LOOK AT THE WATER -- LOOK AT THE SKY ---

RODRIGUES   WE KNOW NOTHING OF THIS BOAT -- ITS STRENGTH -- WE'VE JOINED THESE MEN, KNOWING NOTHING OF ---

GARRPE   IT IS OUT OF OUR HANDS. THE SKY -- NOT THE WATER -- LOOK UP AT THE SKY!

RODRIGUES   BROTHER GARRPE ---

GARRPE   WHAT?

RODRIGUES   CAN YOU SWIM?

(The CRASH of a HUGE WAVE tosses them to one side. They struggle to right themselves, still shouting over the sound ---)

CAN YOU, BROTHER?

GARRPE   YES. AND YOU -- CAN YOU SWIM?

RODRIGUES   (pause) IT IS OUT OF OUR HANDS.

(**GARRPE** throws his arms around **RODRIGUES**, holding him.)

Suddenly, **KICHIJIRO** rushes to the "bow" of the ship. He leans out into the storm -- only a single rope keeping him from falling into the sea. It looks as if he may hurl himself into the water, as he shouts ---)

KICHIJIRO   SANTA MARIA -- MOTHER OF GRACE -- MOTHER OF MERCY -- PROTECT ME FROM MY ENEMIES -- AND RECEIVE ME AT THE HOUR OF MY DEATH!

GARRPE   THE MAN IS A CHRISTIAN!

(**KICHIJIRO** is about to fall into the water, when -- **GARRPE** rushes to him and grabs him, saving his life.)

KICHIJIRO	**GARRPE**	**RODRIGUES**
SANTA MARIA ---	TAKE MY ARM!	GARRPE ---

(The STORM REACHES ITS ZENITH, as ---
RODRIGUES, left alone, terrified, prays aloud, and ---
GARRPE holds a frantic **KICHIJIRO**, trying to make him speak.)

GARRPE	RODRIGUES
HOLD TIGHT NOW -- YOU MUST STAY ALIVE -- AND YOU MUST ANSWER: ARE YOU A CHRISTIAN? ANSWER NOW – NO HARM WILL BEFALL YOU: ARE YOU A CHRISTIAN?!	Trust in the Lord and sing his praise ... With thy whole heart ... With thy whole soul ...

KICHIJIRO I AM KICHIJIRO -- I AM A FISHERMAN---	With thy whole mind ... With thy whole strength ...

GARRPE BUT, THE "SANTA MARIA" – I HEARD IT FROM YOUR OWN LIPS. ANSWER ME: ARE YOU A ---	Trust in the Lord and sing his praise ... With thy whole heart ...

(**KICHIJIRO** breaks free of **GARRPE** and runs to another part of the boat, disappearing. **GARRPE** turns his head back into the storm, with confidence. He crosses himself.)

GARRPE   [cont.] THANKS BE TO GOD.

(ALL SOUND OUT. INSTANT LIGHT SHIFT to ---

A SILHOUETTE ON THE HILLSIDE: INOUE, in profile.
FERREIRA enters -- also in profile -- and stands before INOUE. FERREIRA lifts his hand up in front of him.
INOUE kneels. FERREIRA makes the sign of the cross over INOUE, then places his hand down on INOUE'S head, gently -- blessing him, as lights quickly return to ---

The Ship. Day. The storm has passed. Sunshine. Blue skies.
RODRIGUES and GARRPE are conducting Mass. The SAILORS are kneeling before them. GARRPE a simple, wooden CHALICE in his hand. RODRIGUES holds a small bit of bread. He offers it to the SAILORS one by one as GARRPE speaks.)

GARRPE   Our Lord Jesus Christ, in the night in which he was betrayed, took bread. And having blessed it, he gave it to his disciples, saying:

(Having given bread to all the **SAILORS**, **RODRIGUES** now looks in the direction of **KICHIJIRO**. He approaches **KICHIJIRO**, as **GARRPE** continues speaking. **KICHIJIRO** looks up at him, but does not move.)

Take, eat. This is my body which is given for you. Do this in remembrance of me.

(**RODRIGUES** kneels down in front of **KICHIJIRO**. He offers him a small piece of the bread. **KICHIJIRO** stares at him, stares at the bread, licking his lips with hunger.)

RODRIGUES (to **KICHIJIRO**) Given for you.

(Then, quickly, **KICHIJIRO** grabs the large piece of bread from **RODRIGUES'** other hand and stuffs it into his mouth. Then he turns away, as **RODRIGUES** slowly makes the sign of the cross over him. **GARRPE** offers the wine to the **SAILORS** as he continues.)

GARRPE After the same manner also, he took the cup. And when he had supped, and when he had given thanks, he gave it to his disciples, saying: This cup is the new testament of my blood, shed for you and for many, for the remission of sins. Do this in remembrance of me.

(**RODRIGUES** stares down at **KICHIJIRO**.)

Lord, remember your faithful. In the name of the Father, and of the Son, and of the Holy Ghost. Amen.

(reaching out his arms toward the **SAILORS**)

Pax Christi.

SAILORS Pax Christi.

GARRPE Go in peace. Serve the Lord.

(**RODRIGUES** moves to **GARRPE** as -- The **SAILORS** move away and are gone. **KICHIJIRO** remains, only partly visible, still curled into a ball.)

RODRIGUES   A blessed day. We have been instruments of His hand.

(Silence. **GARRPE** stares at him, moves away.) What is it? What's wrong?

GARRPE   News which the sailors told me this morning.

RODRIGUES   What news?

GARRPE   In Japan, at Shimabara, thirty-five thousand Christians rose up against their feudal lord.

RODRIGUES   Thirty-five thousand! Do you see, brother, the number of believers in Japan is great ---

GARRPE   They were massacred. All of them. Men, women. Children. Murdered by order of the Shogun.

(Long silence. **KICHIJIRO** is now looking up, leaning in.)

RODRIGUES   (quietly) Blessed are those who have died in the Lord. Give them rest from their labors, and let their good deeds accompany them to Heaven.

(**KICHIJIRO** is standing now, looking out into the water.)

GARRPE   And from this sorrow, another. The Shogun has cut off all trade, all travel. As a result of this insurrection, no Japanese may leave the country. And, no foreign ships may enter.

(he looks out to the water)

On penalty of death, we are forbidden to land in Japan.

(**RODRIGUES** and **GARRPE** look to each other. **KICHIJIRO** has lifted something out of the water. It is a handful of small TWIGS, bits of branches.)

KICHIJIRO   (excitedly) Look, here. Twigs and branches. We are near land! And there -- (points to the sky)

That bird! Look! Land is near!

(The **SAILORS** appear, looking into the distance. **KICHIJIRO** points to the horizon as --- **RODRIGUES** and **GARRPE** stand together, looking out at the horizon. Their voices are simple, quiet.)

GARRPE   Two years since we left Portugal. And now Japan in sight.

(**RODRIGUES** looks to **GARRPE**, then back out at the water.)

RODRIGUES   We must be seen by no one.

(The SAILORS quickly remove the crates, dismantling the "ship," and then exit, as lights shift to ---
A Rocky Inlet. Japan. Night. Only **RODRIGUES** and **GARRPE** are visible, standing side by side, peering into the darkness.
The SOUND of WATER lapping quietly against rock.
RODRIGUES and **GARRPE** kneel. They kiss the ground. They make the sign of the cross. Then ... they wait.)

GARRPE   (quietly) No moon tonight. That is in our favor.

RODRIGUES   (also quietly) Where is Kichijiro? Where has he gone?

GARRPE   He leapt from the ship and disappeared ---

RODRIGUES   We should have kept him with us.

GARRPE   He's gone to find the Christians who will protect us ---

RODRIGUES   He's gone to betray us.

(**GARRPE** looks at him.)

I'm certain of it. He'll be given the reward Valignano spoke of.

GARRPE   Brother, he is a Christian. In the storm at sea, he called out "Santa Maria." He is one of our own faith ---

RODRIGUES   Faith could not turn a man into such a coward.

GARRPE   He promised to get us here and he has. We have put our lives in his hands.

RODRIGUES   And he will prove to be our Judas.

(Suddenly, **KICHIJIRO** rushes on, holding a TORCH. His voice shatters the silence. He stands at a distance, pointing excitedly at **RODRIGUES** and **GARRPE**.)

KICHIJIRO   Here they are! Come this way! I've found them for you. Come --- they are right here!

(SOUND OF VOICES approaching ---)

GARRPE   (overlapping **KICHIJIRO**, quietly to **RODRIGUES**) I fear you're right.

RODRIGUES   (also overlapping **KICHIJIRO**) Here, brother, quickly ---

(Fearful of betrayal, **RODRIGUES** and **GARRPE** hide behind something in the darkness.)

KICHIJIRO   They've nowhere to go. Come and take them!

(**KICHIJIRO** continues to point, excitedly, as --- THREE PEASANTS enter. They are **MOKICHI, MATABE** and **ICHIZO** -- but they remain in darkness, their faces not yet seen. Their VOICES stop when they see where **KICHIJIRO** is pointing.
Silence. No one moves. Then, finally …)

MOKICHI   (tentatively) Padré?

(Silence. **RODRIGUES** and **GARRPE** look to each other, as --- **MOKICHI** steps into the light of **KICHIJIRO**'S torch. We see his face for the first time -- filled with kindness, curiosity.)

Padré? Are you there?

(**RODRIGUES** and **GARRPE** emerge from hiding, and are seen by the PEASANTS. Silence.
MOKICHI tentatively makes the sign of the cross, saying …)

Mio Padré.

(**RODRIGUES** and **GARRPE** cautiously approach the PEASANTS.
RODRIGUES makes the sign of the cross.
The PEASANTS all bow their heads.
RODRIGUES and **GARRPE** smile, tears in their eyes.
The PRIESTS and the PEASANTS embrace one another, tentatively, at first
… then joyfully.
KICHIJIRO stands, separate, watching, as ---
The SOUND of DISTANT DRUMMING is heard.)

ICHIZO   (to MOKICHI) <u>We must go before we're seen.</u>

MOKICHI   <u>Yes.</u>

MATABE   <u>Quickly. now ---</u>

MOKICHI   (gesturing to **RODRIGUES** and **GARRPE**) <u>Please follow us.</u>
<u>This way ---</u>

(**RODRIGUES** and **GARRPE** understand. **ICHIZO** takes the torch from
KICHIJIRO and leads the way into the darkness. The PEASANTS and
GARRPE disappear into the night.
KICHIJIRO is the last to walk past **RODRIGUES**. He stops for a moment,
looking at **RODRIGUES** ---)

RODRIGUES   I mistrusted you. I'm sorry ---

(**KICHIJIRO** backs away from **RODRIGUES**, saying ---)

KICHIJIRO   <u>You do not trust Kichijiro. No one trusts Kichijiro ---</u>

(And he is gone, running off after the others, as -- Lights isolate: **RODRIGUES**,
looking out at the water.)

RODRIGUES   "Go into the world and preach the gospel to every creature.
He who believes and is baptized shall be saved; he who does not believe shall
be condemned."

(MUSIC: **"Ave Verum Corpus"**)

My brothers in faith, as I write to you I think of Christ's words to his disciples. And his words bring a picture to my mind. A picture that's been with me since I was a child. The most beautiful picture in all the world:

(PROJECTED ON THE WHITE FABRIC: **The Face of Christ.**
Dark hair, beard. Compassionate eyes. [From the Rembrandt painting: "Christ" -- Bredius # 624]
The FACE looms behind **RODRIGUES** as he speaks.)

The face of Christ.

Those soft clear eyes, filled with trust and compassion. That face which could do no wrong, could utter no word of insult. The face which has always fascinated me, since there is no mention of it in the Scriptures -- no description whatsoever. Like faith, it is left to the imagination. And the face I imagine has been my closest ally, my constant friend. In times of trouble, this face has never abandoned me.

My brothers, such news since we arrived:

(**A Hut, near the village of Tomogi.** A small dwelling place -- with room only for two straw mats on the floor. A small wooden door.
MATABE and **ICHIZO** are putting the MATS in place, readying the hut.
GARRPE is with them, now wearing peasant clothing.
The MUSIC, as well as the FACE OF CHRIST gradually FADE AWAY during the following.)

ICHIZO   (to **GARRPE**) Here, Father. You will be safe here.

RODRIGUES   We are ministering to the people in a village called Tomogi. They are sheltering us in a hut -- hidden high in the mountains.

(**RODRIGUES** changes into the peasant clothing during the following. He continues to speak to the audience.)

On a typical day, two peasants from the village climb the mountain and visit us. They bring us food. We give communion, hear confessions. Then, the next day, another two peasants arrive -- and so on. They come in small groups to avoid arousing suspicion. They've given us clothing to conceal our identity.

These peasants have inherited a very cruel life. What little they grow or earn is taken from them -- as payment -- by the samurai. And, if suspected of being Christian, they are forced to place their foot on a small bronze plaque. This is known as the *fumie*. On the plaque is carved the image of our Lord's face; or that of the Blessed Virgin. By trampling on the *fumie,* they prove to the authorities that they are not Christians.

GARRPE   (to **RODRIGUES**) Matabe and lchizo are their names. Matabe speaks some of our language, saying he learned it from a priest.

RODRIGUES   Ferreira? Did you learn from Father Ferreira?

MATABE   (shaking his head) <u>No.</u>

RODRIGUES   But, do you know of Ferreira? Have you heard that name?

MATABE   Ferreira?

(**RODRIGUES** nods. **MATABE** looks at **ICHIZO** -- who shakes his head "no.")

GARRPE   They've seen no priest in five years -- but have kept their faith alive. (to the PEASANTS)
Are there Christians in the other villages?

MATABE   (to **ICHIZO**) <u>He asks if we know of Christians in other villages.</u>

ICHIZO   <u>It's dangerous to know. We must stay here.</u>

MATABE   It is dangerous to talk to strangers. If found to be Christians, we will be killed.

ICHIZO   <u>There are many informers.</u>

MATABE   There are many informers. They are rewarded by the magistrate.

ICHIZO   <u>We must be careful.</u>

RODRIGUES   This man, Kichijiro, do you know him?

ICHIZO   <u>Kichijiro. Yes.</u>

RODRIGUES   Is he a Christian?

ICHIZO   <u>Yes. His family was killed.</u>

MATABE   His family was put to death -- burned at the stake ---

RODRIGUES   Why?

ICHIZO   <u>They refused to step on the *fumie*.</u>

MATABE   They would not trample on the face of Christ.

RODRIGUES   The *fumie* ...

MATABE   <u>Yes.</u>

RODRIGUES   And Kichijiro? Did he escape?

ICHIZO   <u>Kichijiro ran away. He is a coward.</u>

MATABE   (to RODRIGUES) What are you asking?

RODRIGUES   Kichijiro -- why was he not punished?

(**MATABE** looks at **ICHIZO**, who says nothing, as ---

A KNOCK at the door is heard. The men freeze.

Another KNOCK.

Very quickly, and very quietly, **ICHIZO** throws back one of the mats, and pulls back a piece of wood, revealing ---

A HIDDEN HOLE, under the hut.

More KNOCKING, louder now, as ---

ICHIZO and **MATABE** quickly hide the clerical CLOTHING in the HOLE. They next take hold of **RODRIGUES** and **GARRPE** and begin moving them down into the HOLE. The PRIESTS comply in disbelief, as ---

Suddenly the DOOR OPENS, revealing --

MOKICHI, one of the PEASANTS they met earlier.)

ICHIZO   Mokichi, what is it?

(**MOKICHI** gestures to someone outside the door, and --- **MONICA**, a young peasant woman, enters. She holds a BABY in her arms, wrapped in cloth.)

MONICA   Father, you are here.

MATABE   Monica.

MONICA   My little girl is ill. Can she be baptized so she will go to Heaven?

(Silence. **MONICA** looks at the PRIESTS, hopefully. They turn to **MATABE** to translate.)

MATABE   This, Father, is Monica.

RODRIGUES   (to GARRPE) A Christian name ...

MATABE   Yes. Her child is ill. Can she be baptized, Father -- so she will go to Heaven?

(**RODRIGUES** and **GARRPE** look at one another.)

GARRPE   Of course.

(**MONICA** steps forward, holding her BABY. A small bowl of WATER is brought to **GARRPE** -- who blesses it.
The PEASANTS gather around the BABY.

As the ceremony takes place, RODRIGUES steps away and continues his letter. He holds his ROSARY in his hands.

MUSIC: **"Kyrie Dominicale"** -- under.)

RODRIGUES   My friends in Christ, never have I felt so deeply the meaning of being a priest. Lacking the trappings of the conventional Church -- we become not deterred, but inspired. Without prayer beads to give them, we have taught the peasants to say the rosary using only their fingers. They have carved small, hidden crosses in the back of their Buddhist statues.

(He lifts a pair of SCISSORS to the light. Opens them. Closes them -- noticing an open space formed just below the "hinge.")

A pair of scissors is made so that -- when closed -- the cross of our Lord appears there, in the open space formed by the metal.

With great diligence, the priests before us plunged the spade into this barren soil. And, despite the persecutions, the seed they planted has sprouted forth with vigor.

GARRPE   What is the child's name?

MONICA   Omitsu.

RODRIGUES   God's promise takes root here, in part, because it brings these people the first kindness they have ever known.

(**RODRIGUES** turns and watches the baptism.)

GARRPE   Are all of you gathered here today able and willing to raise this child in God's name?

MATABE   (to **ICHIZO** and **MONICA**)   Are we willing to give this child a Christian life?

ICHIZO, MONICA, MOKICHI   Yes.

RODRIGUES   We have been here for two months, now. And, as we conducted our first baptism, I remembered a strange thing which Valignano had told us.

(MUSIC CONTINUES, as ---
VALIGNANO appears, opposite. He is lit by the WHITE CANDLE he is holding.)

VALIGNANO   This man, Inoue -- the most cruel of the Japanese magistrates -- he himself was baptized into our faith.

(A SILHOUETTE ON THE HILLSIDE: INOUE is baptized by **FERREIRA**, slowly and gracefully, as --- **GARRPE** lifts water onto the BABY'S head.)

GARRPE   And now, Omitsu, in the presence of these witnesses ---

VALIGNANO   It was Ferreira, himself, who conducted the service.

GARRPE   I baptize you in the name of the Father ---

VALIGNANO   What kind of country must that be ---

GARRPE   And of the Son.

VALIGNANO   --- Where a man could turn so completely?

GARRPE   And of the Holy Ghost.

(**VALIGNANO** exits with the lit CANDLE. **RODRIGUES** stares at the SILHOUETTE, as **FERREIRA** makes the sign of the cross over **INOUE**, and --- **GARRPE**, his fingers dripping water, makes a cross on the BABY'S forehead.)

I make the sign of the cross, claiming you for Christ ---

RODRIGUES   I promise you that we will become bolder. That we will find Ferreira and learn the meaning of this mystery.

GARRPE   That you may forever be granted the blessings of his Kingdom.

(The SILHOUETTE FADES TO BLACK.)

RODRIGUES   Your servant in Christ ---

GARRPE   Amen.

RODRIGUES   Father Sebastian Rodrigues.

MONICA, ICHIZO, MOKICHI, MATABE   Amen.

(Sudden POUNDING on the DOOR.
MUSIC OUT.)

ICHIZO   Who is there?

(**KICHIJIRO** opens the door quickly, speaks urgently.)

KICHIJIRO The guards are coming. They are nearing the village!

ICHIZO (to the PRIESTS) Quickly, now. You must hide --

(**ICHIZO** rushes out and is gone.)

MOKICHI How many are there?

KICHIJIRO Three samurai on horseback ---

(**MOKICHI** opens the HOLE in the HUT, pointing down to it.)

MATABE The soldiers are in the village, looking for Christians.

KICHIJIRO Hurry, they're coming!

MOKICHI Hide now, they are looking for you!

RODRIGUES Kichijiro ---

(But, **KICHIJIRO** has already run out the door and disappeared. As the other PEASANTS leave, **ICHIZO** stops and turns back to the PRIESTS.)

MOKICHI Don't worry, Father. No matter what they do to us: we will never betray you.

GARRPE (pause, then to **RODRIGUES**) He tells us not to worry. That no matter what harm befalls them … they will not betray us.

(The PEASANTS exit. Silence.
GARRPE reaches out his hand. **RODRIGUES** looks at him … then understands. He hands his ROSARY to **GARRPE**, who hides it in the hole. **GARRPE** begins to step down into the hole.)

Brother. For our safety, we're to hide.

(**RODRIGUES** does not move.)

Until the danger has passed, we must ---

RODRIGUES   And when will that be?

(Silence. He turns to **GARRPE**.)

Garrpe, we have been too cowardly. Hiding in this hut all day, for months
– while the peasants risk their lives on our behalf. This is OUR fight, OUR
mission -- not theirs. We are God's own hands on earth ---

GARRPE   And, as such, we have performed baptisms, heard confessions
from ---

RODRIGUES   I am embarrassed by our weakness.

GARRPE   What would you have us do?

RODRIGUES   One of us should go to Nagasaki. There we may find more
Christians -- those who knew Father Ferreira.

GARRPE   Do you know the risk in that?

RODRIGUES   We can't be afraid of what they'll do to us, we must ---

GARRPE   (forcefully) I'm not speaking of the risk to us. The risk to the
Church. If we fail, the Church here fails with us. You know that.

(Silence. They stare at each other.)

RODRIGUES   May I have my rosary?

(GARRPE stares at him for a long moment.)

GARRPE   (simply) No. Not till it's safe.

(pause)

We are not bigger than our mission, brother. What you and I desire, what we
think we must do -- none of that is worth putting our mission at risk.

RODRIGUES   Ferreira would do otherwise. He would not sit here,
cowering in fear.

GARRPE   Perhaps he should have.

(pause)

Perhaps then he'd still be among us, spreading the word of our Lord.

(CRASH OF DRUMS, as lights shift quickly to ---
A SILHOUETTE ON THE HILLSIDE: A **SAMURAI** addresses the people
of Tomogi in a loud voice.)

SAMURAI   <u>People of Tomogi: Christianity is an outlawed religion. An
informer has told us that there are members of this forbidden Christian sect
among you. If any among you will name these people, you shall receive one
hundred pieces of silver.</u>

(Silence.)

<u>If you speak now, you will be rewarded. If you refuse, you shall suffer the
consequences.</u>

(Silence, as lights also reveal an area ---
Outside the Hut. A stone slab, used for sitting or as a table, defines the area.
MONICA enters, slowly. Her BABY is strapped to her back.)

<u>SPEAK NOW. NAME THE CHRISTIANS AMONG YOU.</u>

(Silence, as ---
MONICA kneels at the stone slab.)

<u>If you speak, you shall be paid in silver. If you remain silent, my Superiors
demand that I return with three hostages. NOW, WILL YOU SPEAK?</u>

(Still more silence, as ---
MONICA removes the BABY from her back and cradles it in her arms.)

<u>You were given a choice. Now, you have earned the wrath of the Shogun.
Select three men from your village. They will be taken to Nagasaki tomorrow.</u>

(The SILHOUETTE VANISHES, as --- **RODRIGUES** enters. When
MONICA sees him, she lowers her head to her chest.)

RODRIGUES   Monica. What is it?

MONICA   <u>Father, what evil have we done? Why must we be punished?</u>

(**GARRPE** enters.)

<u>How long must we wait before we will we see our Lord's kingdom?</u>

RODRIGUES   (quietly, to **GARRPE**) Do you know her words?

(**GARRPE** kneels down next to **MONICA** -- as she takes the BABY from her back and cradles it in her arms.)

GARRPE   <u>Monica, what has happened?</u>

MONICA   <u>Again, the guards came. Again, they found nothing.</u>

GARRPE   (to **RODRIGUES**) The guards came again to the village -- (to **MONICA**) <u>And then --- ?</u>

MONICA   (crying quietly) <u>Matabe ...</u>

RODRIGUES   Matabe -- yes -- what of him?

(**MOKICHI** enters. **RODRIGUES** and **GARRPE** turn to him.)

GARRPE   What has happened to Matabe?

MOKICHI   <u>The guards asked if priests -- foreign priests -- were being hidden here. No one spoke.</u>

GARRPE   (to **RODRIGUES**) The villagers were asked if they were hiding priests -- foreign priests. No one spoke.

MOKICHI   <u>They pulled Matabe from the crowd, aimed an arrow at his heart -- and asked again. Again, no one spoke.</u>

<u>They shot the arrow through him.</u>

(**GARRPE** lowers his head.)

RODRIGUES   Garrpe ...?

GARRPE   They pulled Matabe from the crowd. They aimed an arrow at him. They asked again if foreign priests were being hidden. This time, when no one spoke ... they shot the arrow through his heart.

RODRIGUES   (quietly, sinking to the ground) Oh, Lord ... oh, Lord make a place for him in your kingdom.

MOKICHI   Matabe ... never betray you.

(Silence. **RODRIGUES** looks up at **MOKICHI**. **MOKICHI** turns and speaks to **MONICA**.)

MOKICHI   The Samurai now demands three hostages. Ichizo and I have agreed to go. We will be taken to Nagasaki.

GARRPE   The Samurai has demanded three hostages. Ichizo and Mokichi have volunteered. They will be taken to Nagasaki.

RODRIGUES   And the third hostage?

MOKICHI   Kichijiro. The people of the village suspect he betrayed them. He was forced to join us.

(**KICHIJIRO** is pushed into the hut by **ICHIZO**.)

RODRIGUES   Kichijiro ---

(**KICHIJIRO** immediately lowers himself to the ground, holding his knees. Fearful.)

GARRPE   The villagers suspect it was Kichijiro who betrayed them. He was forced to be the third hostage.

(A pause, then **RODRIGUES** turns to **GARRPE**.)

RODRIGUES   We've brought them nothing but harm.

GARRPE   We can't abandon them ---

RODRIGUES   The longer we stay, the more danger we bring to this village.

GARRPE   Brother, we ---

(**RODRIGUES** goes to the hole in the hut. He opens it. He removes his ROSARY from the hole. He attaches it to his belt.)

RODRIGUES   To find the lonely and abandoned flock. That was our charge.

(He lifts **GARRPE**'S CRUCIFIX from the hole and offers it to him.)

No more hiding.

(**GARRPE** stares at him, then takes the CRUCIFIX. **RODRIGUES** looks at **GARRPE** and indicates the PEASANTS.)

Ask them where we should go. Ask them!

KICHIJIRO   The Goto islands. There are Christians there. They will welcome you.

(Silence. They all turn and look at **KICHIJIRO**.)

GARRPE   The Goto islands. His home. He says there are Christians there that will welcome us.

RODRIGUES   (approaching **KICHIJIRO**) Will they know of Ferreira there? Father Ferreira?

KICHIJIRO   (nod) Ferreira. Yes.

RODRIGUES   THEY WILL KNOW OF HIM -- YOU'RE CERTAIN?

KICHIJIRO   Yes.

MONICA   And in Hirado. There are many Christians there.

RODRIGUES   Hirado? There are Christians there, as well?

GARRPE   Yes.

RODRIGUES   It's settled, then. We have our destinations. And, whatever the result – whether our mission meets with success or ends in glorious martyrdom -- we shall be the priests which Ferreira taught us to be. We will be the soldiers of Christ.

(**GARRPE** looks at **RODRIGUES** for a long moment. **RODRIGUES** nods, as if to say "tell them." **GARRPE** turns to the PEASANTS.)

GARRPE   Father Rodrigues -- will travel to the Goto Islands. I will go to Hirado.

(The PEASANTS stare at the PRIESTS, then after a moment, each of them nods. **GARRPE** steps toward **MONICA**. He holds his CRUCIFIX in front of him. He looks at **MONICA**. Then, he puts the CRUCIFIX in **MONICA**'S hands.)

May God's strength be with you.

(**MONICA** takes the CRUCIFIX in both hands, holding it with great reverence. She bows, in thanks, as --- **MOKICHI** steps toward **RODRIGUES**, tears in his eyes.)

MOKICHI   Father, if we are ordered to trample …

(**GARRPE** looks at **RODRIGUES**.)

ICHIZO   If the Samurai demands it …

MOKICHI   I had rather my feet were cut off than trample on the holy image. But, if we do not trample on the *fumie*, they will keep taking hostages from our village ---

ICHIZO   They won't stop till they've killed us all.

GARRPE   (to **RODRIGUES**) He asks what to do if they are ordered to trample on the *fumie*. The Samurai will keep taking hostages until they trample on the holy image.

MOKICHI   Father, if they put the *fumie* at our feet, and they order us to ---

RODRIGUES   (to the PEASANTS, firmly) Do not deface the Church.

(gesturing "no")

Don't.

(more gently now)

Be strong and have faith. The Lord God shall not abandon you in your time of need.

GARRPE   But, brother, if the Samurai carries out his threat, if they and their families are killed ---

RODRIGUES   Each death in Christ is a stone which will, in time, become the foundation of the Church.

(Long silence, as **GARRPE** stares at **RODRIGUES**. Then he bows his head in prayer. The others do the same.
KICHIJIRO remains at a slight distance, watching, head not bowed. During the prayer -- unseen by the others – **KICHIJIRO** bows his head and joins them in prayer.)

GARRPE   Dear Lord, accept your servant Matabe into your kingdom, that his faith in you may be rewarded. Teach us all to give and not count the cost; to fight and not heed the wounds; to toil and not seek for rest; to labor and not ask for reward; knowing that with each struggle we do your will. Through Jesus Christ our Lord.

MOKICHI, MONICA, ICHIZO, RODRIGUES   Amen.

(**KICHIJIRO** lifts his head before the others can see that he has prayed. The PEASANTS begin to leave. **KICHIJIRO** is following them off ---)

RODRIGUES   Kichijiro ---

(**KICHIJIRO** stops, turns. The PEASANTS are gone.
RODRIGUES removes his own ROSARY and approaches **KICHIJIRO**. When he holds the rosary out, offering it to **KICHIJIRO** --- **KICHIJIRO** turns and runs off.
A long silence, as **GARRPE** and **RODRIGUES** stare at each other …)

RODRIGUES   God's promise will be fulfilled, brother.

(… then, they embrace, holding each other tightly.)

And, I will see you again.

GARRPE   Yes, but where? In this strange land? Or in our Father's kingdom?

(They part. **GARRPE** looks once more at **RODRIGUES** … then leaves.
RODRIGUES stands, alone, as ---
FERREIRA, in flowing robes, standing downstage in a shaft of beautiful
STAINED-GLASS LIGHT.
MUSIC: **"O Esca Viatorum"**)

FERREIRA   St. Ignatius has left us, his Jesuit followers, a text of *Spiritual Exercises*. They are intended to keep us strong in our service of the Church.

Join me.

(**RODRIGUES** approaches **FERREIRA** and kneels near him. **FERREIRA** raises his hand, as **RODRIGUES** looks up at him.)

Exercise Number Three-hundred Sixty-five: "To arrive at complete certainty
---

RODRIGUES   "To arrive at complete certainty ---

FERREIRA   "I will believe that the white object I see before me is black ---

RODRIGUES   "I will believe that the white object I see before me is black
---

FERREIRA   "If that should be the decision of the hierarchical Church.

RODRIGUES   "If that should be the decision of the hierarchical Church.

FERREIRA   "For I believe that Christ our Lord is ruling and guiding us for our soul's own good."

RODRIGUES   "For I believe that Christ our Lord is ruling and guiding us for our soul's own good."

(**FERREIRA** smiles, warmly. His light fades, as he moves away, saying …)

FERREIRA You're a very good student, Sebastian. Again, now. On your own ...

(MUSIC OUT, as lights reveal ---
A Small Boat. Night. The boat faces downstage, with room enough for only its OARSMAN and **RODRIGUES**. The OARSMAN sits in the back of the boat -- his face unseen, throughout.
The SOUND of WAVES lapping gently against the boat.)

RODRIGUES Spiritual Exercise Number Three Hundred Sixty-Five:

"To arrive at complete certainty, I will believe that the white object I see before me is black -- if that should be the decision of the hierarchical Church.

(**RODRIGUES** moves into the boat and sits, in front.)

"For I believe that Christ our Lord ---

(He stops, looks around in the darkness.)

"For I believe that Christ our Lord is ruling and ---"

(He stops, looks around again. He speaks to the OARSMAN.)

Tell me -- I've been told that just across this water there are Christians. Hidden Christians. An entire village. Is that right?

(No response from the OARSMAN.)

Hidden Christians -- on the island -- a village -- hidden Christians?

(Still, no response from the OARSMAN. Long silence. Finally ...)

"My dear brothers. I write to you still. For you are all that remains of what I knew of the world.

I'm told at one time the missionaries rode into Nagasaki harbor in large ships, and there on the hillside was a great and holy cross, welcoming them. They stepped onto shore and into the arms of a thousand true believers ...

What has become of our glorious dream?

The persecutions have lasted now for over twenty years. The soil of Japan is littered with the bitter laments of its peasants. The blood of its priests. Brother Garrpe walks alone -- somewhere far from here, seeking refuge, fearing betrayal. And I ride across black water, in a rat-infested boat, my life once again entrusted to a stranger. Hidden in the clothes of a peasant, I seek a village forced to hide its faith.

Only the waves welcome us. Constant ... quiet ... and indifferent.

(A very long silence. Only the gentle SOUND of the WAVES is heard, rhythmic and hypnotic.

RODRIGUES looks in various directions, into the distance. Then speaks, simply ...)

Truly, this is the end of the earth."

(**The Shore** -- designated by a strong, tight downlight, downstage of the boat.

In silence, **RODRIGUES** stands, steps slowly out of the boat -- and into the light. He looks into the distance, then turns to discover that ---

The OARSMAN is gone. The boat is gone, as well. **RODRIGUES** stands in the light, as lights also reveal ---

Valignano, standing on the HILLSIDE, addressing a group of [unseen] students.

As **VALIGNANO** speaks, **RODRIGUES** moves about the stage, slowly -- he is hungry, exhausted.)

VALIGNANO   In the final letter we received from Father Rodrigues, he spoke of being taken to an island off the coast of Japan. He was alone. He was without food. He had been granted God's supreme test of faith.

He traveled inland, climbing the rocks, following crude pathways -- in search of the Christian village that awaited him. After several days of no food, and little sleep, he saw the roofs of huts in the distance. He saw smoke rising into the air. Hopeful now, and with his faith still strong within him, he rushed toward the village. And, when he arrived ---

(Lights expand around **RODRIGUES** to reveal ---

A Village in the Goto Islands. Dusk. The village is simply a bare stage.

The SOUND of WIND. The random CALL of CROWS.)

--- it was empty.

Dust swirled on the deserted roads. Cats wandered about, wild and alone – screaming into rooms. The soldiers had been to the village. There were signs of a battle -- doors battered down, cups and plates broken and lying about, clothing hanging lifeless in the wind.

But the huts, like the roads, and like the fields ... were empty.
The villagers had vanished, leaving nothing but the wind whistling through the crumbling huts and the crying of the cats.

(Long silence as **RODRIGUES** stands, taking in the scene.)

He called out in a loud voice ... but no one answered.
Famished with hunger, he looked for food and found none.

And there, it is said, he remained.
He waited.
And, he prayed.

And with that, our news of his mission to Japan came to an end.

(Light out on **VALIGNANO**, as ---
Kneeling with exhaustion and hunger, **RODRIGUES** cries out ---)

RODRIGUES   MY GOD, WHERE ARE YOU? WHERE HAVE YOU ALL GONE?

This, then, is my parish. These abandoned huts and missing persons -- my cathedral, my congregation.

(Strangely -- with alternate bursts of energy, and bouts of exhaustion and despair -- **RODRIGUES** moves about, talking to the nothingness around him.

The growing SOUND of CICADAS, as they fill the air with their droning cries.)

My dear friends in Christ: We are carried here by the very sea which carried our predecessors -- Father Xavier, Father Torres, Fathers Cabral and Valignano and Ferreira.

The sea, then, was all things hopeful. The sea was the voice of God.

But, you ask of me this question: Father Rodrigues, how much does the sea witness? Does it know of the torture of Christians, does it hear their apostasies and register their screams? How, then, can the sea remain silent?

Men are taken away -- Mokichi, Ichizo -- taken from their homes and forced to trample on the holy image, their lives in the balance, their fate unknown.

Matabe is murdered for holding fast to his faith. And the sea -- the beautiful, resolute sea -- pounds the shoreline with impunity, crashing the rocks with a hollow nonchalance.

And again you ask me: good Father Rodrigues, why this silence? How can God witness the persecution of his servants and do nothing?!

(He collapses to the ground. Breathes deeply.)

Forgive me. It is vile need -- it is hunger talking through me. Like our Lord on the cross -- like that ravaged, forgiving face -- my mouth aches with thirst.

Forgive me and keep me in your ...

(Then ... a laugh from **RODRIGUES**. Starting softly, then building to a wild intensity.)

How ludicrous it becomes! A priest in rags, shouting at the silence! The prayers -- the confessions -- the beads and books, the wine and the bread -- how silly it becomes if one lets ---
(he stops)
If one dare imagine ---
(again he stops, serious now)
How ludicrous our lives if in fact ...

(pause)
If in fact God does not exist.

(The SOUND of the CICADAS has FADED AWAY. The stage sits in an absolute and oppressive silence.

RODRIGUES is motionless, dwarfed by the silence.
He looks around. Then ... slowly, achingly ... he lifts his **ROSARY** to his face. Looks at the rosary.
Then ... he kisses it ... as tears stream down his face.)

"And our Lord Jesus Christ said unto them: Pray that ye enter not into temptation. For truly the spirit is willing, but the flesh is weak."

Our Father, who art in heaven, hallowed be thy name. Thy kingdom come, thy will be done, on earth as it is in heaven.

RODRIGUES [cont.]	**VOICE**
Give us this day our daily bread ---	Give us this day our daily bread ---

(A VOICE is heard from somewhere onstage, unseen, hiding. The VOICE is mumbling the prayer along with **RODRIGUES**. **RODRIGUES**, at first, is not aware of it.)

RODRIGUES	**VOICE**
And forgive us our trespasses as we forgive those who trespass against us.	And forgive us our trespasses as we forgive those who trespass against us.
And lead us not into temptation ---	And lead us not into temptation ---

(And now **RODRIGUES** stops, suddenly. He has heard the VOICE. **RODRIGUES** sits, motionless. Then, slowly looks around, fearfully. Seeing nothing, he continues, cautiously ...)

RODRIGUES   But deliver us from evil ---

VOICE   Deliver us from evil ---

RODRIGUES   Who is there?

(pause)

<u>Who is it?</u>

(Silence. He concludes the prayer …)

In the name of the Father ---

VOICE   <u>The Father ---</u>

(Silence.)

RODRIGUES   And the Son ---

VOICE   <u>The Son ---</u>

RODRIGUES   And the Holy Ghost.

VOICE   <u>The Holy Ghost.</u>

(**RODRIGUES** stands, looking now in the direction of the **VOICE**.)

RODRIGUES   Amen.

(A person lifts his head from hiding and we see the source of the **VOICE**: it is **Kichijiro.**)

KICHIJIRO   Amen.

(Standoff. Silence.)

RODRIGUES   Kichijiro ---

Mio Padré. <u>I've come to warn you.</u> Danger. Soldiers.

(pats his own chest)

Kichijiro … protect you.

(**RODRIGUES** stares at **KICHIJIRO**, then … he notices one of **KICHIJIRO**'S bare feet.)

RODRIGUES   Your foot is bleeding. You've cut it.

(**KICHIJIRO** stares at him.)

Where have you been running from?

(**KICHIJIRO** turns and starts to run away, but --- **RODRIGUES** grabs him, firmly, stopping him. Their eyes meet. **KICHIJIRO** stands, motionless.

RODRIGUES quickly tears free a piece of his own CLOTHING. He tears this piece of fabric in two. With the first piece HE WASHES **KICHIJIRO**'S FOOT -- wiping blood from the wound. He wraps the second piece, as a bandage, tightly around the wound, as he speaks …)

You were to be taken to Nagasaki with the other men. As hostages for the magistrate. Why are you here?

(The foot is now wrapped. **KICHIJIRO** whimpers and grunts, backing away. **RODRIGUES** follows him, closes in on him.)

I know you understand what I'm saying. Answer me. Answer me ---

(**KICHIJIRO** pulls a piece of dried FISH from inside his clothing. He offers it to **RODRIGUES**.)

KICHIJIRO   Fish for you. Eat. I've brought it for you. For you.

RODRIGUES   Where are Mokichi and Ichizo? What has become of them?

KICHIJIRO   Please eat. For you.

RODRIGUES   Answer me! Were they taken to Nagasaki? Were they?

KICHIJIRO   (nods)

RODRIGUES   And you were left behind?

KICHIJIRO   (nods) Yes.

RODRIGUES   WHY? DID YOU ESCAPE? WHAT DID YOU DO?

(**KICHIJIRO** is crying, seemingly shrinking down inside himself.)

KICHIJIRO.

(**KICHIJIRO** looks up.)

Tell me.

(**KICHIJIRO** lifts his head and looks at **RODRIGUES**. Then, standing, he looks at the ground.
He lifts one of his feet.
Then ... he slowly lowers the foot onto a piece of ground in front of him. As he does this, tears fall from his eyes.)

KICHIJIRO   Forgive me ---

RODRIGUES   You trampled?

KICHIJIRO   I am not a strong man ---

RODRIGUES   You stepped on the *fumie*. You apostatized.

KICHIJIRO   Forgive me ---

RODRIGUES   And for your betrayal, they let you go free?!

KICHIJIRO   For you. There is danger here. You must have strength.

(**RODRIGUES** stares at him, speechless. He does not take the food from **KICHIJIRO**. Instead, he turns and starts off, quickly, as ---

KICHIJIRO rushes after and tackles **RODRIGUES**. They fall to the ground, wrestling furiously, as **RODRIGUES** struggles to free himself from **KICHIJIRO**'S grip. At a moment when **KICHIJIRO** has the upper hand, he points in the direction which **RODRIGUES** was heading ---)

SOLDIERS. THE SOLDIERS ARE THAT WAY. MIO PADRÉ. CAPTURE. KICHIJIRO – PROTECT YOU.

(**RODRIGUES** stares up at **KICHIJIRO**, then looks quickly off in the direction he has referred to. He releases his grip on **KICHIJIRO** -- who stands, retrieves the piece of FISH, and sets it near **RODRIGUES**. **RODRIGUES**, breathing heavily, stares at **KICHIJIRO**, stares at the offering ---)

Given for you.

(**RODRIGUES** looks up at **KICHIJIRO** ... then grabs the fish, and devours it, hungrily. Desperately.
KICHIJIRO stands behind him, watching.

The SOUND of the CICADAS gradually returns.)

RODRIGUES   (as he finishes eating) What will become of them -- those men you abandoned?

(**KICHIJIRO** does not respond)

Is there not a reward for me, for the betrayal of a priest?!

KICHIJIRO   Silver.

RODRIGUES   Silver?

KICHIJIRO   Yes. Three hundred pieces.

RODRIGUES   Three hundred pieces of silver.

KICHIJIRO   (nods) Yes.

RODRIGUES

(not looking at **KICHIJIRO**)

It's laughable, isn't it? Our Lord was betrayed for thirty pieces of silver. And here the authorities will pay three hundred for the ---

(**KICHIJIRO** suddenly runs off -- in the direction he indicated "the soldiers" were -- and is gone.

RODRIGUES starts to stand, but, instead --- slumps to his knees, weak, resigned. Speaks quietly.

MUSIC: **"Ave Verum Corpus"** -- under.)

"What thou dost, do quickly." Such were our Lord's words to the man who betrayed him.

And with that, our Lord was taken. And tried. And put to death. That glorious martyrdom -- a fate so dearly worshipped; so avidly emulated by the saints.

But, is that why a priest exists? To give his own life and become a martyr? What of preserving his life, at all costs -- so that the flame of faith will not be extinguished? Are there not already too many saints in heaven, and too few on earth?

(**KICHIJIRO** enters. **RODRIGUES** turns to him, quickly -- an accusation. **KICHIJIRO** -- his hands behind his back – stops suddenly when he sees the intensity of **RODRIGUES'** look. **RODRIGUES** speaks quietly, simply …)

They've made a puppet of you. As they did of Judas.

(**RODRIGUES** stands and faces **KICHIJIRO**, accusing him.)

What are you holding? The silver they paid you for my betrayal?

(**KICHIJIRO** stares at him, a look of guilt on his face.)

Well?

(**KICHIJIRO** brings his hands out from behind his back -- he is holding a small container of WATER.

The MUSIC and the FACE OF CHRIST FADE AWAY.)

KICHIJIRO   Water. For you.

(**KICHIJIRO** walk to **RODRIGUES** and offers him the water. **RODRIGUES** stares at him.)

Mio Padré. <u>Don't you trust me?</u>

(**RODRIGUES** says nothing. He takes the water from **KICHIJIRO**. He drinks, slowly at first -- then, voraciously. As he does, **KICHIJIRO** squats nearby and speaks ...)

No one trusts me. Not all men are strong, Father. Some men are born cowards – weak shoots like me which will never grow. Mokichi. Ichizo -- they are strong shoots. They take root, grow. But not me. I am a weak shoot.

(Finished drinking, **RODRIGUES** wipes at his mouth with his hand, licking the moisture from his fingers.)

I am not strong. I am a weak man.

(**RODRIGUES** looks for a long time at **KICHIJIRO** -- who is holding his head in his hands.)

RODRIGUES   Do you want to confess?

(**KICHIJIRO** looks up at **RODRIGUES**.)

For your betrayal -- for stepping on the *fumie?* Do you want to confess?

KICHIJIRO   Confession?

RODRIGUES   Yes.

KICHIJIRO   Confession?!

RODRIGUES   Yes. I will hear your confession.

(**RODRIGUES** beckons to him.
KICHIJIRO moves to **RODRIGUES** and kneels before him. **RODRIGUES** makes the sign of the cross.)

In the name of the Father, and of the Son, and of the Holy Ghost. Amen.

KICHIJIRO   Amen.

RODRIGUES   "Blessed is the man that endureth temptation: for when he is tried, he shall receive the crown of life, which the Lord hath promised to them that love him."

Tell the Lord your sins, that he may hear and forgive you.

KICHIJIRO   I am a weak man. <u>I have sinned against you. At Nagasaki, I trampled on the holy image. Other men are strong, but I am not. I have seen others sent to death and said nothing. I have watched and done nothing.</u>

(As **KICHIJIRO** speaks, with great passion, we see ---

A SILHOUETTE ON THE HILLSIDE: Behind the WHITE FABRIC -- the THREE FIGURES tied to the STAKE, as before. The FOURTH FIGURE stands nearby, holding a LIGHTED TORCH.)

RODRIGUES   Kichijiro, slow down ---

KICHIJIRO   (overlapping, with great fervor) <u>My Father was tied to the stake. Then, my Mother. And my brother. They would not step on the *fumie*---</u>

RODRIGUES   I don't know what you're saying ---

KICHIJIRO   (overlapping) <u>They would not betray their Lord. But I am a weak man. I was afraid. I lifted my foot ---</u>

(The FOURTH FIGURE approaches the STAKE, and begins to ignite it with the LIGHTED TORCH ---)

RODRIGUES   Kichijiro ---

KICHIJIRO   <u>My family screamed out my name -- but I lowered my foot and I trampled! I TRAMPLED! AND I FLED! AND I WATCHED THEM -- TIED TO THE STAKE -- COVERED IN FLAMES -- I WATCHED THEM BURN AND I RAN AWAY ---</u>

(Just as the STAKE is about to be ignited ---

RODRIGUES grabs **KICHIJIRO**, forcefully, by the shoulders – to settle him. At the same moment ---

The SILHOUETTE DISAPPEARS, in an instant.

KICHIJIRO, crying, takes hold of **RODRIGUES** -- clinging to him, desperately. **RODRIGUES** speaks to him, gently ...)

RODRIGUES   Kichijiro. Repeat after me: "Our Lord is hung on the cross."

KICHIJIRO   "Our Lord is hung on the cross."

RODRIGUES   "Our Lord is crowned with thorns."

KICHIJIRO   "Our Lord is crowned with thorns."

RODRIGUES   "Our Lord is crucified for us."

KICHIJIRO   "Our Lord is crucified for us."

RODRIGUES   "Our Lord dies for our sins."

KICHIJIRO   "Our Lord dies for our sins."

RODRIGUES   God, the Father of mercies, has sent the Holy Spirit among us for the forgiveness of sins. Through God's grace alone are we offered pardon and peace. And therefore, through the ministry of the Church in Rome, and the communion of the Saints in heaven ...

(**KICHIJIRO** looks up into **RODRIGUES**' face.)

... I hereby absolve you of all your sins. In the name of the Father. And of the Son. And of ---

(Suddenly, TWO GUARDS rush onstage -- their faces partially covered by their clothing.

They grab **RODRIGUES**, forcefully.

RODRIGUES stares at **KICHIJIRO** for an instant, as the GUARDS prepare to drag him away. **KICHIJIRO** is still kneeling.)

GUARD ONE	**GUARD TWO**
Get up! The magistrate Inoue will see you -- he will see you to the Pit!	Where's your god, now? Why won't your god protect you now?

(**GUARD TWO** SPITS, directly into **RODRIGUES**' face.

GUARD ONE holds up a small BAG and SHAKES IT. The clinking of SILVER COINS is heard. The GUARDS laugh, as ---

The bag is thrown at the feet of **KICHIJIRO**.)

KICHIJIRO   Forgive me. I am a weak man ---

(As **KICHIJIRO** stands and pleads --- **GUARD TWO** rips the ROSARY away from **RODRIGUES** and throws it to the ground.)

| **GUARD ONE** | **GUARD TWO** |
| You will trample like the others --- | Your trinkets will not save you --- |

(**RODRIGUES** is hauled away by the GUARDS, saying nothing, staring at **KICHIJIRO**. When they are gone ---

KICHIJIRO throws himself to the ground -- and picks up the ROSARY. He kisses it. He clutches it to his chest. Tears run down his face as he says ...)

KICHIJIRO   Mio Padré. Mio Padré, forgive me ...

(**A Hill overlooking the Sea. Dawn.** The HUGE SUN from the opening of the play is seen rising behind THREE MAGISTRATES. They appear to be sitting on pedestals, looking down on those below. They remain motionless, imposing.

RODRIGUES wanders on, barefoot, his arms tied behind his back with rope. Disoriented, he stands alone, downstage. He squints into the brilliant sunrise. As he does so ---

The VOICE OF THE [unseen] **INTERPRETER** is heard.)

VOICE OF INTERPRETER   Native Country: Portugal. Name: Rodrigues.

(**RODRIGUES** looks up at the looming MAGISTRATES. He looks around to find the source of the VOICE.)

Said to have come from Macao to Japan.

(**RODRIGUES** says nothing, continues to look around.

Now, from off stage, the SOUND of VOICES SINGING, VERY SOFTLY:
"We're on our way, we're on our way.
We're on our way to the temple of Paradise.
The temple of Paradise is far away.
The temple of Paradise is far away. We're on our way, we're on our way.
We're on our way to the temple of Paradise."

RODRIGUES listens for a moment, then speaks over the sound of the SINGING VOICES.)

RODRIGUES   Where am I? What is this place?

(The **INTERPRETER** enters, a wry smile on his face. He holds a small FAN, which he waves to cool himself.

The SINGING CONTINUES, under …)

INTERPRETER   A lovely view of the sea, don't you think?

(**RODRIGUES** turns and sees the **INTERPRETER**.)

It reflects our kindness toward our prisoners.

(He gestures to the [unseen] crowd around them.)

Please don't let the others bother you. They are only Christians, imprisoned for their beliefs. And now, with a priest in their midst, they watch with great interest.

(Suddenly, he shouts toward off stage ---)

SILENCE!

(The SINGING STOPS, instantly. Silence.)

RODRIGUES   Your words, the way you speak ---

INTERPRETER   Don't be surprised. There are many interpreters like myself. We learned the language from the Portuguese priests. We let them baptize us in exchange for learning, for knowledge.

RODRIGUES   So, you, too, are a Christian?

(The **INTERPRETER** begins untying **RODRIGUES'** hands.)

INTERPRETER   (smiles) Father, your Christianity may trick the peasants -- but it will not trick me. I see through you like glass.

(**RODRIGUES'** hands are now free.)

RODRIGUES   You're not afraid I'll escape?

INTERPRETER   (shakes his head 'no') If you escape, we'll kill your followers. It's that simple.

RODRIGUES   Your hatred of Christianity, your fear of our religion will not make us disavow our ---

INTERPRETER   Father, you misunderstand. Inoue does not fear you. He believes you bring needless suffering to the peasants.

RODRIGUES   You can end their suffering! Set them free!

INTERPRETER   It is not our decision.

RODRIGUES   Then whose is it?!

INTERPRETER   (simply) It is yours.

(The sun has now risen more fully, revealing TWO of the MAGISTRATES to be STONE STATUES.

The THIRD, however, is a MAN. A small BOWL sits on his lap. Now, he begins to move, slightly: with his hands directly above the BOWL -- not touching water -- he begins to very slowly rub the tips of his extended fingers together.

During the following, the **MAGISTRATE** often NODS – seemingly in agreement with **RODRIGUES'** statements.)

If you say a single word, they will be set free.

RODRIGUES   What are you saying?

INTERPRETER   Apostatize.

(Silence.)

RODRIGUES   And if I refuse? Then, will I be killed like the others?

INTERPRETER   Certainly not. We've learned from our mistakes. We no longer provide the peasants with new martyrs.

(pause, smiles)

Perhaps you're not a priest, after all. A priest would have pity on his followers. He would want to end their suffering.

(**RODRIGUES** stares at him, sizing him up.)

RODRIGUES   Punish me alone.

INTERPRETER   (with a wry smile) That's impossible.

RODRIGUES   Why?

INTERPRETER   It is because of you that they suffer.

(TWO PEASANTS are pushed onstage. They fall to the ground. Their hands are tied behind their backs with rope. When they stand, **RODRIGUES** sees their faces …

It is **Mokichi,** and **Ichizo.** They look to him, pleadingly …)

These men -- Mokichi, Ichizo are their names. You know these men, do you not?

(**RODRIGUES** stares at them, saying nothing.)

They deny it -- they are protecting you -- but we know you were in their village, in Tomogi. And this man, caught today as he followed you here.

(Opposite, another MAN is pushed onstage. His hands are also tied behind his back. It is **Kichijiro.**)

Do you have any idea why he would be following you?

(**RODRIGUES** stares at **KICHIJIRO**, saying nothing, as -- **KICHIJIRO** lowers his head, and looks away.

The **INTERPRETER** holds up Rodrigues' ROSARY.)

Christian icons have been found in his possession. Where would he have gotten them?

(Silence. **RODRIGUES** turns to the **INTERPRETER**.)

RODRIGUES   I have traveled thousands of miles from my home, not on behalf of Portugal, not to corrupt the lives of the Japanese or interfere in its government -- but to bring the universal word of our Lord to your people.

(The MAGISTRATE is nodding with approval. Seeing this, **RODRIGUES** gains confidence and resolve as he speaks ---)

If we did not believe that the truth as we know it -- the truth of belief and compassion; forgiveness and grace -- if we did not believe that such truth was universal, why should so many priests endure these hardships? It is precisely because truth is common to all countries and all times that we can call it truth.

INTERPRETER   Father, we are not disputing the right and wrong of your doctrine. In Spain and Portugal what you say may be true. But, Christianity -- as the Japanese have learned it -- is of no value to us.

(pause)

Have you nothing to say? Even here, at this moment, surrounded by the peasants you have put in danger?

RODRIGUES   Nothing I can say will change your mind. And I have no intention of altering my beliefs.

INTERPRETER   Father Ferreira, at one time, said the same thing. Now, the children laugh and call him "Apostate Peter."

(**RODRIGUES** stares at him.)

Yes, he is alive. He lives in Nagasaki. He has taken a Japanese name and a Japanese wife. Since his apostasy, he is happy and at peace.

RODRIGUES   (bitterly) I don't believe you.

INTERPRETER   That is your right.

RODRIGUES   You'll say anything. Invent any lies to entrap us. And no matter how we respond we will be punished.

(The **INTERPRETER** turns to the **MAGISTRATE** and speaks ---)

INTERPRETER   <u>He claims we will entrap him. And no matter what he says, he will be punished.</u>

MAGISTRATE   (in a gentle voice) <u>We would never punish the fathers without reason.</u>

INTERPRETER   He says: We would never punish the fathers without reason.

RODRIGUES   Not according to Inoue. It is his plan to punish us all. If Inoue were here he would punish me instantly.

(Laughter from the **INTERPRETER**. He <u>says something</u> to the **MAGISTRATE** -- who also laughs.)

What are you laughing at?

INTERPRETER   Father, this is Inoue. The Governor of Chikugo.

(**RODRIGUES** turns quickly and looks at the **MAGISTRATE** -- who is, indeed, Inoue.

INOUE smiles a warm smile.)

INOUE   <u>Welcome, Father.</u>

(**INOUE** sets the bowl aside, stands, and extends his hand toward the others. In his hand is a plaque, about eight inches square ...

It is the *FUMIE.*

The **INTERPRETER** takes the *FUMIE* from **INOUE.** He carries it to the center of the stage.
He sets it on the ground.
Then, he addresses the entire [unseen] crowd.)

INTERPRETER   Christianity is an outlawed religion! Let all of you imprisoned here bear witness to these men and their fate!

(**MOKICHI, ICHIZO** and **KICHIJIRO** all look at the *FUMIE.*
Then ... **MOKICHI** and **ICHIZO** look up at **RODRIGUES** ---

RODRIGUES stares at them, motionless.

The **INTERPRETER** turns to the three men.)

It has been reported that you are practicing Christians, all three of you. What is your answer to this?

MOKICHI   I am a Buddhist. I follow the teachings of the monks at our Temple.

ICHIZO   I, too, am a Buddhist. I am not a Christian.

KICHIJIRO   I worship the Buddha.

(The **INTERPRETER** turns to **RODRIGUES,** with a smile.)

INTERPRETER   Three times have they denied you. They assure us that they are practicing Buddhists.

RODRIGUES   Then you have your answer. Let them go ---

INTERPRETER   We shall see.

(He turns to **MOKICHI, ICHIZO** and **KICHIJIRO.**
He points to the *FUMIE.)*

If that is so, trample on the *fumie!*

(The **INTERPRETER** shoves **MOKICHI** forward. He stands in front of the *FUMIE*.

MOKICHI looks up at **RODRIGUES** again, his eyes desperate --- **RODRIGUES** looks at the *FUMIE*, then back to **MOKICHI** ...

Then ... **RODRIGUES** NODS, slightly, to **MOKICHI**.)

Trample!

(A pause, then ... with tears running down his face ... **MOKICHI** places his foot on the *FUMIE*.

Then, he steps back, as ---

ICHIZO is shoved forward. He, too, looks at **RODRIGUES** ... who once again ... after a moment ... NODS. Then, **ICHIZO**, too, in great agony, steps on the *FUMIE*.

KICHIJIRO is then shoved forward. He looks pleadingly at **RODRIGUES**. Then, he too steps on the *FUMIE*.

INOUE looks on, saying nothing. He exchanges a look with the **INTERPRETER**. Complete silence, as ---

The **INTERPRETER** stares at **MOKICHI**, **ICHIZO** and **KICHIJIRO** for a long moment. Then ... a smile comes to his lips. He turns to **RODRIGUES**.)

We are not so easily deceived.

(to the MEN)

<u>Do you think you can deceive us like that? Do you think we are fools?! We heard your breathing become heavy -- we saw the sweat form on your faces.</u>

(The **INTERPRETER** lifts the *FUMIE* and holds it high above his head so that all can see.)

<u>If you are not Christians, then I ask you to SPIT on the cross of your Lord -- and declare that your Blessed Virgin is a WHORE.</u>

(The MEN stare at the **INTERPRETER**, frozen with fear.)

RODRIGUES   What have you told them?

INTERPRETER   To SPIT on the *fumie* and call their Blessed Virgin a WHORE.

RODRIGUES   No, you must stop this, I beg of you ---

INTERPRETER   As I told you, Father: only you can stop this.

(pause)

You need only say one word.

(**RODRIGUES** looks at the MEN. At **INOUE**. At the **INTERPRETER**.

He does not speak.

The **INTERPRETER** shoves him away, with force ---)

Away with you.

(**RODRIGUES** is shoved to **a downstage corner.** He stands in a shaft of light -- separated now from the scene on the HILLSIDE.

The **INTERPRETER** hands the *FUMIE* to **MOKICHI**. He holds it in front of him, trembling.)

<u>Come now. Do as you're told. If you're not a Christian, SPIT ON THE IMAGE.</u>

(**MOKICHI** is shaking with fear, trying to make himself spit on the holy image, as ---

RODRIGUES turns and faces the audience.)

RODRIGUES   My brothers in Christ, I was later told what happened:

Mokichi, tears flowing down his cheeks, was powerless. He could not bring himself to spit on the *fumie.*

(The **INTERPRETER** takes the *FUMIE* from **MOKICHI**, shoves him to the ground, and thrusts the *FUMIE* into the hands of **ICHIZO**. He holds it, crying, fearful, silent.)

Ichizo, too -- despite their threats -- could not deface the holy image. Both men confessed to Inoue that they were Christians.

(**INOUE** smiles.
KICHIJIRO is handed the *FUMIE*. He holds it in front of him. He, too, is crying -- his hands trembling with fear.)

As for Kichijiro …

(**KICHIJIRO** closes his eyes … and SPITS on the *FUMIE*. The **INTERPRETER** instantly unbinds **KICHIJIRO**'S hands – and he runs off, disappearing into the distance.)

… he was set free.

(**INOUE** lifts his hand in the air: The **INTERPRETER** grabs **MOKICHI** and **ICHIZO** and pushes them off stage, as ---

The SOUND of the CRASHING WAVES begins softly … then builds in intensity during the following.)

Later that day, our eyes turned to the sea. As we looked down from our prison on the hillside … we saw Mokichi and Ichizo. The guards were pushing them toward the water's edge. For a moment, they disappeared from view.

(Now, as **RODRIGUES** describes it, lights reveal ---

A SILHOUETTE ON THE HILLSIDE: Behind the WHITE FABRIC -- TWO LARGE CROSSES, with a MAN attached to each. The crosses face away from the audience.)

Then, two large crosses were raised into the air.
Lashed to one was Mokichi.
Next to him, Ichizo.

This was <u>water torture</u> -- the water torture.

At night, when the tide came in, their bodies were immersed up to the chin. At low tide, they withered in the hot sun. And so it was ... day after day ... after day.

That they may die as slowly as possible -- that was Inoue's goal. So all the peasants could witness it. So all would learn what became of Christians in Japan.

(The SILHOUETTE ... very slowly ... FADES TO BLACK.)

For three days, we watched the water crash against them. We watched them grow frail -- till their bodies were nearly indistinguishable from the crosses on which they were hung. Till none of us knew whether they were dead or alive. We screamed from our prison on the hillside: Be strong! We are praying for your soul! Soon you will go to your reward -- soon you will be in Paradise!

But, there was no sound. Only the sea -- the relentless, resolute sea.

(**RODRIGUES** closes his eyes.)

Dear Lord, we pray of you: do not increase their suffering. Have mercy upon them. Carry them with you into your kingdom.

And then, from the blackness of that night ... a voice.

VOICE OF MOKICHI   (singing, quietly, achingly) "We're on our way ... we're on our way ...

(Slowly, LIGHT RISES AGAIN on the **SILHOUETTE**: It has CHANGED -- the BODIES of the MEN are significantly SMALLER, barely distinguishable from the CROSSES themselves.)

"We're on our way to the temple of Paradise ...

RODRIGUES   It was Mokichi. With the last of his strength -- singing a Christian hymn.

VOICE OF MOKICHI   (continuous, overlapping **RODRIGUES**) "The temple of Paradise ... is far away... the temple of Paradise ... is far away ... we're on our way ... we're on our way ... we're on our way ..."

(The SINGING FADES AWAY and is gone.
The only SOUND is the SEA -- calmer now, insistent. The SILHOUETTE of
the CROSSES remains.)

RODRIGUES   The waves engulf the men a final time. The foam breaks on
the sand. And, in the distance, a white bird -- hovering above the sea -- flies
far, far away.

It is over.

(**RODRIGUES** makes the sign of the cross.)

What remains of their bodies is burned -- to leave nothing for the Christians
to worship. Their ashes are thrown onto the water.

(Three shafts of light rise onstage, revealing --
Valignano, Ferreira, and **Kichijiro. VALIGNANO** holds a CANDLE, as
before. They are all looking at the CROSSES.)

VALIGNANO   No death is meaningless. It is a stone which in time will
become the foundation of the Church ---

RODRIGUES   In my head I hear the voices of my Superiors ---

VALIGNANO   They are now with the Lord. Like the Japanese martyrs who
have gone before, they now enjoy everlasting happiness.

(**VALIGNANO** exits with the lit CANDLE.)

RODRIGUES   But, in my heart ... in my heart I hear only the sea. The
murderous, resolute sea.

(He turns and asks of **FERREIRA** ---)

If this be martyrdom -- where is God's heavenly light?! Where are the angels
and archangels blowing their trumpets of glory?!

(**FERREIRA** says nothing, as the light on him fades to black.)

Can it be, is it possible, that as men cry out in anguish ... our God remains
silent?

As silent as the sea.

(Lights fade on **RODRIGUES** and **KICHIJIRO** -- And then on the CROSSES as ---
The WAVES continue to pound the shore.
End of Act One.)

Act Two

"Even the virtuous man can be saved."

-- Shinran

(From the darkness, a CRASH OF DRUMS as lights reveal ---

Inoue, looming upstage. He extends his arm and gestures to an area of the stage below him, causing lights to reveal ---

A Prison Cell. Day. The cell is designated by a few shards of light falling on the floor through the bars.

RODRIGUES is curled on the floor, asleep -- his clothes torn and filthy. He moves a bit, perhaps having a nightmare. **INOUE**'S gesture also produces ---

SOUND: A CACOPHONY OF DEEP, LABORED BREATHING; LOW, GUTTURAL MOANING: and a DEEP, CONSTANT MUSICAL DRONE. This sound is accented -- randomly -- by the SOUND of SHOVELS DIGGING, WHIPS CRACKING, METAL BEING POUNDED. The effect is visceral and terrifying.

INOUE is gone.

After a few moments, the SOUND OF THE CACOPHONY is JOINED by the SOUND of MUSIC: **"Ave Verum Corpus."** As the MUSIC BUILDS, we begin to see ---

A SILHOUETTE ON THE HILLSIDE: FERREIRA and **GARRPE** kneel before **VALIGNANO. VALIGNANO** gives them HOLY COMMUNION -- the "host," the wine -- then makes the sign of the cross over them.

In his cell, **RODRIGUES** stirs, but does not wake, as ---

A FIGURE IN DARK CLOTHING moves slowly toward the CELL. This is **KICHIJIRO**.
He crawls near **RODRIGUES** and watches him as he sleeps. Then, he places an [unseen] OBJECT into **RODRIGUES'** HAND. **RODRIGUES** does not awaken.

The SILHOUETTE FADES AWAY.
The MUSIC has completely replaced the CACOPHONY, filling the theatre with loud and rich sound, as ---

KICHIJIRO looks down upon **RODRIGUES**, watching over him.

From the HEART OF THE MUSIC, an AMPLIFIED VOICE is heard, strong and gentle ...)

VOICE OF CHRIST [MALE]   I will not abandon you. I am with you to the end of time.

(Suddenly, TWO HAND CLAPS, loud and quick, as -- **KICHIJIRO** runs off into the darkness and is gone.
RODRIGUES sits bolt upright, as ---
MUSIC STOPS, abruptly.)

RODRIGUES   What is it? <u>Who is there?</u>

(In the distance, a COCK CROWS.

Now, standing next to **RODRIGUES** is the **INTERPRETER**.)

INTERPRETER   Bad dreams?

(**RODRIGUES** turns to him, startled -- but says nothing. He looks around, breathing heavily.
Then, he looks and notices the object which Kichijiro
put in his hand: it is his ROSARY -- dirty and battered.)

Perhaps that object is the cause of your bad dreams. Who brought it to you?

(**RODRIGUES** does not speak.)

<u>Answer me!</u>

(The **INTERPRETER** stares at him, hard. **RODRIGUES** looks down at the ROSARY. Finally, the **INTERPRETER** extends his hand.)

Be careful, Father ---

(**RODRIGUES** puts the ROSARY in the **INTERPRETER**'S hand.)

--- Be careful who you protect.

(The **INTERPRETER** drops some BLACK CLOTHING into the cell.)

You've been given new clothing.

(gestures for **RODRIGUES** to change clothes)

Please. It's a gift from the magistrate.

RODRIGUES   These are the clothes of a Buddhist monk.

INTERPRETER   Yes. <u>Jittoku.</u>

RODRIGUES   I don't want their gifts.

INTERPRETER   But your own clothes, Father, they are old and torn ---

RODRIGUES   Nor do I want their pity.

INTERPRETER   I assure you, Father. They'll show no pity.

(Silence. They stare at one another. Then, the **INTERPRETER** smiles, warmly -- gesturing again to the clothing.)

Now, please …

(After a look at the **INTERPRETER**, **RODRIGUES** lifts the clothing. During the following, he changes into them.

The **INTERPRETER** uses his FAN to cool himself as he speaks.)

Tell me something. As Buddhists, we believe that everything exists naturally – that the world has neither beginning nor end. But you, Father -- you believe that your God made the world. That he caused it to be.

RODRIGUES   That is true. He is the Creator.

INTERPRETER   Why then did he create evil?

RODRIGUES   He did not ---

INTERPRETER   Is there not evil in the world he created?

RODRIGUES   He created everything for good -- and as part of that goodness, he gave man the power of thought, of decision. When men use that power in the wrong way – that is evil.

INTERPRETER   So, your God is blameless ---

RODRIGUES   That is a ---

INTERPRETER   Your God feels no shame ---

RODRIGUES   Shame?! No -- how can you say ---

INTERPRETER   I should think he'd feel shame.

RODRIGUES   In what way? Shame for what?

INTERPRETER   For the suffering he has caused. If he is loving and merciful -- if, as you say, he created all things for good -- why does he allow his followers to suffer so completely?

RODRIGUES   (a confident smile) I assure you, that is the age-old question of the Church.

INTERPRETER   What, then, is the age-old Answer?

(Silence. **RODRIGUES** has no answer. Then …)

RODRIGUES   Faith.

(Silence.)

INTERPRETER   Father, do you believe that?

RODRIGUES   I do.

INTERPRETER   And do you think your faith is stronger than Ferreira's? That you will not apostatize?

RODRIGUES   Never.

INTERPRETER   Have you been told of the Pit? The place of torture?

(Silence. **RODRIGUES** stares at him.)

I'll show it to you. One day soon.

(The **INTERPRETER** turns and leaves, as ---

The CACOPHONY of PRISON SOUNDS resumes, and ---
A PRISON GUARD enters and removes Rodrigues' old clothing.

RODRIGUES sits, alone in his cell -- his eyes closed.)

MONICA   Mio Padré.

(**RODRIGUES** opens his eyes and sees **MONICA** standing outside his cell. He looks twice to be certain that it is her.)

RODRIGUES   Monica?

MONICA   Yes.

RODRIGUES   (with elation) Let me see you …

(He reaches out his hands. She steps closer. He holds her hands through the "bars.")

Oh, a familiar face, I can't tell you …

MONICA   Mio Padré …

RODRIGUES   Your little girl -- your baby -- where is she?

(**MONICA** does not respond. **RODRIGUES** lets go of her hands and pretends to cradle a baby in his arms ...)

<u>Baby</u>. Your baby -- is she with you?

MONICA   (quietly) Omitsu.

RODRIGUES   Yes, Omitsu -- where is she? Has something happened to her?

(**MONICA** pulls her arms back through the "bars" and wraps them around herself, her head bowed. She is crying.)

Shall we pray? <u>Pray for her?</u>

(**RODRIGUES** kneels, preparing to pray. **MONICA** looks at him, shaking her head "No.")

MONICA   (shaking her head) For Omitsu?

<u>No.</u>

RODRIGUES   Why?

MONICA   Omitsu ...

(she looks to the sky, smiling through her tears)

<u>Omitsu is in Heaven. There is no pain there. No hunger or strife. Only peace.</u>
<u>Only peace and everlasting happiness.</u>

RODRIGUES   Omitsu. <u>Heaven</u> ---

MONICA   (nods, looking to the sky) Omitsu. <u>Heaven</u>.

(Silence.)

RODRIGUES   Yes. She was baptized into God's church. She is with him even now. We will pray for her.

MONICA   No. Pray for us here.

(She indicates herself -- pressing her open palm against her chest. Then, she indicates those in the prison -- gesturing to the area surrounding the cell. As she does so, she speaks with great fervor.)

Please. Pray for those imprisoned here. Pray that our suffering will end. That soon, we will go to our reward in Heaven.

(Again, she indicates herself -- then the other prisoners. As she does so ---

PRISONERS are seen in the SHADOWS, at various parts of the stage. First ONE, then MANY of them. They all wear dark, tattered clothing. They all remain at a distance, looking at **RODRIGUES** from the darkness. Their faces are never seen.)

Mio Padré. Pray ... for ... us ... here.

(MUSIC: **"Kyrie Dominicale"**

MONICA kneels, bows her head, and folds her hands in prayer. **RODRIGUES** stares at her.

Then, in the SHADOWS, the **PRISONERS** begin to kneel -- one by one -- until they, too, are awaiting **RODRIGUES'** prayer.

RODRIGUES looks at the PRISONERS. Then, he begins ...)

RODRIGUES   Heavenly Father, teach us to hold in our hearts the words of the Psalm, one of the joyous songs of David:

[Note: this is from Psalm 146]

"While I live will I praise the Lord: I will sing praises unto my God while I have any being. Happy is he whose hope is in the Lord our God -- who made heaven and earth, the sea and all that is therein, which keepeth the truth forever.

(He stops. With great empathy, he looks around at the praying PRISONERS as he continues. They do not look up when he stops -- they remain steadfast in their prayers.)

"The Lord giveth food to the hungry. The Lord looseth the chains of the prisoners. The Lord ---"

(The **PRISONERS** continue to pray, quietly, to themselves. As they pray, they use their FINGERS -- in lieu of prayer beads -- to say the ROSARY, as ---

RODRIGUES steps OUT OF THE CELL, approaches the audience.)

But, my dear, distant brothers in Christ, I must tell you: As I stand amidst these prisoners and speak to them David's words of praise; as I see the toil and suffering inflicted upon them by the guards --- the words of a different Psalm come into my mind, one of the songs of Asaph:

(fiercely) [Note: this is from Psalm 83]

"Keep not thou silence, O God: hold not thy peace, and be not still. For, lo, thine enemies make a tumult: AND THEY THAT HATE THEE HAVE LIFTED UP THEIR HEADS.

(Lights reveal **Inoue** -- in the distance, looking down on **RODRIGUES**, as before.)

They have taken counsel against thy people, and consulted against thy hidden ones. As the fire burneth the wood, and as the flame setteth the mountains ablaze: so PERSECUTE THEM WITH THY TEMPEST and MAKE THEM AFRAID WITH THY STORM. Let them be confounded and troubled forever; yea, LET THEM BE PUT TO SHAME AND PERISH -- THAT MEN MAY KNOW THAT THOU ART MOST HIGH OVER ALL THE EARTH."

(A CRASH OF DRUMS as ---
RODRIGUES stops, collects himself. He turns his attention back to the PRISONERS.)

Forgive me. I am tempted by thoughts of vengeance.

(pause)

But, don't you see ... all men are not heroes and saints. How many Christians, if only born in another time -- a time free from persecution -- how many of them would have known neither apostasy nor martyrdom, and would, instead, have lived blessed lives of faith until the very hour of their death?

(Silence. Then, **RODRIGUES** steps BACK INTO THE CELL and concludes his prayer to the **PRISONERS**. As he raises his hand, the **PRISONERS** all look up to him.)

"The Lord looseth the chains of the prisoners. The Lord openeth the eyes of the blind, raiseth those that are bowed down, and loveth ye, the righteous. The Lord shall reign forever, unto all generations.

(MUSIC FADES OUT.)

Laudate Eum."

PRISONERS   Praise Him.

RODRIGUES   (very quietly) Praise be to Christ.

(The **PRISONERS** stand and leave the SHADOWS, disappearing once again into darkness. ONE PRISONER remains, at a distance, looking at **RODRIGUES**.

MONICA comes to the cell and puts her arms through the "bars." **RODRIGUES** takes her hands in his.)

MONICA   Thank you, Father.

(With hope in her eyes, she touches her chest with her hand, then gestures to the sky, saying ---)

Heaven. In Heaven we shall see our reward.

(**RODRIGUES** nods, quietly saying ---)

RODRIGUES Heaven.

(**MONICA** leaves, as ---)

The remaining PRISONER walks slowly toward the cell. He is covered in a large, dark blanket. The PRISONER stops near the cell and kneels. **RODRIGUES** begins to make the sign of the cross over him, when ---

The PRISONER removes his blanket and we see his face: it is **Kichijiro.**)

RODRIGUES   Kichijiro ---

(**KICHIJIRO** hands a small bowl of RICE through the "bars" of the cell, saying---)

KICHIJIRO   <u>I've brought rice for you.</u>

(**RODRIGUES** does not move. **KICHIJIRO** is insistent.)

Kichijiro. For you.

(**RODRIGUES** takes the rice, staring at **KICHIJIRO**.)

RODRIGUES   But, why have you ---

(But **KICHIJIRO** is gone, running off into the darkness. **RODRIGUES** watches him go. Looks down at the bowl of rice, as ---

The **INTERPRETER** enters.)

INTERPRETER   Have we a need for more rice?

(**RODRIGUES** is silent.)

I'll see that your portions are increased.

RODRIGUES   Give my food to the Christians. All of it.

(The **INTERPRETER** takes the bowl of rice from him.)

INTERPRETER   And your tea, has it been hot enough?

RODRIGUES   Why this treatment? The peasants are forced to do hard labor, but I am kept here, inside, where I ---

INTERPRETER   We've let you pray with the Christians. Isn't that what you wanted -- the chance to be a priest in Japan?

RODRIGUES   If your plan is to soften me -- if it is to weaken my resolve by seeing to my comfort, I tell you it will not ---

INTERPRETER   (with a smile) Believe me, Father, I would be more than happy to torture you. But the decision is not mine.

RODRIGUES   Is that what you did with Ferreira? Softened his spirit, then tortured him till he apostatized?

INTERPRETER   It did not require torture. He did so willingly. As will you.

RODRIGUES   Never.

(Lights shift to ---
Inoue's Chamber. Evening.)

INTERPRETER   (looks off, announces) His Lordship, the Governor of Chikugo.

(**INOUE** enters. He gestures for **RODRIGUES** to come a bit closer, and to kneel. **RODRIGUES** does so. The **INTERPRETER** stands near by.)

INOUE   I am afraid I have neglected you.

(The **INTERPRETER** TRANSLATES to **RODRIGUES**.)

I have been attending to business in Hirado.

(TRANSLATION.)

Hirado is a lovely place. You should go there, Father, if you get a chance.

(TRANSLATION.)

RODRIGUES   His Lordship speaks as though I were a free man.

[Note: the conceit of these scenes is that INOUE -- having been instructed and baptized by the Portuguese priests – understands their language. Therefore, he does not need the INTERPRETER to translate RODRIGUES' words.]

INOUE   (smiles)

You are more free than most, Father.

(TRANSLATION.)

But, all that enslaves you is a single word. A foot placed on a picture.

(TRANSLATION.)

Many men would envy your position.

(TRANSLATION.)

RODRIGUES   Such as the men slaughtered at Shimabara? The helpless women and children, murdered in the night?

(Silence. **INOUE** stares at **RODRIGUES**. A long silence.)

INOUE   Father Rodrigues, you and the other missionaries do not seem to know Japan.

(TRANSLATION.)

RODRIGUES   And you, honorable magistrate, do not seem to know Christianity.

INOUE   (a smile) I was baptized a Christian. There was a time when I sought the guidance of the Church. But, thirty years have passed -- and the seed which was sown here has withered and died.

(TRANSLATION.)

RODRIGUES   If it dies here, its death will not be the fault of the Church -- but the Japanese authorities who've chosen to punish their own people.

You fear the Church. You fear the hope it brings to the peasants. You fear their allegiance to something with far greater power than you.

(**INOUE** smiles, rubs his fingers together.)

INOUE   You are a wise man, Father. Let me ask you a question which requires the thoughts of a wise man.

(TRANSLATION. **RODRIGUES** nods.)

The Lord of Hirado had four concubines. They lived with him at his castle. The four concubines argued and bickered constantly -- each jealous of the other, each eager to be loved best of all.

(TRANSLATION.)

In turn, each of the concubines would take the man aside and whisper in his ear: "Choose me. And me, alone. Send the others away. Then you and I will live in peace."

(TRANSLATION.)

When the man could stand their bickering no longer, he made his decision. Do you know what he decided?

(TRANSLATION.)

RODRIGUES   If he was a wise man, he sent them all away.

INOUE   (smiles and laughs) Oh, Father -- you please me very much!

(TRANSLATION. A smile, too, from **RODRIGUES**.)

For you see, that man is Japan itself. And the four concubines are England and Holland, Portugal and Spain. Each of them jealously whispering in the ear of Japan, each of them slandering their rivals. So, as you said, Japan is wise to send them all away.

(TRANSLATION.)

RODRIGUES   It is better that he have one lawful wife, than four concubines.

INOUE   And, by this lawful wife -- you mean Portugal?

(TRANSLATION.)

RODRIGUES   No. I mean the Church.

INOUE   (enjoying their argument) Let me ask you, Father: Have you had many wives?

(TRANSLATION … with a smile from the **INTERPRETER**.)

RODRIGUES   (also a smile) On that point, I concede.

INOUE   Speaking as a man who has had many wives, I tell you this:

(TRANSLATION.)

A man cannot love a wife who forces herself upon him. Her affection is unwanted. Her desperation makes her ugly. And, her ugliness will leave her barren.

(TRANSLATION.)

RODRIGUES   We have not forced our religion upon the peasants, they have ---

INOUE   (interrupting) I want you to think about this, Father: That a man should not choose a barren woman to be his wife.

(TRANSLATION. Silence. **RODRIGUES** stares at **INOUE**. **INOUE** looks to the **INTERPRETER**.)

Take him to the wharf.

(The **INTERPRETER** NODS.
INOUE exits.)

INTERPRETER   There is someone he wants you to meet. This man, too, is from Portugal. And, like you, he is a priest. You will have much to talk about, I'm sure.

RODRIGUES   Is it Ferreira? Am I to finally see him?

INTERPRETER   We're going now.

RODRIGUES   Where?

INTERPRETER   To the wharf.

(The **INTERPRETER** and **RODRIGUES** move to a downstage corner, near a tall WOODEN STAKE, as lights shift to ---

The Wharf. Day. The BLUE SEA brilliant in the distance.

The SOUND of WAVES, the CRIES of GULLS.

During the following, the **INTERPRETER** ties **RODRIGUES'** hands to the STAKE behind him. This area is isolated – by lighting -- from the rest of the stage.)

RODRIGUES (as his hands are tied to the STAKE) You said you didn't fear my escape.

INTERPRETER You said you wished to be treated like the other prisoners.

(**RODRIGUES** looks across the stage and sees something approaching in the distance.)

Can you see him coming?

RODRIGUES I can't, yet, see his face. He is with a group of peasants. The guards are shoving them this way.

INTERPRETER Is he the man you've been expecting?

RODRIGUES Yes. I'm sure of it.

INTERPRETER I see.

RODRIGUES He did not renounce his faith! I knew your stories were lies -- he is not in Nagasaki, has not taken a Japanese wife. He is still a priest -- still here among his followers.

(calls across the distance)

Father!

INTERPRETER It's no use ---

RODRIGUES Father Ferreira, I've found you ---

INTERPRETER   He can't hear you. The sea is too loud. The distance too great.

(A MAN is shoved onstage, opposite. He falls to the ground, his face hidden from view. He wears ragged and torn peasant clothing.)

RODRIGUES   Father, I'm here ---

(He stops, suddenly, as ---

The MAN lifts his head from the ground and **RODRIGUES** sees his face … it is **Garrpe.** He is haggard and dirty. His face is bloodied by a cut near his eye.

Stunned, **RODRIGUES** says the name, quietly.)

Garrpe.

INTERPRETER   (smiling) You know this man?

(Silence, as **GARRPE** struggles to stand -- weak with fatigue.)

RODRIGUES   What have they done to him? I want to know. I want to speak to him.

INTERPRETER   You see, Father, I've told you no lies.

RODRIGUES   You toy with us like a cat with his prey. I want to speak to Garrpe. Now.

INTERPRETER   There will be time for that. The guards must first complete their business.

(**GUARD ONE** enters, carrying a rolled-up STRAW MAT. **GUARD TWO** follows, dragging a WOMAN whose hands are tied together with rope. We have yet to see her face.

The GUARDS conduct their business directly in front of **GARRPE**. **RODRIGUES** and the **INTERPRETER** continue to watch from a distance.)

RODRIGUES   What are they doing to her?

INTERPRETER Yesterday, this woman, and the other peasants all trampled on the *fumie.*

RODRIGUES Then why were they not set free?

INTERPRETER A peasant's apostasy means nothing. Our concern is the priests. And, you see, Father Rodrigues: in all of Japan, only two of you remain.

(The SOUND of the SEA grows louder, and is joined by a LOW, CONTINUOUS DRONE, haunting and persistent, as ---

GUARD ONE unrolls the STRAW MAT on the ground. The WOMAN is pushed forward ... and **RODRIGUES** sees her face. It is **Monica.)**

RODRIGUES Monica ---

INTERPRETER Your voice will not carry, Father. Do not waste your strength.

(MONICA is pushed down onto one end of the mat --
her stomach to the ground. Then, during the following, the GUARDS ROLL UP THE MAT ... TRAPPING MONICA INSIDE.

GARRPE watches, helpless.)

Do you know this inlet, Father?

(he points to the HILLSIDE upstage)

Just beyond those rocks. It is very deep. And the waves are strong.

(The MAT is now completely rolled. Only MONICA'S HEAD is visible, protruding from one end. The GUARDS TIE THE MAT CLOSED, tightly, with a ROPE.

GARRPE leans down to touch MONICA, to bless her, but ---

One of the GUARDS shoves him back, away. Then, the GUARDS carry the MAT upstage, to the HILLSIDE.)

(The SOUNDS grow STILL LOUDER.)

RODRIGUES   MONICA ---

INTERPRETER   The Christian fathers talk of mercy ---

RODRIGUES   GARRPE, STOP THEM ---

(**INOUE** appears, standing high on the HILLSIDE. He looks down to **GARRPE**.)

INTERPRETER   (pointing at **GARRPE**)

But where is this father's mercy for these poor peasants?! First this woman, then the others -- one by one, they will be tossed into the sea. This priest, Garrpe -- he alone can save their lives. The Lord of Chikugo is asking him now. He need only say one word.

RODRIGUES   GARRPE ---

INTERPRETER   You may shout all you like. But no man is louder than the sea.

(The SOUND of the SEA, and the DRONE grows VERY LOUD. They are JOINED BY MUSIC: **"Ave Maria"** -- ALSO LOUD.

The stage begins to DARKEN considerably, leaving only the following images prominent: **RODRIGUES**, tied to the stake; GARRPE, opposite; the SILHOUETTE of **INOUE** and the GUARDS on the HILLSIDE: and the vast BLUE SEA behind them.

The **INTERPRETER** exits, leaving **RODRIGUES** alone, straining to free himself from the stake:

In SILHOUETTE, INOUE extends his arms -- reaching out toward GARRPE … asking him.

GARRPE stands, motionless.)

RODRIGUES   (reciting the litany quickly, desperately to himself) Lord, have mercy upon us.

Christ, have mercy upon us.

Lord, have mercy upon us.

Christ, hear us.
God, the Father of heaven -- have mercy upon us ...

(**GARRPE** shakes his head "NO" -- then kneels and prays.

INOUE lowers his arms. Then, he gestures to one of the GUARDS, as ---

RODRIGUES shouts over the SOUND/MUSIC to GARRPE ---)

APOSTATIZE! GARRPE -- YOU MUST! YOU MUST APOSTATIZE!

(The GUARD descends from the HILLSIDE and approaches **GARRPE**, who continues to pray, eyes closed.

The GUARD is holding a *FUMIE*. He places it in front of **GARRPE**. Then, he lifts **GARRPE** to his feet, with force.)

Heart of Jesus, victim of our sin -- have mercy upon us.
Heart of Jesus, our salvation -- have mercy upon us.
Heart of Jesus, hope of those who die in you -- have mercy upon us ...

(**GARRPE** sees the *FUMIE* in front of him. He stares at it.
He looks up to the HILLSIDE, looks at INOUE.
Again, **INOUE** reaches both arms toward **GARRPE** -- waiting ...)

LORD, THERE IS STILL TIME TO SAVE THEM. LORD, HEAR OUR PRAYER. BE NOT SILENT, O GOD!

(Crying, shaking with fear ... **GARRPE** again shakes his head "NO." He steps back, away from the *FUMIE,* wrapping his arms around his body, clutching at himself.

INOUE slowly lowers his arms.
Then, **INOUE** turns and NODS to the GUARDS.)

THERE IS STILL TIME -- EVEN NOW -- PLEASE, LORD -- DO NOT PUT THIS BLOOD ON OUR HANDS ---

(In SILHOUETTE on the HILLSIDE: the GUARDS lift the ROLLED UP MAT in which MONICA is bound.

There is a moment when the MAT -- held by the GUARDS -- is silhouetted against the BLUE SEA ...)

HOW CAN THIS BE? HOW, AS THE FAITHFUL DIE IN YOUR NAME, HOW CAN YOU ---?

(... then the MAT IS HURLED INTO THE SEA, disappearing instantly upstage, behind the HILLSIDE.

The MUSIC and SOUND reach a CRESCENDO, as **RODRIGUES** screams ---)

NOOOOOOOO!!!

(The GUARDS exit, as **INOUE** stares at the SEA.

GARRPE RUSHES TO THE TOP OF THE HILLSIDE.
He is now silhouetted next to **INOUE** -- looking out to sea.

INOUE looks at **GARRPE**, then turns and leaves, as -- **GARRPE**, alone, stares out to SEA for another moment.

Then, GARRPE LIFTS HIS ARMS ... and JUMPS from the HILLSIDE, disappearing into the SEA, as, INSTANTLY ---

LIGHTS SHIFT to RODRIGUES ALONE, and there is --

INSTANT SILENCE.

GARRPE is gone.
The BLUE SEA remains in the distance.
RODRIGUES leans back against the stake, breathing heavily. He cries. He stands there: bound, alone, exhausted.
He speaks to his God.)

Do you not see? Is it possible that you do not see our suffering -- the lives extinguished in your name?

(Silence.)

That you did not see Garrpe? That you did not see him fighting the waves, fighting to save your servant Monica -- whose child he himself baptized in your name? Did you not see him struggle as he was swept away -- further and further -- searching in vain for the straw mat which had sunk like a stone – drifting and screaming and gasping for air until he, too, was gone. Until he, too, was swallowed by the sea. The endless, resolute sea.

(Silence. Then, a burst of laughter from **RODRIGUES**.)

You mock us! You slander us with silence! WHERE ARE YOUR TRUMPETS?

WHERE IS THE GLORIOUS MARTYRDOM WE HAVE BEEN PROMISED? When our Lord Jesus Christ breathed his last -- when on that cross at Calvary he gave up the spirit -- it is written that DARKNESS COVERED ALL THE LAND, and THE VEIL OF THE TEMPLE WAS RENT IN TWAIN FROM TOP TO BOTTOM! Are we no longer your children? Are we all now like Judas -- ARE WE MERELY YOUR PUPPETS?!

(pause; then a fierce, quiet calm)

Two lives. Gone. In this moment -- just now -- two lives have ended … (pause)

… and the world is unchanged.

How are we to reconcile that? At the hour of my death, too, will the cicada still cry, the gulls circle, the waves crash the shore -- relentless and indifferent? Will there be no trace of my time on earth?!

(from his very core)

SPEAK!

(The word itself gives way to tears. And exhaustion.

And, now, amid the silence … the tranquil SOUND of WAVES, lapping the shore. Beautiful, rhythmic, resolute.

The **INTERPRETER** appears behind him. He unties **RODRIGUES**' hands -- freeing him from the stake.)

INTERPRETER   (quietly) It's an awful business. No matter how many times one sees it. Simply awful.

(The **INTERPRETER** leaves, as ---

RODRIGUES walks slowly towards center stage, where he gradually collapses to his knees. As he speaks, the lights shift around him, the "bars" of his cell appear once again, and he is back in ---

The Cell. Night. RODRIGUES slumps to his side, curling into a ball on the floor. He speaks to no one, as ---

The WAVES SLOWLY FADE AWAY, and are replaced by --

The distant SOUND of DEEP, LABORED BREATHING, louder than before. Again, it is accompanied by a LOW, CONSTANT DRONE.

Just outside the cell, behind **RODRIGUES** and unseen to him, is what appears to be a small pile of OLD CLOTHING or BLANKETS.)

RODRIGUES   Listen. The snoring of the guards -- stupid and without care. While, at the same time, the prisoners in their midst fight for their very souls.

I have been thinking about sin. Sin is not what it is thought to be. It is not stealing. It is not the telling of lies.

Sin is for one man to walk brutally over the life of another and be quite oblivious to the wounds he left behind.

Inoue -- who orchestrates this persecution -- is a sinner. But Christ died for him. Kichijiro -- betrayer of his family, drunkard, liar, apostate -- Kichijiro is a sinner. But Christ died for him. The guards who torture the peasants, rape the women, throw the men in boiling water till their skin drops like silk from their bones -- Christ died for them.

It is easy enough to die for the good and the beautiful. The hard thing is to die for the others -- to die for the despicable; the miserable and the corrupt.

Please ... teach me.

(PROJECTED ON THE WHITE FABRIC: **The Face of Christ,** as before, appearing very gradually out of the darkness.

MUSIC: **"Ave Verum Corpus"** -- very softly, under.)

I wanted to save Mokichi, Ichizo -- but I could not.
I wanted to save Monica; I wanted to throw myself in the water, like Garrpe, to save her, to free her from their torture -- but I could not.

(From the pile of CLOTHING/BLANKETS, a MAN emerges, listening to **RODRIGUES** -- staring at him with great compassion. It is, of course, **KICHIJIRO. RODRIGUES** has not yet seen him.)

All I can do is feel pity. But pity is not action.
Pity is not love.

So … please … teach me.

(TWO HAND CLAPS are heard --
MUSIC STOPS ABRUPTLY ---
RODRIGUES sits up, quickly, as morning light reveals ---

The INTERPRETER standing just outside the cell. He is holding a rolled-up STRAW MAT.

The FACE OF CHRIST is gone.)

INTERPRETER   Look at him, Father.

(**RODRIGUES** turns and now sees **KICHIJIRO.**
KICHIJIRO starts to run away, but is stopped by the **INTERPRETER.**
KICHIJIRO whimpers, quietly.)

Hiding in the dark with you. Do you know what he is, Father? He is a dog. You kick him and he runs away.

But he always returns.

(The **INTERPRETER** shoves **KICHIJIRO** -- who falls to the floor, then rises quickly and runs away, fearfully ---)

KICHIJIRO <u>I don't know this man -- I am not a Christian -- I am not ---</u>

(**KICHIJIRO** is gone. The **INTERPRETER** turns to **RODRIGUES**.)

INTERPRETER How are we today?

(**RODRIGUES** stares at him, saying nothing.)

The floor is cold, Father. I've brought you a mat -- it will help you sleep.

(The **INTERPRETER** drops the rolled-up MAT on the ground in front of **RODRIGUES**. He stares at it, sickened. He shoves it away from him.)

At least Garrpe died with courage. You, Father -- you're a coward. You don't deserve to be a priest.

(**RODRIGUES** stares up at him.) Get up. We're going.

(Instant light shift to: Inoue's Chamber. Morning. The WHITE FABRIC is PULLED AWAY, revealing -- **INOUE**, looking down upon **RODRIGUES**.

In the distance, a COCK CROWS.)

INOUE <u>Good morning, Father.</u>

(**RODRIGUES** nods.)

<u>When last you were here I asked you to consider something I said. Have you done so?</u>

(TRANSLATION. **RODRIGUES** nods. Then, **INOUE** nods --
gesturing for **RODRIGUES** to speak.)

RODRIGUES The question of a barren woman being a wife. (pause)

I don't believe the Church is barren. I believe that here -- in this country -- it can bring forth life. It is like a young tree. It must be nurtured. It must be watered and watched with great care.

INOUE <u>It was planted here long ago. Yet it has never taken root. Why?</u>

(TRANSLATION. **RODRIGUES**, his fervor now aroused, begins to answer, but ---
INOUE interrupts him.)

I know your answer, Father.

(TRANSLATION.)

You will say: because it has met with persecution. (TRANSLATION.)

RODRIGUES   (passionately) Yes! Persecution and death! It has never been given a chance to grow!

INOUE   You are wrong, Father.

(TRANSLATION.)

You see, a tree cannot take root in a swamp. And so, your Christianity will never survive in this swamp of Japan.

(TRANSLATION.)

RODRIGUES   What can that mean -- a swamp? Tell me!

INOUE   Japan does not destroy its enemies ... it changes them -- absorbing them like a swamp.

(TRANSLATION.)

We have conquered your Church by transforming it. So, now, Father, your work here is useless.

(TRANSLATION.)

RODRIGUES   But, tell me: WHY MUST YOU FEAR US? We bring only mercy, we bring ---

(**INOUE** raises his hand, stopping **RODRIGUES**.)

INOUE   You are like all the rest, Father. You want it made simple.

(TRANSLATION.)

But, our differences are not religious, and they are not political. What separates us is this:

(TRANSLATION.)

I am Japanese.

(TRANSLATION.)

And that, Father ... that cannot be made simple.

(TRANSLATION, then ---

INOUE turns to the **INTERPRETER** and NODS.
The **INTERPRETER** claps his hands, twice quickly.

A CONCUBINE enters, carrying the BOWL we have seen INOUE use before. The BOWL is placed before INOUE.
WATER is poured into the BOWL.

INOUE gives **RODRIGUES** a final look, and says ...)

Tonight, you will apostatize.

(TRANSLATION, and MUSIC: **"Exsultate Justi"** as --

INOUE slowly, ceremonially, WASHES HIS HANDS. **RODRIGUES** watches, silently.

INOUE is handed a towel. He dries his hands. Then -- he turns away and is gone.

The **INTERPRETER** claps his hands, twice quickly, and --

A WAGON is pushed onstage by **GUARD TWO** -- his face, as always, not identifiable. The WAGON consists of a small wooden platform on four wheels, with a vertical WOODEN CROSS rising from it -- about six feet into the air.

RODRIGUES is tied to the CROSS on the WAGON. His clothes are also torn away, somewhat -- leaving his remaining clothing tattered.)

RODRIGUES   Where are you taking me?

INTERPRETER   Back to the prison. But, this time, I thought you'd like to see the city. And I thought the city would like to see you.

(**The Streets of Nagasaki. Day.**

The WAGON is pushed downstage where it then remains stationary. Their MOTION is indicated by ever-shifting shafts of SUNLIGHT which land, flicker and disappear on RODRIGUES during the following. GUARD TWO stands near the wagon, behind it. The INTERPRETER stands on the ground next to RODRIGUES. The area surrounding them remains in shadow.

The MUSIC is joined by the growing SOUND of the STREETS: VOICES OF RIDICULE, LAUGHTER, SINGING, THE BARKING OF DOGS, THE SQUAWKING OF CHICKENS, ETC. -- continuous and overlapping.)

Look at them, Father! They mock and spit at you. They laugh and call you "Jesus of Nagasaki!" They throw the shit of their animals at you ---

RODRIGUES   Insult me all you like -- it does nothing but strengthen my courage.

INTERPRETER   What courage?! The courage to watch your friends die -- and do nothing?!

(During the following, a PEASANT MAN rushes up from the [unseen] CROWD and places a "CROWN" -- made of twigs and straw -- on RODRIGUES' head. The PEASANT MAN then runs away, laughing. GUARD TWO laughs, as well.

Gradually revealed in the SHADOWS -- his face not seen – is KICHIJIRO. He is crouched low to the ground, trying not to be seen. With intense concentration, he fumbles with a bit of STRING and some small scraps of PAPER in his hands.)

Where are your followers now? You are USELESS, Father. You amount to NOTHING.

RODRIGUES   Did you do this to Ferreira? Did you parade him through the streets -- to mock him?!

INTERPRETER   We hung him in the Pit. That was enough. (**RODRIGUES** looks away.)

Does that disappoint you? Did you imagine he was stronger than that?

RODRIGUES   I imagine nothing anymore! I feel nothing for Ferreira. Nothing but contempt – for had he been stronger, perhaps the faithful would not have lost their way.

INTERPRETER   You are all that remains, Father: you are the last priest in Japan. (with a laugh, to the crowd)

HAIL, THE KING OF THE CHRISTIANS!

(A LOUD, SUDDEN CRACK OF THUNDER. together with a -- A CRASH OF DRUMS, as ---
LIGHTS ISOLATE **RODRIGUES**, and ---
KICHIJIRO, who remains at a distance, trying not to be seen. He continues to fumble with the STRING and PAPER in his hands.
RODRIGUES emits a huge cry to the heavens ---)

RODRIGUES   "ELOI, ELOI, LAMA SABACTHANI?!" I was taught that these words were the prayer of a man about to give up his life, but now my thinking has changed. "My God, why hast thou forsaken me?" -- can it be that these were words of terror?

That in his final hours, our Lord, too, felt the terror of abandonment? The terror of facing the silence of God?!

INTERPRETER   (again with a laugh, again to the crowd) HAIL, JESUS OF NAGASAKI!

RODRIGUES   We are told that he was sentenced to death, then paraded through the city.

(He sees **KICHIJIRO**. Their eyes meet.)

And there, in the back of the crowd: Judas -- his betrayer -- following after him. No one knows why.

(**KICHIJIRO** rushes up to **RODRIGUES** and PRESSES SOMETHING into his [bound] hand, saying quietly ---)

KICHIJIRO   Mio Padré ...

(**KICHIJIRO** runs away, as, simultaneously ---)

INTERPRETER   HAIL, JESUS OF NAGASAKI!

(The **INTERPRETER** claps his hands, twice quickly, and -- **GUARD TWO** unties **RODRIGUES'** hands from behind the CROSS. The WAGON is wheeled off, and ---
THE SOUND OF THE STREETS gradually fade away, as lights shift to ---

The Cell. RODRIGUES stands, alone, one hand still tightly closed into a fist. He slumps to the ground in his cell. He looks around.
Then, he brings his closed fist in front of his face.
He opens his fist -- finding the odd jumble of STRING and PAPER scraps from Kichijiro.
He lifts the string, letting it fall and reveal itself ...

It is a ROSARY.

He stares at it. Then, he clutches it to his chest. He kneels. He touches the PAPER ROSARY "BEADS" as he speaks.)

RODRIGUES   (quietly, eyes closed) "And he came to a place which was known as Gethsemane. And he withdrew from the others; and kneeled down, and prayed, saying: 'Father, if thou be willing, remove this cup from me. Nevertheless ... not my will, but thine, be done.' And there appeared an angel unto him from heaven, strengthening him ..."

(He opens his eyes. He waits. He listens. There is only silence.)

But there are no angels. Only these walls. Only the guards snoring in the distance. All my life, when I felt such silence, when I felt myself becoming lost -- I would close my eyes and think of your face. The most beautiful face that has ever claimed the prayers of man. I would merely close my eyes and …

(His eyes closed, he waits. There is nothing.)

Lord, where are you? Where is your face? Has it become like your image on the *fumie* -- that face which ebbs away with every foot that touches it, rubbed clean with each apostasy -- till your features are softened, and finally, erased?

Lord, is it possible … has your face vanished from my heart?

(He waits. Nothing. Then ---

HAND CLAPS from the darkness nearby -- twice, quickly. **RODRIGUES** turns, immediately, with force ---)

Enough! No more questions from Inoue! No more of this charade -- do you hear me?!

(From the direction of the hand claps, a MAN steps into the light. It is not the Interpreter …

… it is **Ferreira.**

He has a quiet, weary look about him. He wears simple black robes. He stands near the cell, staring at **RODRIGUES**, saying nothing.

A very long silence. Then, finally, quietly …)

Father. Father Ferreira.

(At the sound of this word, **FERREIRA** lowers his head and looks away. More silence.)

At last … I feared I would never see you …

(Long silence. **FERREIRA** continues to look down, away.)

Mio Padré … please … say something. If you have … in your heart … any pity for me … please … Father … say something …

(**FERREIRA** slowly, briefly, looks up at **RODRIGUES**, as --

The **INTERPRETER** enters, followed by a BONZE -- a Buddhist monk in robes similar to Ferreira. The BONZE looks somberly at the ground, throughout.)

INTERPRETER He is no longer a Father. His name is Sawano Chuan. He lives at Saishoji temple. He does the work required of him by Inoue, the Governor of Chikugo.

(The **INTERPRETER** looks to **FERREIRA**, nods. **FERREIRA** lifts his head a bit and speaks. His words are clear and measured. He does not look at **RODRIGUES**.)

FERREIRA I am a useful man. I am useful to this country.

(A long silence. **FERREIRA** continues to look away.)

RODRIGUES Father ... please ... tell me. What are they making you do?

INTERPRETER Sawano Chuan spends his days ---

FERREIRA (a quiet fury, using his own words to convince himself) I spend my days writing. I am adapting a book on astronomy for the magistrate.

Yes, that's what I'm doing. I am of some use. The Japanese are rich in knowledge and learning -- but there are still some things I can do -- some things a Westerner can contribute to this country -- in areas such as medicine and astronomy -- I am doing all I can -- I have procured lenses and telescopes from a Dutch trading ship -- because, you see, astronomy is not a fanciful pursuit, no, it is useful, yes, in navigation, in the study of tides, the cycles of seasons and weather, the planting of crops -- it is a practical science -- so, you see, I am not useless in this country. I can perform some service. I am a useful man. I am.

(Complete silence. The SINGING has FADED AWAY. **RODRIGUES** stares at **FERREIRA**.)

INTERPRETER Tell him of the other book.

(**FERREIRA** does not respond.)

He has written another book. It is called "Kengiroku."

(At the mention of this word, the BONZE looks up – for the first, and only, time in the scene.)

It shows Christianity to be a false doctrine. It refutes the teachings of your so-called Christ.

(**RODRIGUES** stares at **FERREIRA**, who continues to look away.)

Inoue has read it. He praises it. If you have spare time in your cell, you should read it.

RODRIGUES   Don't mock me ---

INTERPRETER   I am teaching you! Isn't it better to be a useful man like Sawano Chuan, than a useless prisoner like yourself?

RODRIGUES   The cruelty! Forcing him to write a book like that -- that is more cruel than any torture I can imagine!

INTERPRETER   Tonight we will show you the Pit.

(turns to **FERREIRA**)

Sawano Chuan.

(**FERREIRA** looks up at him.)

Get your work done quickly.

(The **INTERPRETER** leaves, followed by the BONZE.

RODRIGUES continues to look at **FERREIRA** -- who has not, yet, fully met his gaze.)

FERREIRA   I've been told to persuade you.

RODRIGUES   (bitterly, knowing the answer) To do what?

FERREIRA   To apostatize.

RODRIGUES   (pause) As you did.

(no answer, stronger)

To renounce my faith as you did.

(Silence. **FERREIRA** speaks, as before, with a quiet, measured intensity.)

FERREIRA   They bind your feet and hands. They suspend you, upside-down, from a rope. The blood rushes down through you, you feel it flooding your neck, you hear it pulsing in your ears -- filling your head to bursting. You think that surely -- you pray that surely -- your brain will hemorrhage. Your heart will stop. Your suffering will be over.

And, at that moment ...

(Still not fully looking at **RODRIGUES**, **FERREIRA** gestures for him to approach. **RODRIGUES** moves to the edge of his cell, close to **FERREIRA**.)

At that very moment when you are praying for your own death ...

(**FERREIRA** turns his head, and tilts his neck -- so **RODRIGUES** can see an area just behind each of his ears.)

They take a knife. And they make a small cut. Behind each ear. To relieve the pressure. Now, you can hang there for a very long time. Now, your suffering is incremental and unending. The blood drips from you slowly. Like your life, it trickles away into the darkness of the Pit.

(Silence.)

RODRIGUES   I dedicated myself to the priesthood because of you. Your teaching, your letters sent home to Lisbon from Japan, they spoke of victory -- the growing strength of the Church.

FERREIRA   Perhaps they did. But, what you see before you now is a missionary defeated by his mission.

RODRIGUES   That's impossible. No one can be defeated by it -- for as we sit here now, another priest has boarded a boat in Macao and will come in secret to this country ---

FERREIRA   And he will be captured. And Japanese blood will flow. When will you understand that it is THEY who must die for your foolish, selfish dream?

(pause)

Our religion does not take root in this country.

RODRIGUES   Of course it does! There are some trees which God has planted everywhere. There was a time when the Church was strong here, strong and growing with ---

(**FERREIRA** suddenly turn to **RODRIGUES** and LOOKS HIM IN THE EYE FOR THE FIRST TIME, saying ---)

FERREIRA   WHEN?

(Startled, **RODRIGUES** is motionless, silent. **FERREIRA** is now animated, engaged.

MUSIC FADES IN, SLOWLY: **"O Esca Viatorum"** -- under.)

For 20 years I labored in this country. I know it better than you ever will. This country is a swamp -- do you know what a swamp is? It is not a wasteland -- it is a living thing. A swamp takes whatever enters it -- consumes it -- and changes it to suit its needs.

The Japanese never believed in our Christian God. They believed in their own gods -- enshrined by their history, handed down by their ancestors. We spoke the word "Deus" which they understood as "Dainichi" -- the Buddhist Sun God. So, they worshipped the sun -- as they had before us, and as they will after us. We spoke of the Virgin Mary and they transformed her into Kwannon -- the Buddhist goddess of mercy. They did nothing but add OUR scriptures and sacraments to THEIR existing rituals.

RODRIGUES   I have seen the Church take hold here ---

FERREIRA   You have seen its CARCASS. It has kept its shape -- but has lost its essence.

RODRIGUES   You're lying to me -- you're an apostate here to do their bidding ---

FERREIRA   You are deceiving yourself ---

RODRIGUES   I have watched them pray, watched them receive the sacraments -- I have seen our faith here! With my own eyes, I have seen ---

FERREIRA   (sharply) Sebastian. The white object you see before you is NOT black. We have been fooled by the Church. Fooled into believing that our God, our faith, our customs are without limit -- that their meaning and purpose survive no matter the country, no matter the people.

That, Sebastian, that is a lie.

(Long silence. **RODRIGUES** speaks with a quiet urgency.)

RODRIGUES   On the floor here, there are letters chiseled into the stone. The traces of a prisoner here before me. A man stronger than the both of us. A man whose faith must have burned to the very end. These letters -- "L" ... "A" ... "U" ---

FERREIRA   "Laudate Eum."

(**RODRIGUES** looks at him.)

This was my cell. "Praise Him" I chiseled there -- my hands bloodied and cold.

(pause)

Sebastian, there are other ways to praise him. Ways not ordained by Rome, nor imagined by our Superiors.

(pause)

Think, brother. Had Christ himself been here, what would he have done?

(Silence. **RODRIGUES** stares hard into **FERREIRA**'S eyes.)

RODRIGUES   You are not the Ferreira I once knew.

FERREIRA   No. I am Sawano Chuan.

(The MUSIC is now GONE. SOUND of LABORED BREATHING is heard again, much louder now, as ---

KICHIJIRO runs on, battered and bloody. He throws himself to the ground just outside Rodrigues' cell.

GUARD TWO rushes on after him, yelling ---)

GUARD TWO   Leave at once -- or you'll be beaten ---

KICHIJIRO   Mio Padré -- forgive me -- forgive me my sins!

(RODRIGUES stands. FERREIRA looks on.)

GUARD TWO   You are forbidden to be here ---

(GUARD TWO hits KICHIJIRO viciously across the back with a club. KICHIJIRO cries out in pain, as ---)

RODRIGUES   Kichijiro ---!

(The GUARD drags KICHIJIRO away.)

KICHIJIRO   I am a Christian -- Mio Padré -- I must confess! -- Confession! -- Confession!

(KICHIJIRO'S VOICE trails off and he is gone, as ---
The SOUND of LABORED BREATHING grows still louder.

RODRIGUES turns, viciously, to FERREIRA.)

RODRIGUES   Do you see none of this?! Do you not hear these sounds -- the screams of these peasants -- and worse: the snoring of the guards -- hour after hour -- filling the air ---

(RODRIGUES begins desperately screaming into the darkness, the distance. FERREIRA watches.)

SILENCE! I BEG OF YOU! STOP THIS SNORING -- THIS HEARTLESS

BREATHING! WAKE THEM -- PLEASE -- SOMEONE -- WAKE THEM AND PUT AN END TO THIS MOCKERY!

(The **INTERPRETER** appears quickly, carrying his fan.)

INTERPRETER   <u>What's the matter here?</u>

RODRIGUES   These sounds -- this breathing -- it is a vicious mockery -- you must do something -- you must ---

INTERPRETER   Yes, it's awful, isn't it. But, with one word from you, it will end. There is less than an hour till the cock crows. Do it now. Apostatize.

RODRIGUES   It is not my faith that is weak, listen to me: it is that breathing -- that callous breathing! -- the snoring of the guards.

(The **INTERPRETER** looks at **RODRIGUES** for a long time. Then … he smiles. He turns to **FERREIRA**.)

INTERPRETER   Show him.

(The **INTERPRETER** exits, as ---
FERREIRA extends his hand to **RODRIGUES**. **RODRIGUES** stares up at him … then offers his hand. [His other hand still holds the crumbled paper rosary.] **FERREIRA** lifts him to his feet, as the lights of the CELL disappear and ---

RODRIGUES and **FERREIRA** stand downstage in a single shaft of light. Alone in the midst of great darkness.

The SOUND OF LABORED BREATHING is VERY LOUD now.)

FERREIRA   The sound you hear is not snoring. It is this. It is the moaning of the Christians hanging in the Pit.

(And now, lights upstage reveal ---

The Pit. BEHIND THE WHITE FABRIC, the SILHOUETTE of a MAN is seen:

The MAN hangs from his ankles, his arms and feet bound with rope. He dangles there in the air, twirling slowly, grotesquely.

In the DISTANCE, BEHIND THIS SILHOUETTE are OTHER BODIES HANGING [these are mannequins/shapes] -- SMALLER in size, dangling in the air. The overall effect is that of a hall of torture; hanging bodies reaching into the distance.

RODRIGUES stares at the SILHOUETTES, silent, horrified.)

Do you want to know the reason I apostatized?

(**RODRIGUES** does not respond.)

It was NOT because they hung me in this Pit. For THREE DAYS I was in here – suspended above a hole filled with bones and excrement, the blood dripping out of me slowly -- and FOR THREE DAYS I WAS SILENT. FOR THREE DAYS I DID NOT BETRAY MY GOD!

(**RODRIGUES** has now covered his ears with his arms and hands -- to block out the SOUND, to block out **FERREIRA**. **FERREIRA** grabs him and shakes him ---)

You must hear me now! And you must hear these voices -- just as I did! These are the people for whom GOD HAS DONE NOTHING. Despite our prayers, despite our pleas -- HE HAS DONE NOTHING. WHY SHOULD THESE PEOPLE SUFFER THIS WAY?!

RODRIGUES The Lord has not abandoned them -- he is making a place for them in his kingdom -- though they suffer here on earth, they shall receive his ---

FERREIRA (overlapping) Sebastian, a great shadow is passing over your soul ---

RODRIGUES You will not tempt me -- you will not pile my weakness upon yours ---

FERREIRA It is time you stopped seeing the Church and began seeing the world ---

RODRIGUES I HAVE PRAYED FOR THEM ---

FERREIRA YES, YOU HAVE PRAYED FOR THEM -- JUST AS I HAVE -- NOW, YOU MUST LOOK AT THEM ---!

(**FERREIRA** PULLS ASIDE THE WHITE FABRIC, revealing ---

The Man Hanging in the Pit, no longer in silhouette, now in the flesh. His face is filthy, bloodied. We see the occasional drop of blood fall from the cuts behind his ears. He dangles, hideously, in the air. His eyes are closed. His mouth is open as he gasps for breath.

The SOUND of BREATHING/MOANING is ENORMOUS NOW -- accompanied still by the low, constant DRONE.

RODRIGUES stares at THE MAN. Sickened, crying.)

This is the reason for my apostasy. Do you hear now? Do you see?!

These are the people you have prayed for. These are the people awaiting the mercy of God.

And where is it, Sebastian? Where is their Church -- where is their God?

RODRIGUES   I can't answer any more, I don't know ---

(**FERREIRA** grabs **RODRIGUES**, forcefully, pointing at **RODRIGUES'** CHEST ---)

FERREIRA   HERE! THEIR CHURCH IS HERE. If you believe in your Lord and his teachings – BECOME AS HIM. Act not as his follower, act not as his witness -- ACT AS HE WOULD ACT.

(**FERREIRA** shoves **RODRIGUES** still closer to the Pit. The MAN looms above him now, hanging there hideously, moaning in pain.)

The moment you place your foot on the *fumie...* this man will be taken from here. He will be unbound. Medicine will be administered to his wounds. He will be fed, and clothed, and cared for. And never again will he return to this place of torture.

(**RODRIGUES** looks at **FERREIRA**. Then, he turns and looks at the MAN.)

A priest is taught to live in imitation of Christ.

(**RODRIGUES** continues to stare at the MAN.)

Certainly Christ would have apostatized.

(**RODRIGUES** turns and looks at **FERREIRA**.)

For them. To end their suffering, he would have trampled on the *fumie.*

RODRIGUES   No ---

FERREIRA   For love, Sebastian, for love he would have apostatized ---

(**RODRIGUES** falls to his knees ---)

RODRIGUES   No, never ---

FERREIRA   Yes -- even if it meant sacrificing everything, his entire being.

(**RODRIGUES** lifts his face to the heavens ---)

RODRIGUES   Now, Lord. If ever you held us in your heart -- your priests, your followers, all of us who have honored your word and awaited your gift of salvation ---

FERREIRA   You are hiding, Sebastian ---

RODRIGUES   (overlapping) Now -- if ever, Lord -- prove now your love for the world! Prove now your righteousness ---

FERREIRA   (overlapping) Hiding your own weakness behind the beautiful words of the Church ---

RODRIGUES   It's you who are weak! But, I still believe – I believe in the salvation of these people.

FERREIRA   YOU BELIEVE IN THE SALVATION OF YOURSELF. You think you're better than these peasants -- more worthy in the eyes of God ---

RODRIGUES   You have corrupted my words ---

FERREIRA   You are frightened, Sebastian -- not of Inoue, not of the Japanese -- but of the Church -- that they will call you a traitor as they called me ---

RODRIGUES   Stop it! No more ---

FERREIRA   SO LONG AS YOU FEAR THE CHURCH YOU WILL NEVER SERVE THE LORD ---

(The SOUND of the BREATHING/MOANING, as well as the ongoing DRONE have now reached a CRESCENDO ---

These SOUNDS are JOINED BY MUSIC: **"Exsultate Justi"**

RODRIGUES takes the crumbled PAPER ROSARY from his closed fist and holds it, desperately, as he pleads ---)

RODRIGUES   "KEEP NOT THOU SILENCE, O GOD: HOLD NOT THY PEACE, AND BE NOT STILL" – IN THE NAME OF YOUR SERVANTS -- FOR MONICA AND GARRPE -- MOKICHI AND ICHIZO -- FOR THOSE WHOSE FAITH COULD NOT BE EXTINGUISHED -- WHOSE LIVES WERE STOLEN FROM THEM IN YOUR NAME BY THE MURDEROUS, MERCILESS SEA -- FOR ALL WHO SUFFER HERE, LORD:

SPEAK!

(INSTANT, ABSOLUTE SILENCE.
The VOICES, MUSIC and DRONE immediately VANISH.

RODRIGUES remains on his knees -- breathing heavily, tears in his eyes; exhausted by his pleas, defeated by the silence.

FERREIRA looks at him for a very long time. Finally, when the silence has grown unbearable ...)

FERREIRA   (quietly, gently) You are now going to perform the most painful act of love that any man has ever known.

(**FERREIRA** extends his open hand to **RODRIGUES**. **RODRIGUES** does not move.
FERREIRA gently takes the PAPER ROSARY from **RODRIGUES'** hands. As it slips through his fingers, he does not move, does not look up at **FERREIRA**. Then ---

FERREIRA PULLS THE WHITE FABRIC CLOSED -- restoring

the BODIES HANGING IN THE PIT, once again, to SILHOUETTE.

Still kneeling, **RODRIGUES** does not look up.

Still in silence … **FERREIRA** extends his arm, gesturing offstage [identical to the beginning of the play], and ---

The **INTERPRETER** enters. He carries the *fumie.*

The **INTERPRETER** looks at **FERREIRA**. **FERREIRA** NODS.
The **INTERPRETER** approaches **RODRIGUES**.

The *fumie* is placed on the ground, directly in front of **RODRIGUES**. **RODRIGUES** now looks down at the *fumie,* tears in his eyes. Slowly, he reaches out his hands toward the *fumie.*

He lifts the *fumie* -- holding it at arms length in front of him. LIGHTS BEGIN TO ISOLATE RODRIGUES, alone, as ---

He speaks -- softly, desperately -- to the *fumie* …)

RODRIGUES   My dear Lord and Savior … is this how we meet? Is this how first I see your face? Each day in Japan I have imagined it, longed for it … and now here it is, before me for the first time.

Am I to defile that which I love most of all?

(A very long silence. Then … tearfully …) Teach me …

(Still more silence. Then ---

PROJECTED ON THE WHITE FABRIC: **The Face of Christ.**
The FACE makes the SILHOUETTES of the BODIES HANGING IN THE PIT DISAPPEAR.

MUSIC: **"Ave Verum Corpus"** -- very softly.

From the HEART OF THE MUSIC … TWO AMPLIFIED
VOICES -- one MALE [as earlier] and one FEMALE; one in ENGLISH and one in JAPANESE -- are heard, overlapping one another slightly ---)

[Male] VOICE OF CHRIST   I, more than anyone, know your pain …

[Female] VOICE OF CHRIST   I more than anyone know your pain …

[Male] VOICE OF CHRIST   (gently) Trample …

[Female] VOICE OF CHRIST   (gently) Trample …

[Male] VOICE OF CHRIST   I was born into this world to share your suffering …

[Female] VOICE OF CHRIST   I was born into this world to share your suffering … and, through love, to relieve you.

[Male] VOICE OF CHRIST   And, through love, to relieve you.

[Female] VOICE OF CHRIST   Trample …

[Male] VOICE OF CHRIST   Trample …

(**RODRIGUES** is standing now, still staring at the *fumie*. He closes his eyes, listening to the VOICES. No one else is aware of them.

During the following, **FERREIRA** gently takes the *fumie* from **RODRIGUES'** hands -- and places it on the ground in front of him.

Unseen by the others, **KICHIJIRO** appears, at a distance, watching. He is lit by a single CANDLE he holds in front of him.

Also during the following, a shaft of light reveals -- **INOUE**, also at a distance, also watching.)

[Male] VOICE OF CHRIST   What thou dost, do quickly -- for then your suffering will be at an end.

[Female] VOICE OF CHRIST   What thou dost, do quickly -- for then your suffering will be at an end.

[Male] VOICE OF CHRIST   I will not abandon you.

[Female] VOICE OF CHRIST   <u>I will not abandon you. I am with you till the end of time.</u>

[Male] VOICE OF CHRIST   I am with you till the end of time.

(**RODRIGUES** opens his eyes, looks down at the *fumie* ---)

[Female] VOICE OF CHRIST   (a whisper) <u>Trample ...</u>

[Male] VOICE OF CHRIST   (a whisper) Trample ...

(**RODRIGUES** lifts his foot. As he does so ---

The MUSIC BEGINS TO SLOWLY FADE, and –
The FACE OF CHRIST also BEGINS TO FADE AWAY ---

RODRIGUES takes a deep breath, still looking down at the *fumie,* his foot still in the air ---

At the moment when the MUSIC and the FACE OF CHRIST VANISH COMPLETELY ---

In that STILL and SILENT MOMENT ---

RODRIGUES places his foot on the *FUMIE.*

He closes his eyes. Tears fall down his cheeks.

After a moment, he slowly removes his foot from the image. Quietly, distantly ... a COCK CROWS.

The **INTERPRETER** turns and looks across the distance to **INOUE**.
INOUE NODS -- then exits.

The **INTERPRETER** lifts the *fumie* from the ground, then exits.

FERREIRA looks at **RODRIGUES**, then nods.
RODRIGUES stares back, coldly.
FERREIRA walks away in the silence and is gone.

Now ... quietly, beautifully ... the SOUND OF DISTANT VOICES, SINGING:

"We're on our way, we're on our way.
We're on our way to the temple of Paradise. The temple of Paradise is far away.
The temple of Paradise is far away. We're on our way, we're on our way.
We're on our way to the temple of Paradise."

RODRIGUES does not move.

KICHIJIRO walks quietly toward RODRIGUES from behind, carrying the CANDLE. He holds the candle in front of RODRIGUES -- offering it. RODRIGUES takes it -- then looks up to see who it's from. As soon as RODRIGUES sees KICHIJIRO ---

KICHIJIRO runs off into the darkness -- hiding in the shadows. As RODRIGUES stands, holding the CANDLE ---

BEHIND THE WHITE FABRIC, the HUGE SUN BEGINS TO APPEAR IN SILHOUETTE, very gradually.

Also revealed, in a tight shaft of light, is VALIGNANO. He holds a piece of paper.)

VALIGNANO   Word has arrived from the Church in Rome. Father Sebastian Rodrigues has apostatized.

(As the SINGING CONTINUES ---

GUARD TWO pushes a crude CART across the stage.
Lying in the CART -- wrapped in a dirty blanket -- his face still bloody -- his arms and legs unbound is ...
The MAN who was HANGING IN THE PIT.

The CART does not stop moving. It passes directly in front of RODRIGUES as it crosses the stage.

As the CART passes ... the MAN looks up at RODRIGUES.
RODRIGUES meets his gaze, tearfully.)

Father Rodrigues, at great personal sacrifice, brought God's word to the Christians in Japan. But now, while imprisoned in Nagasaki, he has renounced his faith.

(The MAN says something which only **RODRIGUES** hears …)

MAN HANGING IN THE PIT   (barely audible) Mio Padré …

(The CART is gone. **RODRIGUES** watches it go, then looks back down at the CANDLE in his hands.)

VALIGNANO   May God have mercy on his soul.

(**RODRIGUES** BLOWS OUT THE CANDLE, as --
The SINGING CONTINUES.
VALIGNANO remains lit, as lights also reveal ---

A Room in the Magistrate's Office. Day.
A simple table defines the room.
The HUGE SUN now looms fully IN SILHOUETTE, behind the scene.

The **INTERPRETER** enters, with a NEW ROBE draped over his arm. During the following, he helps **RODRIGUES** CHANGE INTO THE NEW CLOTHING.)

INTERPRETER   Welcome, Father.

VALIGNANO   I have been in Asia now for much of my life. There was a time when the Church in Japan was strong. The lords -- men such as Inoue -- agreed to be baptized … and their subjects followed. But that time is gone. What we have learned – from the example of Fathers Ferreira and Rodrigues -- will serve as a warning to us all:

The differences between our cultures are absolute.

For Christianity to remain in Japan, I now believe it must do so through the Japanese themselves -- through priests who emerge from among their own people.

As for me, I have sent my last priest to Japan.

(LIGHTS OUT on **VALIGNANO**.
RODRIGUES is now newly dressed.)

INTERPRETER   This will be a fine room to work in. We will bring you objects found among the peasants. You will determine if the objects are Christian objects. You will be paid for your work.

RODRIGUES   (quietly, hoarsely) Home.

INTERPRETER   What? I didn't hear you.

RODRIGUES   Portugal.

(pause)

Will I ever see my home?

(The **INTERPRETER** stares at **RODRIGUES** -- then makes a final adjustment to the ROBE.)

INTERPRETER   Let me know if there is anything you need.

(**INOUE** enters. Behind him is **FERREIRA** -- carrying a BOOK in his hands. Behind Ferreira is his JAPANESE WIFE.)

INOUE   Greetings.

(**RODRIGUES** nods, slightly.)

I believe you know Sawano Chuan. And, with him, is his wife.

(TRANSLATION. **RODRIGUES** stares at **FERREIRA**, coldly.)

Honorable Sawano, have you brought your book with you?

FERREIRA   (nods) Yes, my Lord.

(**INOUE** gestures toward **RODRIGUES**.
FERREIRA walks across the room and hands the book
to **RODRIGUES**, as ---)

INTERPRETER   (to **RODRIGUES**) The Honorable Sawano Chuan has brought you something to read. "Kengiroku." The book which shows Christianity to be a false religion.

(In silence, **FERREIRA** hands the BOOK to **RODRIGUES**. **RODRIGUES** looks at **FERREIRA**, throughout.)

INOUE   (to **RODRIGUES**) I have been told you heard voices, Father. That the Face of Christ spoke to you from the *fumie.*

(TRANSLATION. **RODRIGUES** says nothing. He is motionless, holding the BOOK uncomfortably in front of his body.)

Surely you deceive yourself! You are a weak man, Father -- that is why you betrayed your faith.

(TRANSLATION.)

RODRIGUES   You left me no choice.

INOUE   Father, you were not defeated by me. You were defeated by this swamp of Japan.

(TRANSLATION.)

RODRIGUES   No.

(pause)

The struggle with my faith was here -- in my own heart.

INOUE   (with a kind smile) I know your struggle, Father. For the good of my people, I, too, renounced the Church.

(TRANSLATION.

INOUE takes PAPER from the table in front of **RODRIGUES**. He writes something on the PAPER as he speaks.)

Since you will now spend your life in Japan, it will suit you to have a Japanese name.

(TRANSLATION, as --- **INOUE** holds the PAPER in front of **RODRIGUES**, showing him.)

A man here in Nagasaki has recently died. His house has been prepared for you. And you will have his name. That name is: Okada San'emon.

(TRANSLATION, as --- **RODRIGUES** slowly takes the PAPER from INOUE.)

Does that suit you?

(TRANSLATION. **RODRIGUES** says nothing, as he stares at the PAPER.)

Please, let me hear you say your name.

(TRANSLATION. **RODRIGUES** looks up from the paper.)

RODRIGUES   (simply, coldly) Okada San'emon.

(**INOUE** and the **INTERPRETER** smile.)

INOUE   The deceased man has a wife. She will now become your wife.

(TRANSLATION.)

You will be comfortable here, Okada-san. You will be a useful man.

(TRANSLATION. **RODRIGUES** remains silent.)

INTERPRETER   Well? Have you nothing to say?

RODRIGUES   (without emotion) Thank you.

INOUE   (nods, speaks with genuine regret) I assure you, Father -- it can't be helped. This country has changed you, just as it changed your Church. That is our way, Father. That is Japan.

(TRANSLATION. as ---
INOUE exits. The **INTERPRETER** sets Ferreira's BOOK on the table, then exits as well.

RODRIGUES and **FERREIRA** stare at each other across the room. Long silence, then ...)

FERREIRA (quietly) Why this silence between us? We are the same man.

(pause)

You hate me as a man hates his mirror. But, we are inseparable now. Each of us has lost our Church.

RODRIGUES (quietly, simply) And, what of our faith?

(Silence, as **FERREIRA** stares at **RODRIGUES**. Then, followed by his WIFE, he walks the length of the room -- directly past **RODRIGUES** -- and is gone.

RODRIGUES is alone in the room. He looks around. He goes to the table. He sits. He looks at Ferreira's BOOK which is on the table. He begins to open it. Stops. Closes it. Pushes it away.

He buries his face in his hands.

A BONZE enters, carrying a WOODEN BOX. He sets it on the table in front of **RODRIGUES** -- then he leaves.

RODRIGUES lifts his head and sees the box. He reaches into the box and pulls out the first of numerous small OBJECTS, such as: STONES, STATUETTES, CUPS, TOOLS, ETC.

He inspects EACH OBJECT carefully, then sets it aside, as he speaks to the audience.)

A final letter. A letter that will never reach the place I now desire most. My home in Lisbon. Dear friends, my story ends here -- on this unforgiving island in the middle of the sea.

One year has now passed since my apostasy. I remain here in this room, each day, doing this work. In the evenings, the guards take me back to my home.

The Church, of course, expelled me long ago. The children here in Nagasaki pass by my window -- they laugh and call me "Apostate Paul."

(He lifts a group of PAPERS from the table. This is his OATH.)

Recently, I have been writing an oath. This was demanded of me by Inoue.

He suspected I still had followers among the peasants. They were, once again, captured, interrogated and made to trample on the *fumie*.

And, as for me ... a small cut was made.

(touches the back of his ear)

Here.

(the other)

And here.

(pause)

And I -- like Ferreira before me -- was hung in the Pit.

The oath I have written is a disavowal of my religion. It is proof that I have rejected the Church ...

(pause, looks directly at the audience)

... which, of course, I have.

(The **INTERPRETER** enters, carrying PAPERS. The BONZE enters with him, carrying ANOTHER WOODEN BOX. During the following, the BONZE places the OBJECTS which **RODRIGUES** is "finished with" into this BOX.)

INTERPRETER   Good day, Okada San'emon.

RODRIGUES   Good morning.

INTERPRETER   What have we found today?

RODRIGUES   (showing an OBJECT) These initials carved here -- they signify the "Ave Maria." It is a Christian object.

INTERPRETER   (making a NOTE on his papers) Very good. And next?

RODRIGUES   (showing another OBJECT) The Blessed Virgin here, disguised to appear as a Buddhist icon. (and another OBJECT)

And here, if one takes a mirror and looks inside, a tiny cross is carved.

INTERPRETER   (making another NOTE) They are very clever.

RODRIGUES   They are, indeed.

INTERPRETER   Anything else?

RODRIGUES   Let me see.

(**RODRIGUES** reaches into the BOX and removes ---

A pair of SCISSORS -- identical to those seen in Act One. He holds them, looks at them, OPENS them.)

INTERPRETER   Well?

(**RODRIGUES** looks up at the **INTERPRETER**. Then, he CLOSES the SCISSORS and looks at them again.

Silence.)

Anything?

RODRIGUES   No.

(pause)

Scissors, nothing more.

(The **INTERPRETER** does not make a note. Instead, he claps his hands. The BONZE takes the SCISSORS, puts them in his BOX, and leaves.

The **INTERPRETER** stares at **RODRIGUES** for a moment.)

INTERPRETER   Okada San'emon. Have you completed your oath?

RODRIGUES   I have.

(**RODRIGUES** hands the **INTERPRETER** his OATH, as lights shift to ---

A Rock Garden, outside the Magistrate's Office. Sunset.

The SOUND of CICADAS, and occasional BIRDS.

RODRIGUES stands alone, breathing deeply, deliciously of the air.

KICHIJIRO appears, at a distance. He speaks in a whisper.)

KICHIJIRO   Mio Padré.

RODRIGUES   Kichijiro -- no ---

(**KICHIJIRO** looks at **RODRIGUES**, tears in his eyes.)

KICHIJIRO   Please. I am a weak man. I trampled on the face of Christ. Hear my confession.

RODRIGUES   No. I am no longer a priest. I cannot hear your confession.

(**KICHIJIRO** approaches **RODRIGUES**.)

KICHIJIRO   Mio Padré, please -- help me! I am a weak man.

(**KICHIJIRO** lifts his foot and begins to place it on the ground in front of him, slowly -- recreating his apostasy. As he does so, **RODRIGUES** steps in quickly and grabs **KICHIJIRO** forcefully -- stopping him. He holds **KICHIJIRO** by the shoulders, looking into his eyes.)

RODRIGUES   (quietly) Kichijiro -- listen to me. I, too, I am a weak man. I, too, trampled on the face of Christ ... the face I had longed for, the face I had loved.

And at that moment, my heart spoke to him, saying: "Lord, I was in agony and you were silent."

And the voice coming from the *fumie*, coming from the face of Christ said: "I was not silent. I was suffering beside you. I am with you now and forever."

(**RODRIGUES** raises his foot. **KICHIJIRO** looks down at the foot.)

I placed my foot down ... I trampled upon that beautiful face ... and a feeling that came from the heart of my soul rushed through me ...

(And now, from amid the rocks in the garden ...

Water begins to flow. It runs over the rocks, gently. It surrounds **RODRIGUES** and fills a small pool near his feet. The SOUND of its motion is beautiful, tranquil.)

It was the essence of love.

(**KICHIJIRO** -- still staring at **RODRIGUES'** foot -- tears a piece of his own clothing, then kneels -- amid the WATER -- at **RODRIGUES'** feet.

KICHIJIRO begins to WASH **RODRIGUES'** FEET. Slowly, gently. **RODRIGUES** speaks, his voice quiet and confident.)

My anguish ... like a rush of water ... was taken from me. My betrayal, condemned by my fellow priests ... was forgiven by my Lord.

And my soul, having lost its Church ... began to find its faith.
(looking down at **KICHIJIRO**, speaking with certainty)
Our Lord was never silent -- for our lives, to this day, have spoken of him.

Kichijiro. Forgive me.

(**KICHIJIRO** lifts his head and looks at **RODRIGUES**.)

KICHIJIRO   You ... are ... forgiven.

(**KICHIJIRO** removes something from his clothing.
It is **RODRIGUES'** ROSARY -- old and weathered, now. He gives it to **RODRIGUES**.)

RODRIGUES   There are neither strong nor weak men. There are simply men whom faith has chosen. Men who both love and sin; betray and believe.

Quietly now ... I will hear your confession.

(**KICHIJIRO** bows his head and speaks his confession ---

But, we do not hear **KICHIJIRO**'S words ... only the SOUND of the FALLING WATER, as ---

The lights fade slowly to black.

End of Play.)

A Note on *Silence*

In the summer of 1994, I went to Japan with several of my American collaborators to do research for what would become a stage adaptation of *Silence*. Our two-week trip—during which we visited many of the areas depicted in Mr. Endo's novel—was one of the most remarkable and invigorating times of my life. We met with Mr. Endo, who gave his blessing for our project, answered our questions and wished us well. We were educated, inspired, (fed!) and entertained by our Japanese hosts. The group of us—Japanese and American—would sit up late, talking about aspects of the novel, engaged in animated discussions of its meaning and message. We sought out historical contexts; we debated the intentions of the characters; we bantered about key events, images, and phrases. We lit up the night with the kind of energy found only during the heady and intoxicating outset of an adventure. We became a group of artists with full hearts—our heads spinning with Mr. Endo's words, with images of the rugged Japanese countryside and the tenacity of the Christians who risked their lives during centuries when their religion was forbidden.

And, as always, just before we said our good-byes, the entire group looked at me and said: "Good luck. We look forward to reading the play."

That, I suppose, is the terrifying, exhilarating and defining feature of being a playwright: that everyone else goes home and waits for you to make a start. To find the story amid the ideas. And to give that story life.

And that brings me to faith.

Is it impossible for an American author to fully capture the stature, subtlety, and complexity of a Japanese novel like *Silence*? Of course it is. And that, I believe, *is exactly why it must be attempted*. It is an act of faith. Any translation is. Any adaptation is. It is the voice in us which says, "There is something from somewhere else that will speak to my own life." It is an act of faith to believe that the foreign can become proximate; the outlandish can become insightful; the harrowing, enlightening. In taking the time to search elsewhere, we begin—like it or not—to see ourselves. Faith is that thing which makes the invisible seem possible.

Lately, we've grown fond of calling the world a "global village." One appeal of this phrase seems to be its ability to shrink that which overwhelms us—to tame the enormity of the planet through linguistics. But, there is nothing to be gained from making the world "smaller" if it is not, at the same time, made tangible. If we know nothing else, we know that there is a relentless unity to life—that each day brings a series of concurrent trials, agonies and delights found from country to country, across time zones, across oceans. And if we do not venture in, we atrophy. If we don't risk the mistakes inherent in confronting a new culture, we do not learn. And if we do not bring our lessons home with us, we do not grow. Graham Greene stated that "hatred is a failure of the imagination." Likewise, ethnocentrism is a failure of faith.

A friend of mine is fond of saying that "a trip isn't over till you tell it." So, in a sense, *Silence* is the trace of an unforgettable adventure. Doing an adaptation, I suppose, is an attempt not only to travel, but to travel *well*. To arrive with curiosity, proceed with humility, learn with ferocity, and report with accuracy. Like faith, it is a necessary and imperfect science.

I'm humbled by the chance to adapt Mr. Endo's masterpiece. I'm honored to have his blessing. I'm forever indebted to my fellow collaborators. And I am ever so grateful for this journey.

Steven Dietz
17 August 95, Seattle

Afterword

Martin Scorsese

I was given my first copy of *Silence* by Archbishop Paul Moore. We had a special screening of *The Last Temptation of Christ* for all of the religious leaders in the city, and at that time Moore was near the end of his tenure as the Episcopal Bishop of New York. Looking back on it now, I realize that I was also given my first copy of Kazantzakis's novel—by my friend Barbara Hershey—and that I spent many years trying to get both books made into films. In one sense, it's obvious that the two novels "talk to each other." They each deal with faith in the face of doubt and temptation. And then, on another level, they each present unique challenges to any filmmaker that tries to adapt them. Those challenges relate directly to one of the greatest and most powerful aspects of art in general and, I think, cinema in particular.

Cinema is the telling of stories with images and sounds – or, in the case of avant-garde cinema, the embodiment and conveyance of emotion with images and sounds. But that's just a job description. I think that every truly great work of art orients you toward what isn't there, what can't be seen or described or named. It happens differently in different forms of art. In music, in poetry, in painting, universes of emotion and mystery are circled over and felt, like feeling the contours of a passageway in the darkness. In the novel, what is said and described opens the way to what *isn't*, that which can only be intimated, sensed (I'm thinking of the title of one of Samuel Beckett's novels, *The Unnamable*). In the greatest movies, what we see points the way to what we don't see, what we *can't* see. For instance, *2001* is an astonishing sensorial experience, and part of what makes it so astonishing is the powerful presence of what we cannot see or know, what's beyond our understanding. You can *see* the black obelisk, but neither the characters nor the audience can comprehend what it really even *is*. And it's interesting to note that Kubrick and Arthur C. Clarke had a very long and complex explanation of what actually *happens* in *2001* – what the obelisk does, how it appeared on earth and then on the moon, what happens to Dave and how he becomes the Star Child, and so on. And they *suppressed* it – they left it out. What you leave out is just as important as what you leave in. Another, very different example would be Claude Lanzmann's monumental documentary *Shoah*. At the end of *Shoah*, which is nine and a half hours long, you feel like you've seen

Auschwitz and Treblinka, the gas vans and the ovens, the piles of corpses and the blue crystals left by the traces of Zyklon B gas. And you *have* seen it – in your mind. That's the great power of that film: it's about the fact that we can't know the horrors of the death camps, we can only conjure them.

This indication of what isn't there is built into the very practice of filmmaking. I've talked a lot about the magic of being in the editing room, putting one image together with another image and seeing a third image in the mind's eye. Eisenstein called it the "third meaning." And if you take out one or two frames, and add a sound, that third image changes. It's remarkable. To this day, when I walk into the cutting room and look at a sequence for the first time, it fills me with a sense of wonder.

Which brings me back to *Silence*. Endo's novel confronts the mystery of Christian faith, and by extension the mystery of faith itself. Rodrigues learns, one painful step at a time, that God's love is more mysterious than he knows, that He leaves much more to the ways of men than we realize, and that He is always present … even in His silence. What role am I playing, wonders Rodrigues? Why am I being kept alive? When will my martyrdom arrive? Of course, it doesn't. Which means that he will be playing a role that is very different from the one he expected to play. He will not be following in the footsteps of Jesus. He will be taking a less revered path, and therefore playing a very different role. This is the most painful realization of all.

How do I translate the last pages of the novel, as abstract as *Moby-Dick* or *The Idiot*, into images and actions? So how do I film these interior sensations and realizations and emotions? How do I make the mystery of faith, and of the ways of God, cinematically present? The answer is in making the movie—going to Taiwan, working with the actors and the cameraman and the production designer, shooting, and then putting it together in the editing room, adding a frame here and taking one out there, mixing the sound, timing the color, and deciding that it's finished. But on another level, the answer lies with the cinema itself, and its way of pointing us toward what we cannot see.

Contributors

Mark Bosco, a Jesuit priest, is an Associate Professor, holding a joint position in the departments of English and Theology at Loyola University, Chicago, Illinois. Besides teaching and research, he is the Director of Loyola's Joan and Bill Hank Center for Catholic Intellectual Heritage. His main research focuses on the intersection of religion and art, especially on last century's Catholic literary revival in Britain and North America. He is the author of *Graham Greene's Catholic Imagination*, and an editor of two collections, *Finding God in All Things: Celebrating Bernard Lonergan, John Courtney Murray, and Karl Rahner* and *Academic Novels as Satire: Critical Studies of an Emerging Genre*. A new collection of essays, *Flannery O'Connor Among Philosophers and Theologians*, is forthcoming.

Jacqueline Bussie is Director of the Forum on Faith and Life and Associate Professor of Religion at Concordia College in Moorhead, Minnesota. She teaches and publishes in the areas of theology, service-learning, problem of evil studies, Christian ethics, interfaith cooperation, and faith and public life. In addition to numerous book chapter contributions and journal publications, she is a sought-after speaker and workshop facilitator. Her first book, *The Laughter of the Oppressed*, won the national Trinity Prize.

Mark W. Dennis is Associate Professor of Religion at Texas Christian University, Fort Worth, Texas, where he teaches courses in Buddhism, Daoism and Confucianism, religion and violence, and world religious traditions. He earned his Ph.D in Buddhist Studies at the University of Wisconsin in 2006, focusing on early Japanese Buddhism. He has a Ph.D. minor in Japanese literature. He has lived in Japan and India for eight years where he studied Buddhism and Hinduism, and has traveled widely in Asia. His first book was an English translation of the *Shōmangyō-gisho*, a Japanese Buddhist text written in classical Chinese and attributed to Japan's Prince Shotoku (574–622 CE). His current research focuses on the reception history of Japanese Buddhist texts.

Steven Dietz is one of America's most widely produced and published contemporary playwrights. Since 1983, his 30-plus plays have been seen at over one hundred regional theaters in the United States, as well as Off-Broadway. International productions have been seen in numerous countries, and his work has been translated into ten languages. Among his many accolades, he is a two-time winner of the Kennedy Center for New American Plays Award. And he secured the Yomiuri Shimbun Award (the Japanese "Tony") for his adaptation of Shusaku Endo's novel *Silence*. He teaches playwriting and directing at The University of Texas at Austin. In Austin, he regularly directs at ZACH Theatre.

Kevin M. Doak holds the Nippon Foundation Endowed Chair in the Department of East Asian Languages and Cultures, Georgetown University, Washington D.C., where he is also Professor of Japanese Studies. His current research focuses on Catholic intellectuals in twentieth-century Japan, particularly the jurisprudence of Kotaro Tanaka. His recent publications include *Xavier's Legacies: Catholicism in Modern Japanese Culture* and "Hiroshima Rages, Nagasaki Prays: Nagai Takashi's Catholic Response to the Atomic Bombing," in Roy Starrs, ed., *When the Tsunami Came to Shore: Culture and Disaster in Japan* (forthcoming). Doak also serves as co-editor of *The Journal of Japanese Studies*.

Elizabeth Cameron Galbraith is Associate Professor of Religion at St. Olaf College, Northfield, Minnesota. She received her D. Phil. from the University of Cambridge Divinity School in 1992. In 1996 the book that grew out of her doctorate, *Kant and Theology: Was Kant a Closet Theologian?*, was published. Her long-term research interests are the problem of evil (theodicy in particular) and Asian Christianity.

Van C. Gessel is Professor of Japanese at Brigham Young University, Provo, Utah, and former Dean of the College of Humanities. His research and translation work has focused on the writings of Endō Shūsaku. His critical writings include *The Sting of Life: Four Contemporary Japanese Novelists* and *Three Modern Novelists: Sōseki, Tanizaki, Kawabata*. He is the co-editor of *The Shōwa Anthology* and *The Columbia Anthology of Modern Japanese Literature*. *The Samurai, Scandal, Deep River*, and *Kiku's Prayer* are among his translations of Endō's works.

Dennis Hirota recently retired from the Department of Shin Buddhism at Ryukoku University in Kyoto, Japan, where he taught for many years. He has published many books and articles, in both English and Japanese, on Pure Land Buddhism and Buddhist aesthetics.

John Kaltner is the Virginia Ballou McGehee Professor of Muslim-Christian Relations at Rhodes College, Memphis, Tennessee, where he teaches courses on the Bible, Islam, and the Arabic language.

Jeff Keuss is Professor of Ministry, Theology and Culture and Director of the University Scholars Program at Seattle Pacific University, Washington. He has penned several books, the most recent of which is *Blur: A New Paradigm for Understanding Youth Culture*. He is the North American Editor for *Literature and Theology*, and he serves as the co-chair of the Paul Ricoeur Section of the American Academy of Religion.

Frances McCormack is a Lecturer in English at the National University of Ireland, Galway. She secured the University's President's Award for Teaching Excellence in 2009–10, as well as NAIRTL's National Award for Excellence in Teaching in 2011. She is currently Vice-Dean of Learning and Assessment in the College of Arts, Social Sciences and Celtic Studies. She publishes on Chaucer, Old and Middle English literature and the writings of Graham Greene. Her monograph, *Chaucer and the Culture of Dissent*, was published in 2007. She is working on a book on Compunction in Old English Literature, and she currently serves as the Director of the Graham Greene International Festival.

Darren J. N. Middleton is Faculty Fellow in the The John V. Roach Honors College and Professor of Theology and Literature at Texas Christian University, Fort Worth, Texas. Originally from England, he has published widely, offering studies on Nikos Kazantzakis, John Updike, Caribbean dub poetry, postmodern theology and West African Christianity. His latest book, co-edited with Dermot Gilvary, is *Dangerous Edges of Graham Greene: Journeys with Saints and Sinners*. He recently received one of his University's highest honors, the AddRan College of Liberal Arts Award for Distinguished Achievement as a Creative Teacher and Scholar. Currently, he is completing a book on the artistic dimensions of the Rastafari religious movement.

Martin Scorsese is an American film director. He has released over 30 movies, from *Mean Streets* (1973) to *The Last Temptation of* Christ (1988) and from *The Aviator* (2004) to *The Wolf of Wall Street* (2013). He won the Academy Award for Best Director for *The Departed* (2006). Currently, he is filming a cinematic adaptation of *Silence*.

Christopher B. Wachal is Visiting Assistant Professor of English at Marquette University, Milwaukee, Wisconsin. He has written on Graham Greene, Flannery O'Connor, and Shusaku Endo. His current research focuses on Catholic writers in Anglophone West Africa. In addition, he is writing a book about twentieth-century Catholic writers and their reflections on globalization.

Dennis Washburn is the Jane and Raphael Bernstein Professor in Asian Studies at Dartmouth College, Hanover, New Hampshire. He is author of *The Dilemma of the Modern in Japanese Fiction* and *Translating Mount Fuji* and has edited several volumes, including *Word and Image in Japanese Cinema, Converting Cultures*, and the forthcoming *The Affect of Difference: Representations of Race in East Asian Empire*. In addition to his scholarly work he has translated several works of fiction, including Yokomitsu Riichi's *Shanghai*, Mizukami Tsutomu's *The Temple of the Wild Geese*, Tsushima Yuko's *Laughing Wolf*, and a new version of *The Tale of Genji*, forthcoming from Norton.

Christal Whelan is an anthropologist, writer, and filmmaker. Among her books are: *Kansai Cool: A Journey into the Cultural Heartland of Japan*, and *The Beginning of Heaven and Earth: The Sacred Book of Japan's Hidden Christians*. Her documentary film *Otaiya* offers one of the only glimpses onto a community of Japanese Hidden Christians who reside on a small island off mainland Japan in the East China Sea. She is currently working on a book about religious revival, urbanization, and the meanings of nomadism in contemporary Mongolia.

Mark Williams took his B.A. in Japanese Studies at the University of Oxford and a Ph.D. in Japanese Literature at the University of California, Berkeley. He has spent most of his career at the University of Leeds, U.K., where he remains Professor of Japanese Studies. He was Head of East Asian Studies between 2000 and 2004, and Chair of the School of Modern Languages and Cultures between 2006 and 2011. He was also President of the British Association for Japanese Studies, 2008–11. He is currently on secondment as Vice President for Academic Affairs at Akita International University, Akita, Japan. He has published extensively, in English and Japanese. His works include: *Endō Shūsaku: A Literature of Reconciliation; Christianity and Japan: Impacts and Responses* (co-edited with John Breen); *Representing the Other in Modern Japanese Literature: A Critical Approach* (co-edited with Rachael Hutchinson); and, *Imag(in)ing the War in Japan: Representing and Responding to Trauma in Post-war Japanese Literature and Film* (co-edited with David Stahl). He is also the translator of *Foreign Studies* and *The Girl I Left Behind*, two novels by Endō Shūsaku.

For Further Reading

The following lists have no pretensions of comprehensiveness; they simply showcase those materials in Shusaku Endo Studies all or part of which many have found instructive.

Shusaku Endo (English Texts)

—*White Man/Yellow Man*. Translated by Teruyo Shimizu. New York: Paulist Press, 2014.
—*Kiku's Prayer*. Translated by Van C. Gessel. New York: Columbia University Press, 2013.
—*Song of Sadness*. Translated by Teruyo Shimizu. Ann Arbor, MI: University of Michigan Center for Japanese Studies, 2003.
—*The Girl I Left Behind*. London: Peter Owen, 1994; New York: New Directions, 1995.
—*Deep River*. Translated by Van C. Gessel. London: Peter Owen, 1994; New York: New Directions, 1994.
—*The Final Martyrs: Stories by Shūsaku Endō*. Translated by Van C. Gessel. London: Peter Owen, 1993; New York: New Directions, 1994.
—*Foreign Studies*. Translated by Mark Williams. London: Peter Owen, 1989; New York: Simon & Schuster, 1990.
—*Scandal*. Translated by Van C. Gessel. London: Peter Owen/New York: Dodd, Mead, 1988.
—*Stained Glass Elegies: Stories by Shusaku Endo*. Translated by Van C. Gessel. London: Peter Owen, 1984; New York: Dodd, Mead, 1985.
—*The Samurai*. Translated by Van C. Gessel. London: Peter Owen; New York: Harper & Row/Kodansha International, 1982.
—*When I Whistle*. Translated by Van C. Gessel. London: Peter Owen/New York: Taplinger, 1979.
—*A Life of Jesus*. Translated by Richard A. Schuchert. New York: Paulist Press, 1978.
—*Volcano*. Translated by Richard A. Schuchert. London: Peter Owen, 1978; New York: Taplinger, 1980.
—"The Anguish of an Alien." *Japan Christian Quarterly* 40.4 (1974): 179–85.
—*Wonderful Fool*. Translated by Frances Mathy. London: Peter Owen, 1974; New York: Harper & Row, 1983.
—*The Sea and Poison*. Translated by Michael Gallagher. London: Peter Owen, 1972; New York: Taplinger, 1980.

—"Concerning the Novel *Silence*." *Japan Christian Quarterly* 36.2 (1970): 100–3.
—*The Golden Country*. Translated by Frances Mathy. Tokyo: Tuttle, 1970.
—*Silence*. Translated by William Johnston. Tokyo: Sophia University & Tuttle, 1969; London: Peter Owen, 1976; New York: Taplinger, 1979.

Endō Shūsaku (Japanese Texts)

—*Endō Shūsaku bungaku zenshū* (*The Collected Works of Endō Shūsaku*; often cited as *ESBZ*), 15 volumes. Tokyo: Shinchōsha, 1999–2000; an 11 volume series first appeared in 1975.
—*Fukai kawa* (*Deep River*). Tokyo: Kōdansha, 1993.
—*Sukyandaru* (*Scandal*). Tokyo: Shinchōsha, 1986.
—*Samurai* (*Samurai*). Tokyo: Shinchōsha, 1980.
—*Kuchibue o fuku toki* (*When I Whistle*). Tokyo: Kōdansha, 1974.
—*Iesu no shōgai* (*A Life of Jesus*). Tokyo: Shinchōsha, 1973.
—*Bara no yakata, Ōgon no kuni* (*The Rose Pavilion* and *The Golden Country*). Tokyo: Shinchōsha, 1969.
—*Chinmoku* (*Silence*). Tokyo: Shinchōsha, 1966.
—*Ryūgaku* (*Foreign Studies*). Tokyo: Bungei Shunjū Shinsha, 1965.
—*Watashi ga suteta onna* (*The Girl I Left Behind*). Tokyo: Bungei Shunjū Shinsha, 1964.
—*Kazan* (*Volcano*). Tokyo: Bungei Shunjū Shinsha, 1960.
—*Obakasan* (*Wonderful Fool*). Tokyo: Chūō Kōronsha, 1959.
—*Umi to dokuyaku* (*The Sea and Poison*). Tokyo: Bungei Shunjū Shinsha, 1958.

Critical Studies (English Texts)

Ban, I. "Endō Shūsaku's *Chinmoku* and the Potentiality of Korean Christian Literature." *Japan Christian Quarterly* 54.3 (1988): 154–9.
Barcus, James E. "For the Love of God: The Problem of Spiritual Awakening in Endo's *Silence*." In *Performance for a Lifetime: A Festschrift Honoring Dorothy Harrell Brown: Essays on Women, Religion, and the Renaissance*, eds. Barbara C. Ewell and Mary A. McCay, 127–40. New Orleans: Loyola University Press, 1997.
Baurain, Bradley. "Shusaku Endo and the Great Temptation." *Christianity and the Arts* 6.3 (1999): 18–20.
Berkouwer, G.C. *The Second Vatican Council and the New Catholicism*. Translated by Lewis B. Smedes. Grand Rapids, MI: Eerdmans, 1965.
Beverly, Elizabeth. "A Silence That Is Not Hollow: The Mindfulness of Shusaku Endo." *Commonweal* 116.16 (September 22, 1989): 491–4.

Bosco, S.J., Mark. *Graham Greene's Catholic Imagination.* Oxford and New York: Oxford University Press, 2005.

Boxer, Charles R. *The Christian Century in Japan, 1549–1650.* Berkeley, CA: University of California Press, 1967.

Boyer, Nicholaus. *Sacred and Secular Scriptures: A Catholic Approach to Literature.* Notre Dame, IN: University of Notre Dame Press, 2005.

Brophy, Don. *One Hundred Great Catholic Books: From the Early Centuries to the Present.* New York: Blue Bridge, 2007.

Burger, David. "*Kirishitan*—Early Christianity in Japan." *Japanese Religions* 25.1/2 (2000): 162–4.

Burkman, Thomas W. "The Historical Novels of Endo Shusaku: Alien Christianity in the 'Mud Swamp' of Japan." *Fides et Historia* 26.1 (1994): 99–111.

Bussie, Jacqueline Aileen. *The Laughter of the Oppressed: Ethical and Theological Resistance in Wiesel, Morrison, and Endo.* New York: T&T Clark International, 2007.

Carter, John Ross, ed. *The Religious Heritage of Japan.* Portland: Book East, 1999.

Cavanaugh, William. "Absolute Moral Norms and Human Suffering: An Apocalyptic Reading of Endo's *Silence.*" *Logos: A Journal of Catholic Thought and Culture* 2.3 (Summer 1999): 96–116.

—"The God of *Silence*: Shusaku Endo's Reading of the Passion." *Commonweal* 125.5 (1998): 10–12.

Clark, Edward William. *Five Great Catholic Ideas.* New York: Crossroad, 1998.

Cohen, Doron B. "The God of *Amae*: Endo's *Silence* Reconsidered." *Japanese Religions* 19.1/2 (1993): 106–21.

Cooper, Michael. *Rodrigues the Interpreter: An Early Jesuit in Japan and China.* New York: Weatherhill, 1974.

Daly, James J. *The Jesuit in Focus.* Milwaukee, WI: Bruce, 1940.

Davis, Lanta. "Embracing Paradox: A Dialogue of Suffering between John Paul II and Shusaku Endo." *Intégrité: A Faith and Learning Journal* 11.1 (2012): 27–40.

Doak, Kevin M., ed. *Xavier's Legacies: Catholicism in Modern Japanese Culture.* Vancouver, BC: University of British Columbia Press, 2011.

Durfee, Richard E. Jr. "Portrait of an Unknowingly Ordinary Man: Endo Shusaku, Christianity, and Japanese Historical Consciousness." *Japanese Journal of Religious Studies* 16.1 (1989): 40–61.

Elliot, William I. "Shusaku Endo: A Christian Voice in Japanese Literature." *Christian Century* 83.38 (1966): 1147–8.

Endo, Junko. "Reflections on Shusaku Endo and *Silence.*" *Christianity and Literature* 48.2 (Winter 1999): 145–8.

Faessel, Victor A. "Spirit of Christ Inculturated: A Theological Theme Implicit in Shusaku Endo's Literary Works." Review of *Spirit of Christ Inculturated: A Theological Theme Implicit in Shusaku Endo's Literary Works*, by Emi Masi-Hasegawa. *Japanese Religions* 30.1-2 (2005): 148–51.

Fehler, Brun. "Re-defining God: The Rhetoric of Reconciliation." *Rhetoric Society Quarterly* 33.1 (2003): 105–26.

Ferreter, Luke. *Towards a Christian Literary Theory*. Houndsmills: Macmillan Press, 2003.

Flannery, Austin, ed. *Vatican Council II: The Conciliar and Post-Conciliar Documents*. Wilmington, DE: Scholarly Resources, 1975.

Fujita, Neil S. *Japan's Encounter with Christianity*. New York: Paulist Press, 1991.

—"Shusaku Endo: Japanese Catholic Novelist." *Religion and Intellectual Life* 3.3 (1986): 101–13.

Gallagher, Michael. "For These the Least of My Brethren: The Concern of Endō Shūsaku." *Journal of the Association of Teachers of Japanese* 27.1 (1993): 75–84.

Gandhi, Leela. *Postcolonial Theory: A Critical Introduction*. New York: Columbia University Press, 1998.

Gaughan, Richard T. "Apostasy and Redemption in Shusaku Endo's *Silence*." *Publications of the Arkansas Philological Association* 26.2 (2000): 13–22.

Gessel, Van C. "Hearing God in Silence: The Fiction of Endo Shusaku." *Christianity and Literature* 48.2 (Winter 1999): 149–64.

—"Endō Shūsaku: His Position(s) in Postwar Japanese Literature." *Journal of the Association of Teachers of Japanese* 27.1 (1993): 67–74.

—*The Sting of Life: Four Contemporary Japanese Novelists*. New York: Columbia University Press, 1989.

—"Voices in the Wilderness: Japanese Christian Authors." *Monumenta Nipponica* 37.4 (1982): 437–57.

Gessel, Van C., ed. *Japanese Fiction Writers Since World War II*. Detroit, MI: Gale Research, 1997.

Gilvary, Dermot and Darren J. N. Middleton, eds. *Dangerous Edges of Graham Greene: Journeys with Saints and Sinners*. New York and London: Continuum, 2011.

Goebel, Rolf J. "Rediscovering Japan's Christian Tradition: Text-Immanent Hermeneutics in Two Short Stories by Endō Shūsaku." *Studies in Language and Culture* 14 (1988): 157–72.

Goodier, Alban. *The Jesuits*. London: Sheed and Ward, 1929.

Greeley, Andrew. *The Catholic Imagination*. Berkeley: University of California Press, 2001.

Grigore, Rodica. "Shusaku Endo: From the Silence of the East to the Silence of God." *Theory in Action* 3.1 (2010): 7–23.

Hagiwara, Takao. "Return to Japan: The Case of Endō Shūsaku." *Comparative Literature* 48.2 (2000): 125–54.

Hall, Douglas J. "Rethinking Christ: Theological Reflections on Shusaku Endo's *Silence*." *Interpretation* 33 (1979): 254–67.

Hick, John. *Faith and Knowledge*. Eugene, OR: Wipf & Stock, 2009.

—*An Autobiography*. Oxford: Oneworld, 2002.

—*The Fifth Dimension: An Exploration of the Spiritual Realm.* Oxford: Oneworld, 1999.

—*A Christian Theology of Religions: The Rainbow of Faiths.* Louisville, KY: Westminster John Knox Press, 1995.

—*An Interpretation of Religion: Human Responses to the Transcendent.* New Haven: Yale University Press, 1989.

—*Problems of Religious Pluralism.* New York: St. Martin's Press, 1985.

—*God Has Many Names.* Philadelphia: Westminster Press, 1982.

Hick, John, ed. *The Myth of Christian Uniqueness.* New York: Orbis Books, 1988.

Higgins, Jean. "East-West Encounter in Endo Shusaku." *Dialog & Alliance* 1.3 (1987): 12–22.

—"The Inner Agon of Endo Shusaku." *Cross Currents* 34 (1984–5): 414–26.

Hirota, Dennis, ed. *Toward a Contemporary Understanding of Pure Land Buddhism: Creating a Shin Buddhist Theology in a Religiously Plural World.* Albany, NY: State University of New York Press, 2000.

Hoekema, Alle G. "The 'Christology' of the Japanese Novelist Shusaku Endo." *Exchange* 29.3 (2000): 230–48.

Hoeveler, Diane Long. "Shusaku Endo's *Deep River:* Trauma, Screen-Memories, and Autobiographical Confessions." *CEA Critic* 67.3 (2005): 28–40.

Hoffer, Bates. "Shusaku Endo and Graham Greene: Cross-Cultural Influences in Literary Structure." *Language and Literature* 28 (2003): 127–33.

Jasper, David. *The Study of Literature and Religion.* London: Macmillan Press, 1989.

Jay, Paul. *Global Matters: The Transnational Turn in Literary Studies.* Ithaca, NY: Cornell University Press, 2010.

Jenkins, Philip. *The Next Christendom: The Coming of Global Christianity.* Oxford: Oxford University Press, 2002.

JinHyok, Kim. "The Wounded Grace: Memory, Body and Salvation in Endō Shūsaku and Rowan Williams." *The Expository Times* 124.8 (2013): 374–83.

Johnson, Patricia Altenbemd. "Kierkegaard and Endo: The Dialectic of Religiousness." *Union Seminary Quarterly Review* 39.1-2 (1984): 85–99.

Johnston, William. *Mystical Journey: An Autobiography.* Maryknoll, NY: Orbis Books, 2006.

—"Endo and Johnston Talk of Buddhism and Christianity." *America* 171.16 (1994): 18–20.

Kadowaki, Kakichi. "Nichiren and the Christian Way." *Dharma World* 26 (1999): 14–22.

Keuss, Jeffrey F. *Freedom of the Self: Kenosis, Cultural Identity and Mission at the Crossroads.* Eugene, OR: Pickwick Publications, 2010.

—"The Lenten Face of Christ in Shusaku Endo's *Silence* and *Life of Jesus.*" *The Expository Times* 118.6 (2007): 273–9.

—*A Poetic of Jesus: The Search for Christ Through Writing in the Nineteenth Century.* Burlington, VT: Ashgate Publishing, 2002.

Kitagawa, Joseph M. *On Understanding Japanese Religion.* Princeton, NJ: Princeton University Press, 1987.

Kitamori, Kazoh. *Theology of the Pain of God.* Richmond: John Knox Press, 1965.

Koyama, Kosuke. *Mount Fuji and Mount Sinai.* London: SCM Press, 1984.

Lazarus, Neil, ed. *The Cambridge Companion to Postcolonial Literary Studies.* Cambridge: Cambridge University Press, 2004.

Lewell, John. *Modern Japanese Novelists: A Biographical Dictionary.* Tokyo: Kodansha, 1993.

Li, David Leiwei, ed. *Globalization and the Humanities.* Seattle: The University of Washington Press, 2004.

Link, Christopher A. "Bad Priests and the Valor of Pity: Shusaku Endo and Graham Greene on the Paradoxes of Christian Virtue." *Logos: A Journal of Catholic Thought and Culture* 15.4 (2012): 75–96.

Livesey, Frank. "The Jesuit Mission in East Asia: Vision or Mirage?" *Inter-Religio,* 27 (Summer 1995): 2–14.

MacCulloch, Diarmaid. *Silence: A Christian History.* New York: Viking, 2013.

Mase-Hasegawa, Emi. *Christ in Japanese Culture: Theological Themes in Shusaku Endo's Literary Works.* Boston and Leiden, Netherlands: Brill Publishers, 2008.

—"Religion and Contemporary Japanese Novelists–Endo's Concept of God Reconsidered." *Interreligious Insight* 4.4 (October 2006): 20–7.

—"Endo Shusaku's *Deep River*–An Interpretation." *The Japan Mission Journal,* 59.3 (Autumn 2005): 191–5.

—*Spirit of Christ Inculturated*: A Theological Theme Implicit in Shusaku Endo's Literary Works, Lund University, 2004.

—"Image of Christ for Japanese: Reflection on Theology Implicit in Shusaku Endo's Literary Works." *Inter-Religio,* 43 (Summer 2003): 22–33.

Mathy, Francis. "Shusaku Endo: The Second Period." *Japan Christian Quarterly* 40.4 (1974): 214–20.

—"Shusaku Endo: Japanese Catholic Novelist." *Thought* 42 (1967): 585–614.

Matsuoka, Fumitaka. "The Church In the World: The Christology of Shusaku Endo." *Theology Today* 39 (1982): 294–9.

McFadden, William C. "The Broken Silence of Shusaku Endo." *Listening* 25 (1990): 166–77.

Middleton, Darren J. N. "Dead Serious: A Theology of Literary Pilgrimage." *Cross Currents* 59.3 (2009): 300–18.

Murphy, Michael P. *A Theology of Criticism: Balthasar, Postmodernism, and the Catholic Imagination.* Oxford: Oxford University Press, 2008.

Netland, John T. "From Cultural Alterity to the Habitations of Grace: The Evolving Moral Topography of Endo's Mudswamp Trope." *Christianity and Literature* 59.1 (2009): 27–48.

—"'Who Is My Neighbor?': Reading World Literature Through the Hermeneutics of Love." *Journal of Education and Christian Belief* 11.2 (2007): 67–82.

—"From Resistance to *Kenosis*: Reconciling Cultural Difference in the Fiction of Endo Shusaku." *Christianity and Literature* 48.2 (1999): 177–94.

—"Encountering Christ in Shusaku Endo's Mudswamp of Japan." In *Christian Encounters with the Other*, ed. John C. Hawley, 166–81. New York: New York University Press, 1998.

Ninomiya, Cindy. "Endō Shūsaku: Bridging the Gap Between Christianity and Japanese Culture." *Japan Christian Quarterly* 56.4 (1990): 227–36.

Noble, Colin. "Endo Shusaku's Jesus: Introduction to a Japanese Christology." *Crux* 27.4 (1991): 28–32.

Okada, Sumie. *Japanese Writers and the West*. Basingstoke: Macmillan Press, 2003.

Orpett, Susan. "Silences and Voices: The Writings of Endo Shusaku." *Journal of the Association of Teachers of Japanese* 27.1 (1993): 57–8.

Pearce, Joseph. *Literary Converts: Spiritual Inspiration in an Age of Unbelief.* San Francisco, CA: Ignatius, 2000.

Pellegrino, Joe. "Endo's Ethics." *Kentucky Philological Review* 15 (2001): 44–8.

Reichardt, Mary R. *Exploring Catholic Literature: A Companion and Resource Guide*. Lanham, MD: Rowman and Littlefield, 2003.

Reinsma, Luke M. "Shusaku Endo's River of Life." *Christianity and Literature* 48.2 (1999): 195–211.

Rimer, J. Thomas. "That Most Excellent Gift of Charity—Endō Shūsaku in Contemporary World Literature." *Journal of the Association of Teachers of Japanese* 27.1 (1993): 59–66.

Rimer, J. Thomas and Van C. Gessel, eds. *The Columbia Anthology of Modern Japanese Literature*, two volumes. New York: Columbia University Press, 2005–7.

Robinson, Lewis. "Images of Christianity in Chinese and Japanese Fiction." *American-Asian Review* 3 (1985): 1–61.

Ross, Andrew. *A Vision Betrayed: The Jesuits in Japan and China, 1542–1742.* Maryknoll, NY: Orbis Books, 1994.

Said, Edward. *Orientalism*. New York: Vintage, 1979.

Sanneh, Lamin. *Whose Religion is Christianity?: The Gospel Beyond the West*. Grand Rapids, MI: Wm. B. Eerdmans Publishing Company, 2003.

Sano, Hitoshi. "The Transformation of Father Rodrigues in Shusaku Endo's *Silence*." *Christianity and Literature* 48.2 (Winter 1999): 165–75.

Schreiter, Robert. *Constructing Local Theologies*. New York: Orbis Books, 1985.

Schroth, Raymond A. "Shusaku Endo, *Silence*." In *Dante to Dead Man Walking: One Reader's Journey Through the Christian Classics*, 190–3. Chicago: Loyola Press, 2001.

Shafer, Ingrid. "Shusaku Endo and Andrew Greeley: Catholic Imagination East & West." *Midamerica* 18 (1991): 160–73.

Smart, Ninian. *Buddhism and Christianity: Rivals and Allies*. Basingstoke: Macmillan Press, 1993.

Somers, Sean. "Passion Plays by Proxy: The Paschal Face as Interculturality in the Works of Endō Shūsaku and Mishima Yukio." In *Through a Glass Darkly: Suffering, the Sacred, and the Sublime in Literature and Theory*, Holly Faith Nelson, Lynn R. Szabo, and Jens Zimmermann eds, 329–46. Waterloo, ON: Wilfrid Laurier University Press, 2010.

Song, C. S. *Jesus in the Power of the Spirit*. Minneapolis: Fortress Press, 1994.

Startzman, Eugene. "Can there be Faith in Betrayal?" *Christianity Today* 28 (1984): 62–3.

Sugirtharajah, R. S. *The Bible and Asia: From the Pre-Christian Era to the Postcolonial Age*. Cambridge, MA: Harvard University Press, 2013.

Suzuki, Tomi. *Narrating the Self: Fictions of Japanese Modernity*. Stanford: Stanford University Press, 1996.

Takayanagi, S.J., Shunichi. "Christianity in the Intellectual Climate of Modern Japan." *The Chesterton Review* 14.3 (1988): 385–93.

Tokunaga, Michio. "A Japanese Transformation of Christianity: Rambling Notes on Reading Shusaku Endo's *Silence*." *Japanese Religions* 15.3 (1989): 45–54.

Toma, Johnny V. *A Study of the Catholic Priest in Shusaku Endo's Novels: A Rare Glimpse into the History of Japan and Christianity*. Saarbrücken, Germany: Lap Lambert, 2011.

Tracy, David. *The Analogical Imagination: Christian Theology and the Culture of Pluralism*. New York: Crossroad, 1981.

Turnbull, Stephen. "From Catechist to Kami: Martyrs and Mythology Among the *Kakure Kirishitan*." *Japanese Religions* 19.1/2 (1993): 58–81.

Wakabayashi, Bob Tadashi, ed. *Modern Japanese Thought*. Cambridge: Cambridge University Press, 1998.

Walls, Andrew F. *The Missionary Movement in Christian History: Studies in the Transmission of Faith*. Maryknoll, NY: Orbis Books, 1996.

Washburn, Dennis. "The Poetics of Conversion and the Problem of Translation in Endō Shūsaku's *Silence*." In *Converting Cultures: Religion, Ideology and Transformations of Modernity*, Dennis Washburn and A. Kevin Reinhart eds, 345–63. Leiden, Netherlands: Brill Publishers, 2007.

—*Translating Mount Fuji: Modern Japanese Fiction and the Ethics of Identity*. New York: Columbia University Press, 2007.

—*The Dilemma of the Modern in Japanese Fiction*. New Haven: Yale University Press, 1995.

Whelan, Christal. "Loss of the Signified Among the *Kakure Kirishitan*." *Japanese Religions* 19.1/2 (1993): 82–105.

Whitehouse, J. C. *Catholics on Literature*. Dublin: Four Courts, 1997.

Williams, Mark. "Crossing the Deep River: Endō Shūsaku and the Problem of Religious Pluralism." In *Xavier's Legacies: Catholicism in Modern Japanese Culture*, ed. Kevin M. Doak, 115–33. Vancouver, BC: University of British Columbia Press, 2011.

—"Endō Shūsaku: Death and Rebirth in *Deep River*." *Christianity and Literature* 51.2 (2002): 219–39.

—*Endō Shūsaku: A Literature of Reconciliation*. London and New York: Routledge, 1999.

Williams, Philip. "Images of Jesus in Japanese Fiction." *Japan Christian Quarterly* 49.1 (1983): 12–22.

Wills, Elizabeth. "Christ as Eternal Companion: A Study in the Christology of Shusaku Endo." *Scottish Journal of Theology* 45 (1992): 85–100.

Woodman, Thomas. *Faithful Fictions: The Catholic Novel in British Literature*. Philadelphia: Open University Press, 1991.

Worcester, Thomas. *The Cambridge Companion to the Jesuits*. Cambridge and New York: Cambridge University Press, 2008.

Yamagata, Kazumi. "Mr. Shusaku Endo Talks About His Life and Works as a Catholic Writer." *The Chesterton Review* 12.4 (1986): 493–506.

Yancey, Philip. *Soul Survivor: How Thirteen Unlikely Mentors Helped My Faith Survive the Church*. New York: Doubleday; Colorado Springs, CO: Water Brook Press, 2003.

Young, Robert J. C. *Postcolonialism: An Historical Introduction*. Oxford: Blackwell, 2001.

Yuki, Hideo. "Christianity and Japanese Culture." *Japanese Religions* 25.1/2 (2000): 28–35.

Index

This index contains a list of English, Japanese, Sanskrit, and other terms. Japanese terms, excluding proper names, include a parenthetical explanation or translation. Sanskrit terms, excluding proper names, are indicated with a parenthetical explanation or translation preceded by "Sanskrit."